Welcome to
HOW IT WORKS
Annual

Hungry for knowledge? Then learn something new today and fuel your imagination with the expert help of **How It Works**. You'll be amazed by the world of fascinating facts and indispensable information now at your fingertips. Detailed cutaway images will reveal the inner workings of everyday items and other intriguing objects, enabling you to see and understand exactly how they work. Breathtaking photos let you marvel at the beauty and spectacle of the world around you, while informative and entertaining articles will prove no question is too big or too small for the **How It Works** team of brains to answer.

How It Works covers the entire universe across six all-encompassing subject areas: science, technology, transportation, the environment, history and space. From motion-control gaming to glaciers, asteroids to autopilot, dinosaurs to diets, comets to cloning, fossils to fridges and so much more besides, you'll find all the answers you'll ever need. So read on and feed your mind with a nutritious dose of **How It Works**.

Enjoy the book

D1333590

HOW IT WORKS
Annual

Imagine Publishing Ltd
Richmond House
33 Richmond Hill
Bournemouth
Dorset BH2 6EZ
☎ +44 (0) 1202 586200
Website: www.imagine-publishing.co.uk

Editor in Chief
Dave Harfield

Editor
Helen Laidlaw

Design
Kerry Dorsey, Andy Downes, Charles Goddard

Cover images courtesy of:
DK Images, BAE Systems, NASA, Samsung,
Kawasaki, Daimler AG, TranStar Racing, Garmin

Photo Studio
Studio equipment courtesy of Lastolite (www.lastolite.co.uk)

Printed by
William Gibbons, 26 Planetary Road, Willenhall, West Midlands, WV13 3XT

Distributed in the UK & Eire by
Imagine Publishing Ltd, www.imagineshop.co.uk. Tel 01202 586200

Distributed in Australia by
Gordon & Gotch, Equinox Centre, 18 Rodborough Road, Frenchs Forest,
NSW 2086. Tel + 61 2 9972 8800

Distributed in the Rest of the World by
Marketforce, Blue Fin Building, 110 Southwark Street, London, SE1 0SU.

IMAGINE
PUBLISHING

HOW IT WORKS

CONTENTS

VOLUME 2

The magazine that feeds minds!

Sections

🍃 Environment

💡 Technology

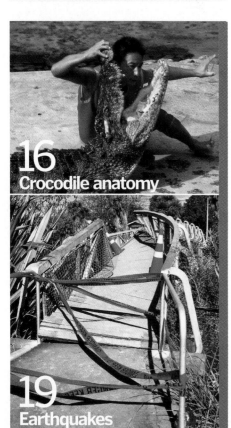

16
Crocodile anatomy

19
Earthquakes

35
Why ticks suck blood

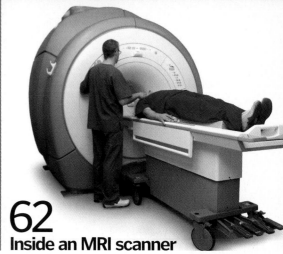

62
Inside an MRI scanner

92
Stealth technology

72
Motion-control gaming

84
Renewable energy

Science

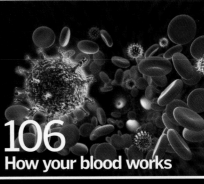

106
How your blood works

116
The power of
magnetism

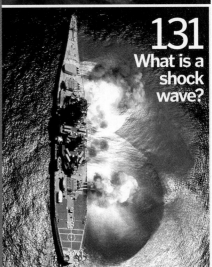

131
What is a
shock
wave?

HOW IT WORKS CONTENTS
VOLUME 2
The magazine that feeds minds!

Space

149 Cat's-Eye nebula

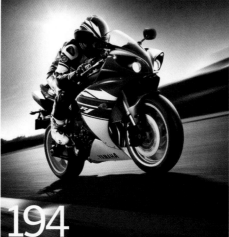
194 Superbikes

204 Battle tanks

199 Automatic transmission

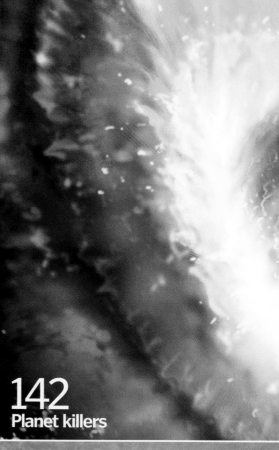
142 Planet killers

176 ALMA telescope

162 Neutron stars

216
Aerobatic displays

236
The cannon

209
Shock absorbers

HOW IT WORKS
ENVIRONMENT
Marvel at the natural world around you

12
Fossils

47
Acid rain

22
Animal camouflage

44
Glaciers

30
The planet's deadliest reptiles

48
Mega tsunamis

38
El nino

18
Crocodiles

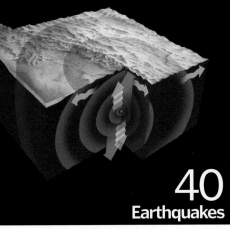

40
Earthquakes

What are fossils?

Obliterating the traditional perception of the origins and evolution of life on Earth, fossils grant us unique snapshots of what once lived on our ever-changing planet

5 TOP FACTS
FOSSILS

4.4
1 The oldest hominid specimen to be uncovered is Ardi, a fossilised set of skeletal remains that have been dated by scientists as being no less than 4.4 million years old.

Controversy
2 Fossil collecting is a popular hobby. However, important or prominent fossils are often sold to collectors instead of museums, leading to the creation of a black market.

Shell
3 One of the earliest realisations of the nature of fossils came from ancient Greek polymath Aristotle, who commented that fossil seashells resembled those of living examples.

Climate
4 Fossils allow scientists to deduce information about the Earth's past climate and environment, as the conditions in which they died are specific to these conditions.

DNA
5 Resin fossils are unique in that they often preserve bacteria, fungi and small fragments of DNA. Animal inclusions tend to be small invertebrates such as spiders and insects.

DID YOU KNOW? Fossils are useful in targeting mineral fuels, indicating the stratigraphic position of coal streams

Adpression
A form of fossilisation caused by compression within sedimentary rock. This type of fossilisation occurs mainly where fine sediment is deposited frequently, such as along rivers. Many fossilised plants are formed this way.

Resin
Referred to as amber, fossil resin is a natural polymer excreted by trees and plants. As it is sticky and soft when produced, small invertebrates such as insects and spiders are often trapped and sealed within resin, preserving their form.

Bioimmuration
Bioimmuration is a type of fossil that in its formation subsumes another organism, leaving an impression of it within the fossil. This type of fossilisation usually occurs between sessile skeletal organisms, such as oysters.

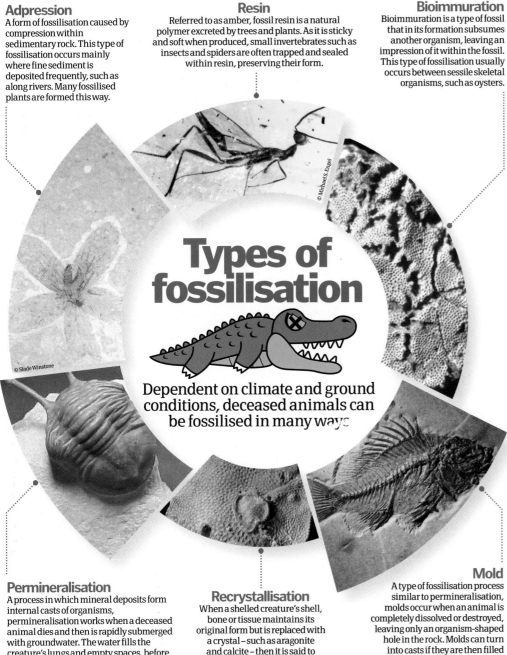

Types of fossilisation

Dependent on climate and ground conditions, deceased animals can be fossilised in many ways

Permineralisation
A process in which mineral deposits form internal casts of organisms, permineralisation works when a deceased animal dies and then is rapidly submerged with groundwater. The water fills the creature's lungs and empty spaces, before draining away leaving a mineral cast.

Recrystallisation
When a shelled creature's shell, bone or tissue maintains its original form but is replaced with a crystal – such as aragonite and calcite – then it is said to be recrystallised.

Mold
A type of fossilisation process similar to permineralisation, molds occur when an animal is completely dissolved or destroyed, leaving only an organism-shaped hole in the rock. Molds can turn into casts if they are then filled with minerals.

Carbon dating
A crucial tool for palaeontologists, carbon dating allows ancient fossils to be accurately dated

Carbon dating is a method of radioactive dating used by palaeontologists that utilises the radioactive isotope carbon-14 to determine the time since it died and was fossilised. When an organism dies it stops replacing carbon-14, which is present in every carbonaceous organism on Earth, leaving the existing carbon-14 to decay. Carbon-14 has a half-life (the time it takes a decaying object to decrease in radioactivity by 50 per cent) of 5,730 years, so by measuring the decayed levels of carbon-14 in a fossil, its time of death can be extrapolated and its geological age determined.

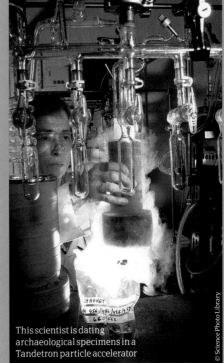

This scientist is dating archaeological specimens in a Tandetron particle accelerator

The origin of life on Earth is irrevocably trapped in deep time. The epic, fluid and countless beginnings, evolutions and extinctions are immeasurable to humankind; our chronology is fractured, the picture is incomplete. For while the diversity of life on Earth today is awe-inspiring, with animals living within the most extreme environments imaginable – environments we as humans brave every day in a effort to chart and understand where life begins and ends – it is but only a fraction of the total life Earth has seen inhabit it over geological time. Driven by the harsh realities of an ever-changing environment, Armageddon-level extinction events and the perpetual, ever-present force of natural selection, wondrous creatures with five eyes, fierce predators with 12-inch fangs and massive creatures

twice the size of a double-decker bus have long since ceased to exist. They're forgotten, buried by not just millions, but billions of years. Still, all is not lost. By exploiting Earth's natural processes and modern technology over the last two hundred years, scientists and palaeontologists have begun to

but, in general, it occurs when a recently deceased creature is rapidly buried by sediment or subsumed in an oxygen-deficient liquid. This has the effect of preserving parts of the creature – usually the harder, solid parts like its skeleton – often in the original, living form within the Earth's crust. The softer parts

"The softer parts of fossilised creatures tend not to survive due to the rapidity of decay"

unravel Earth's tree of life and, through the discovery and excavation of fossils – preserved remains and traces of past life in Earth's crust – piece the jigsaw back together.

The fossilisation of an animal can occur in a variety of ways (see 'Types of fossilisation' above)

of fossilised creatures tend not to survive due to the speed of decay and their replacement by minerals contained in their sediment or liquid casing, a process that can leave casings and impressions of the animal that once lived, but not its remains. Importantly, however, creature fossilisation tends to ▶

> "Excavating any discovered fossil in order to date and analyse it is a challenging, time-consuming process"

be specific to the environmental conditions in which it lived – and these in themselves are indicative of certain time periods in Earth's geological history. For example, certain species of trilobite (an extinct marine arthropod) are only found in certain rock strata (layers of sedimentary and igneous rocks formed through mineral deposition over millions of years), which itself is identifiable by its materials and mineralogic composition. This allows palaeontologists to extrapolate the environmental conditions (hot, cold, dry, wet, and so on) that the animal lived and died in and, in partnership with radiometric dating, assign a date to the fossil and/or the period.

Interestingly, however, by studying the strata and the contained fossils over multiple layers, through a mixture of this form of palaeontology and phylogenetics (the study of evolutionary relatedness between organism groups), scientists can chart the evolution of animals over geological time scales. A good example of this process is the now known transition of certain species of dinosaur into birds. Here, by dating and analysing specimens such as archaeopteryx (a famous dinosaur/bird transition fossil) both by strata and by radiometric methods, as well as recording their molecular and morphological data, scientists can then chart its progress through strata layers to the present day. In addition, by following the fossil record in this way, palaeontologists can also attribute the geophysical/chemical changes to the rise, fall or transition of any one animal/plant group, reading the sediment's composition and structural data. For example, the Cretaceous-Tertiary extinction event is identified in sedimentary strata by a sharp decline in species' diversity – notably non-avian dinosaurs – and increased calcium deposits from dead plants and plankton.

Excavating any discovered fossil in order to date and analyse it is a challenging, time-consuming process, which requires special tools and equipment. These include picks and shovels, trowels, whisks, hammers, dental drills and even explosives. There is also an accepted academic method all professional palaeontologists follow when preparing, removing and transporting any discovered fossil. First, the fossil is partially freed from the sedimentary matrix it is encased in and labelled, photographed and reported. Next, the overlying rock (commonly referred to as the 'overburden') is removed using large tools up to a distance of 6-9 centimetres (2-3 inches) from the fossil, before it is once again photographed. Then, depending on the stability of the fossil, it is coated with a thin glue via brush or aerosol in order to strengthen its structure, before being wrapped in a series of paper, bubble wrap and Hessian cloth. Finally, it is transported to the laboratory.

A europasaurus fossil is examined

THE FOSSIL RECORD

By examining discovered fossils, it is possible to piece together a rough history of the development of life on Earth over a geological timescale

© Wallace63

12 | CAMBRIAN | 542-488.3 Ma

The first geological period of the Paleozoic era, the Cambrian is unique in its high proportion of sedimentary layers and, consequently, adpression fossils. The Burgess Shale Formation, a notable fossil field dating from the Cambrian, has revealed many fossils including the genus opabinia, a five-eyed ocean crawler.

11 | ORDOVICIAN | 488.3-443.7 Ma

Boasting the highest sea levels on the Palaezoic era, the Ordovician saw the proliferation of planktonics, brachiopods and cephalopods. Nautiloids, suspension feeders, are among the largest creatures from this period to be discovered.

© Jlorenzi

10 | SILURIAN | 443.7-416 Ma

With its base set at major extinction event at the end of the Ordovician, the silurian fossils found differ markedly from those that pre-date the period. Notable life developments include the first bony fish, and organisms with moveable jaws.

9 | DEVONIAN | 416-359.2 Ma

An incredibly important time for the development of life, the Devonian period has relinquished fossils demonstrating the evolution of the pectoral and pelvic fins of fish into legs. The first land-based creatures, tetrapods and arthopods, become entrenched and seed-bearing plants spread across dry lands. A notable find is the genus tiktaalik.

© Nils Knötschke

OLD

1. Mrs Ples
An example of one of our common ancestors (australopithecus africanus), Mrs Ples is a remarkably preserved skull. Carbon dating suggests she lived 2.05 million years ago.

OLDER

2. Archaeopteryx
The earliest and most primitive bird to be uncovered, archaeopteryx lived in the late Jurassic period (150-148 Ma) and is often cited as evidence of a transitional fossil between dinosaurs and birds.

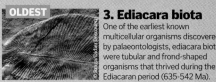

OLDEST

3. Ediacara biota
One of the earliest known multicellular organisms discovered by palaeontologists, ediacara biota were tubular and frond-shaped organisms that thrived during the Ediacaran period (635-542 Ma).

DID YOU KNOW? The minimum age for an excavated specimen to be classed as a fossil is 10,000 years

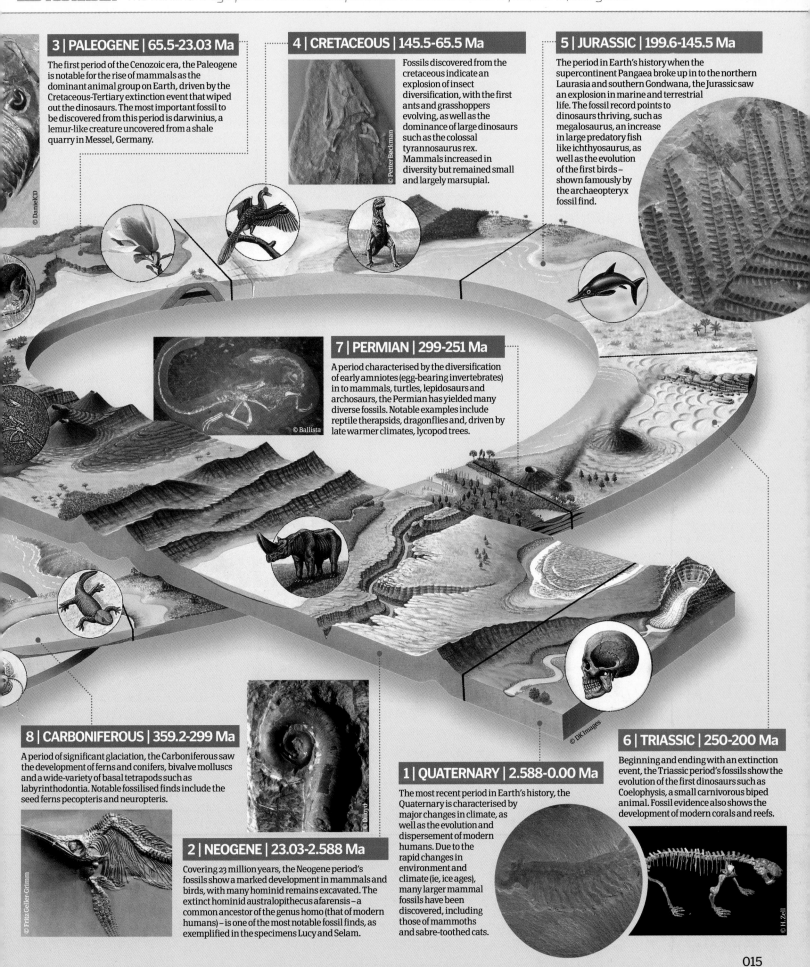

3 | PALEOGENE | 65.5-23.03 Ma
The first period of the Cenozoic era, the Paleogene is notable for the rise of mammals as the dominant animal group on Earth, driven by the Cretaceous-Tertiary extinction event that wiped out the dinosaurs. The most important fossil to be discovered from this period is darwinius, a lemur-like creature uncovered from a shale quarry in Messel, Germany.

4 | CRETACEOUS | 145.5-65.5 Ma
Fossils discovered from the cretaceous indicate an explosion of insect diversification, with the first ants and grasshoppers evolving, as well as the dominance of large dinosaurs such as the colossal tyrannosaurus rex. Mammals increased in diversity but remained small and largely marsupial.

5 | JURASSIC | 199.6-145.5 Ma
The period in Earth's history when the supercontinent Pangaea broke up in to the northern Laurasia and southern Gondwana, the Jurassic saw an explosion in marine and terrestrial life. The fossil record points to dinosaurs thriving, such as megalosaurus, an increase in large predatory fish like ichthyosaurus, as well as the evolution of the first birds – shown famously by the archaeopteryx fossil find.

7 | PERMIAN | 299-251 Ma
A period characterised by the diversification of early amniotes (egg-bearing invertebrates) in to mammals, turtles, lepidosaurs and archosaurs, the Permian has yielded many diverse fossils. Notable examples include reptile therapsids, dragonflies and, driven by late warmer climates, lycopod trees.

8 | CARBONIFEROUS | 359.2-299 Ma
A period of significant glaciation, the Carboniferous saw the development of ferns and conifers, bivalve molluscs and a wide-variety of basal tetrapods such as labyrinthodontia. Notable fossilised finds include the seed ferns pecopteris and neuropteris.

2 | NEOGENE | 23.03-2.588 Ma
Covering 23 million years, the Neogene period's fossils show a marked development in mammals and birds, with many hominid remains excavated. The extinct hominid australopithecus afarensis – a common ancestor of the genus homo (that of modern humans) – is one of the most notable fossil finds, as exemplified in the specimens Lucy and Selam.

1 | QUATERNARY | 2.588-0.00 Ma
The most recent period in Earth's history, the Quaternary is characterised by major changes in climate, as well as the evolution and dispersement of modern humans. Due to the rapid changes in environment and climate (ie, ice ages), many larger mammal fossils have been discovered, including those of mammoths and sabre-toothed cats.

6 | TRIASSIC | 250-200 Ma
Beginning and ending with an extinction event, the Triassic period's fossils show the evolution of the first dinosaurs such as Coelophysis, a small carnivorous biped animal. Fossil evidence also shows the development of modern corals and reefs.

"Pollen is the fine powder produced by the male sex organs of a flower"

Woodpeckers explained

Woodpeckers whack their heads against wood up to 20 times a second, at 1,200 times the force of gravity, without suffering concussion, detached retinas or any other symptoms of head injury. But why?

Woodpeckers' tongues have longitudinal muscles for side-to-side movement when poking around for insects

How does pollen work?

Discover how this 'irritating' flower powder functions, enabling germination

Pollen is the fine powder produced by the male sex organs of a flower. It contains the male gametes (or sex cells). When a grain lands on the stigma of a flower of the same species, a special pollen tube grows from the grain of pollen down through the flower's style to link the sperm cells to the unfertilised eggs in the flower's ovaries. Here germination takes place, as the ovules are fertilised and a seed forms.

Heavier pollen is transferred to plants by insects going from flower to flower. However, the lighter airborne pollen that gets blown from one flower to another is the stuff that causes people with pollen allergies to experience hay fever. ⚙

Holes
Woodpeckers excavate small rectangular holes on the sides of tree trunks, prying off wood to expose tasty beetle larvae and carpenter ants.

Skull
Woodpeckers have a thicker skull than most other birds. It's made of extremely strong yet spongy compressible bone, to help cushion the blow. The beak and skull are linked by elastic connective tissue.

Brain
Unlike human brains, which are floating about in a pool of cushioning cerebrospinal fluid, woodpecker brains are tightly enclosed in the skull with practically no cerebrospinal fluid.

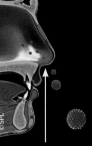

Sex cells
Inside a grain of pollen are the male sex cells, called 'gametes'.

Inner lining
The inner wall of a grain of pollen is the intine. It encloses the sex cells and other vegetative cells.

Outer wall
The protective outer wall is the exine. It has a different patterned structure, depending on species.

Stiff tail feathers
The woodpecker can prop itself up like a tripod, using its strong tail-feather muscles.

Beak
The strong bones that comprise the woodpecker's straight bill are strengthened by a horn-covered beak, which hammers into the wood and bark of a tree at something like 12,000 impacts per day in search of bugs and ants.

Hyoid apparatus
Within the long tongue is a skeletal structure called the 'hyoid apparatus'. This is a collection of small bones supported by cartilage and muscles, which fold up like an accordion and enable the woodpecker to stick its tongue out further.

Third eyelid
Woodpeckers have a thick inner eyelid, which acts as a seatbelt to ensure the bird's eyeballs don't pop out and also prevents tearing the retina. The eye is filled with blood to support the retina.

Zygodactyl feet
For optimum insect foraging, woodpeckers' feet are zygodactyl, which helps them cling onto vertical tree trunks. Zygodactyl means they have two front-facing toes and two back-facing toes.

Hay fever
When someone with a pollen allergy breathes in pollen, chemicals and antibodies are produced and released to fight the infection.

Pollen count
The pollen count is a measure of the number of grains of pollen present in a cubic metre of air. The higher the pollen count, the worse the hay fever symptoms.

LOW	30
MODERATE	30-49
HIGH	50-149
VERY HIGH	149 AND OVER

Barbed tongue
Because a woodpecker probes around inside tree trunks for insects, its barbed tongue needs to be longer than its beak – sometimes up to four times longer. In some species the tongue actually forks in the throat and disappears below the base of the jaw, wrapping up and over the head before rejoining behind the eye socket or nostril.

Neck muscles
A split second before every tap, the dense muscles in the bird's neck contract and distribute the force of the impact away from the skull down through the rest of the body, like shock absorbers.

Best mates...

To lay her eggs, the female frog is stimulated by a special embrace (called amplexus) from her mate, who then fertilises the mass of embryos (spawn) she produces. Although the female can lay up to 4,000 eggs, only a few will survive against the elements and other aquatic predators.

Ligers and tigons

When lions and tigers mate, new species are born

Ligers and tigons are two resultant species that emanate when lions and tigers cross breed. If a male lion mates with a tigress then a liger is born, if a male tiger mates with a lioness then a tigon is born. Both hybrid species are extinct in the wild as their respective habitats lead to minimal interaction, however many examples of both species can be found in captivity across the world in zoos and wildlife parks.

Ligers are now the more prevalent of the two species due to the greater probability of them living past birth, although during the early-20th Century this was not the case. The liger, as with the tigon, shares characteristics from both parent species – ligers enjoy swimming for example, a trait which is associated with tigers, however they also have spots, a characteristic gene of the lion – and tends to be bigger due to imprinted genes. Indeed, the current largest liger in the world weighs over 400 kilograms and is twice the size of its parents. Interestingly, though, tigons tend to suffer from dwarfism rather than gigantism as they always inherit the growth-inhibitory genes from the lioness mother, often weighing only around 200 kilograms.

Unfortunately, due to the hybrid man-made nature of ligers and tigons, growth disorders and degenerative diseases are common, as well as shortened life spans. ✿

Size
Ligers can grow to twice the size of their parents.

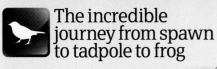

Inherited
Ligers enjoy swimming like their mother, and can have spots like their father.

A male liger in Novosibirsk Zoo, Russia

The life cycle of an amphibian

The incredible journey from spawn to tadpole to frog

4. Tadpole
At six days old, the egg hatches and becomes a tadpole. External gills develop to filter water and take in tiny bits of food. A sucker protrudes beneath the head end, which can suck onto plant matter.

3. Tail bud
The tail bud forms at around the four-day mark. Muscles have begun to develop and the embryo feeds on the yolk inside itself.

2. Mutation
Following a mere matter of hours after the egg has been laid, the metamorphosis has begun.

1. Egg
Several layers of absorbent watery jelly swell to protect a single tiny embryo that has been fertilised by the male frog. Water is vital to the development of these aquatic babies.

5. Internal gills
Nine days into metamorphosis, a flap of skin grows over the external gills and replacement internal gills develop. A spiracle (pore) remains on the left-hand side where water can escape. The tadpole's eyes are not yet fully formed.

6. Hind legs
Next the internal gills develop and a pair of hind legs form.

7. Front legs
The final stage of a frog's development (around 75 days) includes the arrival of front legs and lungs to replace the internal gills. Amphibians can also breathe through their mucous-covered skin.

8. Froglet
For the next one to two years, the young frog's tail will become increasingly short until it's barely a tail at all.

9. Frog
A frog becomes an adult at the tender age of three years. It will breathe using its fully formed lungs and will take to the land to seek out a mate and begin the whole process again.

"Crocodile teeth are only designed for gripping and puncturing"

How crocodiles hunt prey

They outlived the dinosaurs but these hunters are anything but elderly

Crocodiles are often described as living fossils, but despite the fact that their body shape hasn't changed much in the last 200 million years, they are actually some of the most sophisticated reptiles on Earth.

Like all living reptiles, they are cold blooded but that doesn't make them sluggish. Crocodiles have a four-chambered heart and muscles that mimic our diaphragm to ensure they can quickly pump oxygen around their bodies for explosive bursts of speed. Crocodiles are ambush predators; their preferred tactic is to lurk in the river with just their eyes and nostrils visible above the surface and burst out of the water to surprise animals that have come to the bank to drink. If their initial lunge fails, they can chase prey over land at speeds of 17km/h (10.5mph). The galloping gait of the crocodile was dismissed as a folk legend for many years, simply because hardly anyone who witnessed it lived to tell the tale.

Once a crocodile has grabbed its prey, it will drag it into the water and pull it under. Crocodiles need air to breathe but they can hold their breath for 30 minutes and drowning your prey is easier and more reliable than risking it escaping if you unclamp your jaws. Crocodile teeth are only designed for gripping and puncturing; they have no incisors or carnassials to slice meat off a carcass. Instead they will grip a

chunk of flesh with the front teeth and spin violently on their long axis to twist off a bite-sized piece. Crocodiles don't have lips so they can't seal their mouth shut when eating. This means they can't swallow food underwater without drowning themselves so each torn off mouthful has to be brought to the surface and tossed into the back of the mouth.

When food is scarce, their cold-blooded metabolism allows crocodiles to go for as long as two years without eating at all. This, combined with their ability to scavenge rotting meat, was probably what allowed them to survive the event that killed the dinosaurs. ✿

A stealthy croc spies its prey from the water

Eyes
Mounted on the top of the head to allow it to watch the bank while almost submerged. A nictitating membrane protects them underwater.

Teeth
Crocodiles have 64 to 70 teeth, which are replaced continuously throughout the animal's life.

Tongue
A crocodile can't stick its tongue out of its mouth because it is anchored to the floor of the mouth all the way along.

Salt glands
Special glands on the top of the tongue allow crocodiles to excrete salt that builds up in their blood in saltwater environments.

Jaw muscle
The massive muscle and its placement a long way forward of the hinge provides a bite pressure almost twice that of a great white shark.

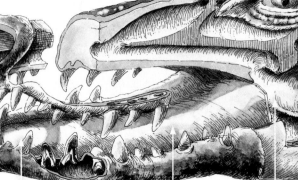

Although the teeth are deadly its the death grip that kills

ON THE MAP

Where to find crocodiles
1 Central America
2 The Amazon Rainforest
3 Sub-Saharan Africa
4 Tropical regions of Asia and the Far East
5 Northern Australia

Let's talk about sex

Crocodiles don't have sex chromosomes. Instead the sex of a crocodile is determined by the temperature at which its egg is incubated. If it is close to 31.6°C it will hatch as a male; anything higher or lower produces a female.

DID YOU KNOW? The largest crocodile in the world is called Utan and measures over six metres long

Anatomy of a river killer

Inside the body of the oldest killer on the planet

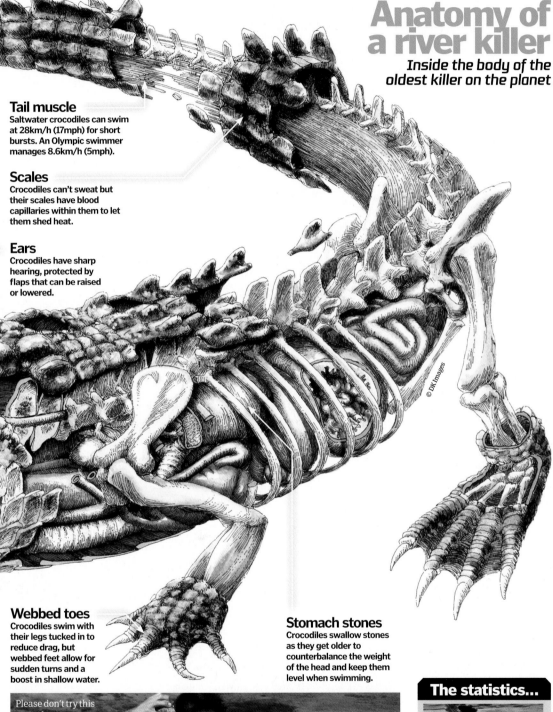

© DK Images

Tail muscle
Saltwater crocodiles can swim at 28km/h (17mph) for short bursts. An Olympic swimmer manages 8.6km/h (5mph).

Scales
Crocodiles can't sweat but their scales have blood capillaries within them to let them shed heat.

Ears
Crocodiles have sharp hearing, protected by flaps that can be raised or lowered.

Webbed toes
Crocodiles swim with their legs tucked in to reduce drag, but webbed feet allow for sudden turns and a boost in shallow water.

Stomach stones
Crocodiles swallow stones as they get older to counterbalance the weight of the head and keep them level when swimming.

Please don't try this one at home

© Cameloctober

Crocodile or alligator?

A field spotter's guide to carnivorous reptiles

Crocodile
Location: Crocodiles live in Africa, Asia, Australia and the Americas, in both fresh and saltwater.

Snout shape: The V-shaped snout is a general-purpose design for catching fish, reptiles and mammals.

Jaws/teeth: The upper and lower jaws are the same width, so the fourth tooth in the lower jaw sticks up.

Colour: Mottled green or sandy yellow, with slightly darker scales along the back and tail.

Skin: Each scale has a pore near the edge, visible even on crocodile handbags and wallets.

© Arfan

Alligator
Location: Alligators are only found in the southern United States and China and vastly prefer freshwater.

Snout shape: A heavier, U-shaped snout provides extra strength for cracking turtle shells.

Jaws/teeth: A wider upper jaw completely covers all the teeth in the lower jaw when the mouth is closed.

Colour: Much darker, sometimes almost completely black, depending on the water quality.

Skin: Alligators only have pores on the scales that are covering the upper and lower jaws.

Fact
A crocodile with a very long, thin snout, is actually a gharial. Caimans look like a slightly smaller alligator, but you can tell them apart because the large scales on their head form a four-four-two pattern, instead of two-two-two.

The statistics...

Crocodile

Type:	Reptile
Diet:	Carnivore
Average life span in the wild:	70 years
Weight:	1,200kg
Size:	4.85m

How rivers

The river's fascinating processes and intriguing features from start to finish

Beginning life in the mountains, rivers form from streams created through precipitation or springs of water that are sourced from groundwater that has percolated the earth. These streams, known as tributaries, then flow rapidly through V-shaped valleys, over rocky terrain and over rock edges as waterfalls. This is the first of three stages any river goes through and is known as the upper course, or youth.

By the second stage – known as the middle course, or maturity – many tributaries will have joined together to form the main body of water that makes up the river. The river meanders at a medium speed across narrow flood plains, which are areas of flat land lying either side of a river. Flood plains are formed when successive flooding causes sediment to be deposited on the banks.

As the river follows its course it carries with it a load, which is made up of rocks, stones, sand and other particles. It is the load that causes erosion as the materials crash against the banks of the river. The load is transported down the river in four ways, depending upon the size of the material. Traction is the rolling of the largest particles across the riverbed, whereas saltation is the bouncing of those slightly smaller. Finer materials are carried along through suspension and some are dissolved within the water and are moved through solution.

The final stage of a river is the lower course, predictably sometimes known as old age. By this time the river has slowed considerably as it heads towards the sea across broad flood plains, finally ending at what is known as the mouth, where the river finally joins the ocean. Deltas are formed as the river then deposits its load. ❀

Waterfall
These are formed over thousands of years as the river erodes away soft rock; the more the soft rock is eroded the steeper the drop becomes.

Flood plain
This is the flat land either side of the river, where floodwater goes and sediment is deposited when the river floods.

Meander
As the river travels its course its load erodes the sides and carves out bends known as meanders.

Deltas, estuaries and the river mouth

The mouth of a river signifies the end of its course and is where the river meets the sea. The 'D' shaped area of sediment that forms at the river mouth is called a delta. Deltas are built up from the bed as the river slows and deposits its load as it reaches the end of its course. The river tends to split as it travels over a delta.

Estuaries are also found at the mouth of a river. In these areas the fresh water of the river meets and mixes with the salt water of the sea. Estuaries are affected by the tide, and the combination of salt and fresh water provides a diverse habitat for many plants and animals.

The delta of the Atchafalaya River on the Gulf of Mexico

The river system

Delta
This is where the river slows down as it reaches the sea and as the water slows it deposits its load. This deposited sediment forms the delta.

Mouth
The mouth is the end of the river, where it widens and joins with the sea. All rivers end this way.

LARGEST

1. Amazon
Location: Brazil
Containing 20 per cent of the planet's fresh water, the Amazon is the largest river in the world based upon the volume of water it carries.

HOLIEST

2. Ganges
Location: India
Hindus make pilgrimage to India's largest river south of the Himilayas to bathe in its water, which is believed to wash away sins.

SHORTEST

3. D River and Roe River
Location: USA
A long controversy resulted in two 200-foot rivers being awarded the title of shortest river in the world.

© Bryce W Harrington 07

DID YOU KNOW? We all live in a river basin. Even if you don't live close to a river, all land drains to a river system

work

Source
It is here the river begins its life, in the form of small streams up in the mountains, which eventually come together to form the main body of the river.

© Science Photo Library

River basin
All of the land around the river is the river basin. The water drains from this land into the river.

A river in the Yamal Peninsula, Siberia that's produced oxbow lakes

Fast-moving current, aided by waterfalls

Oxbow lakes

Oxbow lakes are crescent- or horseshoe-shaped lakes situated at the side of a flowing river. They are formed from river meanders and are the result of lateral erosion cutting into the bends of the river's course where the river is flowing at its fastest. This eventually leads to the two bends joining together and altering the river's course. Deposition also plays a role as sediment builds up on the outside of the bend where the river flow is much slower. As the river breaks through and the bends join, the sediment builds up to cut off the meander and an oxbow lake is formed.

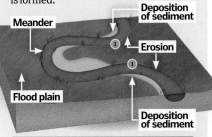

Deposition of sediment

Meander

Erosion

Flood plain

Deposition of sediment

Stage one

As the water flows around the meander it flows fastest at points 1, leading to the materials carried by the river crashing into (and therefore eroding) the bends.

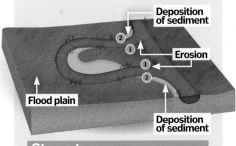

Deposition of sediment

Erosion

Flood plain

Deposition of sediment

Stage two

The river flows slowest at points 2, which leads to deposition of sediment. The continuous erosion at points 1 has led to breakthrough, where the curves of the meander have joined together, changing the flow of the river's course.

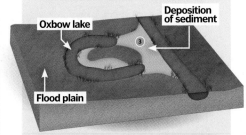

Deposition of sediment

Oxbow lake

Flood plain

Stage three

More deposition at point 3 has led to a crescent-shaped lake being completely separated from the river. This lake is known as an oxbow lake and in time will become a wetland, followed by a meadow where trees and plants will develop.

Animal camouflage

The sneaky secrets of the most amazing animals you've never seen

Almost every animal has a good reason to hide. Going undetected makes it easier to catch food – and easier to avoid becoming someone else's. In any species, the individuals that stand out the most will be the first to be eaten and the last to catch their own dinner, and so natural selection picks the ones with the best camouflage.

There are several different kinds of camouflage. The most basic is to hide under a rock, or in sand or leaves. This is sometimes called 'crypsis', and some animals will incorporate bits of their environment on their bodies to improve the effect. Three-toed sloths have algae growing in their fur, which gives them a dark green hue that helps them hide among the trees. Coral crabs deliberately attach young polyps to their shells so they resemble part of the reef.

The next step is to change your own body colouration. Mammals have a colour pallette restricted to white, black, brown and yellow, but fish, amphibians, reptiles and birds can all produce a vivid array of greens and bright red. Red might not seem like a great colour for camouflage, but lots of seaweed and corals are red, and in fact many sea creatures obtain the red pigment for their bodies by eating the corals and seaweed that they hide among.

Camouflage is a show performed for a few specific observers. Most mammals see in black and white, or only two colours. Primates see three primary colours while birds see four. Insects can see well into the ultraviolet part of the spectrum and many snakes can sense infrared. Choosing the right camouflage is about exploiting the weaknesses in your target's visual system. Even if your colour is a very close match to your surroundings, your outline can still give you away. One of the earliest parts of the brain to evolve was concerned with recognising the edges of things, and most animals still have a dedicated outline recognition brain region. Good camouflage uses contrasting patterns of light and dark, or different colours. These trick the outline recognition system so that it mentally carves up your shape into smaller, irregular blocks. In some environments, there is so little to hide

5 TOP FACTS
MASTERS OF DISGUISE

Pink soft coral crab
1 This crab attaches coral polyps to its own shell as a sort of marine ghillie suit. With matching shell colouration from eating coral, it becomes a walking coral reef.

Sea dragon
2 The leaf-like protrusions on this relative of the seahorse make fast swimming impossible, but they do provide excellent camouflage.

Ghanaian praying mantis
3 Normally green, the Ghanaian praying mantis will moult its skin and change to a black colour after a forest fire, in order to retain its camouflage.

Leaf insect
4 The wide flattened body of the leaf insect looks just like a leaf, and the legs are disguised either as smaller leaves or as bite marks from the main leaf depending on the species.

Gaboon viper
5 A 1.5m snake that's as thick as your arm sounds hard to miss, but the incredibly disruptive pattern perfectly matches the jumble of dried leaves on the African forest floor.

DID YOU KNOW? *Tigers are well camouflaged in the jungle because most of the animals they hunt are green/orange colour blind*

A broadclub cuttlefish

How the cuttlefish gets its spots

Cephalopods – particularly the octopus and the cuttlefish – are the undisputed masters of the quick change. Their skin is packed with specialised cells called 'chromatophores' that change the colour or reflectivity of the skin. Each chromatophore has its own activating muscle and nerve fibre, and these are connected to a part of the brain dedicated to coordinating the complex patterns. Although the chromatophores only contain red, yellow and brown pigments, cuttlefish can create almost any colour by combining different layers of coloured and reflecting cells. Green, for example, is achieved by using an iridescent layer deep in the skin to scatter light back through yellow pigments, which act as a filter. All the layers are controlled independently and simultaneously, so a cuttlefish can change its entire skin colour in less than a second. Chameleons use a similar arrangement of skin cells but the chromatophores are controlled using hormones, rather than nerve impulses, so the change occurs more slowly.

Harmless hoverflies can mimic wasps

Under the skin

Chromatophore
When the cell is relaxed, the pigment forms an inconspicuous dot in the centre. By pulling the radial muscles, the chromatophore is stretched into a larger disc and the colour is visible.

Pigment
Radial muscle fibres

☐ Orange-yellow ☐ Red-orange ☐ Black-brown

Iridophore
Iridophores generate iridescent colours using stacked crystals of translucent guanine proteins as tiny prisms. By altering the angle of the iridophore, the colour changes.

Iridosomal platelet
Nucleus

☐ Pinks ☐ Yellows ☐ Greens ☐ Blues ☐ Silver

Leucophore
Leucophores use the same proteins as iridophores, but instead of stacking them in plates, the crystals are arranged on the surface of the cell. Squeezing or flattening the cell controls how much light is reflected.

Nucleus
Cell body
Transparent refractive granule

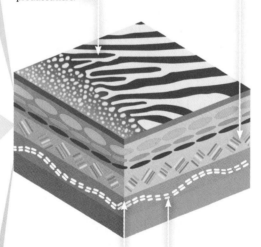

Top layer
Stacked layers of chromatophores contain the three basic pigments. Reds, yellows, browns and black colours are all produced here.

Middle layer
The iridophores create interference patterns to generate shimmering, metallic patterns, and are also used to create blue and green colours.

Mirror granules
The guanine crystals are actually transparent, but by arranging them in tiny beads they act like crushed glass and form a white base.

Base layer
Leucophores are white. White is used as a danger signal by many octopuses, but this layer is also used as a 'base coat' to modify the colours of the chromatophores above.

What's brown and sticky? A stick!

Camouflage is usually about blending anonymously into the background, but there are times when it is better to disguise yourself as something specific. Mimics copy the shape, colouring, movement and sometimes even the smell of another species to fool prey or predators. This is an evolutionary arms race. As predators evolve more and more acute senses to see through the subterfuge, so the mimics must constantly refine their disguise. One of the most common forms of mimicry, Batesian mimicry is where a harmless species pretends to be a dangerous one, such as the many species of hoverfly that mimic stinging wasps. But poisonous species can mimic each other, too. Monarch and viceroy butterflies show this kind of 'Müllerian mimicry' – both are toxic, but they have evolved to mimic each other so that bird predators only have to learn one wing pattern to avoid, rather than two.

behind that this 'dazzle' camouflage is all you have. The Royal Navy used this technique in World War I to make it hard to judge the speed and heading of battleships on the featureless ocean. But the orca, or killer whale, beat them to it by several million years. The bright patches of white on a black body disrupt its outline so that it is not immediately recognised as a threat. Zebras use the same technique, but this time the entire herd merges into one huge zebra that is much more intimidating and confusing to lions and cheetahs.

Sometimes, a purely visual camouflage isn't enough. Procrypsis is the technique of camouflaging your movement. Predators are acutely sensitive to movement, but a typical forest is a whirl of activity and they must quickly tune out the background motions of wind, water and all the non-food animals if they are not to be overwhelmed. Chameleons, leaf insects and preying mantises can exploit this by moving with a rocking motion that mimics the swaying of branches in the wind. Some Pacific octopuses will curl up like a rock, but still manage to move along the seabed by synchronising movement with the back-and-forth patterns of shadow cast by sunlight through the waves.

A monarch butterfly mimics to ward off predators

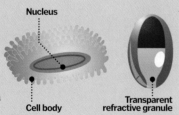

"Camouflage is a show performed for a few specific observers"

Jungle illusionists
An impressive game of hide and seek takes place among the trees

Jackson's chameleon
Technique: Colour and movement
Reason: Hunting
In the lush, high-altitude forests of Kenya and Tanzania, the bright green skin of the Jackson's chameleon blends with the mosaic of thick waxy leaves. Their skin is mottled to break up the animal's outline and has very rough scales to create a thorny, irregular texture. When they perch, their long tail is coiled into a tight circle to help the chameleon look more like a leaf, and they move with a swaying motion to mimic the effect of the breeze through the branches.

Tawny frogmouth
Technique: Disruptive colour pattern
Reason: Defensive
This distant relative of the owl and cuckoo lives in Australia and New Guinea. It eats insects and small frogs by sitting still until food comes within range, and then pouncing. It feeds at night, so the camouflage is to protect it during the day. Perched motionless in the crook of a tree branch or on a dead log, the pattern of its feathers mimics the texture of tree bark.

Bird dropping spider
Technique: Mimicry
Reason: Defensive
This Australian spider catches moths at night by luring them with their own sex pheromones, but during the day it is vulnerable to being eaten by birds. So it disguises itself as the least appetising thing for a bird: their own droppings! The creamy-coloured abdomen with brown stippled patches closely resembles the guano of a bird that feeds on insects.

Jaguar
Technique: Disruptive pattern
Reason: Hunting
Hiding 100kg of big cat in the dense forests of south America isn't easy, but if you are an ambush predator, it's vital that you succeed. Jaguars use a similar rosette pattern on their fur to the African leopard but the rosettes are larger, darker and have a small spot in the middle. The effect is similar to the dappled shade cast by the thick jungle foliage on the forest floor. This makes it very hard to trace the outline of the jaguar, until it moves. And by then, it's too late.

Lying low on the land
The land is home to many sly creatures, so watch your step

Human vision

Lion vision

A lone zebra is easier for lions and other predators to see, compared to when they're huddled together

Israeli sand gecko
Technique: Colour and counter-shading
Reason: Protection and hunting
Sand geckos use the huge surface area on their finger pads to cling to the walls or roofs of rock crevices in the desert. The mottled sandy colour that covers all of their upper surface, including their eyelids, blends against the gritty sandstone rocks. When they are the right way up, hunting insects on the desert floor, their white belly appears to neutralise the shadow cast by their upper body.

DID YOU KNOW?

Chameleon changes
The word 'chameleon' is a by-word for invisibility and camouflage, but most chameleons don't change colour to match their surroundings. Their default colour is already an excellent camouflage and colour changes are used to signal their mood to other chameleons.

DID YOU KNOW? The Indonesian mimic octopus is so good at hiding, it wasn't officially discovered until 1998

Zebra
Technique: Dazzle pattern
Reason: Confusing predators
The African savannah is a difficult place to hide, but the bright stripes of the zebra work in a different way. Instead of making the animal blend into its surroundings, they make it blend into the herd. When threatened, zebras huddle together and the stripes make it difficult to tell where one starts and another ends. Lions and other predators rely on splitting one target away from the herd. The visual clump created by the stripes confuses and acts as a survival technique for the zebra.

Mackerel
Technique: Stripes and counter-shading
Reason: Defensive
Mackerel swim in huge schools. Seen from above, the distinctive striped pattern resembles the rippling pattern of shadow seen in shallow seas. At close range the effect may be similar to the zebra's stripes and make it hard for predators to lock on to any single fish. The counter-shaded belly is common to most fish, making them harder to spot from below against the lighter surface.

Invisible mysteries of the deep
Below the surface of the water lurk a talented band of beasts

Cuttlefish
Technique: Colour changing
Reason: Signalling, hunting and protection
Cuttlefish have the most advanced colour-changing system of any animal. Not only can they change their colour in less than a second, but they can also move from static camouflage patterns to rapidly pulsing displays to hypnotise prey or communicate with other cuttlefish. Their skin can also change the polarisation of the light reflecting off it, important because many marine animals are sensitive to the polarisation angle of light.

Snowshoe hare
Technique: Seasonal colour
Reason: Defensive
During the short Alaskan spring and summer, the snowshoe hare has fur that is standard 'rabbit brown' to blend against the leaves and heather. But this hare doesn't hibernate and a brown animal wouldn't last long on a carpet of snow, with lynx and great horned owls patrolling. So it moults to a winter coat, which is pure white except for a black tip on each ear.

Indonesian mimic octopus
Technique: Colour changing and behavioural mimicry
Reason: Protection and hunting
The mimic octopus is an active predator and can't afford to spend long periods sitting on the seabed pretending to be a rock. But it does have lots of predators of its own, so uses its camouflage abilities to imitate more than 15 other animal species. As well as changing the colour and patterning of its skin, it can also radically alter its texture from smooth to spiny and contort its arms and body to change shape.

Egyptian nightjar
Technique: Colour and pattern
Reason: Protecting its eggs
Birds normally defend themselves against predators by flying away, but the Egyptian nightjar lives in the desert, where there are no trees for roosting. It also eats moths, which means it is active by night. In the day it rests on the sandy ground, but its mottled brown, rather scruffy-looking plumage is almost impossible to spot. The nightjar just looks like a stone or a piece of dried wood. Egyptian nightjars don't even build nests, hiding their eggs beneath their own camouflage.

Stonefish
Technique: Colour and spines
Reason: Ambush
The stonefish catches small fish and shrimp by lying still on the seabed and resembling a stone. When food swims close, it pounces and then goes back to being a stone. To defend itself from its own predators, the stonefish has 13 poisonous spines. Whereas most poisonous animals are brightly coloured as a warning, the stonefish's camouflage means that it's often trodden on by accident, killing a human in two hours.

"Male octopuses die after mating"

The statistics...

© H Zell

Octopus

Class: Cephalopod

Diet: Carnivore

Average life span in the wild: 6 months–5 years

Weight: 0.1-200kg

Size: 3cm–9m

Octopuses

The incredible abilities of this eight-legged wonder of the natural world, exposed

Octopuses are the superheroes of the animal kingdom, with so many amazing abilities and adaptations that it begins to look greedy. They can solve mazes, open screw-top jars and use tools. They can walk, they can swim and they can even jet propel themselves at high speed. They can change colour, imitate other animals, squirt ink, inject poison and jettison their own legs. When you can do all that, who cares if you can predict football results or not?

Although they are molluscs, octopuses don't have a shell or bones and the only hard part of their body is a small beak, made of keratin. This allows them to squeeze through extremely small gaps – an octopus a metre across can pass through a tube the size of a 50 pence coin. Octopuses mainly eat crabs and small fish that they winkle out of crevices in rocks and coral reefs, but they can also tackle small sharks by enveloping the shark's gill openings and suffocating them.

Octopus blood uses a greenish-blue copper pigment called haemocyanin, instead of the iron-based haemoglobin in our own blood. Haemocyanin can't carry as much oxygen as haemoglobin, but it is actually more efficient at low oxygen concentrations and in cold water. Despite this, octopuses have poor circulation and quickly run out of energy. This may be one of the reasons for their intelligence – they don't have the stamina for a prolonged chase and must rely on their cunning.

Male octopuses die almost immediately after mating. The females are even bigger martyrs. They guard their 20,000 eggs for a month and rather than leave the nest to hunt, they will eat some of their own legs. After that, the female dies and the eggs hatch into babies approximately the size of a walnut. ✿

Chromatophores
The colour-changing cells in the skin are funnel-shaped. By squeezing ink into the funnel from a bulb at the base, the octopus can control the size of the coloured dot.

Eye
This looks much like our own, with a lens and an iris but it evolved in a different way. Octopuses don't have a blind spot where the optic nerve passes through, because the retina is positioned differently.

Poison glands
These evolved from salivary glands, and as well as paralysing prey they also soften up the flesh, making it easier to eat.

© Gronk

Colouration
This blue-ringed octopus can change colour to match the sea bed or suddenly flash the bright blue rings to startle predators.

Suckers
Twin rows run the length of the tentacles to allow the octopus to grip and to taste anything it touches.

Jet-propelled

Octopuses normally swim by pulsing their tentacles, like the bell of a jellyfish. This is quite energy efficient but it lacks acceleration, so when an octopus needs a sudden turn of speed it switches to jet propulsion. To do this, they suck water into the mantle cavity and then squirt it at high pressure out of their siphon tube. This is the same way that they circulate water over their gills, so the octopus is really taking a deep breath and then blowing out hard. The siphon is positioned on the side of the octopus's body but it can be steered like the engines of a Harrier jet. Sometimes they use it as a boost when walking as well.

The way forward when the octopus needs a quick burst of speed
©albert kok

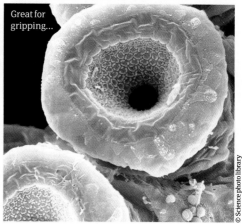
Great for gripping...
© Science photo library

SMART

© Steve Childs

1. Mimic octopus
To scare predators and fool prey, this octopus changes shape and colour to impersonate snakes, jellyfish and even crabs.

SMARTER

© Beckmannjan

2. Common octopus
Several octopuses in zoos have figured out how to undo screw-top jars to get at food inside.

SMARTEST

© Nhobgood

3. Coconut octopus
The only invertebrate to demonstrate tool use, the coconut octopus carries around two halves of a coconut shell and climbs inside when threatened.

DID YOU KNOW? Octopuses have three hearts; two pump blood through the gills, the third serves the rest of the body

Octopus anatomy

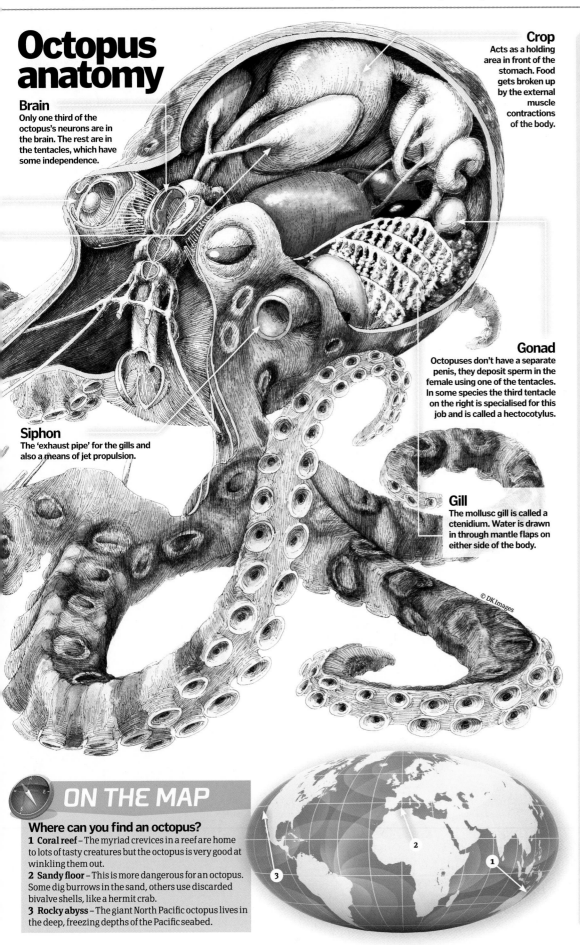

Brain
Only one third of the octopus's neurons are in the brain. The rest are in the tentacles, which have some independence.

Crop
Acts as a holding area in front of the stomach. Food gets broken up by the external muscle contractions of the body.

Siphon
The 'exhaust pipe' for the gills and also a means of jet propulsion.

Gonad
Octopuses don't have a separate penis, they deposit sperm in the female using one of the tentacles. In some species the third tentacle on the right is specialised for this job and is called a hectocotylus.

Gill
The mollusc gill is called a ctenidium. Water is drawn in through mantle flaps on either side of the body.

© DK Images

Defences

All octopuses inject a paralysing poison through their beak to subdue prey. The smaller the octopus, the more deadly the poison. The 10cm blue-ringed octopus can kill a human. Octopuses have lots of predators of their own though, and most of their adaptations are to evade capture. Colour-changing skin cells, called chromatophores, can be used for camouflage or to flash alarming colours to scare predators. Many species also have tiny muscles under the skin to change their texture to resemble spiky coral or fringed seaweed. The mimic octopus will even hold its legs and swim in such a way as to look like a flounder, sea snake or a poisonous lionfish. If that doesn't work, the octopus can squirt a cloud of melanin dye. This provides a smoke screen and also interferes with the sense of smell that most sharks use to locate prey.

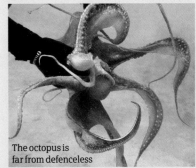

The octopus is far from defenceless

Intelligent legs

With the ability to twist in every direction, and suckers that can grip and release individually, octopus legs are much too complicated to be controlled from a central brain. Instead they operate semi-autonomously. An octopus is like a man holding a bunch of trained snakes; he issues instructions and trusts that they will be carried out, occasionally he has a look to make sure. This means that an octopus doesn't have a very good idea of where its legs actually are at any moment and can't work out the shape of something by feeling it, like we can.

Octopuses can taste through their suckers and can detach a leg and regenerate a new one if they need to give you the slip. One species, the Paper Nautilus, uses a leg to deliver sperm. It detaches and swims across to the female all by itself.

ON THE MAP

Where can you find an octopus?
1 Coral reef – The myriad crevices in a reef are home to lots of tasty creatures but the octopus is very good at winkling them out.
2 Sandy floor – This is more dangerous for an octopus. Some dig burrows in the sand, others use discarded bivalve shells, like a hermit crab.
3 Rocky abyss – The giant North Pacific octopus lives in the deep, freezing depths of the Pacific seabed.

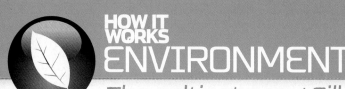

Why swim when you can lay back and read?

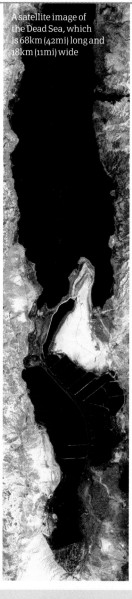
A satellite image of the Dead Sea, which is 68km (42mi) long and 18km (11mi) wide

The Dead Sea

What makes this ocean so much saltier than everywhere else?

The Dead Sea is the second saltiest body of water on the planet. Its water is around eight times saltier than ordinary seawater – and a quarter of the weight of Dead Sea water is salt. Salty water is denser than fresh water, so it's harder to sink in the Dead Sea than regular water. You can even float on your back and read a newspaper.

Salt collects in the Dead Sea because of its geography. The sea lies inland on the border of Jordan and Israel at the bottom of an enormous rift valley. It's the lowest spot on Earth – about 400m below sea level at the water's surface. Only the Jordan River flows into the Dead Sea, and no rivers out. Water can't escape except by evaporation. It's estimated that over 7 million tons of water evaporate each day due to the hot, dry climate. When this water evaporates, it leaves behind the salt it contains. ✿

DID YOU KNOW? The Dead Sea gets its name because only tiny plants and salt-loving bacteria can survive in the salty water.

Silkworms

How and why do these insects produce silk?

Silkworms produce liquid silk internally in two specially evolved glands. These glands feed the silkworm's spinneret, a single exit tube that protrudes from the head, from which the worm can direct the flow of the liquid into a matrix. As the liquid silk exits the spinneret, it hardens on contact with the air to form twin filaments composed of fibroin – a strong protein material – which is then covered with the gummy chemical sericin, excreted from a second pair of glands to cement the filaments together. Silkworms use their produced silk to build a protective cocoon for their metamorphosis into silk moths. Once unravelled, a single cocoon woven by a silkworm can measure up to 900m in length. ✿

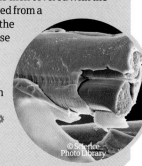

Heated cocoons mean that silk fibres can be woven

© Science Photo Library

Animal moulting

It's the circle of life in all its skin-shedding glory

Creatures throughout the animal kingdom undergo the process of moulting – the replacement of their horns, hair, skin or feathers. Insects moult to allow their growing bodies to expand beyond the constraints of their rigid exoskeleton, forming a new shell in the process and often eating the old one. Most mammals shed their hair in autumn to grow a thicker layer of protection for the winter, and vice versa for the summer.

Birds moult their feathers regularly as they become worn with use, growing fresh new ones in their place. Water birds, however, often lose all their feathers at once and thus the ability to fly, meaning that they must remain hidden from predators until their feathers have re-grown. Camouflaged animals keep their pattern when they're moulting except for decorator crabs, who transfer the camouflage from their old to new exoskeleton. ✿

Out with the old, in with the new…

The timescale of moulting for a southern hawker dragonfly is a little over three hours

5 TOP FACTS
EYES

Eye-spy
1 There are ten eye layouts falling into two categories. Simple eyes have one concave photoreceptive surface, while compound eyes have a number of lenses on a convex surface.

Seven
2 Simple eyes such as those of humans are very common on Earth and have evolved at least seven times from just a small grouping of photosensitive cells.

Mosaic
3 Adult dragonflies can have 30,000 ommatidia, giving them incredibly detailed, mosaic-like images to process. The quantity also grants them excellent movement sensing.

Different forms
4 Compound eyes come in two forms. Apposition eyes work by combining individual points of info together to form an image, while superposition eyes create one whole image.

Cambrian
5 Apposition eyes are almost certainly the original type of compound eye. The oldest eyes found are from the trilobites of the Cambrian Period (542-488.3 million years ago).

DID YOU KNOW? The ommatidia that make up compound eyes are between 5-50 micrometres in size

The head of a carpenter bee clearly showing its compound eye structure

A compound eye as imaged under an electron microscope. Note the numerous individual ommatidium

© Muhammad Mahdi Karim

Inside a bee's eye

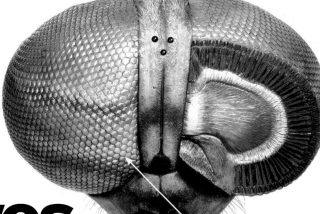

Cornea
The outer part of each ommatidium is overlaid with a transparent cornea that refracts incoming light.

Crystalline cone
Beneath the cornea of the ommatidium is a crystalline pseudocone that helps focus the light further into its body.

Photosensing cells
The inner 90 per cent of the ommatidium contains six to eight long, thin photosensing R cells.

Rhabdom
The portion of the R cells at the central axis of the ommatidium form a light guide, a tube referred to as the rhabdom.

Optic nerve
At the base of the rhabdom it meets an optic nerve which transmits the picture element to the brain.

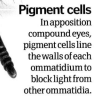

© DK Images

Pigment cells
In apposition compound eyes, pigment cells line the walls of each ommatidium to block light from other ommatidia.

Compound eyes

Allowing for an incredibly wide viewing angle and the detection of fast movement, compound eyes are highly technical biological structures

Compound eyes are made up of numerous small optical systems arranged around the outside of a convex surface. There are two different types of compound eye: apposition and superposition. The former is the more common and works by having each photorecepting system (the eye's ommatidia) independent from every other, each viewing light from just a small part of the overall picture, only to be then pieced together by the brain into a comprehensible whole. This differs from superposition compound eyes where the individual optical systems do not work separately from each other, but rather instead pool their light together to produce one single erect image at the back of the eye.

Indeed, apart from an external aesthetic similarity, with an array of facets positioned around a convex structure, the two compound eye types differ greatly in how they work. The main difference is most evident in how the two eyes' ommatidia process light to form an image. In apposition eyes each ommatidium consists of a thin, tapered tube capped with a cornea, beneath which is a transparent crystalline cone through which rays converge to an image at the tip of its receptive structure, referred to as the rhabdom. Each ommatidium is hexagonal in shape and lined with pigment cells, which act as a light barrier between each tube. Because of this, each ommatidium only receives an incredibly narrow proportion of incoming light from directly in front of it, each contributing a small part of the overall picture.

In superposition compound eyes, however, beneath the optical elements there is a wide transparent clear zone, unimpeded by pigment cells. This means that unlike apposition compound eyes where the ommatidium form small isolated images to be pieced together at the brain, the optical elements in superposition eyes superimpose all light rays received across the ommatidia to form one erect image on a deep-lying retina, only then having the whole image sent to the brain for processing.

There are benefits of each type of compound eye, compared to each other and standard lens-bearing eyes as sported by humans. The main benefits include a very large viewing angle – due to the convex array – fast movement tracking due to the amount of photorecepting units that do not have to individually move to track, and the ability to detect the polarisation of light. However, negatively, because the individual elements are so small, due to the principle of diffraction of light, resolution in compound eyes is considerably worse than in normal variants with large lenses (this is why astronomical telescopes have such large lenses or mirrors). The main benefit of superposition eyes over apposition eyes is their ability to deliver a picture in lower light conditions due to the convergence of gathered light rays. ✿

World's deadliest reptiles

We take a look at the most dangerous reptiles on Earth

From snakes to crocodiles, the deadliest reptiles on our planet have a variety of ways to kill, stun or disable a foe. Some, like the king cobra, possess a fatal amount of venom that they inject into their prey, while others like the saltwater crocodile use their strength to overpower enemies.

Across all corners of the globe lurks a reptile with the potential to cause harm. While some are unjustly feared despite their timid nature, others are not nearly feared enough. Attacks on humans in most cases are rare due to the knowledge of how dangerous these creatures can be. However, they are not unheard of, and when one of these animals is cornered or threatened its aggressive nature can quickly become apparent.

Read on and take a look at five of the planet's most lethal carnivorous reptiles, as we pit them head-to-head to find out which is the most deadly. ✿

King cobra

The largest venomous snake in the world, it strikes fear into the heart of its prey

Fortunately for us, the king cobra is generally shy and will slink away from humans. However, when defending itself or its eggs it is one of the most deadly reptiles known to man. When facing an attacker the cobra is able to raise 1.8 metres off the ground and move forward to attack.

They live in undergrowth present in rainforests and humid jungles. One of their terrifying characteristics is the ability to slide up trees, surveying the area and finding prey from above. They primarily eat other snakes and smaller reptiles, preferably non-venomous snakes. To find prey, it can "smell" nearby chemicals with its forked tongue.

To kill, the king cobra strikes and pierces its prey with its fangs, injecting a lethal amount of venom. A single bite from a king cobra will typically contain 6-7ml of neurotoxin, which is enough to kill up to 20 people. It then devours the creature whole. They are the only snakes that make nests for their eggs, and a female king cobra will lay anywhere from between 20 and 40 eggs at any one time. King cobras are generally found in southeast Asia, with the largest living in Malaysia.

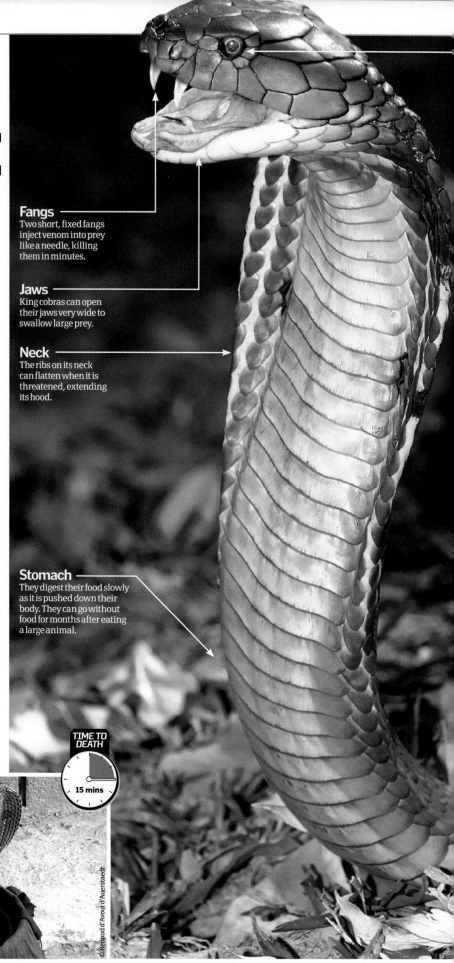

Fangs
Two short, fixed fangs inject venom into prey like a needle, killing them in minutes.

Jaws
King cobras can open their jaws very wide to swallow large prey.

Neck
The ribs on its neck can flatten when it is threatened, extending its hood.

Stomach
They digest their food slowly as it is pushed down their body. They can go without food for months after eating a large animal.

TIME TO DEATH
15 mins

Not the friendliest pet in the world...

© Renaud d'Avout d'Auerstaedt

Cold blooded
1 Reptiles are able to regulate their inner body temperature depending on the environment they are in, helping keep them alive in a number of different places and situations.

Skin
2 Reptiles have a dry and scaly skin that contains high levels of keratin, which prevents water loss and helps regulate the internal body temperature.

Heart
3 All reptiles have a three-chambered heart to pump blood around the entire body, except crocodiles, which have four chambers just like humans.

Eggs
4 Most reptiles lay eggs with a hard shell, and baby reptiles develop within the eggs from which they hatch, requiring both food and air immediately.

Air
5 Although some reptiles reside in or near water, they need a constant supply of air unlike amphibians, which live underwater when they are born.

DID YOU KNOW? There is enough venom in one bite from a king cobra to kill an elephant

King of the cobras

What makes this snake so deadly?

Eyes and ears
King cobras can see 100m away, and although they have no ears they can "hear" sound vibrations.

Skin
They shed their smooth-scaled skin about five times a year.

The statistics...

King cobra
Genus: Ophiophagus
Length: 3.6-5.5m
Weight: 6-9kg
Top speed: 16km/h (10mph)
Life span: 20 years

Kill factor
King cobra

Aggression: Generally shy, but make it mad and you'll quickly discover its bad temper.

Intelligence: Uses its hood, hiss and speed to its advantage when confronted.

Speed: Agile and quick, they can pounce forwards up to an incredible two metres.

Strength: On rare occasions they will use their muscular body to constrict prey.

Other: The fatality rate from its venom is up to 75 per cent, and can be as quick as 15 minutes.

Deadly rating:

Gila monster

The only venomous lizard which lives in the United States is shy but can be very deadly

Found across several states in America, including Nevada and California, the Gila monster is known for being timid but potentially very deadly. Its main source of attack is its venom. The teeth of a Gila monster have grooves which channel the venom into the wounds of its prey. They are average-sized lizards with powerful jaws and short legs adapted for digging.

Identifiable by their characteristic black bodies interspersed with orange, pink and yellow, Gilas are lethargic creatures that spend about 95 per cent of their lives underground in burrows. They eat mainly bird or reptile eggs and on occasion small birds, lizards and mammals. They are commonly thought to be very deadly and dangerous reptiles. However, their venom is primarily used for self-defence. They tend to bite their prey by surprise and come back when the venom has taken effect. Unless threatened, Gila monsters will only attack when seeking a meal.

TIME TO DEATH
1 hour

Caution! Handle with care!

Good looks
A stout body and beadlike scales, the Gila monster tends to reside in harsh desert environments.

Is it a monster?
The human risk is low, but this beast can be deadly

A hungry Gila can deliver a nasty nip

Fatty deposits
Gila monsters store fat in their tails – like a camel does in its hump – to be used during hibernation.

Kill factor
Gila monster

Aggression: Generally run or hide rather than fight.

Intelligence: Coloured scales allow limited camouflage when avoiding predators.

Speed: Sluggish and slow. Avoiding one shouldn't be too hard for a human.

Strength: Quite weak. They use venom to assist in hunting prey.

Other: Although deadly to smaller animals, its venom is rarely fatal in humans.

Deadly rating:

The statistics...

Gila monster
Genus: Heloderma
Length: 30-60cm
Weight: 1.3-2.2kg
Top speed: 24km/h (15mph)
Life span: 30 years

Which parts of the world do our deadly five inhabit?

- King cobra
- Gila monster
- Saltwater crocodile
- Komodo dragon
- Green anaconda

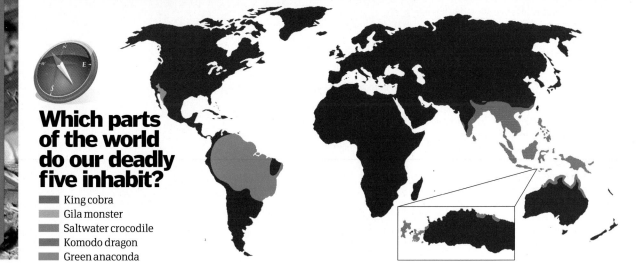

"The saltwater crocodile will typically overpower, drown and then dismember its prey"

Kill factor
Saltwater crocodile

Aggression: Very dangerous, particularly in mating season.

Intelligence: Use very clever hunting tactics.

Speed: Fast swimmers and slow walkers but have a quick leap.

Strength: A powerful bite and a muscular tail. Very strong.

Other: Young crocs are forced out of their home territory by domineering adults.

Deadly rating:
☠ ☠ ☠ ☠ ☠

TIME TO DEATH
60 secs

The statistics...
Saltwater crocodile

Genus:	Crocodylus
Length:	2.1-7.0m
Weight:	408-1,000kg
Top speed:	40km/h (25mph)
Life span:	70 years

Who knew they could do camouflage too?

Tail
The strong tail of a Komodo dragon is often longer than its body.

Kill factor
Komodo dragon

Aggression: Multiple attacks on Indonesian villages back in 2009 showed the dragon's aggressive potential.

Intelligence: Komodo dragons are smart animals, particularly when hunting.

Speed: Appear clumsy but can move as fast as a dog, and are excellent swimmers.

Strength: Weak bite but strong claws, and their tail can knock down large mammals like pigs.

Other: Slow acting but deadly venom. Dragons are typically quite solitary.

Deadly rating:
☠ ☠ ☠ ☠

The statistics...
Komodo dragon

Genus:	Varanus
Length:	2-3m
Weight:	68-91kg
Top speed:	(24km/h (15mph)
Life span:	30 years

Saltwater crocodile

The largest living crocodilian on Earth eats anything, even humans

When tackling large prey or attackers, the saltwater crocodile will typically overpower, drown and then dismember them. The crocodile can hold its prey underwater as it can separate its mouth from its throat, allowing it to open its massive jaw when fully submerged. To finish off its prey it will either drag it to land or hold it above water and swallow it vertically.

They are very intelligent creatures, lurking beneath the surface of the water until potential prey arrives for a drink. Using their powerful tail, they then suddenly leap out of the water and drag their prey back underwater. In the last 25 years they have been responsible for the death of about a dozen people.

They mostly eat small fish and land vertebrates but they are not picky eaters. Any mammal in its vicinity is good food as far as a saltwater crocodile is concerned. They have even been known to attack boats, mistaking them for enemies. Their jaws have a biting force of up to 2,300kg per square inch, the most powerful bite on the planet. On land they use their strong legs to move, while underwater they use their giant tail for propulsion.

They are generally found in brackish (slightly salty) waters such as rivers, swamps and estuaries. They are also occasionally seen in the open sea as they can swim up to 1,000km (620 miles), but they are most commonly found in northern Australia, southeast Asia and eastern India.

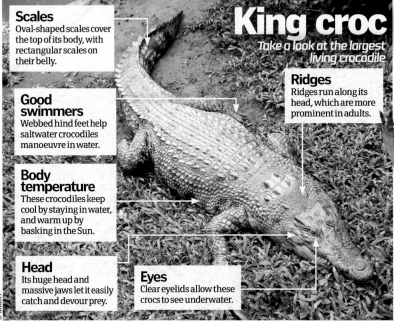

Scales
Oval-shaped scales cover the top of its body, with rectangular scales on their belly.

Good swimmers
Webbed hind feet help saltwater crocodiles manoeuvre in water.

Body temperature
These crocodiles keep cool by staying in water, and warm up by basking in the Sun.

Head
Its huge head and massive jaws let it easily catch and devour prey.

Eyes
Clear eyelids allow these crocs to see underwater.

Ridges
Ridges run along its head, which are more prominent in adults.

King croc
Take a look at the largest living crocodile

© Midori

A beast that can kill in just seconds

DAYS

1. Bite
Some reptiles seep venom into their prey when they bite, coming back to finish off their enemy up to a week later when the venom has taken effect.

Mats Stafseng Einarsen

HOURS

2. Venom
Toxins target the nerves and muscles in prey which provide movement, often rendering animals completely immobile in under an hour.

MINUTES

3. Constriction
Reptiles such as the anaconda asphyxiate their prey by coiling their body around that of the prey, stopping them breathing and killing them in minutes.

DID YOU KNOW? The Komodo dragon was discovered in WWI, when a pilot saw the reptiles after swimming to Komodo Island

Deadly dragon

What makes one of the last living relatives of the dinosaurs so deadly?

Skull
The skull of a dragon is designed to withstand large amounts of stress, so they can stop their prey pulling away.

Poison
Large glands channel venom between the animal's teeth, which then seeps into their prey.

Teeth
60 razor-sharp teeth help them literally tear their prey into shreds, known as pull-feeding.

Claws
Dragons use their long and powerful claws to climb trees, and also to attack prey.

Tongue
The long yellow forked tongue of a dragon detects the chemicals of nearby prey.

TIME TO DEATH
3 days

The world's deadliest hand puppet…

Komodo dragon

The world's heaviest living lizard is also one of the most dangerous reptiles

These huge lizards like to live an isolated existence except during mating season, when males will patrol and defend a territory up to 1.9km (1.2mi) long per day. They are found only on a small group of Indonesian islands in the Flores and Bali seas.

Komodo dragons are cannibalistic, but will also eat large prey such as pigs and deer of a similar size to themselves. Like saltwater crocodiles they are not fussy eaters, and will eat almost anything they can overpower, including other dragons. They are very quick eaters: a 45kg dragon was observed to eat a pig almost its own weight in 20 minutes, equivalent to a human eating 320 quarter-pound hamburgers in the same time.

It was only discovered in 2009 that Komodo dragons possess a deadly amount of venom, which they use to kill their prey. When hunting, a dragon will keep a vice-like grip on its prey with its mouth. Venom then seeps into large wounds on the prey made by the teeth. The prey goes into shock and bleeds to death. Although they have a similar-sized skull to that of a saltwater crocodile, the bite of a dragon is only one-sixth as strong.

Kill factor
Green anaconda

Aggression: Short-tempered reptiles, and even more so when in captivity. Not good pets.

Intelligence: These ambush predators wait for the perfect opportunity to attack prey.

Speed: Slow on land but quick and deadly in the water.

Strength: Capable of killing large animals such as jaguars with their strong body.

Other: One of the few reptiles that gives birth to live young.

Deadly rating:

☠ ☠ ☠ ☠

Green anaconda

The biggest snake in the world is at its most dangerous when underwater

Although its cousin, the reticulated python, might be longer than the green anaconda, it pales in girth comparison, as the anaconda is not only long but also incredibly thick. They are one of the few reptiles where the females outsize the males. They tend to live in swampy marshes and streams in the tropical rainforests of the Amazon and Orinoco basins. On land they are slow and clunky but in water they are reptiles to be reckoned with. Like the saltwater crocodile, they wait submerged in water for prey to approach, using their eyes and nostrils on the top of their head to see around and breathe.

Like the king cobra the green anaconda swallows its prey whole, digesting it as it moves down its body. Its teeth are angled backwards, so that once it has bitten its prey, any attempts to escape will only impale the animal further. They feed on animals as large as jaguars and also pigs and deer. Their main method of attack is constriction; they are known as nonvenomous constrictors. They wrap their bodies around prey and squeeze until asphyxiation occurs. Again, they can go months without eating after a large meal.

Giant snake

Why this massive reptile can be so dangerous

Attack
When killing prey, the green anaconda coils around and constricts its prey until it can no longer breathe.

Mouth
The green anaconda can open its mouth through a jaw-widening 180 degrees.

Body
These nocturnal creatures have a characteristic olive-green body covered in black spots.

Head
Narrow head is small when compared to its thick, muscular body.

Eyes and nose
Green anacondas can still see and breathe when almost fully submerged.

The statistics…
Green anaconda

Genus:	Eunectes
Length:	6-9m
Weight:	132-227kg
Top speed:	21km/h (13mph)
Life span:	10 years

TIME TO DEATH
2 mins

Antenna
Grasshopper antennas tend to be much shorter than their body and consist typically of 10-20 segments, covered with tiny sensory hairs that are known as sensilla.

Wings
Grasshoppers have two pairs of wings at the fore and hind of the abdomen. Hind wings can be used for flight, while the fore wings are for noise production.

Femora
The elongated hind femurs allow it to leap great distances, as well as produce noise by rubbing its outer ridges on its fore wings.

Mandibles
Tearing pinchers used to shred grasses, plants and crops, the mandibles can chew food and instigate mechanical digestion.

Abdomen
Abdomen size and shade develops according to age and gender – females are larger than males. Females have an ovipositor, a tubular egg-laying structure, at the rear.

Grasshoppers

Renowned for their jumping prowess, grasshoppers are a diverse species of insect

Similar to the locust and cricket, the grasshopper is a species of insect in the orthoptera order, however it is non-migratory and tends to exist in isolation (ie, it does not swarm), meeting up generally only to mate.

Grasshoppers consist of a long abdomen (females are equipped with an ovipositor for laying eggs), short forelegs, powerful hind legs (responsible for its jumping prowess), two pairs of wings and a short antenna. Its nervous system is controlled by a series of ganglia, a collection of nerve cells located in each part of the body – the largest occurring in the head. Information is fed to the ganglia via its antenna, sensilla (tiny exterior hairs) and cerci (paired appendages at its rear). Sound is detected by a pair of tympanal organs, a set of membranes stretched across a frame, and backed by an air sac and sensory neurons.

Grasshoppers are herbivores and tend to eat grasses, plants and leaves, dissected by their mandibles. Food is digested in a series of three guts – the stomodaeum, mesentreron and proctodaeum – running from the fore of the abdomen to the rear respectively. Food is broken down by a selection of secreted enzymes including amylase, protease, lipase and invertase. Reproduction occurs through a lengthy ovulation process (up to nine months), with eggs laid by females typically a few inches underground.

There are currently roughly 11,000 species of grasshopper recorded worldwide, and they tend to be found residing in tropical forests and grassland planes. ✿

A female grasshopper laying her eggs in sand. Female abdomen tips are fitted with two pairs of triangular valves to ease the digging process

How do squid swim?

The jet propulsion system that powers squid though water

To move itself through water a squid will emit constant, steady bursts of fluid to provide the necessary acceleration. Squid are able to take water into their mantle and expel it at a high rate, reaching speeds of up to 40km/h (24mph) after expelling 94 per cent of their fluid.

Shaped like a torpedo, the rear body of a squid lets it travel almost like a rocket. By quickly compressing the mantle, a jet of water shoots out behind the squid. The force of this jet moves the squid forwards, allowing it to drift until it comes to a stop, when the process is repeated. To refill the cavity, elastic tissue in the mantle works in tandem with radial muscles to bring in water, in addition to the pressure of incident water as the squid moves. During feeding, the squid swims in the other direction using its arms, allowing it to easily grab prey.

To quickly evade predators, squid can hyperinflate their mantle cavities, expanding them beyond their normal size. This allows for a quick and sudden intake of water that can be rapidly expelled for a fast getaway. ✿

Method of propulsion

Mantle
As the squid prepares to propel itself, the walls of the mantle expand to bring in water, filling the mantle cavity inside.

Cavity
Powerful muscles in the walls of the mantle contract and pressurise the water in the cavity.

Steering
To change its direction it uses two fins at its tail end, in addition to altering the direction of the jet.

Funnel
A one-way valve known as the funnel allows water to be stored for jettison at a later period.

Expel
The water is spurted out near the squid's head, propelling it backwards through the water.

These jet-propelled swimmers can reach speeds of 40km/h (24mph)

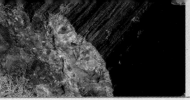

Petrified forest
The world's biggest concentration of fossilised trees can be found in Petrified Forest National Park, Arizona, US. Here, huge logs 60 metres long and three metres in diameter were rapidly buried by sediment, causing them to decay very slowly. Silica deposits in the ground water eventually replaced all the wood, leaving perfect replicas of the original trees. The forest was uncovered in the Seventies.

DID YOU KNOW? *Certain species of tick can cause tick paralysis from a salivary neurotoxin*

Fossil trees step-by-step

The formation of fossilised trees

Why does wood turn to stone after thousands of years under water?

Ancient vegetation like trees, plants and other organic matter can be preserved over many millions of years. In fact, entire fossilised landscapes have been discovered in recent times. You might wonder how wood can survive for all these millions of years, but the fact of the matter is, the wood itself has long gone. What remains are minerals that replaced the wood in the same shape, form and patterns. ❂

© Science Photo Library

1. Tree dies
Say you have a lush forest some 100 million years ago, and the climate suddenly alters dramatically, killing the trees. A dead tree will fall to the ground, and in some cases a swamp will develop and cover up the tree, preventing it from decaying properly.

2. Submerged
If the tree is covered up quickly enough, it will maintain its original shape under the mud. As the cells in the wood begin to break down and deteriorate, they will become hollow. The swamp is rich in minerals (calcite and sillicon), and this calcium-rich water will seep into the spaces in the wood.

3. Calcified
When the swamp water evaporates, the minerals will be left behind where the old wood once existed.

4. Rock
The properties of the original tree no longer exist. Instead, a calcified (or petrified) rock log sits in its place.

Why do ticks suck blood?

Discover how these little bloodsuckers make a tasty meal of their warm-blooded hosts

Ticks are extremely small parasites that feed on the protein-rich blood of other animals through a process called 'hematophagy'. As they are arachnids they have eight legs, the first pair of which features a special sensory pit called the 'haller' organ, which can sniff out prey. After finding a suitable host, the tick anchors itself to the unwitting victim using its claws as well as its spiny legs and the special sucker pads on its feet. To puncture the skin and get to the blood, the tick uses its two fang-like chelicerae, and then extends a long serrated proboscis called a 'hypostome'. The hypostome makes it difficult to remove an attached tick as, like a fishhook, it's covered with backwards-pointing barbs. The tick then sucks up blood until its body, also known as the 'idiosoma', is so bloated it can't take any more – this can take several days. ❂

Engorged
This image shows a tick filled with blood.

Ticks can swell to many times their size after feeding

© Science Photo Library

How to remove a tick
Always consult a doctor if you are at all concerned about a tick bite. However, it's best to remove a tick as soon as possible, as they carry such infectious diseases as lyme disease. You should avoid touching the tick, so it's a good idea to use tweezers or wear protective gloves. Then, firmly but gently, take hold of the arachnid as close to the skin as possible and pull it straight out – don't wiggle or twist, as the delicate mouthparts can break off in the skin.

Once the tick has been removed, clean the area with antiseptic (soap and water will do) to help reduce the chance of bacteria and infection.

The water cycle

Rain falling today has spent billions of years travelling between Earth's clouds, oceans and ice

The water, or hydrological cycle is the Earth's water recycling system. Since water rarely escapes the planet or arrives from space, the water cycle keeps rivers relentlessly flowing into the oceans and the atmosphere supplied with clouds and rain. Without it, life simply couldn't exist.

The water cycle circulates water between the oceans and atmosphere, sometimes via the land. When ocean water is heated, it turns into water vapour, which rises into the atmosphere and is carried by winds. The vapour cools at some point and forms clouds. Around 78 per cent of the rain, snow and other forms of precipitation falling from these clouds goes straight back into the ocean. The rest falls over the Earth's continents and islands.

Some of this water runs into rivers and lakes and is carried back to the sea. Water also seeps back to the oceans through deep soil and rocks, becoming the Earth's groundwater. Water falling as snow over the polar ice sheets can be buried, sometimes for millions of years, until it reaches the sea via slow-moving glaciers.

Water that stays in shallow soil can be lifted back into the atmosphere when it warms. Alternatively, plants may suck up soil water through their roots and return it to the atmosphere through their leaves. When animals eat plants, they take the water into their bodies and expel it into the air in their breath.

Humans are increasingly altering the water cycle on land by building cities and flood controls, and capturing water for drinking, agriculture and industry. ✿

How the water cycle works

Loss from vegetation
Plants contribute about ten per cent of the water in the atmosphere by losing water drawn from the ground through their leaves by transpiration.

Ocean water evaporation
Ocean water is heated, evaporates and rises into the atmosphere as water vapour. The vapour cools as it rises and, at some point, condenses and forms clouds.

Water processes explained

Condensation
When you breathe on a cold window and it fogs up, you're seeing condensation in action. It's the process by which water vapour in the air turns back into liquid water when it cools down. Atmospheric water vapour condenses on salt, smoke and dust particles to form clouds.

Infiltration
Infiltration is where water seeps into the ground rather than running across it. Once in the ground, the water stays in shallow soil layers or moves deeper to form groundwater. Dry, loose soils on flat ground will absorb more water than steeply sloping hard surfaces or already wet soil.

Ancient science

1 People first mentioned the water cycle around 2,000 years ago. One of the oldest Hindu scriptures, the Chandogya Upanishad, said "rivers... lead from sea to sea."

Drop to drink

2 Most people get water from rivers and lakes, which form just 0.014 per cent of the world's water. The rest is mainly in the oceans (96.5 per cent), ice or underground.

Olympic deluge

3 A small thunderstorm can produce, on average, 2,000 tons of rain in just 30 minutes. That's enough to fill an Olympic-sized swimming pool.

Earliest water

4 Liquid water may have existed on Earth for 4.4 billion years. The water in your glass is almost as old as our planet and significantly older than the dinosaurs.

Slow moving

5 Water can spend more than 10,000 years locked up in deep groundwater or the polar ice sheets, but just a few days in the atmosphere.

DID YOU KNOW? The Sun powers the water cycle, moving around 15.5 million tons of water through the atmosphere every second

The River Indus is now some 30 kilometres wide in places

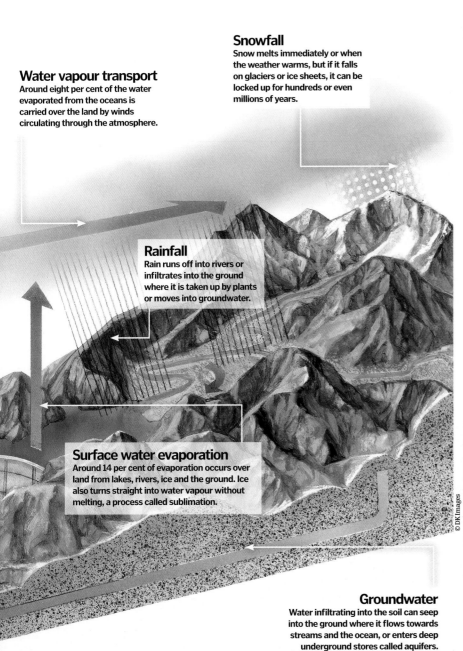

Water vapour transport
Around eight per cent of the water evaporated from the oceans is carried over the land by winds circulating through the atmosphere.

Snowfall
Snow melts immediately or when the weather warms, but if it falls on glaciers or ice sheets, it can be locked up for hundreds or even millions of years.

Rainfall
Rain runs off into rivers or infiltrates into the ground where it is taken up by plants or moves into groundwater.

Surface water evaporation
Around 14 per cent of evaporation occurs over land from lakes, rivers, ice and the ground. Ice also turns straight into water vapour without melting, a process called sublimation.

© DK Images

Groundwater
Water infiltrating into the soil can seep into the ground where it flows towards streams and the ocean, or enters deep underground stores called aquifers.

When the water cycle lets us down

Floods affect tens of thousands of people each year, as is evident from the devastating monsoon flooding across Pakistan in 2010. The flood, which affected some 20 million people, was the result of the heaviest monsoon rains in the area for generations. On 8 August 2010 the River Indus burst its banks, sweeping away entire communities. While it's normal for Pakistan to receive half its annual rainfall (250-500mm) during the monsoon months of July and August, the country was reportedly bombarded with 300mm on 29 July alone. The Met Office suggests several possible reasons for the unusually heavy rains, including changes to upper atmosphere airflow, active monsoon systems, and La Niña (El Niño in reverse).

Serious floods, like those seen in Pakistan during July and August 2010, can cause catastrophic destruction

Runoff
Water flowing down tarmac roads into curb-side drains after a storm is an example of the process of runoff. Rain that doesn't evaporate or infiltrate into soil or rock also flows down small channels as runoff. The channels merge into streams that, eventually, join rivers flowing downhill to the sea.

Evaporation
Wet clothes hung outside dry by evaporation, the process by which liquid water turns into vapour when heat energy breaks bonds between its water molecules. Soaking a T-shirt keeps you cool on a hot day because since evaporation uses up heat energy from the air, it reduces nearby temperatures.

Precipitation
Precipitation is a catch-all term for water falling from clouds to the earth. It covers rain, snow, hail and so on. Precipitation happens when water vapour condenses on airborne particles as droplets. These grow bigger by, for example, collisions until they become so heavy they fall to the ground.

Transpiration
Plants – like humans – breathe out water vapour, a process called transpiration. During transpiration, water drawn into a plant's roots is carried to the leaves where it evaporates. How much plants transpire varies depending on air temperature, humidity and incoming sunlight. Higher temperatures and stronger sunlight mean more transpiration.

"Scientists still struggle to fully understand El Nino, when it is coming and why it occurs"

The El Nino phenomenon explained

What is El Nino?

The weather-altering phenomenon unveiled

El Nino is the presence of warm surface water along the western coasts of South America (especially Peru), due to an altering of normal winds in the southern hemisphere. In an El Nino year, the trade winds that blow towards Australia either greatly reduce, die completely, or in extreme years even reverse. This stops the ocean current from pushing warm water towards Australia, and instead the higher waters on the Australian coast ebb back towards Peru. This increases both the sea temperature and level on the South American coast. The changes in the area also mean that the convectional uplift and resulting rainfall which normally occurs in Australia moves to the Peruvian coast.

Scientists still struggle to fully understand El Nino, when it is coming and why it occurs. Each one is different and how the atmosphere reacts each time varies. Due to these varying conditions and irregularity, the cause of El Nino is not completely understood. While we know it is caused by wind change, little more is certain.

El Nino occurs roughly every four to seven years and lasts on average between 12 and 18 months. However, in recent years it appears to be increasing in regularity. Closely linked with the El Nino phenomenon is that of La Nina. In La Nina years normal conditions of the Pacific are heightened, due to extra strong trade winds. This means the waters of Peru are much colder than normal, and the convectional rain of eastern Australia is heavier. ✿

Conditions during El Nino

- Weaker or even reversed trade winds
- Warmer seawater in western South America
- Higher sea level on the Peruvian coast
- More rainfall in South America
- Drier conditions in Australia

Conditions during La Nina

- Colder than normal sea water off the western South American coast
- Heavy rain and flooding in Australia
- Warmer than normal sea temperatures off the eastern coast of Australia
- More tornadoes during spring and summer

Drier conditions during El Nino can produce drought

El Nino vs normal

Normal yea

Convectional uplift
Rainfall occurs where warm, moist air rises, cools and condenses.

The Walker Loop
The air then returns and sinks, forming the Walker Loop.

Trade winds
Trade winds blow westwards, blowing warm water with it across the Pacific.

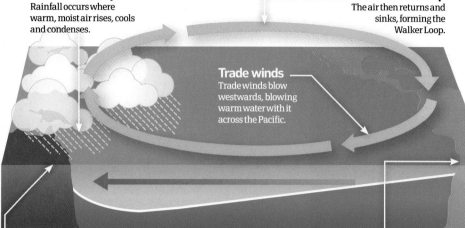

Australian conditions
Due to the pressure of trade winds, the water is about 50cm higher and 8°C warmer in Australia than Peru.

El Nino convectional uplift
Rising air also moves eastwards, causing convectional uplift and rainfall at the Peruvian coast.

Peruvian condition
Cool, nutrient-rich water pulled up from below by the westward-moving wind

El Nino year

El Nino trade winds
Trade winds drop or stop completely, or in some years totally reverse.

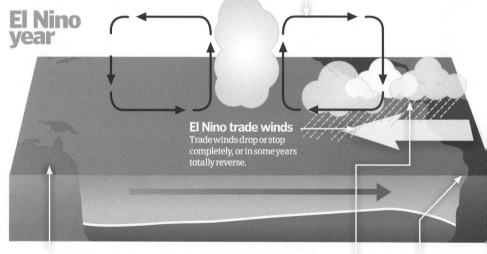

El Nino Australian conditions
Conditions can become very dry in Australia, and even lead to drought.

Increased convection
As the warm water travels eastwards, it creates more convection and therefore storms along the way.

Sea condition
Due to the drop in winds the war sea water ebbs back from Austral causing about a 30cm rise in Per

El Nino by satellite

These satellite images show sea height during El Nino in 1997

1. The beginning
The sea level is high off the coast of Australia, as you can see by the red and white. The sea level is low off the coast of Peru, as demonstrated by the blue.

3. The main event
This diagram shows El Nino at its height. The sea at the Peruvian coast is far deeper than normal now the water has made its way across from Australia. Blue can be seen near the Australian coast, where the sea level is shallower.

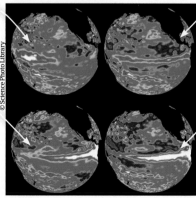

© Science Photo Library

2. On the move
The water across the Pacific becomes deeper, as the water from the Australian coast begins to travel eastwards towards Peru with the dying down of the trade winds. This is shown by the red strip.

4. On its way back
As the trade winds begin to pick up again, the water moves back from the Peruvian coast to its rightful place on the Australian coast. This is shown by the red strip beginning to ebb westwards.

Hippo jaws

Why do these water-dwelling creatures open their mouths so wide?

A hippo may open its mouth wide as a sign of aggression, similar to other animals such as lions and baboons. Opening their jaws shows others their fearsome set of weaponry: their teeth.

Although hippos eat vegetation, they do not use their teeth to do so. Their giant canines and incisors are used only for killing. Instead, they use their huge lips to rip grass from the ground for consumption. A hippo is able to spread its lips through a jaw-dropping 150 degrees and up to 1.2m (3.9ft) in width. The strength of a hippo's jaw muscles – a bite force of 1,800lb – is such that it can use its fearsome teeth to bite a crocodile, human, or even a small boat in half. ✿

The skull of a hippopotamus contains tusk-like canines as long as your arm

Each of a hippo's two lips is about 0.6m (2ft) wide

Incisors
Razor-sharp incisors can rip through the skin of a hippo's latest meal.

Jaw-dropping
A hippo can spread its gums to an enormous 1.2m (3.9ft).

Yawn
The apparent 'yawn' of a hippo is actually a display of aggression and alerts others to its aggressive mood.

Canine
The tusk-like canines of a hippo are not only used as weapons, but also warn off potential predators when displayed.

© Raul694

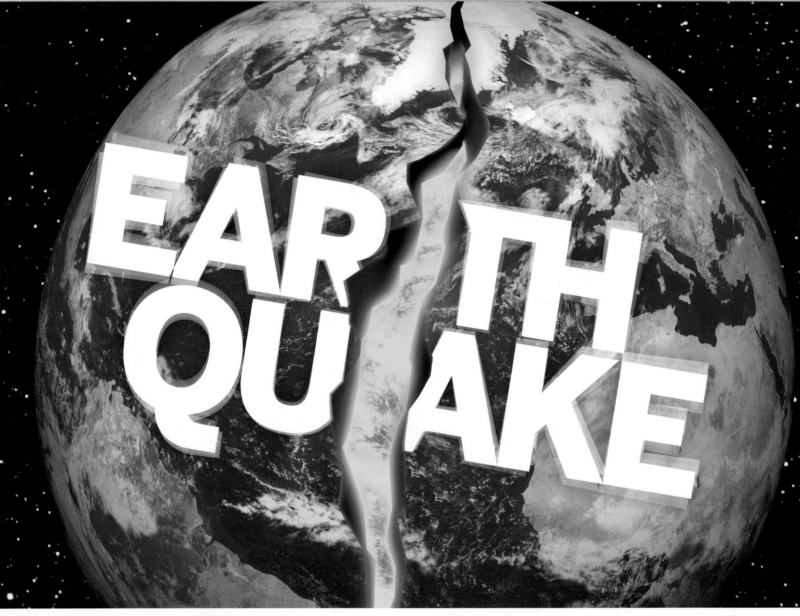

EARTH QUAKE

Discover why this sudden release of pressure can flatten cities and spawn giant waves

Even if you've never felt an earthquake, you'll know they can be devastating. Films like *2012* feature 'mega quakes', where gaping fissures swallow people and buildings. Real-life earthquakes are less dramatic than those in the movies, but they're still one of nature's worst natural hazards. Unstoppable and terrifying, big quakes strike with little or no warning, flattening cities and killing tens of thousands of people.

Most of the world's earthquakes occur at the boundaries between the Earth's huge crustal plates. These boundaries are called faults, and the plates – of which there are 15 of varying different sizes here on Earth – jostle on the planet's surface like the pieces of a giant, floating jigsaw puzzle. In some parts of the world, these crustal plates grate past each other. In other places, they collide or are pulled apart. Faults break open as

these rigid plates move and exert forces great enough to crush and tear solid rock.

As the plates move about, the rock slabs at either side of faults are dragged past each other. But rocks are jagged and uneven, meaning there's lots of friction between them. This friction causes the rocks to become locked together. Pressure builds along the fault as the plates grind along, squeezing and stretching the rocks until, eventually, they break and lurch forward. Huge amounts of pent-up energy are unleashed, and it's the resulting snap that is an earthquake.

The point at which the Earth's crust first breaks is called the earthquake focus. This is usually many miles below the Earth's surface. The epicentre is the point on the surface located directly above the focus.

The released energy speeds through the Earth in the form of shock waves.

There are three main types of shockwave: primary, secondary and surface waves. Primary waves radiate fastest from the earthquake focus. Secondary waves arrive later and surface waves arrive last. The surface waves travel near the Earth's surface, rocking the ground and causing the widespread devastation wrought by the largest earthquakes. People barely feel primary or secondary waves.

The size of an earthquake is defined by its magnitude – this is a measure of the energy released. Magnitude isn't a simple measurement of the relationship between earthquake size and energy. Increasing the magnitude by one increases shock wave size by ten times and total energy released by about 30 times. So for example, a magnitude eight earthquake is a billion times more powerful than a magnitude two. Quite an unimaginable thought.

5 TOP FACTS
EARTHQUAKE

Lotta quaking
1 Around 18 major earthquakes and 20,000 smaller earthquakes happen every year worldwide – that's 50 earthquakes greater than magnitude 4.5 every day.

The big ones
2 'Mega quakes' above magnitude 10 are impossible – no fracture in the Earth's surface is long enough to store the vast energies. The biggest ever was 9.5.

Heart shaker
3 Earthquakes can occur almost anywhere. The 1931 Dogger Bank earthquake was felt throughout the UK – a woman died of a heart attack and a church spire spun around.

Deadly waves
4 2004's Indian Ocean tsunami was among the world's most devastating natural disasters. It killed at least 200,000 people in 14 countries and had waves up to 30m high.

Living dangerously
5 Tokyo, Japan, lives with the constant threat of earthquakes. Several quakes happen daily and a catastrophic quake strikes about every 70 years.

DID YOU KNOW? *The Richter scale is being replaced by a more accurate measurement, the Moment Magnitude scale*

Faults: cracks in the Earth

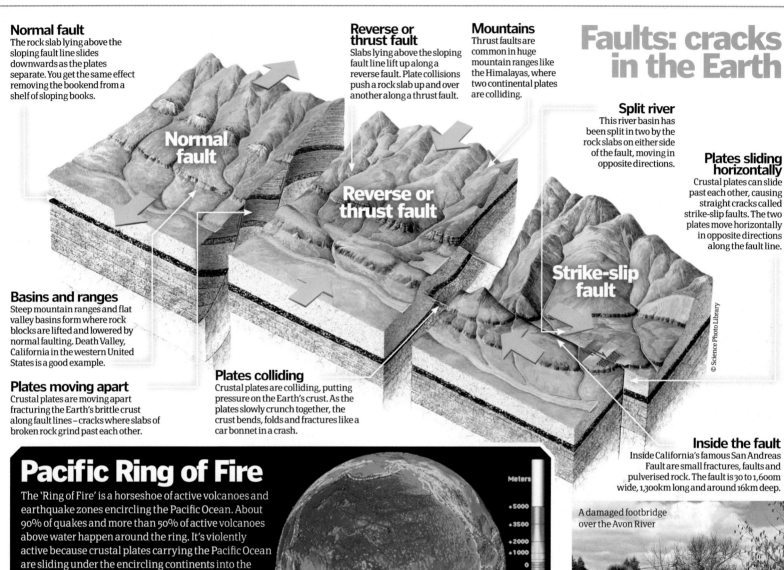

Normal fault
The rock slab lying above the sloping fault line slides downwards as the plates separate. You get the same effect removing the bookend from a shelf of sloping books.

Reverse or thrust fault
Slabs lying above the sloping fault line lift up along a reverse fault. Plate collisions push a rock slab up and over another along a thrust fault.

Mountains
Thrust faults are common in huge mountain ranges like the Himalayas, where two continental plates are colliding.

Split river
This river basin has been split in two by the rock slabs on either side of the fault, moving in opposite directions.

Plates sliding horizontally
Crustal plates can slide past each other, causing straight cracks called strike-slip faults. The two plates move horizontally in opposite directions along the fault line.

Basins and ranges
Steep mountain ranges and flat valley basins form where rock blocks are lifted and lowered by normal faulting. Death Valley, California in the western United States is a good example.

Plates moving apart
Crustal plates are moving apart fracturing the Earth's brittle crust along fault lines – cracks where slabs of broken rock grind past each other.

Plates colliding
Crustal plates are colliding, putting pressure on the Earth's crust. As the plates slowly crunch together, the crust bends, folds and fractures like a car bonnet in a crash.

Inside the fault
Inside California's famous San Andreas Fault are small fractures, faults and pulverised rock. The fault is 30 to 1,600m wide, 1,300km long and around 16km deep.

© Science Photo Library

Pacific Ring of Fire

The 'Ring of Fire' is a horseshoe of active volcanoes and earthquake zones encircling the Pacific Ocean. About 90% of quakes and more than 50% of active volcanoes above water happen around the ring. It's violently active because crustal plates carrying the Pacific Ocean are sliding under the encircling continents into the Earth's interior. The crust is broken into many rigid plates, which drift across hot rock below. The grinding and melting of the oceanic crust as it's forced down near the Pacific coast creates volcanoes and earthquakes.

Key
Colour scale: Ocean depth/land elevation in metres
Red dots: Earthquake epicentres with a magnitude greater than or equal to 5 since 1980
Yellow lines: Plate boundaries

Meters
+5000
+3500
+2000
+1000
0
-1500
-3000
-5000
-7000
-9000

© Science Photo Library

A damaged footbridge over the Avon River

It's interesting to note that earthquake damage isn't directly related to magnitude. Deep, distant earthquakes shake the ground less than close, shallow earthquakes because the energy released at the focus has had a chance to disperse. Big earthquakes often cause longer tremors. For example, an earthquake in 1949, which had a magnitude of 7.1, shook the ground for 30 seconds, while a magnitude 8.3 earthquake in 1964 lasted five minutes.

The majority of the shuddering during an earthquake is caused by Rayleigh waves. These surface waves roll along, convulsing the Earth's crust. The ground heaves up and down and from side to side much like water waves in the ocean. Earthquakes can shake the ground violently enough to open large fissures but, unlike in the movies, these don't crunch closed around people's bodies and legs.

Big, long-lasting surface waves created by large earthquakes can topple buildings, crack roads and buildings and even trigger landslides. Well-built, earthquake-proof buildings on solid bedrock usually suffer substantially less damage than urban areas built on loose debris and sediments. Water-saturated sediments can behave like quicksand when shaken, where loose grains move apart and flow like a liquid. In Niigata, Japan, 1964, earthquake-resistant buildings tumbled onto their sides when the ground underneath liquefied.

The population faces additional hazards once the shaking stops. Fires break out where the ground convulsions sever gas and electricity lines or destroy flammable objects. Nearly 90 per cent of the damage in the 1906 San Francisco earthquake was due to fire. Lives can be endangered and rescue efforts thwarted by collapsed bridges,

© Martin Luff

"Tsunamis can reach speeds of 970 km/h in the deep ocean"

▶ burst water pipes, broken containers of hazardous chemicals and aftershocks.

Aftershocks are the less powerful earthquakes following the main tremor, when faults shift and readjust after the release of energy and stress. You could think of a tremor as the ground breathing a big sigh of relief. Major earthquakes are usually followed by several noticeable aftershocks within the first hour or so. The number of aftershocks drops over time. However they can happen months, years or decades after the quake.

Undersea earthquakes can be as devastating as those on land, if not more. Fault movements can displace huge volumes of water, which crash to shore as killer waves called tsunamis. An undersea earthquake near northern Indonesia triggered the Indian Ocean tsunami in 2004 – the world's biggest for at least 40 years. At least 120,000 people in Indonesia alone were killed by the giant waves. Rescue teams cleared up bodies for weeks afterwards. The final death toll was over 200,000.

Tsunamis can reach speeds of 970km/h (602mph) in the deep ocean, depending on water depth. As the tsunami races into shallower water, it slows down and can reach a mammoth 30m high when it hits shore. The first sign may be water rushing out to sea, sometimes beyond the horizon, leaving the sea floor bare. The sea pours back onshore as a series of towering waves or a rapidly rising tide. Warning signs such as these can save lives. A ten-year-old British girl saw the sea hurtling away from the beach at a resort in Phuket, Thailand in 2004 and warned her mother and staff that a killer wave was coming. She'd learned about tsunamis in school a fortnight before. ✿

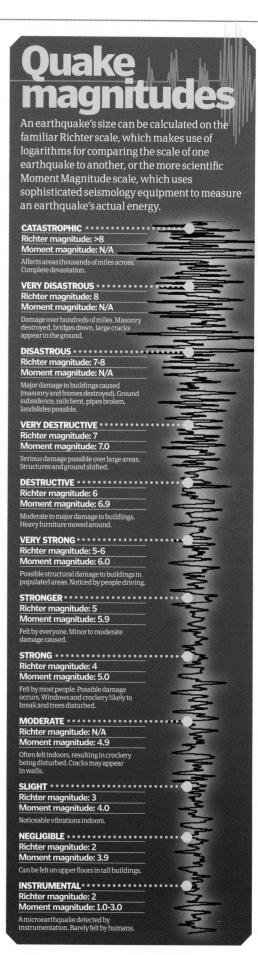

Quake magnitudes

An earthquake's size can be calculated on the familiar Richter scale, which makes use of logarithms for comparing the scale of one earthquake to another, or the more scientific Moment Magnitude scale, which uses sophisticated seismology equipment to measure an earthquake's actual energy.

CATASTROPHIC
Richter magnitude: >8
Moment magnitude: N/A
Affects areas thousands of miles across. Complete devastation.

VERY DISASTROUS
Richter magnitude: 8
Moment magnitude: N/A
Damage over hundreds of miles. Masonry destroyed, bridges down, large cracks appear in the ground.

DISASTROUS
Richter magnitude: 7-8
Moment magnitude: N/A
Major damage to buildings caused (masonry and frames destroyed). Ground subsidence, rails bent, pipes broken, landslides possible.

VERY DESTRUCTIVE
Richter magnitude: 7
Moment magnitude: 7.0
Serious damage possible over large areas. Structures and ground shifted.

DESTRUCTIVE
Richter magnitude: 6
Moment magnitude: 6.9
Moderate to major damage to buildings. Heavy furniture moved around.

VERY STRONG
Richter magnitude: 5-6
Moment magnitude: 6.0
Possible structural damage to buildings in populated areas. Noticed by people driving.

STRONGER
Richter magnitude: 5
Moment magnitude: 5.9
Felt by everyone. Minor to moderate damage caused.

STRONG
Richter magnitude: 4
Moment magnitude: 5.0
Felt by most people. Possible damage occurs. Windows and crockery likely to break and trees disturbed.

MODERATE
Richter magnitude: N/A
Moment magnitude: 4.9
Often felt indoors, resulting in crockery being disturbed. Cracks may appear in walls.

SLIGHT
Richter magnitude: 3
Moment magnitude: 4.0
Noticeable vibrations indoors.

NEGLIGIBLE
Richter magnitude: 2
Moment magnitude: 3.9
Can be felt on upper floors in tall buildings.

INSTRUMENTAL
Richter magnitude: 2
Moment magnitude: 1.0-3.0
A microearthquake detected by instrumentation. Barely felt by humans.

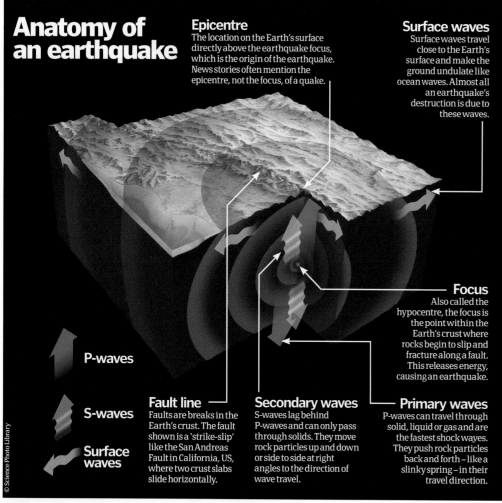

Anatomy of an earthquake

Epicentre
The location on the Earth's surface directly above the earthquake focus, which is the origin of the earthquake. News stories often mention the epicentre, not the focus, of a quake.

Surface waves
Surface waves travel close to the Earth's surface and make the ground undulate like ocean waves. Almost all an earthquake's destruction is due to these waves.

Focus
Also called the hypocentre, the focus is the point within the Earth's crust where rocks begin to slip and fracture along a fault. This releases energy, causing an earthquake.

P-waves

S-waves

Surface waves

Fault line
Faults are breaks in the Earth's crust. The fault shown is a 'strike-slip' like the San Andreas Fault in California, US, where two crust slabs slide horizontally.

Secondary waves
S-waves lag behind P-waves and can only pass through solids. They move rock particles up and down or side to side at right angles to the direction of wave travel.

Primary waves
P-waves can travel through solid, liquid or gas and are the fastest shock waves. They push rock particles back and forth – like a slinky spring – in their travel direction.

© Science Photo Library

Shock waves at the Earth's core

P-waves
P-waves can travel through the core

S-waves
S-waves can't penetrate the liquid outer core

Weak P-waves
Some P-waves bounce off the solid inner core

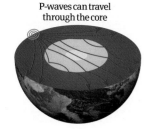
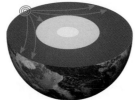
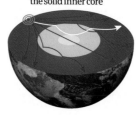

Head to Head
DESTRUCTIVE EARTHQUAKES

DEADLIEST

1. Shensi Province earthquake, China, 1556
More than 830,000 people died in this quake, which flattened city walls and temples, and was felt 800km (500mi) away.

LARGEST

2. Great Chilean earthquake, Chile, 1960
The Valdivia or Great Chilean quake had a magnitude of 9.5, making it the most powerful ever recorded.

COSTLIEST

3. Kobe earthquake, Japan, 1995
This quake is possibly the costliest natural disaster to hit one country. It caused more than US $100 billion of damage.

DID YOU KNOW? Taking cover under a sturdy desk could save your life if you're stuck indoors when an earthquake strikes

The Parkfield Experiment

Subject to an earthquake of magnitude 6.0 or higher on average every 22 years, Parkfield in California is one of the most seriously affected places on Earth for tectonic activity. Lying straight across the epic San Andreas Fault, one of the longest and most active faults in the world, the town has seen massive destruction since its formation in the 19th Century. So much so, in fact, that the United States Geological Survey has instigated a state-of-the-art experiment in Parkfield, to better understand the physics and potential of earthquakes. Take a look at the activities going on at Parkfield

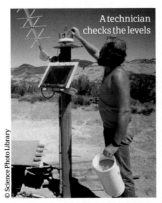

A technician checks the levels

© Science Photo Library

Laser to measure surface movement by bouncing beams on reflectors
A hilltop laser near Parkfield measures movement of the Earth's crust. Red and blue laser light is fired at 18 reflectors located several kilometres away. The system converts the time the light takes to bounce back into distance travelled. It can measure movements of 1mm over about 6km.

Satellite relaying data to US Geological Survey
The US Geological Survey, which monitors natural hazards, constantly receives data from the Parkfield sensor network. Scientists can be aware of an earthquake within minutes. Sensor measurements are recorded on computer and transmitted to a satellite. There's no need to visit the instruments on foot, except for maintenance.

Sensors in water well to monitor groundwater level
Fluctuating groundwater levels can indicate that rocks are being squeezed or stretched. Monitoring pressure on rocks helps scientists monitor the risk of an earthquake. Groundwater levels are monitored in eight wells around Parkfield. Water level, air pressure and rainfall measurements are made every 10 to 15 minutes.

Strainmeter to monitor surface deformation
Strainmeters spot changes in the shape or size of rocks placed under pressure by movements in the Earth's crust. They can detect the crust stretching by 2.5cm in more than 25,000km by monitoring changes in the volume of liquid in a borehole, or calculating the distance between two points.

© Science Photo Library

PARKFIELD
Pop 34

Seismometer in hole to record microquakes
Seismometers are instruments for measuring ground movements. Nine seismometers sit in boreholes a few hundred metres underground near Parkfield. They can detect smaller earthquakes than surface instruments because they're less exposed to noise.

Magnetometer to record magnetic field
As the Earth's magnetic field alters before a quake, magnetometers measure changes in local magnetic fields. There are magnetometers located at seven sites around Parkfield.

VIBROSEIS truck that probes the earthquake zone
A 14-ton truck is used to map rock layers underground without a hole being dug. The truck concentrates its weight on a short pole and shakes for several secs. Scientists record vibrations bouncing back to the surface. How the vibrations are reflected underground vary with rock type and thickness.

Near-surface seismometer to record larger shocks
Seismometers can detect ground movements during earthquakes and turn them into electrical signals. The Parkfield region is bristling with seismometers, with 14 arranged in a T-shape around 1-2km across, monitoring how shock waves travel during earthquakes.

Arrows show crustal plate movements along the San Andreas Fault
The Pacific plate and North American plate are grinding past each other at a rate of about 3.5cm each year along California's San Andreas Fault. At current rates, San Francisco will lie next to Los Angeles in 15 million years.

Creepmeter to record surface movement
Creepmeters detect fault movement by measuring the distance between two pillars standing at either side of a fault. Measurements are made electronically by calculating the angle of a wire stretched between the pillars. There are 13 creepmeters in the Parkfield area, with one in the epicentre of past Parkfield earthquakes.

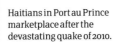

Haitians in Port au Prince marketplace after the devastating quake of 2010.

"Glacial erosion involves abrasion and plucking"

Glaciers in Wrangell St Elias National Park, Alaska

Briksdalsbreen, one of the best-known arms of the Jostedalsbreen glacier

Glacier power

Discover the awesome Earth-shaping power of gigantic rivers of ice

Glaciers are huge rivers or sheets of ice, which have sculpted mountain ranges and carved iconic peaks like the pyramid-shaped Matterhorn in the Swiss Alps. The secret of this awesome landscape-shaping power is erosion, the process of wearing away and transporting solid rock. Glacial erosion involves two main mechanisms: abrasion and plucking. As glaciers flow downhill, they use debris that's frozen into the ice to sandpaper exposed rock, leaving grooves called striations. This is the process of abrasion. Plucking, however, is where glaciers freeze onto rock and tear away loose fragments as they pull away.

Today glaciers are confined to high altitudes and latitudes, where the climate is cold enough for ice to persist all year round. During the ice ages, however, glaciers advanced into valleys that are now free of ice. Britain, for example, was covered by ice as far south as the Bristol Channel.

You can spot landforms created by ancient ice. Cirques are armchair-shaped hollows on mountainsides, which often contain lakes called tarns. They're also the birthplaces of ancient glaciers. During cold periods, ice accumulated in shady rock hollows, deepening them to form cirques. When two cirques formed back-to-back, they left a knife-edge ridge called an arête. Pyramidal peaks were created when three or more cirques formed. Eventually the cirque glacier spilled from the hollow and flowed downhill as a valley glacier. This glacier eroded the valley into a

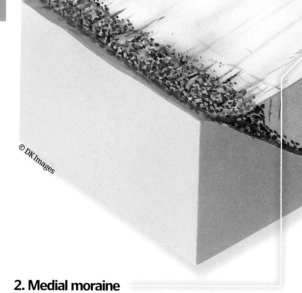
© DK Images

8. Snout
The end of the glacier is called its snout, perhaps because it looks like a curved nose. The snout changes position as the glacier retreats and advances.

2. Medial moraine
A medial moraine is a debris ridge or mound found in the centre of a valley, formed when two tributary glaciers join and their lateral moraines merge.

U-shape, with steep cliffs called truncated spurs. When the glacier melted, tributary valleys were left hanging high above the main valley floor.

Hard rock outcrops in the valley were smoothed into mounds orientated in the direction of ice movement. Rock drumlins are shaped like whalebacks, adopting a smooth, convex shape. Roche moutonnée have a smooth upstream side, and a jagged downstream side formed by plucking. Where valley rocks varied in strength, the ice cut hollows into the softer rock, which filled with glacial lakes known as paternoster lakes.

Modern-day glaciers are found where it's cold enough for ice to persist all year round

BEAUTIFUL

1. Landscape Arch, USA
This delicate natural arch – Earth's third largest – is only 2m (6.5ft) thick at its narrowest, but spans a whopping 90m (295ft).

LIVELY

2. Transgondwanan Supermountains, Gondwanaland
Nutrients eroded from a giant mountain range 600 million years ago may have helped Earth's first complex life to develop.

SPECTACULAR

3. Grand Canyon, USA
The Grand Canyon was eroded into the Colorado Plateau by the Colorado River, as mountain building uplifted the plateau.

DID YOU KNOW? Ten per cent of the world's land is covered by ice, compared to about 30 per cent during the last ice age

Spotter's guide to lowland glaciers

When you stand at the bottom, or snout of a valley glacier, you can see landforms made of debris dumped by the ice. The debris was eroded further up the valley and transported downhill, as if on a conveyor belt. Meltwater rushing under the glacier sculpts the debris heaps.

The snout is the place in the valley where the glacier melts completely. This changes over time. If the glacier shrinks, it leaves a debris trail behind. Should it grow again, it collects and bulldozes this debris. To understand why the snout moves up and downhill, you need to see glaciers as systems controlled by temperature and snowfall. On cold mountain peaks, snow accumulates faster than the glacier melts. As ice flows into warmer lowlands, melting begins to exceed accumulation. The snout advances or retreats depending on whether inputs of snow exceed ice loss from the system by melting.

1. Lateral moraine
Lateral moraines are made from rocks that have fallen off the valley sides after being shattered by frost. When the glacier melts, the moraine forms a ridge along the valley side.

3. Terminal or end moraine
An end moraine is a debris ridge that extends across a valley or plain, and marks the furthest advance of the glacier and its maximum size.

7. Erratics
Erratics are boulders picked up by glaciers and carried, sometimes hundreds of kilometres, into areas with a different rock type.

6. Braided streams
These streams have a braided shape because their channel becomes choked with coarse debris, picked up when the stream gained power during periods of fast glacier melt.

4. Recessional moraine
A recessional moraine is left when a glacier stops retreating long enough for a mound of debris to form at the snout.

5. Outwash plain
Outwash plains are made of gravel, sand and clay dropped by streams of meltwater that rush from the glacier during the summer, or when ice melts.

Inside an ice-carved valley

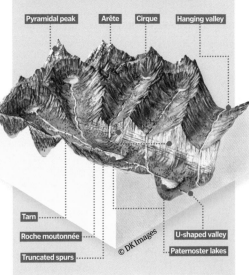

Pyramidal peak · Arête · Cirque · Hanging valley · Tarn · Roche moutonnée · Truncated spurs · U-shaped valley · Paternoster lakes

© DK Images

An aerial shot of a glacier

How does a glacier move?

Glaciers can only move, erode and transport debris if they have a wet bottom. Polar glaciers are frozen to the bedrock all year round and typically move around 1.5 metres (5 feet) per year, as ice crystals slide under gravity. In temperate climes like the European Alps, however, glaciers can slide downhill at 10-100 metres (30-330 feet) per year, due to the fact that meltwater forming under the glacier during mild summers acts as a lubricant.

If meltwater accumulates under a glacier, the ice can race forwards at up to 300 metres (990 feet) per day. During the fastest recorded surge, the Kutiah Glacier in Pakistan sped more than 12 kilometres (7.5 miles) in three months.

HOW IT WORKS
ENVIRONMENT
"The crocodile death roll is a unique method to feed off previously killed prey, not a method to kill them"

Crocodile tactics / Snakeskin / Whirlpools

Death rolls
How crocs employ this tactic

Commonly misunderstood, the crocodile death roll is a unique method to feed off previously killed prey, not a method to kill them. The most famous user of the death roll is the Nile species of crocodile, common to the Nile River in Egypt. Here, crocodiles use their camouflage and speed to grab large prey and drag them into the water. Once there, the crocodile proceeds to drag the target underwater, holding it there until it drowns. Once the prey is dead, the crocodile then performs the death roll in order to tear large chunks of flesh off its body quickly and efficiently. To do this, it buries its large teeth into the creature's flesh, before rolling its body 360 degrees. The muscular force of the crocodile's body in partnership with the sharpness of its teeth proceed to tear the prey open, something that would prove difficult within the water while stationary. ✿

Marsh crocs basking in the sun

A close-up view of a snake's shedded skin

Why do snakes shed their skin?
How and why do these slippery reptiles moult so frequently?

Snakes shed their skin for two main reasons. The first is to facilitate continued growth. This occurs as snakeskin does not grow in partnership with the snake itself, unlike in humans, where millions of skin cells are shed each year continuously on a microscopic, unseen level. On the contrary, snakes cannot shed skin in this microscopic way, necessitating them to literally outgrow the outer layer of skin whole on a frequent basis. The frequency that snakes shed their skin is largely dependent on the stage of life cycle they are in, with sheddings incredibly frequent during infancy and teenage years (bi-monthly in some species), but slowing to a couple of times per year as adults.

The second reason why snakes shed their skin is to preserve their health. Poor living conditions (lack of humidity, lack of vegetation, excess heat, and so on) as well as an inadequate food source can lead to skin damage and parasites. If left unchecked for a long period of time in the wild, this would be highly detrimental to the snake's well being. By shedding its skin, the snake can mitigate these potentially damaging conditions and start anew.

Interestingly, however, the shedding process brings with it complications. For the week or two preceding the shedding, the snake's vision is impaired due to the loosening of the skin's outer layer, and the week or two after the event, the new outer layer is soft and vulnerable to attack from predators. For this reason, snakes tend to be overly protective around sheddings, and largely inactive if possible. The snake initialises each shedding by rubbing itself against a sharp object such as rock, to pierce the outer layer of skin. ✿

Whirlpools
The often deadly vortex explained

Whirlpools are formed by the rising and falling of fast-flowing water through ocean channels on the seabed. Due to this, tsunamis – as seen in Japan in 2011 – are major whirlpool creators, with their massive waves receding quickly away from the shoreline. If this massive quantity of water is funnelled into narrow channels, a whirlpool can form, with a powerful vortex sweeping water towards its centre in a downdraught. While whirlpools can be dangerous, with rare cases of people drowning in them, there have been no reported cases of boats actually being sunk in their vortices. ✿

Naruto whirlpools, located in the Naruto Strait channel

TORRENTIAL

1. Hurricane Mitch (1998)
During Hurricane Mitch, America was soaked by 127cm (50 inches) in a few hours, causing mudslides and flash flooding.

POTENT

2. Acid snow
The effects of acid precipitation falling as snow can be more severe than rain. Rapid snowmelt in spring can cause a shock of acidity to lakes and rivers.

NON-EXISTENT

3. Atacama desert
There is no record of rain having ever fallen over some of the weather stations in the Atacama desert.

DID YOU KNOW? *Volcanic eruptions are the primary culprit for naturally releasing acid rain-causing gases into the atmosphere*

Where does acid rain come from?

We've all seen the effects of acid rain on limestone statues, but how does this damaging substance form?

All rainwater is a little bit acidic, because the carbon dioxide present in the atmosphere dissolves in water and forms carbonic acid. Stronger acid rain, however, can damage stone structures and can also be harmful to crops, as well as polluting waterways. It forms in the atmosphere when poisonous gases emitted by human activities combine with the moisture within rain clouds.

Fossil-fuelled power stations and petrol/diesel vehicles give off chemical pollutants – mainly sulphur dioxide (SO_2) and nitrogen oxides (NOx) – which when mixed with the water in the air react and turn acidic. ✿

Acid rain in action

2. Wind
The gases are carried on the wind to higher ground, towards rain clouds.

3. Gases dissolve
Upon combining with the water vapour (water and oxygen) in the rain clouds, the gases react to form weak but potentially damaging acid. Sulphur dioxide from industry becomes sulphuric acid.

4. Acid rainfall
When acid rain falls it can damage plant life, infiltrate waterways and erode buildings and statues.

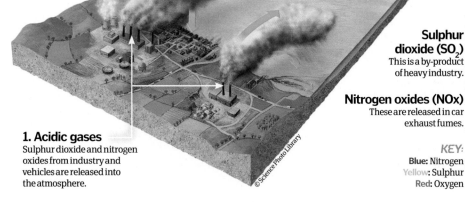

© Science Photo Library

1. Acidic gases
Sulphur dioxide and nitrogen oxides from industry and vehicles are released into the atmosphere.

Oxidation of sulphur and nitrogen

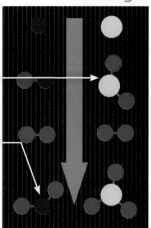

Sulphur dioxide (SO_2)
This is a by-product of heavy industry.

Nitrogen oxides (NOx)
These are released in car exhaust fumes.

KEY:
Blue: Nitrogen
Yellow: Sulphur
Red: Oxygen

What is a mirage?
How does this optical illusion bring invisible distant objects into view?

Commonly seen in the desert or at sea, a mirage is an optical phenomenon associated with light refraction. As light rays pass from a distant object through one material and into another, their refractive index changes, which alters the speed at which the rays travel. This is known as 'refraction' and it causes the light rays to bend and change direction. So when light passes from a layer of denser cool air through to a layer of less-dense warm air, refraction occurs. Due to the curvature of

the Earth, the bent light rays can bring otherwise obscured objects beyond the horizon into view above it, in line with the viewer.

The 'vision in the desert'-type mirage is known as an 'inferior' mirage. These mirages make objects appear much closer than they are, and light coming from objects on the horizon will appear as images down on the ground. They occur when the ground is so hot that it warms the air just above the surface. Light rays passing from the overlying cool air through to this warmer air near the surface will

bring a distant object into view at a closer range. Where the light would normally go to the ground, it goes up to meet the viewer's eyes.

Conversely, 'superior' mirages can make an image of an object appear unfeasibly high off the ground. This occurs when a layer of cool air sits beneath a layer of warm air (ie, over an area of ice or very cold water, such as the poles). Because the cold air near the ground is denser than the air higher up, light is refracted downwards, bending the light rays towards the viewer's eyes. ✿

How a mirage is formed

Superior mirage
A superior mirage appears high in the sky, making the object beyond the horizon visible to the viewer.

Seeing the invisible
Due to the curvature of the Earth, this village, which is situated beyond the horizon line, is concealed from the viewer.

Bending the light
Because the cold air near the surface is denser than the warmer air overlying it, light rays passing from the object through the air are refracted.

© Science Photo Library

Mega tsunami

Among the most epically destructive forces on Earth, tsunamis cause catastrophic levels of carnage, unearthing trees, levelling buildings and ending life. Delve to the bottom of the ocean to understand their causes and formation

Tsunamis form through a complex, multi-stage process that emanates from the massive energy release of a submarine earthquake, underwater or coastal landslide, or volcanic eruption.

The first stage in this formation begins when the tectonic upthrust caused by the quake or impulse event causes massive amounts of ocean water to be displaced almost instantaneously. This action kick-starts a simple series of progressive and oscillatory waves that travel out from the event's epicentre in ever-widening circles throughout the deep ocean. Due to severe levels of energy propagated from the impulse, the waves build in speed very quickly, reaching up to an incredible 805km/h (500mph). However, due to the depth of water, the speed of the waves is not visible as they expand to have incredibly long wavelengths that can stretch between 96-192km (60-120mi). Because of this, the wave amplitudes (the wave height) are also very small as the wave is extremely spread out, only typically measuring 30-60cm (11-23in). These long periods between wave crests – coupled with their very low amplitude – also mean that they are particularly difficult to detect when out at sea.

Once generated, the tsunami's waves then continue to build in speed and force before finally approaching a landmass. Here the depth of the ocean slowly

5 TOP FACTS
TSUNAMIS

Harbour wave
1 In Japanese the word tsunami literally translates as 'harbour wave'. Tsunamis are a frequent occurrence in Japan, with over 195 recorded throughout history so far.

Ancients
2 It was the Greek historian Thucydides who first linked tsunamis to earthquakes. However, their exact cause remained speculative until the 20th Century.

Brakes
3 Out at sea tsunamis travel incredibly quickly, often clocking up over 800km/h. This speed slows as it reaches the shoreline, often being reduced to around 80km/h.

Quick draw
4 The first part of a tsunami to reach land is referred to as a 'trough'. Here water along the shore recedes dramatically in a mass drawback, exposing normally submerged areas.

Monitoring
5 Due to their destructive nature, tsunami-related activity is monitored by specialist observation centres such as the Pacific Tsunami Warning Center in Honolulu.

DID YOU KNOW? The earthquake that generated the 2004 Indian Ocean tsunami was the fifth most deadly in history

How a tsunami forms

4. Approach
As the tsunami waves approach the coastline of a landmass they are slowed dramatically by the friction of their collision with the rising seabed. As the velocity lessens, however, the wavelengths become shortened and amplitude increases.

5. Impact
Finally, with the wavelength compressed and heightened to large levels (often between five and ten metres), the giant waves collide with the shore causing massive damage. The succeeding outflow of water then continues the destruction, uprooting trees and washing away people and property.

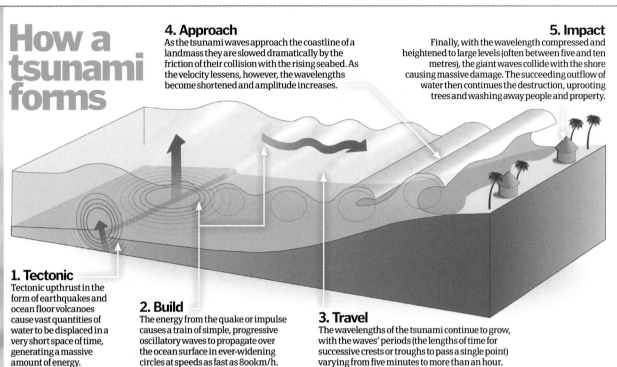

1. Tectonic
Tectonic upthrust in the form of earthquakes and ocean floor volcanoes cause vast quantities of water to be displaced in a very short space of time, generating a massive amount of energy.

2. Build
The energy from the quake or impulse causes a train of simple, progressive oscillatory waves to propagate over the ocean surface in ever-widening circles at speeds as fast as 800km/h.

3. Travel
The wavelengths of the tsunami continue to grow, with the waves' periods (the lengths of time for successive crests or troughs to pass a single point) varying from five minutes to more than an hour.

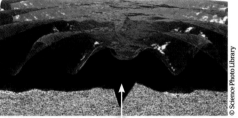
© Science Photo Library

© Science Photo Library

Cause
Tsunamis initiate when an earthquake causes the seabed to rupture (bottom centre), which leads to a rapid decrease in sea surface height directly above it.

Effect
As the tsunami reaches the shore the shallow, long and exceedingly fast waves pile up, reducing the wavelength and increasing their height dramatically.

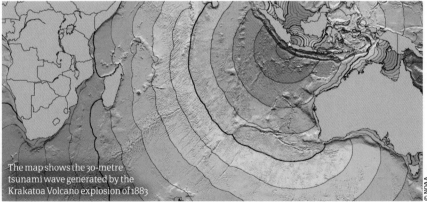
The map shows the 30-metre tsunami wave generated by the Krakatoa Volcano explosion of 1883
© NOAA

No need to ask what this sign means

TSUNAMI
RUTA DE EVACUACION
ROUTE OF EVACUATION

Head to Head
HISTORIC TSUNAMIS

BIG

1. Messina
The Messina earthquake of 1908 triggered a large tsunami 12 metres high that levelled entire buildings and killed more than 70,000 people in Sicily and southern Italy. The earthquake that generated it measured 7.5 on the Richter scale and caused the ground to shake for between 30 and 40 seconds.

BIGGER

2. The Valdivia earthquake
The Valdivia earthquake of 1960 caused one of the most damaging tsunamis of the 20th Century. Thousands of people were killed by it and it stretched as far as Hilo, Hawaii. Measuring 9.5 on the Richter scale, the earthquake caused waves up to 25 metres to assault the Chilean coast. The earthquake also triggered landslides and volcanic eruptions.

BIGGEST

3. Lituya Bay
After an earthquake caused a landslide at the head of Lituya Bay, Alaska, in July 1958, a massive tsunami was generated measuring over 524 metres in height, taller than the Empire State Building. Amazingly, despite the awesome height of the tsunami, only two fishermen operating in the bay were killed by it.

begins to reduce as the land begins to slope up towards the coastline. This sloping of the seabed acts as a braking mechanism for the high-velocity tsunami waves, reducing their speed through colossal friction between the water and the rising earth. This dramatic reduction in speed – which typically takes the velocity of the tsunami to 1/10th of its original speed – also has the effect of reducing the length of its waves, bunching them up and increasing their

amplitude significantly. Indeed, at this point coastal waters can be forced to raise as much as 30 metres above normal sea level in little over ten minutes.

Following this rise in sea level above the continental shelf (a shallow submarine terrace of continental crust that forms at the edge of a continental landmass) the oscillatory motions carried by the tsunami are transferred into its waters, being compressed in the process. These oscillations under the

pressure of the approaching water are then forced forwards towards the coast, causing a series of low level but incredibly fast run-ups of sea water, capable of propelling and dragging cars, trees, buildings and people over great distances. In fact, these run-ups are often responsible for a large proportion of the tsunami's damage, not the giant following waves. Regardless, however, following the run-ups the tsunami's high-amplitude waves continue to slow ▶

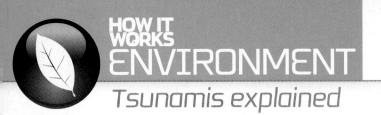
"Due to severe levels of energy propagated from the impulse, the waves build in speed very quickly"

▶ and bunch into fewer and fewer megawaves before breaking at heights between five and ten metres over the immediate coastline, causing great damage and finally releasing its stored energy.

Due to the severe hazards that tsunamis pose, research into their causes and tracking of their formation has increased through the 20th and 21st Centuries. Currently, the world's oceans are monitored by various tsunami detection and prevention centres, such as the NOAA (National Oceanic and Atmospheric Administration) run Pacific Tsunami Warning Center (PTWC) based in Honolulu, Hawaii.

Set up back in 1949, the PTWC utilises a series of tsunami monitoring systems that delivers seismic and oceanographic data to it on a daily basis, with information transferred to it and other stations by satellite connection. This is one of two American-run centres that monitors the Pacific Ocean and it is responsible for detecting and predicting the size and target of any approaching tsunamis.

Tsunami prevention has also seen advances as construction techniques and materials have developed over the past century. Now areas that are prone to tsunamis, such as Japan's west coast, are fitted with large-scale sea walls, artificial deep-sea barriers, emergency raised evacuation platforms and integrated electronic warning signs and klaxons in coastal resorts and ports.

Areas that have been affected by tsunamis in the past are also fitted with physical warning signs and have specific evacuation routes that best allow for large numbers of people to quickly move inland. Unfortunately, however, despite many advances being made to ensure prone areas are protected and warned in advance, due to the transcontinental nature of generated tsunamis, remote or under-developed areas are still affected regularly, the consequences of which were evident following the disastrous 2004 tsunami in the Indian Ocean that claimed over 200,000 lives. ✿

A tsunami early-detection buoy is removed from the ocean for maintenance

The DART II tsunami detection system
Introducing the system and technology that aids scientists in detecting upcoming tsunamis

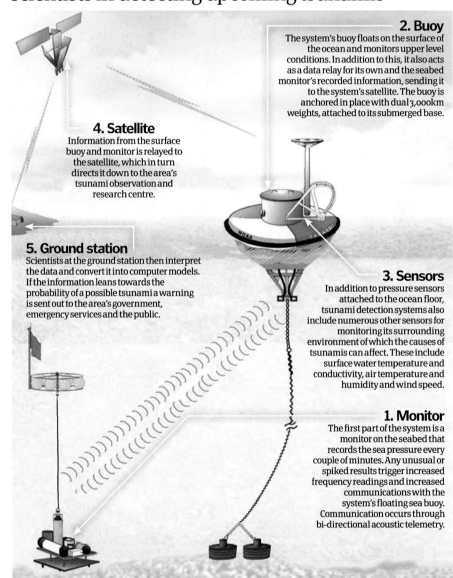

2. Buoy
The system's buoy floats on the surface of the ocean and monitors upper level conditions. In addition to this, it also acts as a data relay for its own and the seabed monitor's recorded information, sending it to the system's satellite. The buoy is anchored in place with dual 3,000km weights, attached to its submerged base.

4. Satellite
Information from the surface buoy and monitor is relayed to the satellite, which in turn directs it down to the area's tsunami observation and research centre.

5. Ground station
Scientists at the ground station then interpret the data and convert it into computer models. If the information leans towards the probability of a possible tsunami a warning is sent out to the area's government, emergency services and the public.

3. Sensors
In addition to pressure sensors attached to the ocean floor, tsunami detection systems also include numerous other sensors for monitoring its surrounding environment of which the causes of tsunamis can affect. These include surface water temperature and conductivity, air temperature and humidity and wind speed.

1. Monitor
The first part of the system is a monitor on the seabed that records the sea pressure every couple of minutes. Any unusual or spiked results trigger increased frequency readings and increased communications with the system's floating sea buoy. Communication occurs through bi-directional acoustic telemetry.

The devastated Marina beach in Chennai after the Indian Ocean tsunami struck

A tsunami emergency evacuation platform in Japan

DID YOU KNOW? The 2004 tsunami released 1,502 times the energy of the Hiroshima atomic bomb

The 2004 Indian Ocean tsunami

Claiming the lives of over 200,000 people, the Indian Ocean tsunami of 2004 was literally off-the-scale in terms of both damage and destruction

The 2004 tsunami striking the coast of Thailand

On 26 December 2004, an undersea megathrust earthquake caused a huge earth subduction and triggered a series of devastating tsunamis that ravaged almost all landmasses bordering on the Indian Ocean, killing over 230,000 people in 14 different countries. The hypocentre of the main earthquake was approximately 160km (100mi) off the western coast of northern Sumatra and emanated from the ocean floor 30km (19mi) below the area's mean sea level. Here, a massive rupture in the ocean floor caused massive tectonic plate movement – an event felt as far away as Singapore – as well as the creation of numerous secondary faults that elevated the height and speed of generated waves to titanic levels.

The fallout from the earthquake and resulting tsunami was the worst for over 50 years, with the event releasing a total of 1.1×10^7 joules of energy. This level of energy release was comparable to 26.3 megatons of TNT, over 1,502 times the energy released by the Hiroshima atomic bomb. Indeed, the rupture was so severe that the massive release of energy was so great it slightly altered the Earth's rotation, causing it to wobble on its axis by up to 2.5cm.

Further, when the British Royal Navy vessel HMS Scott surveyed the seabed around the earthquake zone with a multi-beam sonar system, it revealed that it has drastically altered its topography. The event has caused 1,500m ridges to collapse into massive landslides kilometres long. The momentum of the water displaced by tectonic upshift had also dragged massive million-ton rocks over 10km on the seabed and an entirely new oceanic trench had been exposed.

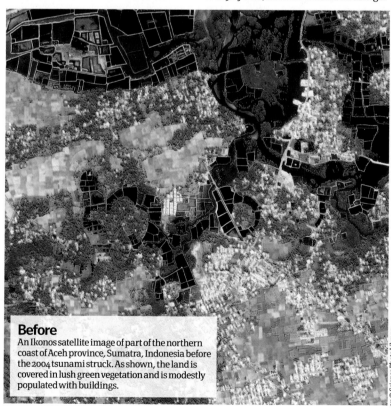

Before
An Ikonos satellite image of part of the northern coast of Aceh province, Sumatra, Indonesia before the 2004 tsunami struck. As shown, the land is covered in lush green vegetation and is modestly populated with buildings.

After
An Ikonos satellite taken on 29 December 2004, three days after the tsunami struck. As can be seen now, almost all of the immediate coastline was completely submerged and the huge, lush plains of vegetation have been severely encroached upon and washed away. Many buildings have also been submerged or destroyed.

2x © Science Photo Library

TECHNOLOGY
Modern gadgetry and engineering explained

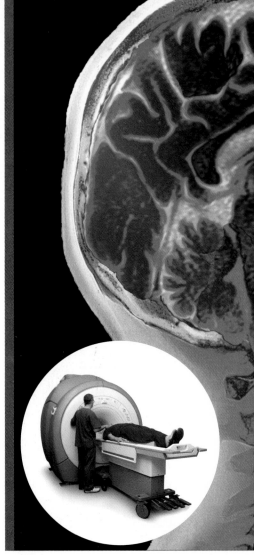

54 Social networks

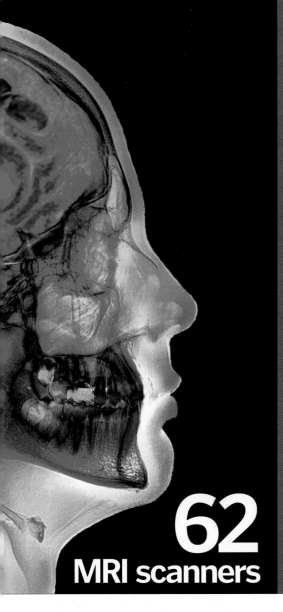

62
MRI scanners

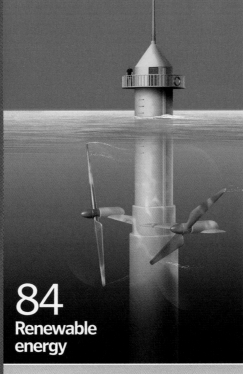

84
Renewable energy

72
Motion-control gaming

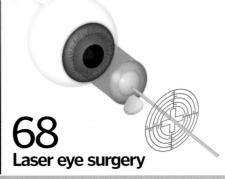

68
Laser eye surgery

92
Stealth technology

Social networks

Discover the technical side of the social media sites that keep us connected with friends around the world

At the heart of many social networking platforms, such as Facebook, is a software tool called the Application Programming Interface (API). This enables multiple communities of users to create an open architecture for sharing data (including photos, tags, events and so on) between communities as well as other applications. Content created in one place can be posted and updated in numerous locations on the internet, creating a web of dynamic information.

At the core of this web is a set of rules and specifications that the social network's software (ie the network's web pages) can liaise with in order to transmit and share information. In essence, the rules dictate the structure of the social web around a user (and accessible by them), granting permissions and access, as well as dictating information relevant to them (their friend's photos, pages, and so on).

For the rules to work – certainly when they are operating based on Hyper Text Markup Language (HTML, the building block code of any webpage) – each point on the social network's web must be represented as an 'object' with a unique ID code. For example, on Facebook your profile page is an object with a unique code. Therefore, if another user wishes to view your profile, to do so they must acquire that code – as dictated by the network's rule-base – in order for the connection to take place. This is facilitated by Facebook's software interface, allowing that person to click on your profile link to fetch that object. This is also why people who have not been granted permission to access a person's full details (ie, they are not 'friends') cannot see that data. Their relationship on the social graph, as dictated by the API's rules, does not allow them to fetch that object, as they have not been granted an 'access token'.

Everything on a Facebook page – be it photos, events, news, comments or links – are classed not only as objects by the API, but are instead directly and indirectly connected by the social graph. Furthermore, there are various different types of connections for various objects, ranging from movie choices and audio/video tags through to groups and news feeds – each linked by the API's rules across the social graph (ie the map by which all users are connected).

Where Facebook's system gets really smart is in its utilisation of an object/connection ranking formula referred to as EdgeRank, an algorithm that charts all interaction between objects, and ranks them accordingly. So, for example, if you

5 TOP FACTS
SOCIAL NETWORKING

Real estate
1 Social network giant Facebook is currently building a data centre in Oregon, USA, measuring 307,000 square feet; the scale of the building has doubled in the past year.

Followers
2 Pop star Lady Gaga currently holds the record for having the most Twitter followers, with over eight million people tracking her regular updates.

$50 bilion
3 Following investment from Goldman Sachs and a wealthy Russian investor, it has been estimated that Facebook is worth a whopping $50 billion.

My decline
4 In the first half of 2010 it was estimated that visits to MySpace halved from 10 million to 5 million, as social networking rival Facebook grew in popularity.

Tweets
5 As of 1 January 2011, it was estimated that 110 million tweets were posted to Twitter every day from the 200 million registered users on the site.

DID YOU KNOW? Facebook experiences roughly 2,000 photo uploads every second – that's just short of 173 million per day

Facebook map

This map of the world was created by linking people on Facebook with their friends in other cities

Paul Butler, an intern at Facebook, created this map of the world using only the connections between friends on the social network. Without using the map of the world as a template, the connections gradually began to show the borders of countries, continents and coastal lines.

The effect works by a sample of 10 million random pairs of friends being taken from the Facebook database. Linking them to each other's city and calculating the number of friends between those cities gives a brightness intensity of how many connections a specific region has to another, some intercontinental and some within the same country.

The outline of the world shows the connections between users of the social network, giving a clearly identifiable map of Earth. Countries such as China and Russia are almost invisible, with a very small Facebook userbase.

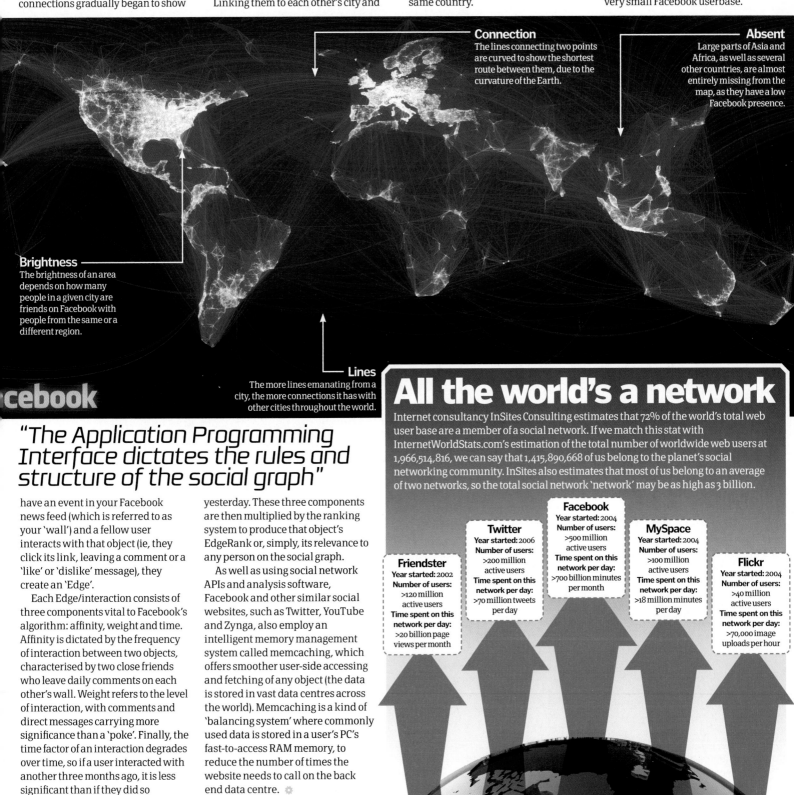

Connection
The lines connecting two points are curved to show the shortest route between them, due to the curvature of the Earth.

Absent
Large parts of Asia and Africa, as well as several other countries, are almost entirely missing from the map, as they have a low Facebook presence.

Brightness
The brightness of an area depends on how many people in a given city are friends on Facebook with people from the same or a different region.

Lines
The more lines emanating from a city, the more connections it has with other cities throughout the world.

cebook

"The Application Programming Interface dictates the rules and structure of the social graph"

have an event in your Facebook news feed (which is referred to as your 'wall') and a fellow user interacts with that object (ie, they click its link, leaving a comment or a 'like' or 'dislike' message), they create an 'Edge'.

Each Edge/interaction consists of three components vital to Facebook's algorithm: affinity, weight and time. Affinity is dictated by the frequency of interaction between two objects, characterised by two close friends who leave daily comments on each other's wall. Weight refers to the level of interaction, with comments and direct messages carrying more significance than a 'poke'. Finally, the time factor of an interaction degrades over time, so if a user interacted with another three months ago, it is less significant than if they did so

yesterday. These three components are then multiplied by the ranking system to produce that object's EdgeRank or, simply, its relevance to any person on the social graph.

As well as using social network APIs and analysis software, Facebook and other similar social websites, such as Twitter, YouTube and Zynga, also employ an intelligent memory management system called memcaching, which offers smoother user-side accessing and fetching of any object (the data is stored in vast data centres across the world). Memcaching is a kind of 'balancing system' where commonly used data is stored in a user's PC's fast-to-access RAM memory, to reduce the number of times the website needs to call on the back end data centre.

All the world's a network

Internet consultancy InSites Consulting estimates that 72% of the world's total web user base are a member of a social network. If we match this stat with InternetWorldStats.com's estimation of the total number of worldwide web users at 1,966,514,816, we can say that 1,415,890,668 of us belong to the planet's social networking community. InSites also estimates that most of us belong to an average of two networks, so the total social network 'network' may be as high as 3 billion.

Friendster
Year started: 2002
Number of users:
>120 million active users
Time spent on this network per day:
>20 billion page views per month

Twitter
Year started: 2006
Number of users:
>200 million active users
Time spent on this network per day:
>70 million tweets per day

Facebook
Year started: 2004
Number of users:
>500 million active users
Time spent on this network per day:
>700 billion minutes per month

MySpace
Year started: 2004
Number of users:
>100 million active users
Time spent on this network per day:
>18 million minutes per day

Flickr
Year started: 2004
Number of users:
>40 million active users
Time spent on this network per day:
>70,000 image uploads per hour

"Banks of super-fast servers maintain a fast, stable connection between the software and remote data"

How social networks keep us connected

Home Your Profile My Account Privacy

Search

Anatomy of a social network

The major elements of a social media site and how they work

How It Works
Edit My Profile

- News Feed
- Messaging
- Events / Calendar
- Friends List

User profiles

When social networking sites want to share profile information between each other and connect, they rely on the fact that the same 'type' of data is used by convention across different services or sites. But how can one system talk to another when it may be programmed in a different computer language and different core operating system?

Much of the common data that is shared (eg, your name, your contacts and your favourites) will be exchanged as a result of what is known as syntactic analysis, or as it is commonly known in computer science, 'parsing'.

Not as complex as it sounds, parsing is the division of data into smaller parts so that it can be formatted into 'tuples', which are individual values in a table. For example, the address 33 Richmond Hill, Bournemouth, UK could be labelled as number, road name, city and country. By collating this data, Facebook is able to create a map of people within a specific network and link them together.

Twitter

They may seem similar, but the differences between Twitter and the status updates on Facebook are more than apparent when you take a look at the framework of each website. Twitter employs the use of a programming language known as Ruby On Rails (RoR) used by many large websites. It allows Twitter to quickly handle the constant requests it receives from users, as millions of posts are 'tweeted' every hour. RoR simplifies multiple codes into easy applications, handling the front end of the site, the web layout itself.

Twitter also employs the use of Scala, another programming language which supports the back end of the website. While RoR is used to adapt to the constant Tweets, Scala supports the website's servers and keeps the general framework ticking over. It handles the vast number of Tweets regularly sent to the website, and interacts with the information stored at Twitter's own data centre.

News feeds

Social networks use mathematical algorithms to dictate the relevance of any news story by assigning them a rank. A news story's rank is usually dictated by its affinity to a user – ie, is it an event planned by their close friend? – its weight, such as whether the user was mentioned in the news story, and chronological timeframe, with older stories being less worthy. On social networks such as MySpace and Facebook, news feeds are connected to almost every aspect of a user's profile, with even distant, third-hand connections (such as a friend of a friend commenting on a picture including the user) being mapped on the service's social graph.

Howitworksmag
Posting our status here allows other users to comment and 'like' our status
10 minutes ago - Like - Comment

Grabbing attention - A user can view posts chronologically or by popularity on the 'Most Recent' and 'Top News' tabs
9 minutes ago - Like

Popularity contest - The more closely connected you are to somebody, the higher their post features in your 'Top News'
6 minutes ago - Like

Write a comment...

Pokes

- **Simon Gladstone** – Poke back
- **Beatrice Smalling** – Poke back

Connections are key

Every action between users on Facebook further intensifies the connection two friends have with one another. This allows Facebook to tailor events, news and status updates to specific friends depending on who or what they have the most interactions with. For example, 'poking' a friend or accepting an invite to an event will show your affinity to them, strengthening the connection, and the stronger your Facebook friendship becomes the more Facebook will link the two of you in future.

Sarah's images
Images, videos and textual information are stored in data centres
10 minutes ago - Like - Comment

Data handling

Due to the large quantity of uploaded information by users, such as videos, pictures and text, social networks require large amounts of storage and processing power. Large-scale industrial data centres are commonly used to store heavy data such as videos – as can be seen in the 307,000 square feet centre being built by Facebook in Oregon, US – while cloud-based networks (location-independent shared servers) are increasingly being used to handle lighter material. Banks of super-fast servers are used to maintain a fast and stable connection between the software and the remote data. In addition, to minimise the footprint of any piece of stored data, many social networks feature conversion software code built into the user interface, to ensure overly large files are not uploaded and those that are are optimised for the web.

Updates

Twitter users do not see the most popular posts by others, rather just the most recent.

Trending

If a particular topic is garnering a lot of attention, through use of tools such as hashtags, which appear in the search engines, it will appear

HowItWorksmag Bournemouth
@HowItWorksmag
The science and technology magazine that knows minds
http://www.howitworksdaily.com

HowItWorksmag
Find out all about the gorgeous McLaren MP4-12C right here
http://wp.me/pjFL55-J8

HowItWorksmag
How It Works eMag Vol.1: For those who missed out on the early

One for the album
More than 100 million photos are uploaded to Facebook every day and 99 per cent of people using Facebook have uploaded at least one photo. People celebrated New Year 2010 on Facebook by uploading a record 750 million photos over that weekend.

MySpace

Many other social networks use a similar underlying framework to that of Facebook to provide an interactive environment for their users. MySpace, one of the most popular social networking sites on the internet, handles its large volume of traffic by redirecting page requests through an UltraDNS system, which accesses a large volume of storage and application servers upon which the website is based.

Like Facebook, MySpace allows users to create a hub of friends with whom they can share information and send messages. The difference, however, is that each user profile on MySpace is its own individual webpage, usually the web address followed by the person's username (for example, www.myspace.com/howitworksmag), allowing anyone on the internet to have access to their profile. Facebook, on the other hand, stores each profile within the website, and only members who are logged in can view them.

Intelligent adverts

Specific advertisements can be tailored to a user's personal data using relational database management systems, which act as servers and provide multi-user access to a number of databases. Using programs such as Google AdWords, advertisers can examine statistics relating to how users came to click on a particular website. The company knows how users used a particular search engine result, or paid for an advertisement to get to a site. It can then also examine how many people 'convert' from visiting a website's initial landing page to becoming spending customers for a particular product or service.

Google has built new mechanics into web searches, enabling advertisers to target people who are searching for their product. Tailoring advertisements to the search terms that people use on Google and then sending visitors to the right page on a site means that users get to see the content they've searched for and website owners keep visitors for longer. Social networking portals allow advertisers to target people based on age, profile, marital status and preferences, making them increasingly commercially focused.

Targeting demographics

Male

In a relationship

24-30 in a relationship

Everybody's changing

Each user can tailor their privacy settings to deny access.

Blocking

You can block specific users who may be trying to gain sensitive information.

Posts

Only people you've befriended will usually be able to see your status updates and profile, unless your settings allow them to be viewed by 'friends of friends'.

200 million
The number of mobile users of social networks worldwide has tripled in the last year alone.

Jan 2010   mid 2010   Jan 2011

In a relationship?

This Valentine's Day, surprise your loved one with a beautiful hand-delivered bouquet from Flowers Forever.

Social networking on the move

Facebook, on the other hand, largely relies on PHP, a general scripting language that is fairly unsimplified. It uses specific lines of code, similar to HTML, to perform a particular request. This difference allows Twitter to operate quicker, as it relies on a constant flow of Tweets, whereas Facebook focuses more on the storing and accessibility of 'Profiles' and connections between friends.

User interface
Dedicated, optimised software interfaces allow social networks to be accessed efficiently.

Real-time
Always-on connections allow real-time status and profile updates.

Fetch and retrieve
An increased bandwidth allows for remote content to be shared or downloaded quickly.

Chat services
Messaging chat services have been around since the earliest Bulletin Board Services (BBS) in the early-Seventies, as a precursor to email. Social networking sites have taken advantage of improved broadband connections to allow users to be able to chat in real-time.

Individual Facebook servers queue a user's messages and send them into their web browser via a programming language known as Erlang. This regularly deletes old chat messages and constantly updates the chat window, but when the user minimises the live conversation, Erlang will 'sleep' (work slower) until the user reactivates the window.

Chat (online) Friends: 5

"Anyone trying to break into the system would have to scour the encrypted servers one by one"

Paying online with confidence

Pay online without revealing your credit card details

Jargon buster

Server
A server is a computer dedicated to linking other computers or electronic devices together, which in large companies tend to operate in banks (groups).

Interchange
Interchanges are small fees charged by banks and companies involved in a transaction, in order to facilitate their processing.

Linux
An operating system (like Windows or iOS) used extensively worldwide in servers and supercomputers, due to its speed and security.

PayPal

The technology behind these secure online payments

PayPal works by utilising thousands of separate servers running the Linux operating system, literal 'blocks' of servers that can be redistributed to perform different tasks in tandem with one another. These thousands of servers connect with an offline database of customer information to transfer data back and forth between payee and recipient. However, the servers don't share information with each other, so anyone trying to break into the system would have to scour the heavily encrypted servers

one by one to piece together the relevant data. This separation of the servers allows PayPal to remain secure while quickly processing the millions of payments it receives, as it would be almost impossible to obtain access to the different servers simultaneously to gather data.

The process is best shown through a step-by-step transaction. When a product is bought, the buyer – who has supplied PayPal with their bank details – authorises a transaction via credit card or cheque to debit their account for the purchase price.

This transaction is handled directly by PayPal, which contacts the seller's bank, credit card association and card issuer, paying the various interchange fees necessary to process it. The seller's money is then deposited into a dedicated PayPal account. This process is mirrored for the merchant, but is processed on a completely separate server for security reasons. Finally, after a set period of time, the money is transferred to the buyer's account in another completely separate transaction across another server. ✿

Your payment options	PayPal sends the money	Recipient receives the money

- Credit card
- Bank account
- PayPal balance
- PayPal plus credit card
- PayPal buyer credit

YOUR SECURE PAYPAL ACCOUNT

- People
- Online stores
- eBay

1. Method
PayPal accepts many different types of payment method, from cheque to credit card. The type of payment affects the amount of interchange fees that are paid and processing time.

2. Interest
PayPal makes money by accruing interest on banked payments, as well as direct fees charged according to an item's value.

3. Exchange
PayPal payments are not restricted just to online stores and auction houses, with people able to directly wire funds to any other person with an email address.

DID YOU KNOW?

The first hairdryer

Inspired by the early vacuum cleaner, in 1890 French inventor Alexandre Godefoy invented the electric hairdryer. He noticed that the sucking motion of the vacuum cleaner could also be used as a time saver in the beauty department. Vacuum cleaners may be used to suck up air and dust, but they also have a warm exhaust (heat from the motor), which Godefoy identified as a method of drying hair.

DID YOU KNOW? A number of hairdryers now feature ceramic heating elements

Manufacturing optical fibre

How does a large glass cylinder become a tiny thread of flexible glass?

The tiny filament of glass at the core of a length of optical fibre starts out as two tubes. These tubes are made from fused quartz glass, which is mainly silica and gives it flexible properties. First the glass tubes are dipped in corrosive hydrofluoric acid to remove any oily residues, they are then placed in a pair of lathes that spin and heat both tubes with a hydrogen and oxygen flame. When the tubes turn white they are nearing peak temperature and at 2,000°C the tubes melt together to form one longer tube.

This longer tube is placed in another lathe where it is turned and heated by a burner before being injected with chemical gases containing liquid forms of silicon and germanium. The heat and gases cause a chemical reaction that leaves a fine white soot inside the tube. As the burner travels up and down the length of the tube the soot fuses to create a solid glass core. The outer glass tube will form the cladding around the core.

Continued heating softens the tube and the new glass inside until the tube collapses in on itself. What you now have is a solid rod called a preform. To thin the preform, it is placed vertically in a drawing tower. This device heats one end of the rod to 2,000°C until the glass softens and becomes a honey-like consistency. As the glass melts it stretches under its own weight and becomes a very tall, thin glass fibre.

Pulleys and lasers are used to measure the precise tension and diameter of the fibre, which should be just 125 micrometres thick. The fibre is then passed under an ultraviolet lamp to bake on a protective outer jacket. The finished optical fibre is then rolled onto massive drums.

Optical cladding
Protecting the inner glass core is another layer of glass that has a lower refractive index than the core. The whole glass element is 125 micrometres across.

Inner core
The glass component of optical fibre is highly refractive, causing total internal reflection. This core measures just eight micrometres across, about the size of a human hair.

Total internal reflection
The high refraction of the glass core and the low refraction of the outer jacket trap light in the core of the fibre so that little to no light is absorbed. This is called total internal reflection.

Plastic jacket
This layer is the last line of defence against damage – such as scratches – to the fragile internal contents. This brings the total diameter of the fibre up to 400 micrometres.

Protective buffer
A resin coating is baked on to protect the delicate glass thread within from moisture damage. With the addition of this layer, the diameter is now 250 micrometres.

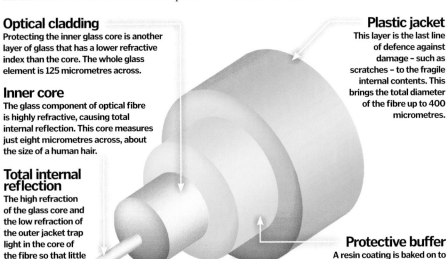

Temperatures up to 2,000°C help create the glass fibre

© Science Photo Library

Be warned: hairdryer results may vary

Hairdryers

How do these domestic appliances create an instant blast of hot air?

The main parts of a hairdryer are a motor-driven fan and an electrically heated element (a very long wire coil with resistance). The element heats up when an electric current flows through it, because electrons bump into the metal atoms in the wire, increasing the vibrations of these atoms. When air from the fan blows through the barrel, the element radiates heat that warms the air up. The hot air passes out through the open end of the dryer (the nozzle), and the user can then direct this hot air onto their hair to speed up the evaporation of water from the surface of the hair.

Fan motor
Electricity enables the electric motor to spin, which powers the fan.

Wire screen filter
At both open ends are filters to prevent lint and dust from clogging up the motor as air is sucked in from the back end.

Nozzle
This is the open end through which the hot air escapes.

Direction of airflow

Barrel

© Science Photo Library

Element (resistor)
This nichrome wire coil heats up when electricity flows through it, because the motion of the molecules inside speed up.

Fan
An electrically powered fan blasts air down the barrel of the hairdryer over the heated element.

Switches
Modern hairdryers have an on/off switch, an air speed control and temperature regulators.

Power source

Modern vending machines can accept banknotes and credit cards as well as coinage

Coin-operated vending machines

How do they recognise the money you insert?

Coin-operated vending machines work by detecting inserted coins through physical and electronic mechanisms. When a coin is inserted into the vendor's slot, it travels down a specially angled chute. It is angled to generate a set amount of momentum for the travelling coin. The currency then passes through an electromagnetic field generated by an electromagnet that surrounds the chute, generating an electronic signature according to its chemical composition. If this signature doesn't match one of the vendor's computer's known set of signatures (the different coin values) the coin is not logged by the system, but rejected.

Once through the electromagnetic field, the travelling coin must then cross the reject chute to be accepted by the vendor. To do this, the coin must be travelling at the correct momentum as dictated by the chute, with coins travelling too slowly or quickly stopped with physical barriers. This ensures that only official, known currency is accepted – coins which are too light, too heavy or too big or small are physically stopped, as they do not travel down the chute at the pre-designed speed. If coins pass both checks, they are logged and accepted by the vending machine and function accordingly; if either check fails, however, the coin is rejected and sent down a second chute for collection. ✿

Physics
Regardless of the coin's signature, inserted coins must then pass over the reject hole. To do this, the coin's size and forward momentum must be consistent with that of the design of the machine.

Electronics
Inserted coins then pass through an electromagnetic field, creating a distinct electronic signature according to their metal composition.

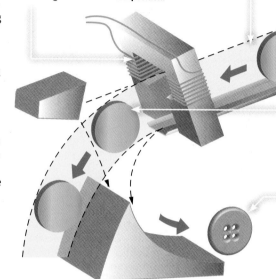

Coins
Coins vary in weight, size and chemical composition. When they are inserted into the machine, they proceed down a specially angled chute.

Duds
Foreign, forged or non-currency is therefore either rejected on chemical grounds (its electronic signature) or physical grounds (its weight and size) and sent down a reject chute for collection.

How copies are made

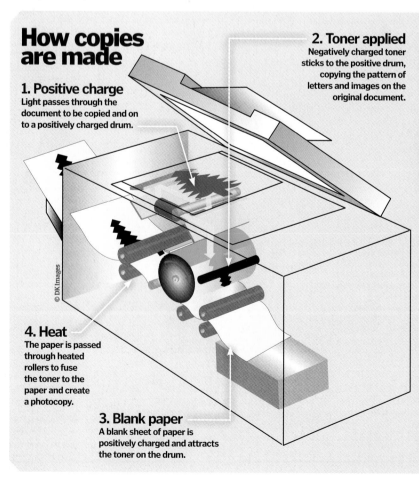

1. Positive charge
Light passes through the document to be copied and on to a positively charged drum.

2. Toner applied
Negatively charged toner sticks to the positive drum, copying the pattern of letters and images on the original document.

4. Heat
The paper is passed through heated rollers to fuse the toner to the paper and create a photocopy.

3. Blank paper
A blank sheet of paper is positively charged and attracts the toner on the drum.

© DK Images

Photocopiers

How do these common office instalations duplicate pages?

The method employed by most modern office photocopiers is xerography – using electrostatic charges and heat to print the required image on paper. The device uses light (hence the 'photo' in photocopier) to increase the electrical conductivity of certain substances. Selenium, which is usually a poor electrical conductor, is often used as it allows for the free flow of electrons in an electric current when light is incident upon it.

Inside the copier is a drum coated in a substance such as selenium. As light passes underneath the document to be copied, it imprints the image on the document onto the drum using negatively charged ink known as toner. More electrons flow where the light reaches as they are not blocked by text or an image, and vice versa, altering the pattern of the ink on the drum. A blank piece of paper with a positive charge attracts these negative ink particles back from the drum, which are then fused onto the paper with heat to produce a copy of the original document. ✿

How not to use a photocopier...

5 TOP FACTS
LIGHTHOUSES

Fame
1 The builder of the Lighthouse of Alexandria, Sostratus – disobeying orders from the pharaoh Ptolemy – engraved his name and a dedication to the sea gods on the tower base.

Academia
2 The technical term for the study of lighthouses is 'pharology', a word derived from Pharos, the island upon which the great Lighthouse of Alexandria once stood.

War
3 George Meade built many notable lighthouses in the US during the classical lighthouse period. He is remembered in history as the winning general in the Battle of Gettysburg.

Tallest
4 The tallest lighthouse in the world is the Yokohama Marine Tower in Yokohama, Japan. The structure flashes alternately green and red every 20 seconds.

Elemental
5 Originally lighthouses were lit merely with open fires, only later progressing through candles, lanterns and electric lights. Lanterns tended to use whale oil as fuel.

DID YOU KNOW? The historic Lighthouse of Alexandria on the Pharos Island, Egypt, could be seen from 30 miles away

A reassuring sight for sailors throughout history

A fixed Fresnel lens without its outer shell

© Hannes Grobe

Fresnel lens
The Fresnel lens allows for a light source to be amplified way beyond its standard imitable ability in a certain direction and done so with fewer materials than a conventional spherical lens. It achieves this by redirecting light waves through a series of prisms arranged in a circular array, with steeper prisms at the edges and flatter ones near the centre.

Lighthouses

Including some of the most impressive man-made structures in the world, lighthouses have played a pivotal life-saving role throughout history

Lighthouses work by rhythmically flashing a rotating light in order to transmit a visual signal to surrounding vessels. This is done so that conditions that provide poor visibility can be mitigated by approaching sailors, allowing them to safely manoeuvre while close to the shore. The individual pattern of flashes or eclipses – referred to as the light's character – determine the transmitted message and these can range from collision warnings to weather reports, directional guidance to the position of other vessels and structures. The breadth and types of characters a lighthouse can use is determined by the International Association of Lighthouse Authorities in Paris.

Lighthouse construction emanated from the practice of lighting beacon fires upon hilltops, something first referenced in Homer's *Iliad* and *Odyssey* in the 8th Century BC. However, it was not until 280 BCE, when the architect Sostratus built the Great Lighthouse of Alexandria on the island of Pharos, Egypt, that man-made lighthouse structures began to be built across the entire globe. Since then the style and complexity of the structure, light source and fuel has changed greatly, with intricate designs formed dedicated to advancing the light-saving technology. How It Works takes a closer look at a classical lighthouse and its constituent components. ✿

Light source
Early lighthouses used open fires and large candles to create light. During the classic period of lighthouse usage, lanterns burning animal oils were common. Gas lamps were also used around the turn of the 20th Century. Modern lighthouses use electric lamps and bulbs.

Rotational crank/ machinery
The rotational ability of the lamp was classically generated by a hand crank, which would be wound by the lighthouse keeper up to every two hours. In modern lighthouses the lamps are powered by diesel electric generators.

Lantern room
Arguably the most important aspect of the lighthouse, the lantern room is the glassed-in structure that sits at the pinnacle of the tower. Commonly, lantern rooms are fitted with storm panes and metal astragal bars in order to withstand the harsh weather conditions it is exposed to, as well as a ventilator in the roof to remove any smoke and heat caused by the lamps within – obviously, smoke is not an issue with electric lamps. Lantern rooms are often surrounded by a gallery, which is used for cleaning the windows.

Tower
Lighthouse towers are usually either built onshore or directly on the seabed. This is best shown in the caisson method, where an open-ended cylinder is sunk and filled with concrete to form a solid base. However the latter is less common due to the erosion suffered by sea waves. Towers have a distinctive shape and colour – often a top-tapered, white tower – to help sailors identify them. Within the tower it is also common to find the lighthouse's service room, the place where the fuel/generator is kept.

Gallery
The gallery is the lighthouse's circular, external platform that is often wrapped around one or two levels. It is used for human observation and also as a maintenance platform for cleaning the lantern room's windows.

"Physicists and engineers use and manipulate the basic laws of physics"

Using magnets to see what's inside

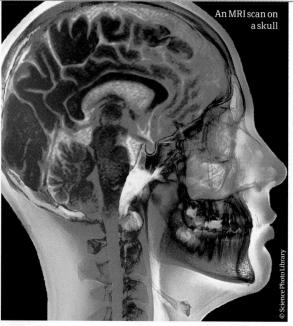

An MRI scan on a skull

© Science Photo Library

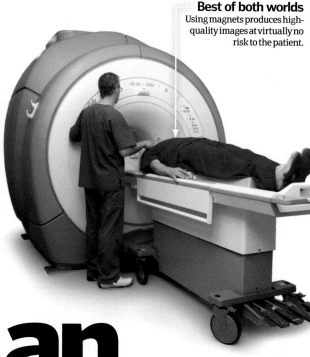

Best of both worlds
Using magnets produces high-quality images at virtually no risk to the patient.

Planning from the detail

The detail provided by MRI scanners enables doctors of all specialties to plan their treatment. When footballers damage their knees, an MRI scan will tell if the ligaments are ruptured. Knee surgeons can then reconstruct the damage, often via keyhole incisions (arthroscopically). MRI scans are used to characterise a variety of tumours, such as those of the rectum (the lowest part of the colon) and within the brain. MRI gives enough detail to determine the size and stage of the tumour. This helps specialist surgeons plan whether the tumour is resectable, and also how to perform the operation.

The MRI's key lies in its ability to differentiate soft tissues – it can even tell the difference between infected and normal tissues. Infections within bones are best identified using MRI, and then surgeons can plan whether to treat with antibiotics, an operation, or if the infection is spread too far, an amputation.

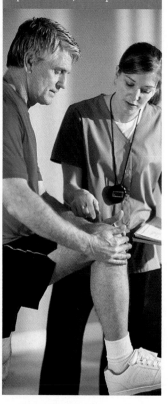

Inside an MRI scanner

When doctors need the highest quality images possible they turn to MRI scanners, but how do they work?

Doctors often plan treatments based on imaging. X-rays, ultrasound and CT scans provide useful pictures, but when the highest quality images are needed, they turn to MRI scanners. While CT scanners use x-rays and therefore expose the patient to radiation, magnetic resonance imaging (MRI) uses powerful magnets and is virtually risk free.

MRI scans are obtained for many medical conditions, although since they are expensive and complicated to interpret, they certainly aren't as easy as taking a chest x-ray. Examples for which they are used include planning surgery for rectal cancers, assessing bones for infection (osteomyelitis), looking at the bile ducts in detail for trapped gallstones, assessing ligamental damage in the knee joints and assessing the spinal cord for infections, tumours or trapped nerves.

Physicists and engineers use and manipulate the basic laws of physics to develop these incredible scanners for doctors to use. MRI scans provide such details because they work at a sub-molecular level; they work on the protons within hydrogen atoms. By changing the position of these protons using magnetic fields, extremely detailed pictures of the different types of pictures are obtained. Since these pictures rely on the tiny movements of these tiny particles, you need to lie very still during the scan. ✿

Slice by slice images

Specially wound coils, known as gradient coils, allow for the detailed depth imaging which creates the slice by slice pictures. While the main superconducting magnet creates a very stable magnetic field, these gradient coils create variable magnetic fields during the scan. These fields mean that the magnetic strength within the patient can be altered in specific areas. Since the protons realign at different rates in different tissue types, the relationship between the strength of the field and the frequency of the emitted photons is different for various tissues. Detecting these differences allows for very detailed images.

Powerful computers outside the main machine then reconstitute all of this data to produce slice by slice imaging. Depending on what's being scanned, 3D reconstructions can then be created, such as for brain tumours.

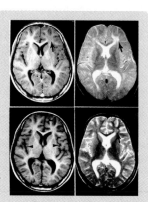

5 TOP FACTS
MRI SCANNERS

Careful
1 Due to the powerful magnets, any metal objects left in the room can be pulled towards the magnet and can harm patients. Examples have included oxygen cylinders and chairs.

Pacemakers
2 Pacemakers were absolute contraindications to MRI scans; modern pacemakers and implantable defibrillators, however, are being designed to be 'MRI safe.'

The most modern
3 MRI scans can be combined with PET scans. These PET-MRI scans produce anatomical and functional images, such as assessing for extent of tumour growth and tumour activity.

Now that's cold
4 The coils of the superconducting magnets are cooled to lower their resistance. Liquid helium cools them to near absolute zero (around -270°C).

Mobile MRI
5 Mobile MRI scanners can go to the patients. They are based in big articulated lorries and can be stationed outside hospitals to provide extra scanning capacity.

DID YOU KNOW? *Around ten per cent of patients are too claustrophobic for conventional MRI scanners*

Radiofrequency transmission
A radiofrequency transmission causes the protons to flip around, and then turning this off causes the protons to re-align. This movement releases energy that is detected by the scanner to create pictures.

Enhancement
Contrast agents are used in addition to enhance the contrast between tissue types. For looking at joints such as the shoulder or knee, contrast can be injected directly into the joint prior to the scan. For the blood vessels, an intravenous contrast is injected during the scan.

Bang bang!
The gradient coils are switched on and off rapidly and alter the magnetic field in specific tissue areas. As they switch on and off, the coils contract and expand by tiny amounts. This produces a loud noise which is heard as a series of loud bangs.

Looking for tumours
Since the protons in different tissue types return to their normal state at different rates, they give off different frequencies of energy and so contrast between different types of tissues can be seen. This allows identification of a brain tumour from normal cells.

Gradient coils
These coils produce much weaker, variable magnetic fields compared to the superconductors. These gradient fields are specifically targeted to certain tissues, allowing for depth and detailed tissue type differentiation.

The MRI scanner

It's a big, hi-tech machine and there are different varieties all around the world, found in hospitals, medical research centres and even zoos, but they all work on common principles of manipulating the laws of physics

Superconducting magnets
These powerful magnets create very stable magnetic fields, which align protons within the body's hydrogen atoms. The magnets are cooled to near absolute zero and so are well insulated from the patient.

The tunnel
The tunnel which the patient lies in is very narrow; some patients don't fit. There are small lights and a radio with headphones to keep you comfortable.

The computer
Once the changes in energy have been detected within the scanner, they are transmitted to powerful computers outside the scanner, which transform the data into useful images.

Lie here
The patient lies down on a narrow plastic 'table' outside the machine, which is then advanced slowly into the tunnel.

© Philips Achieva 3.0T TX images courtesy of Philips

MRI atoms
It's a matter of reading the alignment

Line up please
Hydrogen atoms contain just one proton and emit tiny magnetic fields. When placed in a stronger magnetic field (the one produced by the magnets), these protons line up in the direction of the field.

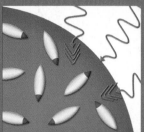

Flip and spin
The scanner emits a radiofrequency through the patient, which flips the spinning direction of these aligned protons. The frequency is at just the right pitch, producing a 'resonance' energy (hence magnetic resonance).

Flip back
Once the radiofrequency is removed, the protons degrade back to their original positions. As they do so they release tiny amounts of radiowave energy in the form of photons. It is these changes that build the detailed pictures.

Converting to pictures
Different magnetic strengths produce different frequencies in the protons, which are also affected by the different type of body tissues. The resultant energy given off by re-aligning the protons is interpreted by a computer to produce detailed images.

© Science Photo Library

Coronal
The coronal plane divides the body into anterior (front) and posterior (back) halves.

Transverse
The transverse plane is a horizontal plane that divides the body into superior (upper) and inferior (lower) parts.

Sagittal
The sagittal plane moves down the midline of the body and divides it into left and right.

You'll need to be an expert to know what you're looking at

Which direction?

Medical teams need to communicate using the same terms so they are clear what they are looking at. The cross-sectional images produced by MRI scanners are extremely complex, but this is why they are so useful. The terms to the left are the imaginary lines that provide cross-sections. The planes can be moved across the body to look at whole organs or areas.

Touch-screen tablets

© Samsung

The world at your fingertips... and it's not too far from the truth! © Samsung

Speed
1 Tablets work using processors that are on average two thirds slower than laptops, but they are still faster because they do not have to power CD drives and hardware keyboards.

Apps
2 Some apps are very similar to popular desktop titles, but often cost very little. With tablets selling by the million, developers can make their money by volume.

Multi-tasking
3 Multi-tasking on tablets is achieved by freezing apps when they are not in use, therefore freeing up precious memory for the currently running apps.

Voice
4 Tablets aren't made for voice calling, but Skype and other services let you use Voice Over IP as long as wireless data is available. A phone's still needed for general calling.

Growth
5 The growth of tablet sales is now starting to impact netbook and laptop sales with some believing that the tablet will dominate the entire computer market in the future.

DID YOU KNOW? Tablets are independent, but the iPad needs to be hooked up to a desktop computer on first use for it to work

Tablets are less powerful than laptops but can be more useful. Find out how they work and what they can do for you

A tablet is a cut-down version of a laptop. Besides having no physical keyboard, it also uses operating systems designed to allow instant online access and an environment closer to the smartphone in design than a desktop operating system. Its great advantage is portability alongside battery lives that can reach up to ten hours, which makes it ideal to work on when out and about or to play on when on a long-distance flight.

Apple brought the tablet form to the attention of the world with the iPad in 2010 and this contrasted greatly with the previous failed efforts of Microsoft to make Windows fit this form factor. It is technically much less powerful than laptops, but this is, ironically, also its biggest advantage. By focusing on allowing the user to consume and create in the simplest of ways they take away most of the maintenance involved in running a standard laptop and still manage to let you do everything you want to via cheap third-party apps. This also makes the tablet much faster than a laptop for most tasks.

The Apple iPad and Samsung Galaxy Tab are currently the most powerful tablets available, but that will no doubt change in the very near future. ✿

© Apple

Movement
An accelerometer is built into the device, which senses the orientation that it is being held at.

Flush
Most screens are built to be flush to the surround to allow navigation and touch all the way to each edge.

Protection
A protective layer is applied to the screen which is made from materials resistant to scratches.

Touch
The capacitive technology reads the electrical current from a finger to analyse placement.

Resolution
Apple's iPad has a screen resolution of 1024x768 pixels. This isn't that high, but results are impressive.

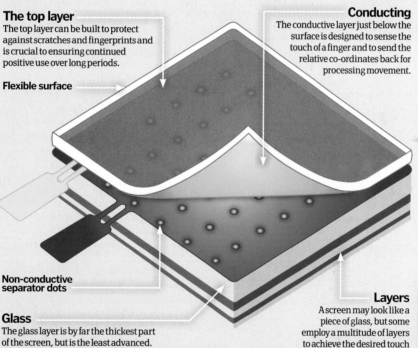

The top layer
The top layer can be built to protect against scratches and fingerprints and is crucial to ensuring continued positive use over long periods.

Flexible surface

Conducting
The conductive layer just below the surface is designed to sense the touch of a finger and to send the relative co-ordinates back for processing movement.

Non-conductive separator dots

Glass
The glass layer is by far the thickest part of the screen, but is the least advanced. All of the clever stuff happens elsewhere.

Layers
A screen may look like a piece of glass, but some employ a multitude of layers to achieve the desired touch and viewing performance.

How does the screen work?

Capacitive screens, which the iPad and most high-end tablets use, are designed only to work with objects that are conductive, such as fingers. This has the advantage of making them feel extremely natural to use. However, you do lose the preciseness of a stylus. The technology can sense the exact movement of a finger and when more than one finger is used it can determine the distance between them and the range of movement to accomplish tasks such as rotating or pinching and zooming photos.

You may be surprised to know that these screens carry an electrical charge that is disrupted by your finger, which carries a different charge. This is how the conductive layer just below the surface can work out where the fingers are placed. A special coating is often applied to the screen, which resists scratches and fingerprints and is so thin that it's not viewable by the human eye. In-plane switching can also be employed to increase viewing angles by decreasing the amount of scattered light across the screen, allowing you to almost view text and images when holding the screen at a 90° angle to your eyes.

How does it connect to the internet?

A tablet can connect to the internet in two ways: Wi-Fi and in some cases 3G. Wi-Fi is a lot quicker but has to rely on the proximity of a router or a public hotspot. If a tablet has 3G capability, it will also require a suitable data plan to allow access anywhere. These can be expensive, but the setup does offer an advantage few laptops have, which is almost universal internet connectivity. The efficiency of the operating systems and browsers, which were originally designed for slower smartphones, means that they run very quickly provided 3G coverage is available.

HOW IT WORKS

"There is a lot of advanced technology squeezed into the Galaxy Tab"

Tablet hardware

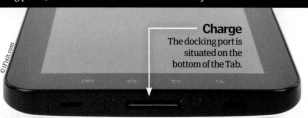

©Apple

Tablets are almost always closed systems that allow little upgrading of the internal parts. Some have expansion card slots to increase the available storage and there are accessories available such as external hardware keyboards and desk chargers, but on the whole they are designed to be used as they come out of the box. They do not have CD drives or USB ports because mechanical media can slow down overall performance whereas the Flash-based memory inside a tablet is extremely fast. This also enables them to run smoother and quicker than laptops and desktops with better specifications. Many can be attached to a TV for video playback, which is achieved via the small built-in graphics processors. On the outside they are built to last with either aluminium or strengthened plastic used to house the otherwise fragile internals. The key to a tablet's speed and strength is the lack of moving parts, which also makes them extremely reliable.

©iFixit.com

Charge
The docking port is situated on the bottom of the Tab.

Tablet software

Almost all current tablets run the Android operating system, which was designed for smartphones. The iPad runs iOS, which Apple also uses on the iPhone. They both rely on third-party apps to offer flexibility and these can be installed in seconds by downloading them from iTunes or the Android Market. Once installed they act in solitude with some clever programming enabling them to take advantage of specific hardware functions. They are not compatible with each other, but the larger publishers are supporting both operating systems with the same titles. Apple produces Pages and Numbers for the iPad which gives full Office document editing and there are also a number of Office apps available for Android tablets. Magazines are becoming a popular genre in the tablet world with the iPad offering more titles than the rest.

© Apple

What's inside the Samsung Galaxy Tab?

How does the flagship Android tablet manage to do so much in such a small space?

It would be easy to think of the Galaxy Tab as a very large Android smartphone, but that would be to ignore the thought that Samsung has put into designing the product. Designing a small tablet that still offers a usable experience is not easy, but some clever technology has been squeezed in to enable this to happen. The seven-inch super TFT screen has been designed by aligning the molecules of the liquid crystal to a perfect parallel, which allows for a wide viewing angle up to 170 degrees. This technology, while not new, is also power efficient which helps the battery produce up to seven hours of video playback on one single charge. This is backed up by the 1GHz Hummingbird processor, which uses incredibly close placement of the circuitry on board to increase clock speeds resulting in minimal power drain. The inclusion of an HSDPA chip produces a mobile data speed of up to 7.2Mbps to rival many home broadband connections and the Broadcom chip takes care of Wi-Fi and Bluetooth, enabling almost constant connections to the outside world.

The built-in gyroscopic sensor is able to sense exactly how the Tab is being held by sensing the exact position of a tiny vibrating object in relation to the X,Y and Z axes. This is particularly useful for advanced gaming and augmented reality apps, which are designed to use this technology wherever possible. The front and rear cameras are not well specified, but are useful for snapshots or for video calling, which utilises the front camera and the HSDPA or Wi-Fi connectivity. There is a lot of advanced technology squeezed into the Galaxy Tab, but it remains lightweight at only 380 grams. It is also half the weight of an iPad thanks to the plastic outer shell that has been used to cover the multitude of components. It may not look classy – and is a very lo-tech material – but it certainly helps reduce the overall weight of this flagship tablet.

SAMSUNG

Phone Readers Hub Navigation
Music Video Calendar

Simple
Flick between screens with just the swipe of a finger.

Internet
Using 3G connectivity, accessing the internet is immediate.

Browser Application

© Samsung

SMALLEST

© Dell

1. Dell Streak
Is it a big smartphone or a small tablet? Opinion seems to be divided over the five-inch screen form factor at this time.

IN THE MIDDLE

© Samsung

2. Samsung Galaxy Tab
The Tab uses the seven-inch screen form factor, which aims to offer a tablet experience while maintaining portability.

BIGGEST

© Apple

3. Apple iPad
With a 9.6-inch screen the iPad lets you enjoy web browsing and many other tasks more than the others, but at the cost of true portability.

DID YOU KNOW? The Tab offers full Adobe Flash compatibility, which does not natively work on the iPad

The Tab teardown

Plastic
The lightweight plastic body helps to reduce the overall weight of the Tab greatly.

Rear camera
The rear-facing camera is diminutive in size, but still packs in three megapixels of power alongside auto focus and an LED flash.

Screen
The super TFT LCD screen offers improved image quality and a wide viewing angle. The pixel density is higher than on the iPad screen.

Connectivity
This tiny chip brings mobile connectivity to the party. Support for up to 7.2Mbps data speeds is included thanks to the HSDPA implementation.

Battery
The 4,000mAh battery is huge and capable of delivering seven hours of video playback and up to ten hours of talk time.

9:02 AM

Places

Market

Apps
Easily purchased from the Android Market.

Power
The 1GHz processor produces excellent speed and is also designed to be as power efficient as possible.

Memory
Up to 32GB of flash memory is built in to the Tab, which complements the microSD expansion slot.

Speakers
The Tab has two built-in loudspeakers, which help deliver a superior stereo sound. The positioning also makes it less likely to cover them with your hands.

Tab vs Pad

Apple's iPad and Samsung's Galaxy Tab are at opposite ends of the scale in terms of size, weight and operating system. They have similar goals, but the Tab's Android OS is open and iOS on the iPad is very much closed. Along with the materials and builds, the differences are numerous

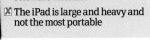

Samsung Galaxy Tab
- ☑ Small and light; much more portable than the iPad
- ☑ Two cameras for snaps and more personal communication
- ☑ 3G connectivity built in as standard

- ☒ The plastic cover feels a little cheap for the price
- ☒ Expensive and only one model available
- ☒ Android OS is not completely refined for the tablet form yet

Apple iPad
- ☑ Stunning build quality and a beautifully designed screen
- ☑ Many magazine and news publications already support the format
- ☑ The optional keyboard turns it into a mini-laptop

- ☒ Expensive for the 3G-enabled version and locked to a contract
- ☒ Little choice for customising the software interface
- ☒ The iPad is large and heavy and not the most portable

The statistics...

Galaxy Tab

Height: 120mm

Width: 190mm

Depth: 12mm

Weight: 380kg

Display: 1024 x 600 pixels

OS: Android 2.2 (Froyo)

Processor: 1GHz ARM Cortex A8

Memory: 16 / 32GB

Battery: 4,000mAh

Camera: 3MP (rear) + 1.3MP (front)

Pricing: £517 ($807)

Learn more
For more info and images of the exposed Galaxy Tab, visit the gadget surgeons at ifixit.com who kindly contributed photos and findings for this article.

ifixit

"A flap is sliced on the surface of the cornea and folded out the way"

Central heating

How a combi boiler heats your home and your water with no need for a separate hot water storage tank

The heat source for a central heating system is the boiler. 70 per cent of UK households now use a combination, or combi boiler to heat their homes and their water – all in one compact unit. Inside the boiler, water is heated by a metal heat exchanger and pumped into a closed system of pipes that loop around the home to radiators in each room. By using a combi boiler, if you turn on your hot tap, water from the mains is heated as needed, with no need for a large and obtrusive storage cylinder.

All modern boilers fitted in the UK are condensing boilers, which are more fuel-efficient because they re-use the heat energy that in a non-condensing boiler would be expelled through the flue. The water is heated as it flows through the pipes inside one (or sometimes two) heat exchangers, which are suspended in hot gases over the burner's flames, maximising the heat transfer from the burner. In a combi, the temperature of the flue gases is reduced to 50-60°C (rather than the 120-180°C in a non-condensing boiler), and most of the gas leaves the flue as water vapour while the rest is drained away as condensate, or water. ✿

Hot water
Hot water is delivered at mains pressure. As soon as the hot tap is turned on, the water flow is detected by the gas burner, which uses electric sparks to ignite the gas that heats the water as it runs back and forth over a heat exchanger.

Boiler
The combi boiler can be programmed to switch the central heating on and off at desired times and at a specific temperature. A pump inside the boiler transports water through the radiators.

Cold mains
The combi heats water direct from the mains as and when it's required. There's no need for a coldwater storage tank.

Radiators
The temperature of a room's individual radiator can be controlled using a thermostatic radiator valve.

Thermostat
A room thermostat is used to control the temperature of the water in the system.

Combination boiler central heating system

LASIK eye surgery...

Cornea
Once tissue has been removed, the flap is folded back onto the cornea and heals quickly.

UV laser
Pulses of ultraviolet laser light vaporise surface tissue, reshaping the cornea.

Bull's-eye
A laser projects a target on the eye at which the UV laser beam can aim.

Flap
A special surgical knife slices a flap open on the surface of the cornea.

Retina
After surgery, light rays entering the eye are focused to a point on the retina, producing a much clearer image.

DID YOU KNOW? LASIK is a kind of refractive laser eye surgery used to treat near- and far-sightedness and astigmatism.

Laser eye surgery

How can a laser beam correct a patient's poor vision?

People with defective eyesight can undergo laser-assisted in-situ keratomileusis (LASIK) eye surgery to correct their vision. LASIK involves using an ultraviolet laser beam to remove tissue and alter the shape of the cornea at the front of the eye. If, for example, the cornea is not perfectly spherical, light rays entering the eye won't focus on a single point on the retina – and it's this that causes the diminished vision. However, by reshaping the patient's cornea, light rays can be refracted, or bent as they pass through the cornea to focus light properly.

A computer maps the shape of the patient's cornea before calculating exactly how much tissue needs to be removed. Using a fine knife called a microkeratome, a flap is sliced on the surface of the cornea and folded out of the way. The main laser light doesn't penetrate the eyeball, but rather it pulses, vaporising the tissue on the surface of the cornea. The flap is then folded back and heals without the need for stitches, resulting in instantly improved vision. ✿

BIG

1. Six-string electric guitar
Whether a Fender Stratocaster or Les Paul, this instrument provides a sound big and versatile enough for pop or rock.

BIGGER

2. Doubleneck electric guitar
This extravagant twin-necked variant provides a normal six-string electric and the more twangy 12-string equivalent.

BIGGEST

3. Electric bass guitar
Biggest in build of the electric guitar instruments, it has a longer neck and thick strings for that deep bass.

xx images © Fender muscial instruments corp

DID YOU KNOW? *Many famous players 'coil tap' or rewire their pickups 'out of phase' to achieve signature tones*

Electric guitars

The science behind how an electric guitar produces that iconic loud sound

Slash doing his fretwork homework
© daigooliva

As opposed to an acoustic equivalent, which uses a hollow body to amplify the vibrating strings, a solid-body electric guitar requires a set of pickups to project the sound.

It uses a principle of electromagnetic induction to translate the movement of metal strings into a very small electric current within a set of pickups. These tightly wound magnetic coils are positioned directly under the area where the player strums and usually contain a set of six pole pieces that sit directly below each string. When the string is plucked it induces a voltage fluctuation inside the pickup, which is then channelled out of the instrument down a lead and into an amplifier. The wattage of the guitar amp largely defines the volume with big live acts using powerful 16 speaker stacks to achieve maximum loudness.

Players also boost the raw guitar signal with effects units or foot pedals that apply layers of distortion for achieving that distinctive crunching rock sound. ✿

Strings
Electric guitars typically have six metal strings open tuned to the standard EADGBE sequence, thick to thin or bass to treble.

Fretboard
The playing surface where notes are formed is divided into 22 intervals known as frets with metal strips called fretwire.

The pickups
Tightly wound magnetic wires that emit an electric current when the string is plucked.

Selector switch
A three- or five-way toggle switch, that changes between rhythm and treble or a combination of the pickups.

Body
Found in varying shapes and either of a flat or archtop profile, the essential guitar electronics are located here.

The bridge
This metal piece of hardware anchors and maintains the string height above the body of the guitar and pickups.

The nut
A strip of plastic or bone that saddles the strings from the headstock and down the neck to the bridge.

Machine heads
These wind the strings around the capstan and increase tension to achieve the desired pitch.

Neck
Fronted by the fretboard, this is typically a separate piece of wood that is bolted or glued to the body.

Truss rod
An adjustable metal bar running through the neck to prevent warping and set the necessary bow in the fretboard.

Scratchplate
Also known as a pickguard, this removable die-cut piece of plastic protects the body from possible plectrum scratches during play.

Volume and tone pots
These are resistors used to vary the pickup output to control volume and tone for each pickup.

© DK image

Wound for sound

We know that the vibrating steel strings generate an electric current within the pickups, but the frequency of this current is proportional to certain characteristics of the string itself. The wavelength of the oscillations change as the strings are plucked at various frets, and the player uses tension with the fretting hand to shorten the length of the string at each interval of the fret board. This changes the vibration pitch passing above the pickup to create the notes needed to form the chords. A thicker 'gauge' of string tends to offer a louder output and heavier tones, while factors such as how the string has been wound also influence the final sound.

© Science photo library

Electric guitar strings often consist of a steel core wound with nickel-plated steel wire

Pressure cookers

How do they cook food so quickly?

Pressure cookers work by raising their internal temperature above a saucepan's capabilities. They achieve this by hermetically sealing their internal structure through a lid/gasket clamping system that restricts the escape of steam and liquids below a pre-set temperature. Through this the pressure within the pan increases massively and allows the internal liquid to rise to a higher temperature before boiling, thereby cooking food faster. Maximum pressure is controlled by a regulator fitted into the lid, which only releases steam when it reaches its pre-set pressure level. In case the regulator gets blocked, a safety valve is also fitted into the lid, which will open if pressure levels increase beyond the regulator's maximum. ✿

Pressure cookers are hermetically sealed pots

Water filters

Removing impurities from water

There are multiple types of water filters, which through physical, chemical and biological processes remove impure substances from water. The most common type of filtration system is that which uses granular-activated carbon, usually in the form of charcoal sheets. The charcoal is treated with an oxidisation process that opens up millions of tiny pores between its carbon atoms, increasing – due to its large porous surface – its ability to absorb (chemically bond with) particulate matter from the water. Once the carbon sheet is saturated with impurities, it's then cleaned by heating it in a furnace. Carbon-based systems are commonly found in household water filters.

Another method used mainly in laboratory or industrial settings (where macromolecular solutions need to be purified) is ultrafiltration. This works by generating hydrostatic pressure to force liquid against a semi-permeable membrane. Solids and solutes of high molecular weight (ie, larger than a water molecule) are caught by the system's membrane while water and low molecular weight solutes pass through into the collection area. This allows the geometry of the membrane to be varied according to local conditions and severity of impurities. ✿

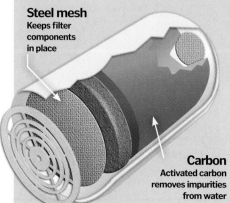

Steel mesh
Keeps filter components in place

Carbon
Activated carbon removes impurities from water

The filter removes impurities from water

Metal detectors

Discover how to locate buried treasure using magnetism

The most common metal detector uses a Very Low Frequency (VLF) technology to search for hidden objects. It employs one of the basic laws of electromagnetism, that an object in an alternating magnetic field (switching from north to south polarity) will create an oscillating field of its own in opposition. A transmitter coil emits this field, switching at a frequency of thousands of times per second. A device known as a magnetometer within a receiver coil can detect magnetic pulses pushed upwards from the object underground in response, and alert the user of the metal detector via a beep, or on screen.

By cleverly employing a process known as phase shifting, the VLF detector can deduce what sort of object is beneath the surface. This method works by calculating the time difference between the frequency of the transmitter's field and the corresponding response from underground. This all depends on how easily the object conducts electricity, and once this is known its composition can then be approximated. ✿

How to detect metal

Control box
Here the circuitry and controls for the user to operate the detector are located, as well as a jack to connect headphones.

Shaft
The shaft allows the detector to be adjusted to an optimum height, while also connecting the controls to the coil.

Transmitter coil
An alternating magnetic field that is emitted from the transmitter coil causes metallic objects to emit their own detectable field.

Stabiliser
Constantly swinging the detector can be hard work, so a stabiliser often wraps around the arm to help keep it steady.

Receiver coil
The receiver detects an object's magnetic field. The stronger the field received, the closer the object is to the surface, and vice versa.

5 TOP FACTS ESPRESSO MACHINES

First
1 The first espresso machine was invented by Angelo Moriondo of Turin, Italy. This was a mass-brewing machine, and largely unlike the individual pulling machines of today.

Waves
2 According to the Specialty Coffee Association of America, we're in the 'third wave' of coffee – it was mass produced, mass marketed and is now being refined.

Roast
3 Espresso is simply a unique method for brewing coffee. Any bean can be used with any level of roast, each giving a flavour dependent on origin and processing technique.

Caffeine
4 It's often thought that a shot of espresso contains more caffeine than a cup of filter coffee. In fact, its reduced size means people consume roughly two-thirds less.

Base
5 Due to its intense and deep flavour, the espresso is used as the base for many other coffee beverages, including the Corretto, Bicerin, Guillermo and Ristretto.

DID YOU KNOW? The first espresso coffee machine was patented in 1884

Espresso machine teardown

Take a look at the core components of a mid-range home espresso machine

© iFixit.com

Pressure pump
As with most espresso machines, water is drawn from the tank by a pump. This is ensured by a pressure differential between the pump core and water tank.

Boiler
Consists of a housing shell (to hold water), a heating coil (to bring water from the tank up to optimal temperature) and dual thermal sensors to monitor steam and water temperature.

Portafilter
Unlike pro-grade espresso machines, the Barista machine uses a pressurised portafilter rather than a commercial one. This ensures that consistent pressure is generated automatically – regardless of coffee grind and tamp level – creating consistently decent espressos for the amateur user.

Water tank
This is a simple storage area for unpressurised water, which is filled manually by the user prior to operation.

Steamer
As well as heating up water for pressurised filtering through coffee, the machine's boiler also generates steam for heating/frothing milk. This facility is accessed and controlled through the steam wand.

Espresso machines

The science and technology behind a silky smooth espresso

Espresso is a brewing method for coffee that, through the filtering of ground coffee through highly pressurised water, generates an intense, deep and syrupy caffeinated beverage. Standard filter coffee is brewed using a drip method – heated water is simply poured over coffee grinds and allowed to filter through them under gravity alone, absorbing their oils and essences. However, espresso is a considerably more complex brewing method that involves many stages of preparation and production. These variables, which can have a dramatic impact on the finished product, include water temperature, pressure level, filter type, tamp level (how much the ground coffee is compacted before brewing), fineness of the bean grind, type of grinder, freshness of the beans and type of bean roast.

For the espresso machine brewing process, the beans, which have been grown and roasted, are first ground into incredibly fine, uniform grains using a grinder. Next the grains are compacted by a tamper (a weighted device used to compress the grains) into the

coffee machine's portafilter, a basket device used to control the flow of water filtered through the grains. On home espresso makers, this filter is usually the pressurised variety, which is designed to automatically compensate for poor/uneven grind and tamps. The espresso machine's pump then draws water from its tank into its boiler for heating to the correct temperature. Advanced machines use a 'roller coaster' technique, where the ideal temperature is maintained in a constant process of water heating, temperature checking, boiler disconnection, temperature checking and water reheating. This means that the water temperature constantly fluctuates either side of the ideal, resulting in a faster ideal temperature pick-up time when water is required for an espresso.

Finally, the water is pressurised and forced through the filter and coffee grains. The heat and pressure of the water extracts and emulsifies the essences of the ground coffee, producing a thick, syrupy liquid topped with a layer of crema – a fine-celled foam imbued with the taste and aromatic properties of the bean. ✿

A large, multi-faucet espresso machine, as used in coffee houses

© Rainer SXC Schmidt

MOTION CONTROL GAMING

Find out how motion-sensitive controllers have revolutionised the way we play videogames

5 TOP FACTS
MOTION-CONTROLLED VIDEOGAMES

Wii Fit
Format: **Wii**
1 No more cheesy workout DVDs – *Wii Fit* revolutionised exercising at home, hitting the jackpot with its appeal to women and seniors.

Rock Band
Format: **Multiformat**
2 With Electronics Arts' answer to *Guitar Hero*, you can live out your musical stardom fantasies in the privacy of your own living room.

Heavy Rain
Format: **PlayStation 3**
3 This popular grown-up thriller mystery game now includes Move functionality as well as the usual control-pad interaction.

Sports Champions
Format: **PlayStation 3**
4 Compete solo or against friends in six sports including archery and volleyball. Can you beat the top scorers in the online leaderboards?

Grease
Format: **Wii**
5 This title uses all of the Wii's functionality to create a great party game – use the Balance Board to dance and the microphone to sing along.

DID YOU KNOW? *PlayStation Move sales reached 1.5 million units in one month in Europe alone*

At Christmas 2006, the UK went wild for the Nintendo Wii – people queued through the night, stores sold out and now 6 million consoles have been sold on these shores alone. By Christmas 2010, motion-control videogame systems were back on the nation's wish-lists as the technology stepped up a notch. In September 2010, Sony released the Move controller for PlayStation 3 and in the November, Microsoft launched Kinect, the first controller-free system. Now, **How It Works** opened each one up to find out how they work.

Let's start with movement detection: to register its exact position, a handheld controller needs a system that can detect motion and speed in three-dimensional space, along with any tilt and twist. The controllers contain tiny accelerometers, micro-electro-mechanical systems (MEMS), which measure acceleration but ignore the effect of gravity. Interestingly, we have biological accelerometers in our ears, the cantilevered beams are tiny hairs (cilia) wafting around in fluid like reeds in water.

MEMS accelerometers consist of tiny strands of silicon attached at one end (cantilevered beams) inside a charged field. The MEMS device measures capacitance (how much charge is stored) so when the beam moves from its neutral position, the change in capacitance can then be used to calculate acceleration.

On Earth, all objects at rest and near the surface are pulled towards the planet with a force of 1G, so manufacturers calibrate their accelerometers to adjust for this. However, it does mean that your Wii won't work properly if you take it on

The controllers...
Here's a quick overview of what each controller does

Microsoft Kinect
Not so much a controller as just a camera that sends out an infrared 'net', meaning every move you perform is mimicked on screen.

PlayStation Move
Working along similar lines to the Wii, the Move features an attractive Orb and will have more appeal to serious gamers.

Nintendo Wii Remote
The device that brought motion control into the mainstream, the Wii has been incredibly successful since its launch in 2006.

holiday with you to the moon. Information from the accelerometers is processed in the controller's microchip and beamed back by Bluetooth, wirelessly, to the sensor.

It's all very well being able to locate the controller in space, but what about movement around the controller's axis? Adding gyroscopic sensors to a controller adds another three dimensions of movement detection: as well as the X, Y and Z planes used to locate the controller, gyroscopes detect movement of the controller

around its central axis: pitch (up/down tilt towards the screen), roll (twist) and yaw (aiming the controller to the left or right of the screen). A basic version of this same technology is used in mobile phones to change the image from portrait to landscape depending on which way up the device is held, the iPhone 4 being a perfect example of this technology currently put to extremely good use.

Gyroscopes are an ideal way to detect motion about a central axis – the orientation of a spinning or vibrating gyroscope attached to a low-friction mount remains the same regardless of movement in the surface to which the mount is attached.

There are different types of MEMS gyroscope sensors – the sensor inside the PlayStation Move contains a set of three tiny tuning fork shaped pieces of quartz placed at mutually perpendicular angles in a charged field. The quartz is piezoelectric so when a current is applied, the forks vibrate. Rotation about the axis of the forks changes the forces at work in the crystal: the plane of vibration stays the same but the frequency of the vibrations changes. Detectors monitor capacitance fluctuations in the charged field to calculate movement of the controller relative to the forks.

Motion-control systems combine the data from their internal gyroscopes and ▶

Player interaction reaches a new level with motion-controlled gaming

© Microsoft

Gyroscope evolution
A new spin on modern gaming

Did you have a spinning top toy? Set it going and it will spin for ages before eventually skidding across the floor. Gyroscopes aren't just a cunning toy for persuading kids that physics is fun; their intriguing properties have many useful motion-detection applications.

The first mechanical gyroscope was built in Germany in the 19th Century and developed by the French physicist Léon Foucault for his investigation of the Earth's rotation. Mechanical gyros like this are used for stabilisation in aeroplanes and boats but they're relatively large and heavy. It wasn't until manufacturers were able to build micro-sized gyros that they appeared in all kinds of electronics devices. Did you ever wonder how a two-legged robot or a Segway scooter stays upright? Both use silicon micro-gyros.

The gyroscope sensor chips are now so small and light that they're widely used in digital cameras for image stabilisation, in mobile phones for screen orientation and in movement-control games where the user twists the handset.

Mechanical gyroscope – the rotating disk spins inside pivoted support rings ('gimbals')

►accelerometers to produce super-accurate information about location in space (X, Y and Z planes), and movement about the controller's axis (pitch, roll and yaw). For extra precision, some systems also throw in a micro-compass (like those used in GPS and satnav systems).

So once the device has accurately detected motion, this needs to be translated to movements that fit on the screen. The system used by Nintendo's Wii uses infrared tracking to determine the cursor's position on the screen. The sensor box above the screen has sets of five infrared (IR) LEDs at both sides. These, together with the IR detector at the top-end of the Wii Remote, mean that the controller's position can be triangulated relative to the screen. So if the LEDs are detected towards the top of the Wii Remote's field of view, the cursor is displayed at the bottom of the screen and vice versa. IR LEDs are used because regular visible light-emitting diodes would be too difficult to pick out from other light sources, especially the screen.

Instead of infrared tracking, Sony's PlayStation Move uses a camera to track visible light from the glowing orb on top of the handheld controller. When it comes to recognising who is actually playing, systems now incorporate a rather ingenious face and voice recognition feature so players don't have to register or pick an avatar. For face recognition, the PlayStation's EyeCam captures a clear shot of the player's face and then maps individual characteristics onto a face template to store in the system's memory. It detects faces using the same technology used first in Sony cameras for 'smile recognition'.

Motion controllers contain microphones not just for sing-along games but also for voice commands and player recognition. So how does this work? Voice-recognition technology is well-established in communications and accessibility software. The sound waves created by speech become vibrations in the microphone, which are converted to digital signals. The processor removes 'noise' from the data-stream (by subtracting a reading of the 'background' noise in the room) and then breaks down the data into unique speech sounds or 'phonemes' – there are roughly 50 phonemes in the English language. The processor then compares the data to its stored library of phoneme combinations to work out which words were said.

So what about all those notoriously tricky words in English, which are spelled differently but sound the same (otherwise known as homophones)? In order to decide which homophone to register, the processor is also equipped with a context-checker – it analyses the words around the homophone, checks the combination against stored

1. Move the Wii-mote
Hold the controller as you would a regular table tennis bat – you can even achieve a backhand.

2. Friends not required
Contrary to promotional images of Wii gaming, 2.4 children or a large group of smiley friends aren't necessary. Nice though.

© Nintendo

examples and then selects the spelling that's, statistically, most likely. The software is also advanced enough to recognise a number of different accents, and the latest videogame systems 'recognise' individual players by storing each user's unique pitch variations, giving you a personal gaming experience every time you turn the console on.

Every different language requires its own library that can delay the release of products using this technology. In 2010 Microsoft Kinect was initially available in US and UK English, Japanese and Mexican Spanish – with the speakers of other languages having to wait until 2011 for updated versions.

With regard to what's next for videogame controllers, developers are hard at work on three-dimensional games (for use with 3D television screens), eye-gaze direction detection and other mind-bogglingly futuristic technology. As handsets become increasingly unnecessary and producers create a wider range of videogames, there will be plenty to satisfy both casual and hardcore gamers. ✿

© Nintendo

THE ORIGINAL

1. Nintendo Wii
The original mass-market motion-control gaming gizmo. A sell-out at Christmas 2006 and still very popular, especially thanks to its upgrades.

© Nintendo

THE COMPETITION

2. Sony PS3 Move
Released in September 2010, Sony's controller is lighter, more accurate and prettier, with its colour-changing light orbs.

© Sony

THE NEXT GENERATION

3. Microsoft Xbox Kinect
No need for batteries, the Kinect does away with a controller. The sensor detects movement, speech and individual players.

DID YOU KNOW? Since its launch in 2006 the Nintendo Wii has sold 75.3 million units worldwide

Nintendo Wii
The console that caused a gaming revolution

Inside a Wii-mote

Nintendo connector
Port for plugging in attachments such as the nunchuk.

Battery clips

Accelerometers (reverse of board)
Used to locate the controller in 3D space.

IR sensor
Detects IR radiation from the LEDs in the console.

Scan button
Can only be accessed internally – used to reset the Wii-mote after repair or updates.

Capacitor
Stores energy to be used when the battery connection is lost.

Vibrator motor

Audio processing chip
This is a stowaway. This chip currently isn't used but might be in future as games develop.

Bluetooth chip
Transmits data to the Wii console.

Speaker and 'rumble pack' (reverse of board)
Provide feedback from events on screen, such as hitting a ball.

© Nintendo

REAL WORLD

The Wii Remote (Wii-mote) uses a three-axis accelerometer to monitor movement sideways, up and down, forward and back. Two sets of infrared LEDs on the Wii console are detected in the Wii-mote and triangulated to determine the cursor or character position on screen.

Nintendo released the Wii MotionPlus device to enhance the Wii-mote – this adds a three-axis 'tuning fork' gyroscope to better detect twisting and tilting movements of controller itself (pitch, roll and yaw).

IN GAME

Using the Wii Remote is fairly intuitive. Slip the strap over your wrist and hold it like a remote control, usually with your thumb on the A-button near the top and your index finger on the B-button on the back.

The movements you perform do depend on the game, for example, hold and swing it like a tennis racket, a golf-club or a bowling ball, thrust it like a sword, or even steer it like a car. The wealth of options is endless.

3. The avatar smashes the ball
The arm of the on-screen character mimics your arm. At least it isn't quite so publicly embarrassing if you trip over the table and fall on your bum...

Inside a capacitive accelerometer
Turning your world around has never been so technical

Capacitance
Capacitance is a measure of ability to store electric charge. It depends on a system's physical dimensions and its electrical permittivity.

Detector chip

Fixed plate

Liquid or gaseous silicon dielectric

Flexible silicon bar (free at the ends)

Direction of acceleration

Fixed plate

Calculations
The detector registers capacitance fluctuations, converts them into distances and calculates acceleration.

Increased capacitance
If there's more space between a plate and the bar, more charge can be stored so the capacitance is greater.

Accelerometer
In an accelerometer, there are two pairs of plates: the flexible silicon bar functions as a second plate for each of the fixed plates.

"Motion detection takes place both in the EyeCam and in the Move controller itself"

PlayStation Move
The console king ups its game

Move

3. Dual controllers
Either one or two controllers can be used for virtual archery.

4. Fire
Release the trigger to release the on-screen arrow.

5. Realistic action
Using two controllers more accurately mimics the physical movements.

Become a real-life Robin Hood in no time at all

© Sony

Move

2. Player two waiting
As soon as it's player two's turn, the EyeCam will detect another Orb being moved.

1. Ready, aim...
Player one's front arm positions the bow while the rear arm draws back the string.

x5

Grab Arrow!

IN GAME

Hold the controller like a microphone with your index finger on the trigger button, and make sure the EyeCam can 'see' the light orb on top.

In the Archery on *Sports Champions*, reach over your shoulder to collect an arrow, bring it over your head and then draw back, releasing the trigger to shoot.

Two controllers can be used to make the movements more realistic – for example, in Archery, the front controller stays still, aiming for the target, while the other draws the bow and releases. In Gladiator Duel, the arm holding the front controller is the shield, while the back controller is the sword.

REAL WORLD

Motion detection takes place both in the EyeCam and in the Move controller itself. The EyeCam tracks the Orb's movement in three dimensions: up/down, left-right (the X and Y planes) and depth (the Z plane). Because the orb is a fixed size, the processor calculates how far away it is using simple laws of perspective: the smaller it appears, the further away it is.

Inside the controller, accelerometers and gyroscopes collect further information about motion including tilt and twist, transmitting this data via Bluetooth to the PS3. The orb contains three LEDs to produce different colours. If you're playing solo, the Move selects the optimum colour to contrast with your surroundings. In multiplayer games, different colours differentiate the players and colours also provide visual feedback on hits and misses.

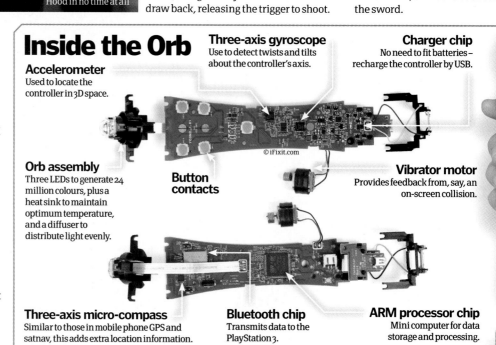

Inside the Orb

Accelerometer
Used to locate the controller in 3D space.

Three-axis gyroscope
Use to detect twists and tilts about the controller's axis.

Charger chip
No need to fit batteries – recharge the controller by USB.

Orb assembly
Three LEDs to generate 24 million colours, plus a heat sink to maintain optimum temperature, and a diffuser to distribute light evenly.

Button contacts

Vibrator motor
Provides feedback from, say, an on-screen collision.

© iFixit.com

Three-axis micro-compass
Similar to those in mobile phone GPS and satnav, this adds extra location information.

Bluetooth chip
Transmits data to the PlayStation 3.

ARM processor chip
Mini computer for data storage and processing.

SONY

You've been framed!
Kinect's body-tracking web-style camera technology is capable of not only zooming in and following the player around the room, it can also detect a second person and will then pan out to watch both people at once. And if another person enters the room the camera will reframe the picture to fit everyone in.

© Microsoft

Kinect

1. It's you!
Your on-screen avatar will mimic your every movement.

2. Swing away
Swing your leg and your in-game character will kick the ball.

IN GAME

With no controller to hold, the Kinect is simple: once you've enrolled, just move your body, gesture or speak. Scroll through virtual libraries by waving your hand or speak the name of a video you want to watch. In multiplayer quizzes, clap to 'buzz in' and answer by speaking. The Kinect can track up to six players, with a maximum of two actively moving to control a game.

3. Get involved
You're the controller when it comes to Kinect, what could be more natural?

History of motion control

Anyone remember *Duck Hunt*, with the annoying dog who chuckled when you missed the ducks? If you played with light guns and used a joystick back in the Eighties, you were using the very first motion-control gaming systems.

Nintendo achieved spectacular flops in the early-Nineties with the Power Glove and the Virtual Boy 3D system (not gender-biased, it was named like the Game Boy) which was worn on the gamer's head. Not a good look, it didn't catch on.

Sony's Move technology is the modern evolution of its EyeToy gizmo – essentially a camera that detected faces and grafted them onto characters in games. Cute but gimmicky.

Flight simulators are a successful example of motion-control technology and are used in both education and games.

Microsoft Kinect
Forget controllers, the future is here

REAL WORLD

With the Kinect switched on, you only need to appear in its field of view to 'sign in'. On first use, the sensor must be calibrated – it scans the room, tilting to 'see' the floor plane and enrols players by storing their body dimensions and facial details. Whereas the Move tracks the light-orbs, the Kinect assigns 20 tracking points on your body. Thinking of crash-dieting or radical surgery? You'll need to re-enrol.

The Kinect's RGB camera monitors players' movements while a processor compares them to its library of hundreds of moves. To detect depth, the system constantly projects infrared radiation, which reflects off objects in the room. The IR camera in the Kinect detects the reflections to create a 'view' of the playing space with objects nearer the sensor appearing a brighter colour. It's not like IR thermal imaging used in night-sight gadgets that detect body heat – it's more similar to the technology is used in landscape mapping.

Kinect

Who says it doesn't make you look cool?

© Microsoft

Inside Kinect

Microphone
All four mics face downwards to keep the front of the box looking sleek. One mic is positioned here on the left...

Microphones
...the other three mics are on the right. Kinect developers tested dozens of arrays to arrive at this optimum configuration.

© iFixit

IR projector
Constantly beams IR radiation into the playing space.

IR camera
Detects IR radiation from the projector reflecting off objects. The information is sent for processing to map the playing space.

Motor
The heavy base unit prevents the Kinect tipping over – it contains the motor, which tilts the sensor and operates the camera's zoom.

RGB camera
This ordinary digital camera detects visible light and sends images for identification and processing.

4. Detection
Every move you perform will be picked up by the camera.

> "The heart of Ocado's operation is its central distribution warehouse"

The system in place at Ocado is maintained by 150 programmers

Shopping online explained

The UK's foremost online supermarket, Ocado, is now ten years old, 'check out' the technology and systems used to get groceries to your door

Online supermarkets that deliver produce to customers via the web are growing in popularity. With no high-street stores, retailers like Ocado rely on a web-based interface that's directly linked to a huge automated warehouse. This allows customers to select their groceries remotely from their computer, or through their smartphone with a special app. Delivery is then scheduled for home transit.

The heart of Ocado's operation is its central distribution warehouse, an automated hub of activity that revolves around a state-of-the-art, ten-mile-long conveyor belt system. The robotic conveyor belt is controlled by a central software-guidance system that directs colour-coded crates through the depot's aisles. Each container is fitted by the system with three open plastic bags and is routed to pass selected produce, according to their barcodes. The system also determines packing patterns – with heavier goods packed at the bottom of bags – as well as the order in which crates should be loaded into transit vans, dependent on delivery time.

Transit to a customer's home is handled by a series of custom-built Mercedes-Benz vans, each with air conditioning to help maintain produce freshness during transit. Routes are co-ordinated from Ocado's communications hub, where computer software liaises with GPS satellites to plan an optimal delivery path according to local traffic conditions and distance to target. If a delivery is located at an elongated distance from the central warehouse, orders are carried to smaller, local hubs, then passed over to region-specific vehicles for final delivery.

Online shopping step-by-step

2. Produce
Online supermarkets source produce directly from individual companies, as well as brand ranges from notable high-street shops. This produce then arrives in bulk to a central pick and packing warehouse.

4. Shipping
Product shipping is usually handled by air conditioned vans to ensure that groceries remain fresh during transit. Vans proceed from the warehouse directly to a user's home or, if distance is lengthy, to a local distribution hub for secodary onward transit.

Home: 15 Min.

1. User interface
Storefronts are web interfaces, directly accessible by personal computers and smartphones. They allow customers to search textually and visually for products, as well as book a delivery slot. Sites often include video recipes, product bundles and price comparison stats.

3. Warehouse
The centre of operations is the distribution warehouse, usually a semi-automated conveyor belt system that sorts orders. The system software is linked to the user interface, receiving orders from customers for picking as well as updating stock levels.

5. Communication
Van transit is conducted via GPS link to a communications hub, where routes are planned and updated remotely, taking advantage of traffic updates and accident reports. This allows for specific time slots to be granted.

Let there be light
The lighter was invented before the match. While chemist Johann Wolfgang Döbereiner invented the lighter in 1816, a true self-igniting match did not arrive until John Walker's invention in 1827.

© Sebastian Ritter 2006

Disposable lighters

How are these miniature, portable flames produced?

Inside almost all modern disposable lighters is butane, used for its practical physical properties that make it a liquid at high pressure but a gas when released into the air. This means it can be stored as a liquid within the lighter, made of welded plastic to provide a high-pressure vessel. Decreasing the pressure by pressing a button and opening a hole allows a small amount of butane to escape in its gaseous state.

As butane is highly flammable, a small hot spark will ignite the narrow stream of gas and create a controlled flame. To create the spark, a piezoelectric crystal generates an electric charge when compressed or struck by a small hammer in the lighter mechanism. This allows a voltage to be created between two wires and ignite the gas. Other lighters strike flint against a metal when a wheel is quickly turned with the thumb, causing friction and creating a spark. ✿

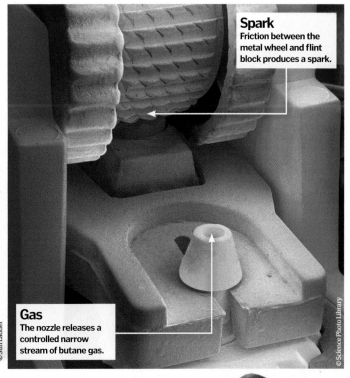

Spark
Friction between the metal wheel and flint block produces a spark.

Gas
The nozzle releases a controlled narrow stream of butane gas.

© Sun Ladder

© Science Photo Library

Bathroom scales

Now we can say "the scales must be broken" with confidence

Inside a spring-activated bathroom scale is an arrangement of four levers running from each corner to the centre of the scale. When you stand on a bathroom scale, a set of brackets distributes your weight and spreads it across the levers. There are four levers because the weight needs to be spread evenly to prevent the instrument from becoming damaged, but they work together as one.

A long lever is attached to a fixed end of the scale where the person stands, and their weight is transferred to a spring system at the other end of the scale. The force exerted on the spring is less than their weight due to a ratio determined by the length of the wheel. For example, a ratio of 1:10 will mean an 80kg person only exerts 8kg of force on the spring, so it can be made much smaller to withstand the force. This spring then turns a dial, which is calibrated to point to the right weight. ✿

Spring and scale

Weight
A weight is applied to the scale very close to a fixed point to reduce the force exerted on the scale.

Ratio
The distance from the fixed end to the spring determines a ratio, which minimises the force on the spring.

Dial
The expansion of the spring moves a cog that causes the dial to turn, with the correct weight pre-calibrated into it.

Spring
The force of the weight pushing down at the other end of the lever stretches the spring.

"Human waste contains bacteria that can spread disease"

What happens after you flush?

Primary clarifier
Solids settle to the bottom of the tank, while the remaining liquid waste is sent to the aeration tanks.

Aeration tanks
Air pumped into the tanks promotes the growth of microorganisms that feed on the remaining organic matter in the waste.

A sewage treatment plant

The treatment of sewage consists of pre-treatment, primary and secondary processes. The aim of the treatment plant is to accelerate how these wastes would be dissipated and processed in the natural world.

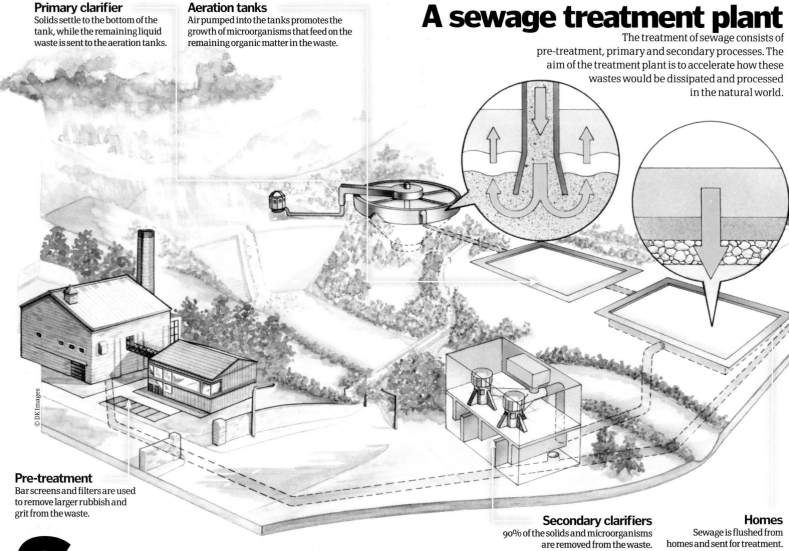

© DK Images

Pre-treatment
Bar screens and filters are used to remove larger rubbish and grit from the waste.

Secondary clarifiers
90% of the solids and microorganisms are removed from the waste.

Homes
Sewage is flushed from homes and sent for treatment.

Sewage treatment

How our waste products are processed to provide pure water and prevent the spread of fatal diseases

When you go to the toilet and flush away your waste, how is it treated to stop it polluting our environment? Up until the 19th Century, no one really cared where it went, but with the growth of towns and cities, human waste became a huge problem.

Besides toilet paper and other solid material sent down the loo, solid human waste contains harmful bacteria that can easily spread disease, as well as phosphates and nitrogens that encourage the growth of algae when it is released into bodies of water. The algae fouls waterways and blocks light, thereby preventing the ability for fish and other creatures to see or breathe properly. The waste also reduces the oxygen in water due to the decomposition of bacteria. This, along with its dirty colour and the stink it

causes due to the release of hydrogen sulphide gas caused by its nitrogen-rich bacteria, all make our waste highly unpleasant and deadly to our environment and ourselves.

The solution in the developed world was to link the new flushing toilets to vast underground sewage systems, to take the waste away from the towns to rivers or the sea. This just moved the problem away from the towns, but in

the 20th Century sewage treatment plants were developed and improved. These treatment plants separate the solids from the liquids, and the waste that cannot be processed and recycled is sent to landfill or incineration.

Strict laws and regulations in the developed world control where and how treatment plants discharge waste, but in many countries sewage is still released without any type of treatment. ✿

5 TOP FACTS
SEWAGE

The great stink
1 The introduction of flushing loos in London caused a pong in 1858. The extra water flowing into the city's 200,000 cesspits caused untreated sewage to pour into the streets.

Purity
2 80% of countries have low standards of water purity, and in the developing world especially one in six people still don't have access to clean drinking water.

The state of China
3 While the number of Chinese sewage treatment plants is steadily increasing, 55% of China's sewage is still not treated. There are only around 2,000 plants in the country.

Explosive manholes
4 In American cities there have been reports of manhole covers exploding into the air. This is likely due to heat from electrical cables, gases and the odd stray spark underground.

New York
5 New York City has 14 sewage treatment plants that deal with 1.4 billion tons of waste a day. The average person in the US produces 14kg of solid waste a week.

DID YOU KNOW? In the USA, 40,000 sanitary sewer overflow (SSO) events happen a year

Typical sewage treatment systems

1. Overflow
An excess of rainwater entering the sewer system can overwhelm sewage plants. Various methods are used to drain it away without treatment, or to store it in retention basins or huge concrete tanks. It can then be filtered and sent for further treatment.

2. Solids
Bar grids and screens are used to remove solid items of rubbish that can include leaves and litter. Smaller screens are used in chambers where grit and sand can be allowed to sink to the bottom and removed. These solids are either incinerated or sent to landfill.

3. Fat and grease
To remove these products, air is pumped into a chamber where the fat and grease rise to the surface. Pumps take away this fatty scum, to tanks where it is collected and removed.

4. Primary clarification
These tanks allow any fat, grease or oil to rise and for sludge to settle at the bottom. Scrapers send the primary sludge downwards, where it's collected and pumped for further processing.

5. Aeration
Air is pumped into this tank to encourage the growth of aerobic microorganisms. They feed on the organic matter that remains in the waste from the primary clarifier.

6. Secondary clarification
This works like the primary clarifier, which removes the microorganisms grown in the aeration tank. Solid sludge at the bottom of the tank is sent for sludge digestion, and at the surface the clean water is sent on for further treatment. The remaining waste is sent back to the aeration tank.

7. Disinfection
The water from aeration still needs to be purged of hazardous microorganisms. Chlorine has been a common chemical used to disinfect water, but it can produce residues that are harmful to aquatic life and may be carcinogenic. The water therefore has to be dechlorinated. An alternative is to subject the water to ultraviolet light, or to use ozone instead of chlorine.

8. Sludge digestion
The sludge consists of water and oxygen-hungry, foul-smelling organic matter. Inside the enclosed tank, anaerobic bacteria that live without oxygen make the sludge inert. It is a slow process that can be sped up by heating the tank between 25°C and 40°C.

9. Drying and sludge finishing
The inert sludge can be dried and dewatered in a separate chamber, and sent for incineration or landfill. In both cases, precautions have to be made to prevent pollution of the environment by this material. To kill the pathogens in dewatered sludge, hydrated lime $Ca(OH)_2$ or quicklime CaO is added to it to produce bio solid fertiliser.

10. Gases
When sludge is being digested and dried it produces a mixture of gases, which mainly consist of up to 70% methane and 30% carbon dioxide, along with a small amount of nitrogen and hydrogen. These gases can be collected and used to heat the sludge or power the plant.

Waterborne diseases

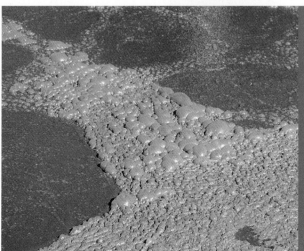

Waterborne diseases are spread by damaged or non-existent sewer systems, pollution and natural disasters. They tend to be caused when animal and human urine or faeces gets into the water supply and encourage the proliferation of deadly viruses and bacteria.

Diarrhoea is a common symptom of waterborne disease. Every day at least 5,000 children die of diarrhoea-related diseases due to bad sanitation. Diarrhoea exhibits itself as frequent evacuation of watery faeces and can last several days. Cholera bacterium in untreated water causes severe vomiting and diarrhoea, leading to dehydration and

life-threatening consequences. If diarrhoea-infected faeces should enter the water supply, it helps to spread the disease even further in the population.

Arsenic in water supplies can cause cancer of the kidney, lungs, bladder or skin. For example, in Bangladesh the World Health Organization estimates that 77 million people are exposed to high levels of arsenic in groundwater, which is the main source of fresh water.

Unsanitary water, food and hygiene standards can also cause hepatitis A and C. This causes an inflammation of the liver and is highly contagious.

Beer pumps explained

How is beer transported from keg to glass?

Beer pumps are pressurised systems used to transfer beer from its transportation keg, cool it via a refrigeration unit and deliver it to taps. The central component is the chiller unit, a multi-compartment tank filled with liquid glycol (commonly used as an antifreeze), through which coiled pipes are wound. Through these pipes beer is drawn by the unit's pump, cooling it as it goes through the glycol tanks until it reaches drinking temperature. Glycol is used rather than water due to its much lower freezing point, allowing beverages to be cooled. ✿

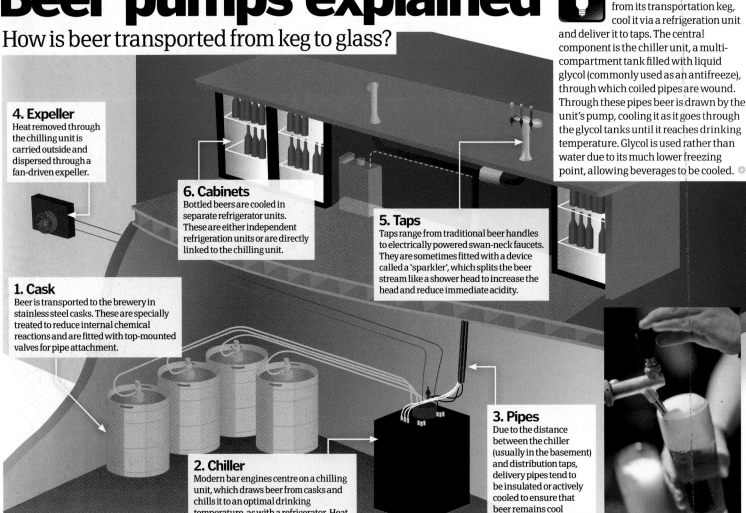

4. Expeller
Heat removed through the chilling unit is carried outside and dispersed through a fan-driven expeller.

6. Cabinets
Bottled beers are cooled in separate refrigerator units. These are either independent refrigeration units or are directly linked to the chilling unit.

5. Taps
Taps range from traditional beer handles to electrically powered swan-neck faucets. They are sometimes fitted with a device called a 'sparkler', which splits the beer stream like a shower head to increase the head and reduce immediate acidity.

1. Cask
Beer is transported to the brewery in stainless steel casks. These are specially treated to reduce internal chemical reactions and are fitted with top-mounted valves for pipe attachment.

3. Pipes
Due to the distance between the chiller (usually in the basement) and distribution taps, delivery pipes tend to be insulated or actively cooled to ensure that beer remains cool during delivery.

2. Chiller
Modern bar engines centre on a chilling unit, which draws beer from casks and chills it to an optimal drinking temperature, as with a refrigerator. Heat is transferred to an external expeller.

Seismographs

The machines that allow even the tiniest quakes to be recorded

A seismograph is an instrument that is capable of measuring the intensity of an earthquake by recording seismic waves, producing a digital or analogue printout of the scale of vibrations known as a seismogram.

The basic principle of a seismograph is that a pen fixed to a stationary pendulum hovering above a piece of paper will draw a line of oscillation as the ground beneath it moves in an earthquake. The larger the wave line it draws, the stronger the earthquake. However, this method is restricted to archaic seismographs, which commonly weighed upwards of a ton in order to overcome the friction between pen and paper and produce a visible reading.

Most modern seismographs employ electromagnetism to reduce the size and improve the accuracy of the seismograph. A coil wrapped around the pendulum creates an electric current within a magnetic field, which can be amplified electronically to produce a magnification of the vibrations as high as 1 million times and reduce the pendulum weight needed to overcome friction. ✿

P waves
The first squiggles are the primary waves, which push and pull the Earth and arrive first at up to six kilometres (3.7 miles) per second.

How to read a seismogram
What do the lines produced by a seismograph actually mean?

Surface waves
Slower than S waves, surface waves move the ground horizontally (Love waves) and vertically (Rayleigh waves).

Frequency
The closer the lines are tells you how frequently the waves are produced, helping to locate the earthquake's epicentre.

Amplitude
The height of a line is the amplitude of the wave, where larger lines correspond to the more destructive waves.

S waves
Larger lines denote secondary waves, travelling 4km (2.4 mi) per second and moving the Earth from side to side.

5 TOP FACTS
TOILET TECH

Lav
1 'Lavatory' comes from Latin 'lavatorium', which comes from 'layo', which translated to modern English means 'I wash'. Today, the word describes a washing/bathing area.

Dunny
2 'Dunny' is the Australian term for an outside toilet. The word derives from the British word 'dunnekin', meaning dung house. The person who empties it is called a dunnyman.

Class
3 The precursor to the modern flush toilet was invented by English courtier John Harington in 1596. However, it didn't enter widespread use for another 300 years.

Duo
4 One of toilet's more recent advances has been the 'duoset' flushing mechanism. The first gives a smaller flush for urine, while the second gives a larger flush for faeces.

Sustain
5 Due to large amounts of water used per person each day on flushing (90 litres/19.8 gallons on average), rules have been introduced to reduce the amount used by toilet systems.

 DID YOU KNOW? The first pay toilet in the United States was installed in Terre Haute, Indiana, in 1910

Handle
When the handle is pushed the fill valve opens, allowing water to refill the tank.

Tank fill tube
Water is drawn up from the mains supply system here.

Flush valve flapper
A rubber plug, the flush valve flapper allows the tank to refill with water between flushes.

Trapway
Waste is carried away from the toilet and into the sewer system via the trapway.

Overflow tube
To prevent the tank from overflowing, an overflow tube carries water into the bowl.

Chain
Connected to the toilet's handle, the chain raises the flush valve flapper, allowing water to enter the bowl and trapway.

"The release of the tank's water creates a vacuum effect that depressurises the trapway"

Rim holes
Spaced evenly along the toilet bowl's rim, these holes help water to be evenly distributed during a flush.

Siphon jet
A secondary stream of water from the tank that bypasses the bowl, the siphon jet adds power to the flush.

Toilet technology explained

Ever wonder about water closets? Here are the facts about flushing…

 Modern flush toilets work in two main stages. First, in order to empty waste from the bowl, a complex flush mechanism is activated. This section is contained within the toilet's tank – the part of the toilet positioned above the bowl – and is initiated when a user presses the toilet's handle. Once pushed, the handle pulls up a chain connected to a flush valve – a rubber stopper that acts as a gateway to the bowl, siphon and trapway. The water in the tank, which has been filled via a filler tube from the mains supply, then exits the tank and descends into the bowl. It follows a rim shelf perforated with equidistant holes, as well as a smaller secondary passage directly into the toilet's siphon – the kinked pipe that sits between the trapway and the bowl.

The release of the tank's water occurs in roughly three seconds, which creates a vacuum effect that depressurises the trapway, generating a large suction force that drags the contents of the bowl down into the sewerage system.

Once flushed, the toilet's tank needs to refill itself for further use. First, now the tank is devoid of water, the flush valve falls back down onto the gateway to the bowl. This reseals the tank. Next, the tank filler valve is switched on either electronically or by a traditional ball cock (a float mechanism that pivots on an axle to open the filler valve when the water falls). This allows water to re-enter the tank through the filler tube, filling it to a preset level, as well as down the overflow tube to refill the bowl. The filler valve is then shut once more, either by the rising of the float or by another

control system. Finally, the refilling of the tank re-pressurises the siphon and trapway, blocking any gases and waste from re-entering the system. It re-creates a large water surface area in the main bowl, ready for reuse.

© Andrew Dunn; www.andrewdunnphoto.com
BOTH
Dr Who was not impressed with his new TARDIS…

War of the water closets

For years, a secret war has been raging over the proper way to hang toilet paper…

In 1989, a survey of American habits discovered that 68 per cent of people questioned staunchly preferred the 'over' toilet paper orientation. They cited that it is easier to grab, allows the design to be clearly seen and is more hygienic, as there is less chance the user will brush their dirty hands against the WC's wall while reaching for it. Advocates of the 'under' orientation cited it grants a tidier appearance, unrolls less easily by accident and is harder for a pet or child to tamper with.

US comedian Jay Leno and advice columnist Ann Landers have had their say. Leno states that: "if people don't have it right [over], they obviously don't know which way it's supposed to go," while Landers writes: "The toilet paper needs to be hung down along the wall."

OVER?

OR UNDER?

2x © Elya

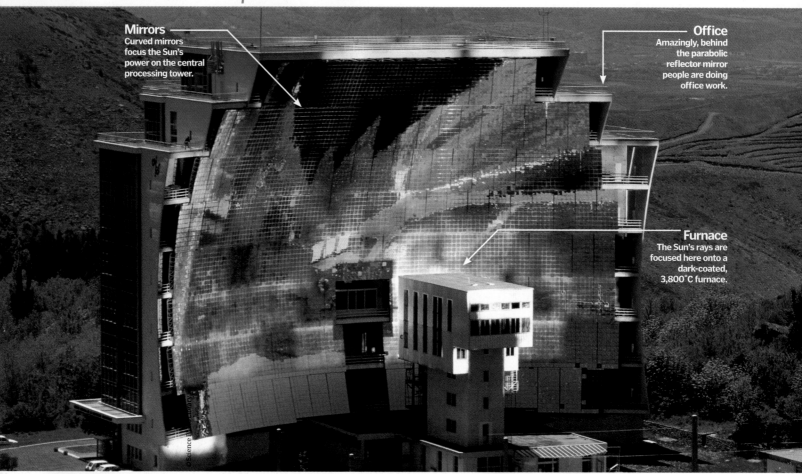

Mirrors
Curved mirrors focus the Sun's power on the central processing tower.

Office
Amazingly, behind the parabolic reflector mirror people are doing office work.

Furnace
The Sun's rays are focused here onto a dark-coated, 3,800°C furnace.

Renewable energy

With the Earth's supply of fossil fuels perpetually declining, new and exciting energy systems are being designed to exploit sustainable resources

Each year the global population is increasing at an exponential rate, creating a ravenous demand for energy. Fossil fuels cannot sustain this and it is forcing governments across the globe to re-evaluate how they are going to provide power for future generations.

Luckily, right now numerous systems are being designed and developed worldwide to address this issue, demonstrating novel and creative methods of exploiting the renewable resources with which the Earth is blessed. Harnessing the power of sunlight, wind, rain, tides and geothermal heat, these technologies are slowly repositioning the balance of power away from finite resources and towards sustainable ones, mitigating long-held fears over a world post-oil and delivering power generation on a domestic as well as industrial level. Let's take a closer look at some of the most promising solutions out there. ✿

An operational Pelamis Wave Energy Converter being buffeted by ocean waves

5 TOP FACTS
RENEWABLE ENERGY

Megawatt
1 The world's largest wind turbine is the Enercon E-126, which has a rotor diameter of 126 metres. The E-126 turbine is rated at a whopping six megawatts.

Year-on-year
2 The worldwide investment in renewable energy capacity has risen exponentially year on year, going from $104 billion in 2007 to a very impressive $150 billion in 2009.

African
3 Kenya is the current world leader in the number of domestic solar power systems installed per capita, with over 300,000 12-30 watt systems sold each year.

Greenest
4 The current world leader in renewable energy production is China, who in 2009 produced 682 TWh of electricity through water, wind, biomass and solar.

Future
5 Recent estimates by scientists forecast the world to run out of most fossil fuels by 2070, with natural gas the first to go, followed quickly by oil and coal.

DID YOU KNOW? The largest solar power station in the world is situated in the Mojave Desert, California

Hydraulic ram
The hydraulic rams resist the motion of the waves, which in turn pump high-pressure hydraulic fluid into the unit's hydraulic motors.

Heave hinged joint
The position for the section's horizontal axis joint.

Sway hinged joint
The vertical axis is connected here to the Converter's other sections.

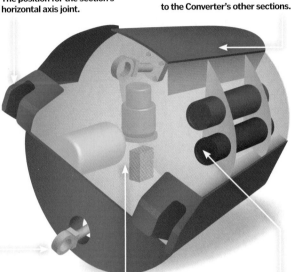

Platform
Taking energy out of a flowing water current generates a major thrust reaction (around 100 tons per MW). Because of this, the monopole tower is drilled deep into the bedrock of the seabed for stability.

Tubular tower
The steel, monopole, tubular tower is submerged at the heart of Strangford Lough and provides a solid structure for the rotors to protrude from.

Generators
Housed within the SeaGen tower, the generators convert the rotational movement of the rotor blades into electricity.

Twin-axial rotors
Measuring 16 metres in diameter, SeaGen's rotors are huge and sport a patented system that allows their blades to be pitched through 180 degrees.

Solar furnace
Generating power from sunlight

The Odeillo-Font-Romeu solar power station in the Eastern Pyrenees, France. Positioned in front of the reflector (out of view here) is an array of 63 flat orientating mirrors that automatically track the motion of the Sun, reflecting incident radiation onto the parabolic reflector mirror. The reflector consists of 9,500 mirrors that concentrate the Sun's rays onto a dark-coated furnace at its focus (central tower). The system is capable of producing thermal power of 1,000 kilowatts, and achieving a temperature of 3,800 degrees Celsius within the furnace.

Motor/generator set
The hydraulic motor converts the hydraulic fluid pumped into it by the rams into torque and rotation in order to drive the unit's generators.

High-pressure accumulators
This allows the Pelamis's pump mechanism to be a manageable size and also to operate quicker, allowing it to moderate demand and smooth out the wave's pulsations.

Pelamis Wave Energy Converter

The Pelamis Wave Energy Converter from Pelamis Wave Power is a system designed to generate renewable electricity from ocean waves. The system consists of a semi-submerged, articulated structure (180 metres long and four metres in diameter) consisting of cylindrical sections linked by joints. These joints, under the pressure of wave-induced motion, move and are resisted by hydraulic rams, which pump high-pressure fluid through hydraulic motors to drive electrical generators and produce electricity. This energy is then fed from each joint down an umbilical and then carried back to shore in a single large seabed feed. Each Pelamis Converter is rated at 750kW and on average a unit will produce 25-40 per cent of that rating annually, which is the annual electricity demand for roughly 500 homes.

A second-generation Pelamis Wave Energy Converter at the European Marine Energy Centre, Orkney

SeaGen tidal generator

The SeaGen tidal generator from Marine Current Systems is an operational – albeit prototype – tidal system based in Strangford Narrows, Northern Ireland. The system consists of twin 16-metre in diameter, submerged axial-flow rotors, which are attached to a central machine and control tower that is fixed to the seabed. Both rotors on the SeaGen sport a unique feature that allows the blades to be pitched through 180 degrees, allowing them to operate in both tidal directions. Appearing like an upside-down submerged windmill, SeaGen works by converting high velocity currents into usable electricity throughout the tidal cycle – much like how a windmill utilises the power of the wind to rotate its sails. Indeed, its large-scale rotors – aided by the 400 million gallons of water that flow past it twice a day – can develop a rated power of 1.2 MW at a current velocity of 2.4m/s. This gives SeaGen the ability to deliver about 10 MW per tide, which annually amounts to 6,000 MWh of energy.

SeaGen is capable of raising its rotors out of the water in order to make maintenance easier

A wind farm 28km off the shore of Belgium's part of the North Sea

Operation
The turbine's generator, gearbox and yaw-control mechanism are housed here.

Wind turbines
Taking the power-generating capabilities of windmills to the next level

One of the world's most developed renewable energy systems, wind turbines take the mechanics of a traditional windmill and upscale them dramatically in order to extract energy from wind and convert it into electricity. The most common wind turbine in production is the horizontal axis variety. These consist of a main rotor shaft and electrical generator at the top of large, tapered, cylindrical towers. This type of turbine works by allowing the wind to rotate its three fixed blades in order to generate mechanical, rotational energy, which is then in turn converted into electrical energy by the installed electrical generator. The slow-to-fast rotation of the rotor and blades is aided by an installed gearbox, which allows for a smooth transition in speeds dependent of wind strength. Wind turbines are often installed in areas of high wind – such as coastal areas – en-mass in massive wind farms, the largest of which in the world is the Roscoe Wind Farm in Roscoe, Texas, which has an epic 627 turbines and total installed capacity of 781.5 megawatts.

An Enercon E-126, the largest wind turbine in the world, situated in Germany

Generator
The turbine's generator converts the rotor's rotational energy into electrical energy to be sent to the grid or storage device.

Gearbox
Helps initiate the rotor's movement and then aids its velocity dependent on wind speed to maximise energy conversion.

Inside a turbine

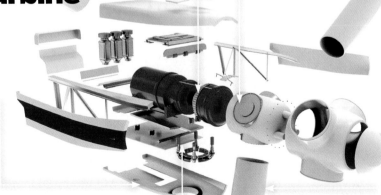

Tower
The turbine's tall tower is a crucial element of its design as in areas with high wind shear the overall wind speed can increase by 20 per cent and the power output by 34 per cent for every 100 metres of elevation.

Nacelle
The direction of the nacelle is dictated by a yaw control mechanism and it is designed to be as streamlined as possible in order to reduce turbulence behind the turbine.

Blades
The turbine's rotor blades are often adjustable, allowing for their angle of attack to be adjusted dependent on wind direction. This allows the turbine to collect the maximum amount of wind energy for the day or season.

Head to Head
DOMESTIC RENEWABLE ENERGY SYSTEMS

MOST EXPENSIVE

1. Solar
Solar panels offer an established form of energy generation on a domestic level. However, they are expensive and are only useful when the weather is fine.

MOST INTRUSIVE

2. Wind
Small wind turbines can be bought and attached to the roof of buildings to supply a small amount of electricity each year. They are cheap but currently inefficient.

MOST CONSISTENT

3. Water
If you are lucky enough to live by a stream or river, small water turbine generators allow you exploit its gentle amble for a small and ensured power return.

DID YOU KNOW? Two solar updraft towers have been approved for construction so far, one in Namibia and the other in Spain

Geothermal power plants

Geothermal energy is power extracted from heat stored inside the Earth. The heat is generated from radioactive decay, volcanic activity, core convection and solar energy absorbed at the Earth's surface. Geothermal power plants work by pumping water down a borehole into hotspots a few kilometres beneath the Earth, then forcing it out of a second borehole into a steam turbine to produce electricity.

A diagram of a geothermal power plant showing the drilling of a borehole to a depth of 5km. At this depth, a layer of water has formed from rainwater draining through the ground (blue arrows). The water is heated by magma, and the borehole enables the energy of the heated water to be extracted.

A. Injection well
B. Hot water to district heating
C. Porous sediments
D. Observation well
E. Crystalline bedrock

Pump house
Production well
Heat exchanger
Reservoir
Turbine hall

A
B
C
D
E

4,000-6,000m
0-1,000m
500-1,000m

© Fisch'X'Ytrottier/Siemens

1. Tower
The central tower acts as a flue to draw hot air through the turbines, as well as housing the plant's machinery and generator.

4. Turbines
The updraft tower is fitted with multiple turbines at its base that suck the hot air inwards from under the collector membrane to generate electricity.

3. Collector membrane
This is made from clear plastic, and while allowing a large proportion of the Sun's rays to pass through it without reflection, almost completely traps the heated air beneath it, adding an accumulative effect.

2. Thermal storage
During the day the Sun's rays heat air under the collector membrane to high levels. At night heat radiated from the ground is better contained under the collector.

Day

Night

Solar updraft towers

An elegant system to exploit solar energy, the solar updraft tower works by combining the chimney effect – where cold air is drawn upwards by reduced local pressure – the greenhouse effect and a wind turbine. The power plant works by trapping air heated by the Sun under a large greenhouse-like circular membrane, which, through convection and the chimney effect, causes the hot air to be sucked in towards and up the central tower. As the hot air travels up the tower the airflow drives a selection of turbines that in turn produce electricity. Definitely one to watch in the future…

Interview

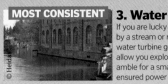

How It Works spoke to Kamil Shar from Sanyo Solar about the exciting new sustainable systems becoming available for home use

How It Works: Energy efficiency is crucial for solar cells, how efficient are Sanyo Solar's modules?

Kamil Shar: The energy conversion efficiency for modules is essentially the barometer for quality and this is really the core feature of our product, offering a lot of value for the end users on a domestic level. It is the residential market that we are focusing on primarily and the reason for that is because of the module's high efficiency we are able to offer more value in a limited space installation area. So your average terraced house can only get up to a 2kW system size and if they are trying to achieve that with lower-quality modules they wouldn't have enough space to make that installation. With our new HIT modules we can achieve a record energy conversion efficiency of 23 per cent at the R&D level; on a domestic level 21.1 per cent.

HIW: How has the conversion efficiency for solar panels been progressing, has it been developing incrementally?

KS: It has been incremental. Previous to that it was around 20 per cent and before that the number rose fast only in the last five to ten years. That is mainly due to the amount of investment we are putting into our R&D, as the market has grown massively over the past couple of years in Europe.

HIW: What level of power is one of your modules going to provide the average domestic consumer and how is created energy used?

KS: The way that the system works in the UK as of 1 April 2010 is we have a subsidiary system called the feed-in tariff and how that works is that if you have a solar installation on your roof it will be connected to the national energy grid. So, any electricity you are generating and not using will be fed back into the grid. The dynamics of the feed-in system benefit self generation as the government has set a tariff of 40 pence for every kW hour of electricity generated and that amount is paid to the system owner whether they use the electricity or not.

HIW: So the user isn't generating electricity that can only be used in their own home, it can be fed into the grid and used anywhere?

KS: That is correct. However, if there is an electricity demand in the house when the electricity is being generated then it will be used to power that household. But if there is no one in at the time or no energy is required it will be fed into the grid. So what we are suggesting to people who invest in our systems is that they should alter their energy habits to generate electricity and use it during the daytime, as it is free and also grants you the tariff all at the same time.

HIW: In Britain it is not particularly sunny, would that jeopardise the 21.1 per cent conversion efficiency?

KS: The figures are generally measured based on industry criteria so all module manufacturers would have to conform to certain criteria when they are measuring cell conversion efficiency, that way everyone is on an even playing field and we are not promoting statistics from Spain in the UK. So, yes, dependent on conditions there'd be fluctuations but they are impossible to quantify, as we wouldn't know how much light there was one day to the next.

HIW: How efficient can silicon solar cells actually become? It is currently 21.1 per cent but is there a theoretical cap or barrier that cannot be overcome?

KS: Currently, 29 per cent is the theoretical maximum for these crystalline-based technology.

HIW: When do you think that figure is going to be hit?

KS: It's very hard to predict as the closer you get to 29 per cent the harder it is to achieve it. It will be achieved, but will be dependent on technological advancement and R&D investment. However, with even a current solar setup now, such as our module and system, users would see a positive return on the initial outlay after eight to ten years and then for the next ten to 12 years, because the feed-in tariff is fixed for 20, they'd be generating income of roughly ten per cent the initial outlay, all the while benefiting from free electricity.

One of Sanyo Solar's 21.1 per cent efficient HIT modules

Desperate times call for desperate measures

CAT FOOD

Can openers

Crucial for extracting tasty foodstuffs, can openers have developed evermore refined and easy-to-use designs

Rotating wheel, plier-grip can openers work by transferring the rotational movement of their key handle – which is rotated by the user – into a circular cutting wheel in order to pierce and cut the lid. To do this the opener uses a system of three gears: two spur gears to transmit the rotational motion of the key to the cutting wheel – which can also step up the force applied – and one feed gear to guide its cutting path round the rim.

In order to further stabilise the grip of the can between the feed gear and the cutting gear, the plier-type handle also allows the user to transfer tension to the cutting plane. The cutting wheel tends to be made from high-grade steel capable of breaking the resistance threshold of the softer lid material and is manufactured with sharp, tapered edges for a clean cut. ✿

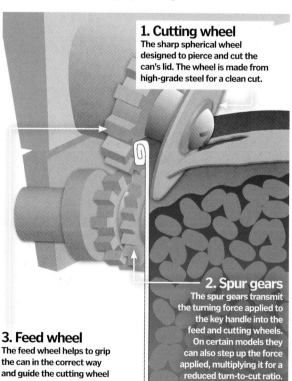

1. Cutting wheel
The sharp spherical wheel designed to pierce and cut the can's lid. The wheel is made from high-grade steel for a clean cut.

2. Spur gears
The spur gears transmit the turning force applied to the key handle into the feed and cutting wheels. On certain models they can also step up the force applied, multiplying it for a reduced turn-to-cut ratio.

3. Feed wheel
The feed wheel helps to grip the can in the correct way and guide the cutting wheel around its circumference.

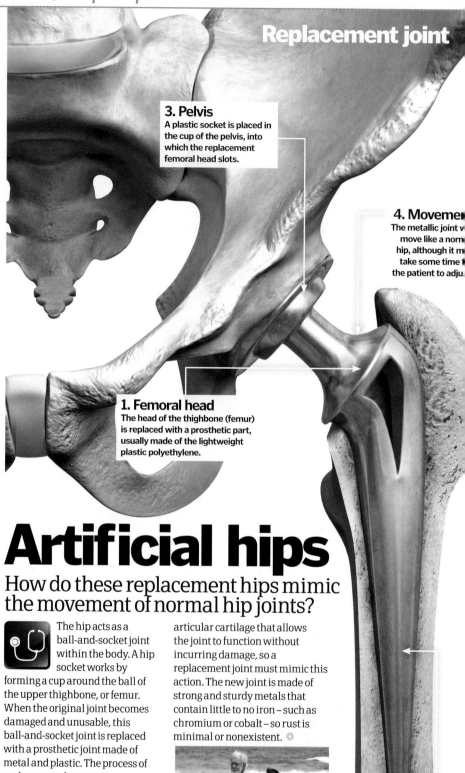

Replacement joint

3. Pelvis
A plastic socket is placed in the cup of the pelvis, into which the replacement femoral head slots.

4. Movemer
The metallic joint v move like a norm hip, although it m take some time the patient to adju.

1. Femoral head
The head of the thighbone (femur) is replaced with a prosthetic part, usually made of the lightweight plastic polyethylene.

2. Femur
A cobalt-chrome or titanium prosthesis replaces the femur and attaches to the new femoral head.

© Science Photo Library

Artificial hips

How do these replacement hips mimic the movement of normal hip joints?

The hip acts as a ball-and-socket joint within the body. A hip socket works by forming a cup around the ball of the upper thighbone, or femur. When the original joint becomes damaged and unusable, this ball-and-socket joint is replaced with a prosthetic joint made of metal and plastic. The process of replacement, known as arthroplasty, involves removing the part of the thighbone that connects to the pelvis.

An artificial hip provides a new ball for the femur bone, which is usually made of the lightweight plastic polyethylene. The replacement pelvic socket is composed of the same material. The upper thighbone joint is originally made of tough and sleek

articular cartilage that allows the joint to function without incurring damage, so a replacement joint must mimic this action. The new joint is made of strong and sturdy metals that contain little to no iron – such as chromium or cobalt – so rust is minimal or nonexistent. ✿

Artificial hips can offer a new lease of life

Harp

1 Inventor Bartolomeo Cristofori, named his invention the gravecembalo col piano e forte, translated from Italian to English to mean 'harpsichord with soft and loud'.

Tense

2 By the late-19th Century piano string tension had been determined at 16 tons, however due to developments in the 20th Century, 30 tons is now possible.

Super-grand

3 The largest piano to buy is the Fazioli F308, a grand piano over 3.08m. A fourth pedal brings the hammers closer to the strings, decreasing volume while maintaining tone.

Spruce

4 High-quality pianos use quarter-sawn, defect-free spruce boards to make their soundboards. The spruce is dried over time for the best vibration and energy transfer.

Chamber

5 The piano was wildly popular in the 18th Century, spurred by musicians such as Mozart and Clementi. It became the instrument of choice for chamber music and concerts.

DID YOU KNOW? *The invention of the piano is credited to Bartolomeo Cristofori in 1709*

How does a piano work?

What goes on inside one of the most popular musical instruments on the planet?

Pianos work by transmitting the vibrational energy of taught wire strings into a soundboard, which in turn converts the vibrational energy into sound. The piano achieves this through both its construction materials and action mechanisms. Pianos consist of five main parts: the frame, soundboard, strings, hammers and keys. The frame is constructed from metal and serves as a stable, immobile platform from which its strings (metal wires) and soundboard (vibration to sound conversion mechanism) can vibrate efficiently. Steel is used as it helps mitigate unwanted vibrational energy being transmitted to the rest of the piano and surrounding area, a problem that leads to distortion of produced sounds. The hammers act as a striking mechanism, and when the piano's keys are pressed by the player, they rise to strike their corresponding strings in order to produce vibrational energy.

The physics of the piano work in a chain-reaction. When a key on the keyboard is pressed, a complex system of jacks, pivots and levers raise a suspended hammer upwards to strike an overhung string, as well as a string damper (a felt block) that, once the string is stuck, comes into contact with the string and ceases its vibration. In the short time between the hammer striking the wire and damper ceasing its motion, the vibrational energy is carried down the string and over a 'bridge', a raised bridge-shaped structure over which the string is tightly stretched. The bridge receives this vibrational energy and transfers it into the piano's soundboard, a wooden board chosen for its resonant properties that through the principle of forced vibration vibrate at exactly the same frequency of the struck string. Consequently, due to the large, expansive size of the board, the quiet tone created by the string is increased, and produces a loud note. ✿

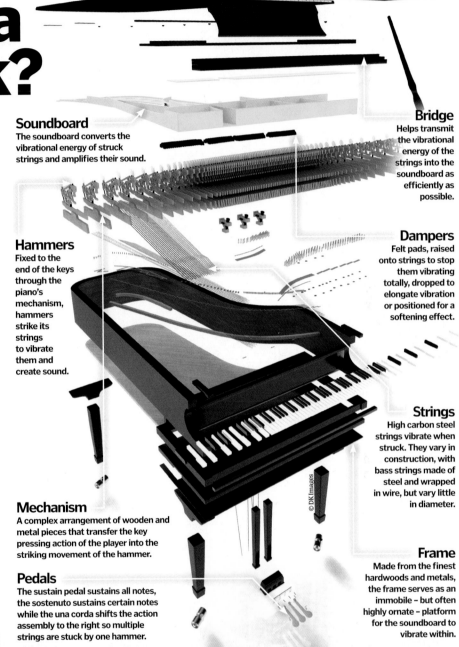

Soundboard
The soundboard converts the vibrational energy of struck strings and amplifies their sound.

Bridge
Helps transmit the vibrational energy of the strings into the soundboard as efficiently as possible.

Hammers
Fixed to the end of the keys through the piano's mechanism, hammers strike its strings to vibrate them and create sound.

Dampers
Felt pads, raised onto strings to stop them vibrating totally, dropped to elongate vibration or positioned for a softening effect.

Strings
High carbon steel strings vibrate when struck. They vary in construction, with bass strings made of steel and wrapped in wire, but vary little in diameter.

Mechanism
A complex arrangement of wooden and metal pieces that transfer the key pressing action of the player into the striking movement of the hammer.

Frame
Made from the finest hardwoods and metals, the frame serves as an immobile – but often highly ornate – platform for the soundboard to vibrate within.

Pedals
The sustain pedal sustains all notes, the sostenuto sustains certain notes while the una corda shifts the action assembly to the right so multiple strings are stuck by one hammer.

© DK Images

© Gryffindor

A classic example of a grand piano, fitted with soft, muffler and damper pedals

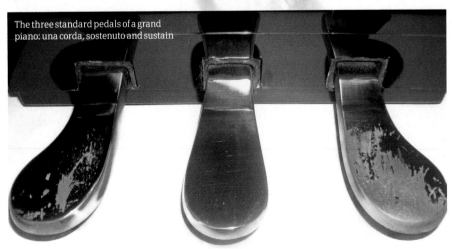

The three standard pedals of a grand piano: una corda, sostenuto and sustain

"Fridges rely on the simple notion of evaporation, absorbing heat when a liquid changes its state"

How your food stays cool

Refrigerators are one of the most vital household appliances, keeping food cool and fresh. But how do they work?

To achieve their cooling effect fridges rely on the simple notion of evaporation, absorbing heat when a liquid changes its state. This evaporation is the central principle of the refrigeration cycle, a perpetual loop in which a refrigerant is forced to change state in order to invoke heat absorption.

The cycle begins with the refrigerant in a vapour state, which is then pressurised in an internal compressor. This compression forces the refrigerant to heat up before being sent outside the fridge into a condenser and expelled into the surrounding area, cooling the refrigerant vapour in the process and condensing it into a highly pressurised liquid state.

This liquid is then sucked through an expansion valve and back into the low-pressure fridge compartment causing the refrigerant to boil (refrigerants have low boiling points), vaporise and drop in temperature, cooling the compartment in the process. The cycle then begins again, with the low-pressure refrigerant vapour being sucked up into the compressor. ✿

Optimum fridge temperature is between 0 and 5°C

5. Compartment
As it boils (refrigerants have low boiling points) the refrigerant vaporises and cools the main compartment of the fridge before being sucked back into the compressor to begin the cycle again.

4. Expansion valve
Once condensed, the liquid refrigerant is sucked into an expansion valve and back into the low-pressure fridge compartment, causing it to boil.

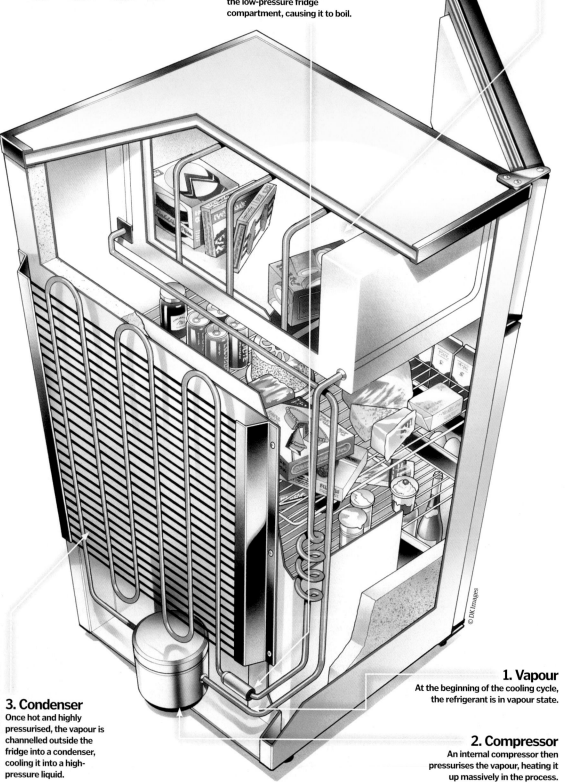

© DK Images

3. Condenser
Once hot and highly pressurised, the vapour is channelled outside the fridge into a condenser, cooling it into a high-pressure liquid.

1. Vapour
At the beginning of the cooling cycle, the refrigerant is in vapour state.

2. Compressor
An internal compressor then pressurises the vapour, heating it up massively in the process.

Head to Head NATIONAL LANDMARKS

CLASSIC		SYMBOLIC		ICONIC	
	**1. Eiffel Tower** The 7,300-ton, 324m (1,063ft) tall tower was designed by – and named after – Gustave Eiffel. It was the tallest man-made structure until 1930.		**2. Statue of Liberty** The 93m (305ft) tall, torch-bearing statue opened in 1886 to visitors who can sightsee from the crown of the statue.		**3. Sydney Opera House** After 30 years of planning and building, this was finally opened in 1973. Its unique shell-like roofing has made it an icon of Australia.

DID YOU KNOW? It takes 500W to rotate the London Eye fully loaded with 800 people. That's the power used by six light bulbs

The EDF Energy London Eye

A world-famous landmark that casts an iconic eye over London

The London Eye was designed to celebrate the arrival of the millennium. It took seven years to design and build and opened to the public on 9 March 2000.

The Eye was such a unique engineering task that different parts of it were built throughout Europe. The capsules were built in France, the main structure in Holland, the cables in Italy, the hub and spindle in the Czech Republic and the rim bearings in Germany.

The whole wheel was assembled horizontally over the River Thames, next to Jubilee Gardens. The riverbed had to be surveyed in detail before work platforms could be put in place and they had to make sure they didn't disrupt any river traffic. The rim was built in large sections that were floated up the Thames on barges. The height of the river had to be monitored, to ensure that they could pass under any bridges on the way to the construction site.

Europe's largest floating crane, the Taklift 1, lifted the sections from the barges onto the work platforms, where they were attached to the hub and spindle by steel cables. The A-frame legs of the structure are set in 33m (108ft)-deep concrete foundations and are hinged at the base. Once the main A-frame was fixed to the hub and spindle, the hinges allowed the whole 1,900-ton structure to be lifted into its vertical position. It took a week to lift the wheel in several stages into its present position. Tension cables set in 1,300 tons of concrete foundation were used to anchor the wheel in place. Capsules were then fitted to the outside of the rim.

The rim is rotated by sets of standard lorry tyres powered by hydraulic motors. As the wheel turns in one direction, the capsules have their own motors to slowly rotate them in the opposite direction to keep them level.

Spoke cables
Rim and hub are attached by 64 radial cables. There are eight rotation cables, which apply tension when the wheel turns in one direction, and eight cables for the opposite direction.

Hub and spindle
The 23m (75ft)-long cast steel spindle consists of eight sections welded together.

Capsules
Rotate in opposite direction to the main wheel to keep level. Each has an entry door at the rear of the capsule.

Compression/ tension base
The former supports the A-frame structure while the latter acts as the foundation for the back-stay cables.

Back-stay cables
Four of these cables anchor and stabilise the A-frame to its concrete base.

The structure of the Eye

Rim
The rim of the Eye is constructed from hundreds of steel tubes welded together in triangular sections.

Boarding platform
Gates ensure that passengers board the rotating wheel in an orderly fashion.

Restraint towers
Two towers guide the rim as it nears the platform, and carry hydraulic restraint guides to halt it in high winds.

Pier and collision protection boom
These are designed to protect the wheel from any river vessels that might accidentally hit the structure.

A-frame legs
These support the 1,200-ton structure. They stand at an angle of 65° and are 58m (190ft) high and 20m (66ft) apart at the base.

© Marks Barfield Architects

Passenger capsules

1. Circular rings are attached to the outside rim of the wheel.

2. The rings each contain a circular-toothed rail.

3. An underfloor motor drives the toothed rail to keep the capsule level as it rotates.

4. The 32 panels of glass on each aerodynamically shaped capsule consist of two sheets of 6mm (0.24 in) glass that sandwich a layer of high-strength clear plastic.

5. The capsules contain their own temperature and air-conditioning systems.

6. Each capsule is fitted with camera and radio links to the ground.

Rotation of the Eye

Capsules
The toothed wheel of the drive motor engages with the circular rails that surround the capsule, rotating 360°.

Main wheel
The wheel rotates round the hub, which consists of two rings of roller bearings with a lifespan of some 200,000 hours.

Driving the rim
Four sets of drive units consist of four lorry tyres. They grip either side of the flat running beam that runs along both sides of the rim.

How to stay under the radar

The statistics...

Sea Shadow

Manufacturer:	Lockheed
Length:	50 metres
Displacement:	572 tons
Top speed:	28 knots
Crew:	10
Decommissioned:	2006

Crew space
With room for only 12 bunks, a microwave, fridge and table, Sea Shadow was clearly not built for comfort.

Stealth technology

From the B-2 to Batman, the look and feel of modern warfare has been visibly changed by stealth technology

Stealth technology refers to a range of different industries in pursuit of one goal: that of making objects less visible. For hundreds of years, visible referred to the purely optical. However, after WWII proved radar's effectiveness at detecting faster-moving assaults, it was clear something had to be done about it. At a stroke, stealth came to include all forms of visibility, from sonic to infrared and of course radar.

Radar cross section (RCS) is a measurement of how detectable an object is to radar: the higher the RCS, the more visible it is. RCS can be reduced in many ways, from designing less prominent shapes to inventing less pervious materials or simply coating the object in reflective paint.

Altering the shape of a craft to minimise RCS involves examining every single part of it – from the wings and tail that protrude the furthest, to every bump on its surface or accessory that might generate a radar signature. The first aircraft to benefit from this approach was the U-2 spy plane, which proved highly effective at evading Soviet detection during the early Cold War. A string of stealth aircraft followed, from the Lockheed Martin F-117 to today's fourth-generation jet fighters like the F-22 Raptor.

However, RCS – for all its merits – is only a measurement of static visibility. As a craft moves, it constantly displays different angles and surfaces. For this reason, shape shifting is not the only focus of stealth technology.

MOST ANTICIPATED

1. Zumwalt-class Destroyers
The US Navy's next stealth class (due in 2013) will take the place of a battleship with optional railgun (as soon as someone builds one!)

© US Navy

MOST DELAYED

2. HMS Helsingborg
Sweden's much-heralded stealth ship took 14 years to show up and still lacked some key features when launched in 2009.

MOST INFLUENTIAL

3. FS Surcouf
The French navy's La Fayette frigate class set the stealth boat standard of clean superstructures, neat angled sides and radar-absorbent materials.

© Frank Dubey

DID YOU KNOW? Radar-absorbing materials are substances that can be added to existing objects to make them less visible

Radar-absorbing materials (RAM) can be added to an existing object to make it less visible. Compared to the vast costs of engineering new shapes or materials, RAMs can make a significant difference for relatively little money, which is why all stealth vehicles now make use of them.

The cheapest and most widely available RAM is iron ball paint, a coating of tiny iron or ferrite-coated spheres that converts radar energy into heat that can be naturally dissipated by the object being concealed. After coverings, there are linings such as foam absorbers, which are used to line any enclosure that needs to be insulated from electromagnetic radiation. Made from layers of carbon-injected foam, absorbers can be cut to virtually any thickness or size, making them cost effective, but not particularly portable.

Finally, there are custom-built casings and coverings such as Salisbury screens – a three-level design consisting of a metallic ground plane, a precisely engineered electrical insulator and a thin, glossy screen. Salisbury screens and their bigger offspring Jaumann absorbers work by splitting the radar wave into parts, which are then either diffused or cancelled out by other reflections of the original wave. Such customised casings are highly technical, expensive and inflexible in the field – one reason why this level of stealth protection is beyond the means of all but the most valuable of consignments. ✿

How not to be seen
Before stealth there was camouflage – but only just

Camouflage was a relatively recent addition to human conflict, developed as late as the Boer War (1899-1902). The need for soldiers to remain unseen resulted in a variety of materials, colourings and styles being developed to help them blend into various terrains, the most famous being the 'ghillie suit' (modelled on the right). As snipers came to be used as spotters for artillery or laser-guided strikes, most recently in the Gulf Wars, the camouflage upon which they rely is more important today than ever before.

Colour me invisible
Ghillie suits are usually khaki or grey but they can be coloured to match any terrain: jungle, desert or arctic conditions.

All stand together
Ghillie suits are worn by snipers and their spotters to avoid detection while moving, stationary and lining up the shot.

Stick-men
Camouflage relies on colour and texture. It may feature mud, twigs or leaves from terrain that the sniper customises himself.

Spots or stripes
When not hand-made by the sniper, ghillie suits come in several pieces, which are glued or stitched to a standard uniform.

Lonely at the top
Despite its futuristic styling, the US Navy has been trying to donate Sea Shadow to a maritime museum since 2006...without success.

Hang on a moment...
If you think you've seen Sea Shadow before, it was the inspiration for the stealth ship in the Bond film *Tomorrow Never Dies*.

SWATH hull
Sea Shadow is built around two submerged twin hulls, each with their own propeller, stabiliser and hydrofoil.

Under connections
Two struts connect the hull to the raised section of the ship. This gives stability in waves of up to six metres.

Sea Shadow IX-529
Never fully commissioned by the US Navy, Sea Shadow was a working concept of how future stealth ships should be built

Active camouflage
Some animals can change their colour, so why can't we?

Active camouflage works by mimicking the background terrain, not approximately (as a ghillie suit would) but precisely, including changes that occur to the background itself – for instance, day becoming night. There are many ways of approaching this, most have relied on the way the object is lit or the way it reflects light back. Recent advances in organic light emitting diodes (OLEDs) promise to allow virtually any image to be projected onto virtually any surface. This would revolutionise active camouflage, but we are at least several years from a functioning adaptive 'stealth suit'.

"Can you see me now?"

"Nothing has matched the F-22's speed, blistering firepower and state-of-the-art stealth technology"

How to stay under the radar

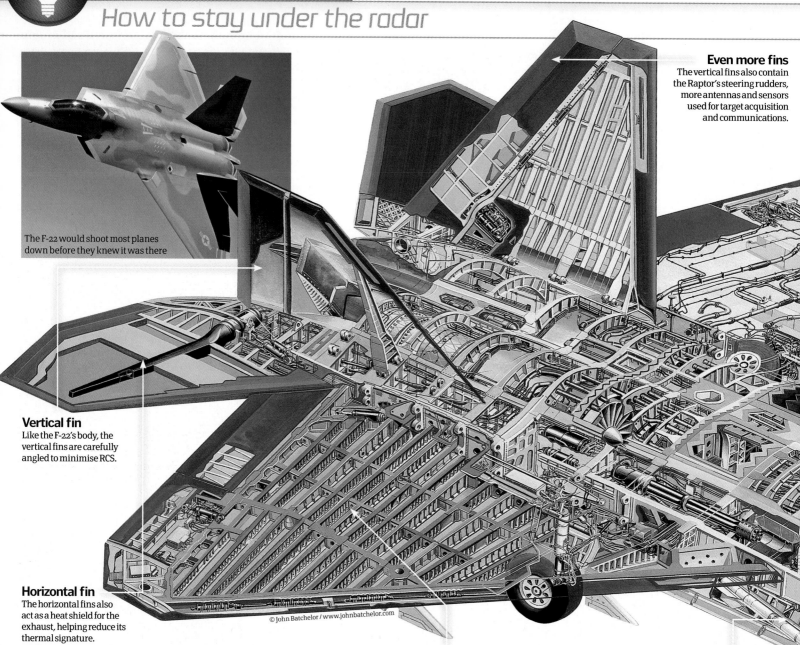

The F-22 would shoot most planes down before they knew it was there

Even more fins
The vertical fins also contain the Raptor's steering rudders, more antennas and sensors used for target acquisition and communications.

Vertical fin
Like the F-22's body, the vertical fins are carefully angled to minimise RCS.

Horizontal fin
The horizontal fins also act as a heat shield for the exhaust, helping reduce its thermal signature.

© John Batchelor / www.johnbatchelor.com

Wings
The titanium and composite wings feature large edge flaps that make the F-22 capable of extreme angles of attack of over 60 per cent.

Sidewinder missiles
Launch bays must be concealed for stealth. Sidewinder missiles, for instance, are ejected from beneath the wings.

F-22 Raptor

This United States Air Force jet is still shrouded in secrecy and remains the most state-of-the-art stealth plane in the sky

Stealth planes have been around since the Fifties, but nothing has matched the F-22's combination of speed, blistering firepower and state-of-the-art stealth technology.

Unveiled in 1997, the F-22 has many technical and design secrets still protected by a US export ban. However, we do know that every bit of the technology it contains has been either designed or tested for stealth. From the concealed surface-to-air missiles to the revolutionary Signature Assessment System that

warns the pilot when the plane's radar signature has changed through wear or combat, the F-22 is king. It may not have the lowest RCS in the skies, but when combined with its powerful M61A2 Vulcan Gatling gun, AIM-120 and Sidewinder missiles and multiple bomb payload, it's hard to envisage much else standing up to it. Neither is the Raptor's stealth capability all about radar, having been designed with five types of visibility in mind – including infrared, acoustic, and radio.

And if you're thinking all this can't come cheap, you'd be right. In 2006 the cost of the F-22 was estimated to be $361 million per aircraft, its $65 billion programme cost making it one of the most expensive aircraft ever produced. Hardly surprising, then, that in more budget-conscious times, the Raptor's shock-and-awe capability was deemed out of kilter with the more modest threats America now faces. As a result, it is due to be replaced in 2014 by the smaller, cheaper F-35 Lightning II.

The F-35 Lightning II will replace the F-22 when it completes its testing phase

DEADLIEST

1. B-2 bomber
By no means the quickest, the B-2 could still drop 80 500lb guided bombs or 16 B83 nuclear bombs in a single pass, probably before anyone realised it was there.

MOST VERSATILE

2. F-35 Lightning
The F-35 is being lined up to replace the super-expensive Raptor, thanks to its lower cost and versatility, including both vertical and horizontal take-off models.

FASTEST

3. Sukhoi PAK FA
Still under development, will the Soviet PAK FA's top speed of Mach 2.1 finally take the F-22's 'ultimate stealth fighter' crown to Russia? Only time, and cash, will tell.

DID YOU KNOW? The true cost of the F-22 is estimated to be $361 million per plane

Every bit of technology the F-22 contains has been designed for stealth

Take the strain
Structural loads are absorbed by five titanium bulkheads running through the F-22's middle adding to the plane's significant weight.

Antennas
For maximum sleekness, even antennae have to be concealed in the F-22's wing and tail sections.

Air intake
The distinctive air intakes channel air up and around the engines. Extra intakes concealed inside can be opened when speed is needed.

Head up display
The F-22's HUD is the pilot's main flight instrument. Built by GEC, it's one of the highest-tech black and white displays in existence.

Active Array Radar
The AN/APG 77 radar changes frequency more than 100 times per second to minimise interception.

Aircraft shape
Altering the shape of an aircraft is still the most effective means of outsmarting radar

Normal planes
Radar works by transmitting radio waves outwards – any reflected energy that bounces can be used to calculate the radar cross section (RCS) of the object that made it. Stealth planes are shaped so as to allow radar signals to be reflected away or absorbed by the fuselage, giving the illusion that no object is there.

Stealth planes
However, every time an object moves, a different facet becomes visible to radar. This explains why stealth planes are so angular in parts (the nose, wings and tail) yet ultra-smooth everywhere else. Basically, anything that interferes with RCS – including weapons systems, engines and antennae – must be concealed or camouflaged.

The Active Array Radar is key to avoiding detection

A US export ban still protects many of the F-22's technical and design secrets

© US Air Force

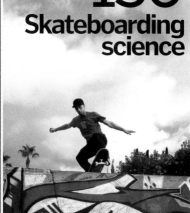

categories explained
Biology Chemistry Physics General

HOW IT WORKS
SCIENCE

130
Evaporation
vs steam

130
Skateboarding
science

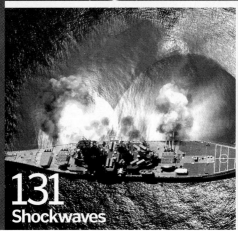

131
Shockwaves

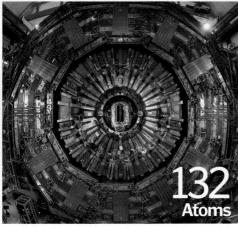

132
Atoms

THE WAR AGAINST KILLER GERMS

They might be a hundred times smaller than the tip of a needle, but evolution has endowed these microorganisms with killer skills

BACTERIA PROTOZOA FUNGI VIRUSES

By the end of his impressive and accomplished life, the industrialist/aviator/filmmaker Howard Hughes was undone by a paralysing fear of germs. He saw them everywhere: microscopic swarms of bacteria, parasites and viruses on every surface, infecting his body with untold horrors. To his credit, Hughes wasn't completely nuts. A close look at even the healthiest patch of human skin would reveal a rich diversity of microbial life, including some bugs with the potential to do great physical harm.

A microbe is any single-celled organism, whether plant, animal, fungus or bacterium. Viruses are usually considered microbes, even though they aren't cells themselves, but rather bundles of RNA that invade and hijack healthy cells. Microbes are literally everywhere. Your body is home and host to hundreds of trillions of microbes, inside and out. Your intestinal tract alone holds 100 trillion bacteria, far outnumbering every tissue, blood and bone cell in your entire body. Microbes thrive in warm, moist conditions, but are some of the only life forms that can survive in the planet's most extreme places, like the glaciers of Antarctica or the red-hot plume of an underwater volcano. Scientists divide microbes into four broad categories: bacteria, protozoa, fungi and viruses. If a microbe has the ability to make us sick (pathogenic), like some bacteria and most viruses and protozoa, we call it a germ.

Of those hundreds of trillions of microbes living on or inside your body, a significant percentage of them are germs. The good news is that germs typically exist in small enough quantities that the immune system can neutralise them before they cause disease. Sometimes, however, germ colonies breach our defences and flourish.

The definition of disease is when cells in your body stop functioning properly. One of the many causes of disease is infection, when a germ enters the body (through the digestive, respiratory or circulatory systems), multiplies rapidly and begins to inhibit normal cell function. Some protozoa like the malaria parasite colonise red blood cells and rupture them, leading to severe anaemia, while some bacteria like

5 TOP FACTS
USES OF GERMS

Food and drink
1 Fermentation is the process by which yeast/bacteria convert sugars and carbohydrates to alcohol and CO_2. Without these germs, we'd never have bread, beer, wine, cheese or vinegar.

Medicine
2 The most famous fungus in history is penicillium notatum, the first antibiotic. Penicillin isolated from the fungus prevents bacteria from forming new cell walls.

Renewable fuel
3 A start-up in California has engineered bacteria to ferment renewable feedstock (grains, grasses, etc) into diesel fuel. Ethanol is chemically similar to alcohol.

Sewage treatment
4 Water hyacinths have the uncanny ability to soak up raw sewage. Bacteria live on their roots, breaking down organic matter into nutrients the plants can use.

Warfare
5 In 500 BCE, archers would dip arrowheads in a putrid mix of dung, snake venom, human blood and decomposing flesh to poison the enemy with a potent microbial mix.

DID YOU KNOW? Bacteria and other prokaryotic cells make up 90 per cent of the total combined weight of all ocean life

Toothbrush
Is your toothbrush located less than two metres from your toilet bowl? According to research by Charles Gerba, the microbiologist synonymous with bathroom germ hunting, a flushing toilet sends an aerosol cloud of pathogenic bacteria into the air, landing and remaining on surrounding surfaces, including your befouled brush.

Bar nuts
The *London Evening Standard* randomly tested bar snacks from six London bars and restaurants, and found varying levels of bacterial contamination by familiar culprits like enterobacteria (from faecal matter), E coli and coliform bacteria. The more the bowl of snacks had been picked over, the more tainted its contents.

The filthiest of the filthy…
Take a look at which everyday items are covered with the most bacteria… you might be a bit surprised by the results

Human skin
Bacteria are the predominant microbes on your skin, numbering in the order of one trillion. According to the Human Microbiome Project, which is genetically coding all microbes on the human body, your skin is home to 100 different species of bacteria, 19 of them in that nasty spot behind your ear.

Bank note
Dirty money, indeed. According to several recent studies, paper money is home to a wide variety of microbes, including traces of pathogenic bacteria like E coli, staphylococcus aureus and salmonella. But before you boil all of your cash, note that microbial levels on money aren't that different to those on human skin.

Toilet seat
For most of us, toilet seats are the gold standard of filthiness. We would sooner drink week-old expired milk than touch a public toilet with our bare hands (feet are very effective). However, according to the experts, not only is a toilet seat the cleanest item in a public bathroom (the floor is the worst), but it also carries fewer bacteria per inch than your computer keyboard or your mobile phone.

Mobile phone handset
Give that iPhone a wipe. According to a number of high-profile experiments, mobile phones carry more pathogens than public toilet seats. It turns out that the buzzing warmth of handheld gadgets is the perfect breeding ground for germs on your hands, face and in your mouth – even the truly gnarly ones.

© Science Photo Library

"Some bacteria like E coli emit toxins that destroy cells along the intestinal or urinary tracts"

E coli emit toxins that destroy cells along the intestinal or urinary tracts. Some of the most common symptoms of disease – fever, vomiting, sneezing, coughing and diarrhoea – are not directly caused by the microbes themselves. It's just your immune system trying to fight off the infection by killing or physically expelling the little beasties.

Of course, not all microbes are bad. Life itself began four billion years ago as a form of bacteria, and it was an ancient type of cyanobacteria that was the first to perform the magic act of photosynthesis, turning sunlight into oxygen. Even today, microbes are the miniature factories that regulate and recycle the essential building blocks of life. When an organism dies, its carbon is salvaged and recycled into the environment by a host of microbes, including bacteria and fungi. Bacteria in the soil 'fix' nitrogen from the air and make it available to plants. Phytoplankton, composed of both protozoa and cyanobacteria, transform CO_2 into solid, reusable carbon compounds. And bacteria in our intestines, notably lactobacillus acidophilus, help us better digest and extract nutrients from food.

Unfortunately, the few seriously nasty microbes give the rest a bad name. Infectious disease caused by microbial infections kills more people worldwide than any other single cause. Just think of the diseases that can trace their roots to a viral, protozoan or bacterial infection: HIV, TB, malaria, pneumonia, sleeping sickness and historical pandemics like the bubonic plague, Spanish flu and smallpox. The discovery of antibiotics (penicillin itself was derived from a fungus) has saved countless lives, but overuse of them has resulted in even more virulent and drug-resistant strains of bacteria, including so-called 'superbugs' that spread in hospital settings and target the critically ill and the elderly.

Microbial infections are a rightful cause for concern, but let's not get all Howard Hughes about it. The best protection is to keep your hands clean with soap and water and to keep your hands away from your face. Get all of your vaccinations and vaccinate your children (a surprising number of adults die from chicken pox every year, usually contracted by their unvaccinated child). Take these simple everyday precautions and your well-evolved immune system should take care of the rest. ✿

"Sometimes germ colonies breach our defences and flourish"

Types of germs

Some germs act like miniature predators or parasites, while the rest just divide and conquer

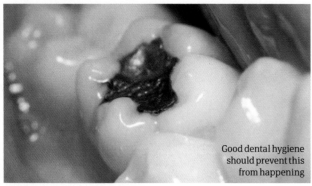

Good dental hygiene should prevent this from happening

Bacteria

Bacteria are some of the smallest and oldest life on Earth. Fossil evidence of these single-cell organisms dates back 3.5 billion years and may represent some of the first life on the planet. Bacteria live everywhere and can thrive in the most extreme cold and heat, but they love the warm comfort of the human body. Only one per cent of known bacteria are harmful to humans, but we know a few of them too well: strep throat, E coli, botulism, the list goes on. Good bacteria help plants and animals extract nutrients from food and soil. Bacteria cells have no walled-off nucleus, just a nucleoid with a single chromosome containing a closed circular strand of DNA.

EXAMPLE: Tooth cavities
This isn't an old wives' tale. Strains of bacteria in the mouth, such as lactobacillus acidophilus, feed on sugars and release lactic acid. If you don't clean your teeth regularly, the acid will eat away at the minerals in the surface, forming an infected hole called a cavity.

Structure of bacteria

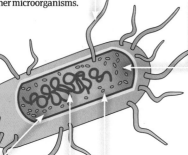

Flagella
One or more whip-like flagella propel the bacterium through its environment.

Fibrae and pili
These protein tubes extend from the body of the cell to help it attach to surfaces and interact with other microorganisms.

Cytoplasm
The contents of the cell float in cytoplasm, a gel composed of water, salts and organic molecules.

Storage granules
Prokaryotic cells don't contain membrane-bound organelles, but granules hold nutrients for later use.

Nucleoid
Lacking the membrane of a true nucleus, this is a bundle made from a supercoiled strand of circular DNA.

Ribosomes
Ribosomes are protein factories of prokaryotic bacteria cells, the same function as served in eukaryotic cells.

Fungi

Biologists have only identified 100,000 species of fungi out of what could be millions in existence. Most fungi exist as microscopic networks of cells, but their colonies can grow so large that we can see them with the naked eye: on the surface of spoiling food, rotting logs, or as the large fruiting bodies we call mushrooms. Fungal cells grow in elongated tubes called 'hyphae' that branch off and interconnect. Humans have learned to use fungi to ferment beverages and foods (yeast) and create life-saving drugs (penicillin), but some fungi can cause rashes (athlete's foot, jock itch, yeast infections), allergies and chronic lung diseases.

EXAMPLE: Fungal infection
The fungus known as 'tinea' thrives in the warm and wet confines of human skin. If left unchecked, colonies will grow rapidly, causing irritation and inflammation of the skin underneath. Tinea pedis is the fungus that loves the space between your toes, causing itching, dryness and cracking.

Structure of a yeast cell

Yeast bud
Species of yeast such as saccharomyces cerevisiae (beer, wine and bread), reproduce by asexual budding.

Septin ring
This tight ring of proteins forms during cytokinesis, when the cytoplasm of the mother yeast cell divides.

Microtubule
Beaded filaments of protein that direct movement of organelles and cell growth and budding.

Fimbriae
The tiny 'hairs' on the surface of a yeast cell don't allow it to move. Instead, fungi grow, reproduce and spread.

©SPL

Nucleus
A yeast cell is eukaryotic – its nucleus and organelles are bound by a cell membrane and its DNA is tightly packed within the nucleolus. Some fungi have multiple nuclei.

Mitochondrian
The mitochondria are the powerhouse of the yeast cell, converting nutrients into energy to fuel the cell's growth and reproduction.

Protozoa

Protozoa are the world's smallest animals. Amoebas are the most famous protozoa, shape-shifting blobs that engulf their prey (bacteria, microfungi) and digest them in stomach-like sacks called 'vacuoles'. Most protozoa are parasites or predators, including the infamous plasmodium falciparum, which causes malaria.

EXAMPLE: Amoebic dysentery
In the case of amoebic dysentery, a person ingests a mature cyst of the protozoan parasite entamoeba histolytica, usually from food or water contaminated within fecal matter. Once the cyst reaches the intestinal tract, it releases trophozoites, active amoeba that burrow into the intestinal lining, causing violent diarrhoea and sometimes even death.

Malaria infection cycle

1. Blood meal
An infected female anopheles mosquito feasts on human blood. She releases sporozoites – immature malaria parasites in her saliva – into the blood stream.

2. Liver infection
The sporozoites, a type of parasitic protozoa, travel through the blood stream to the liver, where they infect cells.

3. Reproduction
Through asexual reproduction, the malaria protozoa split in two, forming haploid versions called merozoites.

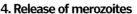

4. Release of merozoites
Eventually, the sheer volume of merozoite infection in the liver cells causes them to burst, sending forth a flood of parasites into the bloodstream.

CONTAGIOUS

1. Tuberculosis
The leading killer of women worldwide, the mycobacterium tuberculosis bacteria is estimated to infect a new person every second.

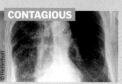

MORE CONTAGIOUS

2. Black Death
In the mid-14th Century, the Black Death – caused by either the bubonic plague bacteria or a virus – killed between 75 and 200 million people worldwide.

MOST CONTAGIOUS

3. Spanish Flu
The 1918 global flu pandemic killed 40 million people. Shockingly, otherwise healthy people could die within hours of the first symptoms.

DID YOU KNOW? *Through carbon fixation, plankton (protozoa) and cyanobacteria produce half of the planet's available carbon*

Viruses

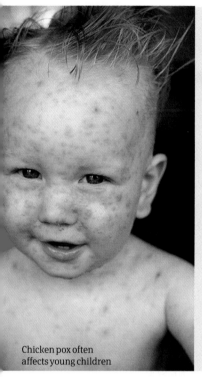

Viruses are the smallest germs of all. In fact, they aren't even cells – just molecules of genetic material (DNA or RNA), which are coated in a protective shell of protein. They come in all different shapes (rods, spheres, multi-sided, even little 'tadpoles') and, unlike other microbes, are almost always bad for you. Viruses target individual types of cells, attaching to landing sites on the cell surface. The virus then injects molecules of DNA or RNA into the cell, which directs the cell to produce even more virus particles before destroying itself. Diseases spread by viruses range from the common cold to smallpox, hepatitis, polio, ebola and HIV.

EXAMPLE: Chicken pox

Chicken pox is caused by the varicella zoster virus, a highly virulent germ (infection rates are as high as 90 per cent) that first attacks the cells at the back of the nasal passages before spreading through the blood stream to nerve and other tissue. In most healthy children, the body's immune system fights off the virus, often causing fevers and body aches in addition to the trademark itchy pox. However, the varicella virus can lie dormant in nerve cells, emerging later in life as shingles, chicken pox's more painful cousin.

Chicken pox often affects young children

Structure of the influenza virus

© SPL

Lipid envelope
When the influenza virion is enveloped by the host cell, the virus particle derives a second protective layer from the host's plasma membrane.

Capsid
In all viruses, the genetic material is surrounded by a protective protein shell called a capsid.

Nucleoprotein
The entire structure of the flu virus is essentially an RNA delivery system. At the heart of the virion (virus particle) are seven or eight pieces of single-stranded RNA.

Hemagglutinin
The surface of the virion is covered with glycoprotein spikes, 80 per cent of which are hemagglutinin, which helps the virus attach to cell walls.

Neuraminidase
These glycoprotein spikes facilitate the release of newly formed virus particles from the host cell. New antiviral drugs block the function of neuraminidase, slowing the spread of the virus.

---

8. Infection of the mosquito
Within the body of the mosquito, the gametes form zygotes, which develop into oocysts to produce more sporozoites, which migrate to the mosquito's salivary glands to begin the cycle all over again.

7. Gametocyte formation
Some of the merozoites evolve into gametocytes, which are cells that can produce male and female gametes.

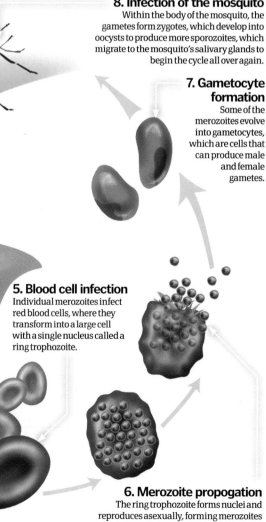

5. Blood cell infection
Individual merozoites infect red blood cells, where they transform into a large cell with a single nucleus called a ring trophozoite.

6. Merozoite propagation
The ring trophozoite forms nuclei and reproduces asexually, forming merozoites and causing the first symptoms of malaria.

Natural defences

The human body acts as the best line of defence against viruses and germs

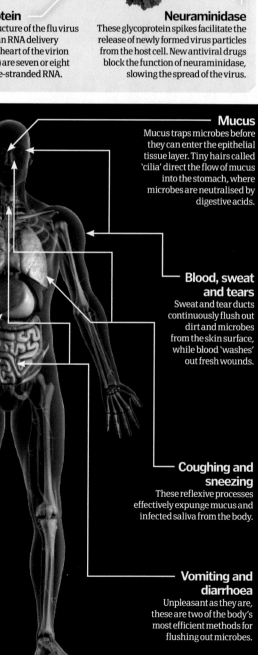

Skin
Not only is the skin a physical barrier to invading germs, but it even secretes toxic lipids that kill microbes.

White blood cells
Once a T-cell or B-cell has met an antigen, it never forgets how to respond, building up our immunity to an increasing variety of microbes.

'Good' bacteria
Your body is bathed in bacteria, inside and out, many of which help to keep the bad guys in check by physically or chemically inhibiting the spread of pathogens.

Mucus
Mucus traps microbes before they can enter the epithelial tissue layer. Tiny hairs called 'cilia' direct the flow of mucus into the stomach, where microbes are neutralised by digestive acids.

Blood, sweat and tears
Sweat and tear ducts continuously flush out dirt and microbes from the skin surface, while blood 'washes' out fresh wounds.

Coughing and sneezing
These reflexive processes effectively expunge mucus and infected saliva from the body.

Vomiting and diarrhoea
Unpleasant as they are, these are two of the body's most efficient methods for flushing out microbes.

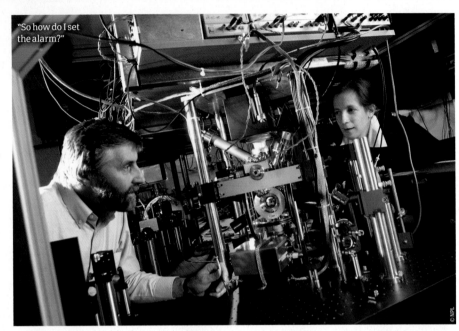

"So how do I set the alarm?"

© NPL

Atomic clocks

You'll never be a nanosecond late again

To make precise calculations of time, an atomic clock measures the number of oscillations between an electron and the nucleus in an atom.

An electron can jump to another shell within an atom if it gains or loses a specific amount of energy. This transition – known as a quantum jump – releases or absorbs the energy in the form of measurable electromagnetic radiation.

The frequency of these transitions allows an atomic clock to keep an accurate reading of time. Modern-day atomic clocks rely on the caesium atom, which is known to have 9,192,631,770 transitions per second.

In early atomic clocks, magnets were used to control the oscillation of specific atoms inside a beam tube. Now, lasers are used to collect and oscillate millions of atoms within a magnetic field. These atoms are pushed up and down in a fountain to detect their energy changes and take an accurate reading of time. ✿

 Learn more

The National Physical Laboratory **www.npl.co.uk** is the UK's National Measurement Institute. Visit the website to learn more about precise weights and measurements.

Vertical
Two lasers throw the ball a metre high and gravity brings it back down.

Probe laser
The atoms are now emitting their optimal energy at the natural resonant frequency of a caesium atom.

Microwave cavity
Microwave signals are tuned to varying frequencies until the atoms are releasing their maximum energy.

Lasers
Six lasers push a gas of caesium atoms into a ball, cooling them to a temperature near absolute zero.

Detector
The frequency of the caesium atom is kept constant and used to define the second.

Calories

We eat them and burn them, but what are they?

A calorie is a unit of potential energy equivalent to 4.184 joules. It is defined as being the amount of energy needed to increase the temperature of one gram of water by 1°C.

In many areas, such as the labelling of food products and fitness machines, kilocalories (4,184 joules) are used in place of calories. When a calorie is burned, energy is released in a process known as complete combustion. In the human body, the organs function by using this energy.

Calories are a necessity for the human body, with the average adult requiring more than 2,000 kilocalories to actively function per day.

The intake of energy through food and drink is balanced against the energy used by the body. Excess calories which are not used are stored as fat for use at a later time. Consuming more calories than you burn will lead to weight gain. ✿

5 TOP FACTS
BURNING CALORIES

1 Shopping
On average, an hour of shopping will burn 200 kilocalories.

2 Filing
Up to 170 kilocalories can be burned an hour by filing while sitting.

3 Eating
Although consuming calories, the body will also use about 130 kilocalories per hour when sitting and eating.

4 On the phone
Getting angry or excited while talking on the phone can burn up to 120 kilocalories an hour.

5 Gum
Chewing sugarless gum burns up to an additional 11 kilocalories an hour as the jaw is continuously moved.

A beefburger with all the trimmings can contain up to 400 kilocalories

High calorie foods can affect your weight

Head to Head
FATHERS OF MOTION

GREAT-GRANDFATHER | **1. Aristotle**
Around 330 BC, Aristotle correctly asserted that all Earth objects would only continue to move while they are being acted upon by a force.

GRANDFATHER | **2. Galileo Galilei**
Unprecedented work on the motion of objects and gravity in the early-17th Century were just some of Galileo's numerous ground-breaking achievements.

FATHER | **3. Sir Isaac Newton**
Newton's laws of motion coming decades after G work, provided the basis our understanding of kir energy and momentum.

DID YOU KNOW? Kinetic energy is measured in joules and momentum in newtons, the latter being a unit of force

Kinetic energy and momentum

We go through the forces and motions with these fundamentals of physics

A collision like this will give both cars a new amount of momentum

Any object that is said to have motion has kinetic energy, which is defined as half the mass of an object multiplied by its velocity squared. It quantifies the work that the object could do as a result of its motion. Rolling a bowling ball, driving a car, or a glass falling from a table are all examples of kinetic energy at work, with each possessing a specific amount at any given point. The faster or more massive a body is, the more kinetic energy it will subsequently have. An object at rest is said to have potential energy, which is converted to kinetic energy when it actually begins to move. The kinetic energy can then be converted into other forms such as thermal or sound energy when it is acted on by another force, colliding with another object or accelerating for example.

As an object accelerates it gathers momentum, which is defined as mass x velocity. The driver of a moving car must apply brakes to stop the car as it has gained momentum and will continue to move forwards unless it is acted on by another force such as friction or contact with another body. Like kinetic energy, the greater the mass or velocity of an object, the greater its momentum. A force acting on a moving object will change its momentum, such as when two cars collide; the result of the collision will see each object with a new amount of momentum, which will depend on their initial mass and velocity. ✿

4. Change in momentum
Although the mass of the bullet doesn't change, its velocity decreases as it passes through the pencils, lowering its momentum and kinetic energy.

6. External force
The pencils and debris continue to move with their gained momentum until they are acted upon by another force.

Object in motion
Both kinetic energy and momentum are the measure of the motion of a body. The former is the energy created when a force accelerates a mass, while momentum is the product of a body's mass and velocity.

1. ½mv²
As the bullet travels through the air, its kinetic energy is defined as half its mass times its velocity squared.

3. Mass and velocity
As the bullet makes its forward motion its momentum transfers to the material in the pencils.

2. Energy transfer
The kinetic energy of the bullet transfers to heat (friction) and sound energy as it passes through the pencils.

5. Conservation of energy
Energy can neither be created not destroyed, so the kinetic energy of the bullet must transform into other states.

7. Conservation of momentum
The total momentum must remain constant, so the debris and pencils gain momentum equal to that lost from the bullet.

Kinetic energy =

$$\text{Kinetic energy} = \frac{\text{mass of object} \times (\text{velocity of object})^2}{2}$$

Momentum =
mass of object x velocity of object

"Each day the kidneys will filter 150-180 litres of blood"

Kidney function

How do your kidneys filter waste from the blood to keep you alive?

Kidneys are bean-shaped organs situated halfway down the back just under the ribcage, one on each side of the body, and weigh between 115 and 170 grams each, dependent on the individual's sex and size. The left kidney is commonly a little larger than the right and due to the effectiveness of these organs, individuals born with only one kidney can survive with little or no adverse health problems. Indeed, the body can operate normally with a 30-40 per cent decline in kidney function. This decline in function would rarely even be noticeable and shows just how effective the kidneys are at filtering out waste products as well as maintaining mineral levels and blood pressure throughout the body. The kidneys manage to control all of this by working with other organs and glands across the body such as the hypothalamus, which helps the kidneys determine and control water levels in the body.

Each day the kidneys will filter between 150 and 180 litres of blood, but only pass around two litres of waste down the ureters to the bladder for excretion. This waste product is primarily urea – a by-product of protein being broken down for energy – and water, and it's more commonly known as 'urine'. The kidneys filter the blood by passing it through a small filtering unit called a nephron. Each kidney has around a million of these, which are made up of a number of small blood capillaries, called glomerulus, and a urine-collecting tube called the renal tubule. The glomerulus sift the normal cells and proteins from the blood and then move the waste products into the renal tubule, which transports urine down into the bladder through the ureters.

Alongside this filtering process, the kidneys also release three crucial hormones (known as erythropoietin, renin and calcitriol) which encourage red blood cell production, aid regulation of blood pressure and aid bone development and mineral balance respectively. ✿

Inside your kidney

As blood enters the kidneys, it is passed through a nephron, a tiny unit made up of blood capillaries and a waste-transporting tube. These work together to filter the blood, returning clean blood to the heart and lungs for re-oxygenation and recirculation and removing waste to the bladder for excretion.

Renal cortex
This is one of two broad internal sections of the kidney, the other being the renal medulla. The renal tubules are situated here in the protrusions that sit between the pyramids and secure the cortex and medulla together.

Renal artery
This artery supplies the kidney with blood that is to be filtered.

Renal vein
After waste has been removed, the clean blood is passed out of the kidney via the renal vein.

© DK Images

Ureter
The tube that transports the waste products (urine) to the bladder following blood filtration.

Renal pelvis
This funnel-like structure is how urine travels out of the kidney and forms the top part of the ureter, which takes urine down to the bladder.

Renal medulla
The kidney's inner section, where blood is filtered after passing through numerous arterioles. It's split into sections called pyramids and each human kidney will normally have seven of these.

Renal capsule
The kidney's fibrous outer edge, which provides protection for the kidney's internal fibres.

DID YOU KNOW?

Two for the price of one

We are thought to have two kidneys because they are so crucial to our survival, the second is purely a 'back up'. Having two organs obviously increases our chances of survival and reproductive fitness.

DID YOU KNOW? *Around 0.07% of the population are born with more than two kidneys*

Nephrons – the kidneys' filtration units

Nephrons are the units that filter all blood passing through the kidneys. There are around a million in each kidney, situated in the renal medulla's pyramid structures. As well as filtering waste, nephrons regulate water and mineral salt by recirculating what is needed and excreting the rest.

Proximal tubule
Links Bowman's capsule and the loop of Henle, and will selectively reabsorb minerals from the filtrate produced by Bowman's capsule.

Collecting duct system
Although not technically part of the nephron, this collects all waste product filtered by the nephrons and facilitates its removal from the kidneys.

Glomerulus
High pressure in the glomerulus, caused by it draining into an arteriole instead of a venule, forces fluids and soluble materials out of the capillary and into Bowman's capsule.

Bowman's capsule
Also known as the glomerular capsule, this filters the fluid that has been expelled from the glomerulus. Resulting filtrate is passed along the nephron and will eventually make up urine.

Distal convoluted tubule
Partly responsible for the regulation of minerals in the blood, linking to the collecting duct system. Unwanted minerals are excreted from the nephron.

Renal artery
This artery supplies the kidney with blood. The blood travels through this, into arterioles as you travel into the kidney, until the blood reaches the glomerulus.

Renal vein
This removes blood that has been filtered from the kidney.

Loop of Henle
The loop of Henle controls the mineral and water concentration levels within the kidney to aid filtration of fluids as necessary. It also controls urine concentration.

Renal tubule
Made up of three parts, the proximal tubule, the loop of Henle and the distal convoluted tubule. They remove waste and reabsorb minerals from the filtrate passed on from Bowman's capsule.

The glomerulus

This group of capillaries is the first step of filtration and a crucial aspect of a nephron. As blood enters the kidneys via the renal artery, it is passed down through a series of arterioles which eventually lead to the glomerulus. This is unusual, as instead of draining into a venule (which would lead back to a vein) it drains back into an arteriole, which creates much higher pressure than normally seen in capillaries, which in turn forces soluble materials and fluids out of the capillaries. This process is known as ultrafiltration and is the first step in filtration of the blood. These then pass through the Bowman's capsule (also know as the glomerular capsule) for further filtration.

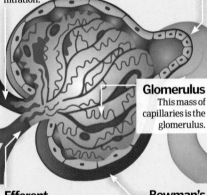

Afferent arteriole
This arteriole supplies the blood to the glomerulus for filtration.

Proximal tubule
Where reabsorption of minerals from the filtrate from Bowman's capsule will occur.

Glomerulus
This mass of capillaries is the glomerulus.

Efferent arteriole
This arteriole is how blood leaves the glomerulus following ultrafiltration.

Bowman's capsule
This is the surrounding capsule that will filter the filtrate produced by the glomerulus.

What is urine and what is it made of?

Urine is made up of a range of organic compounds such as proteins and hormones, inorganic salts and numerous metabolites. These by-products are often rich in nitrogen and need to be removed from the blood stream through urination. The pH-level of urine is typically around neutral (pH7) but varies depending on diet, hydration levels and physical fitness. The colour of urine is also determined by these factors, with dark-yellow urine indicating dehydration and greenish urine being indicative of excessive asparagus consumption.

94% water

6% other organic compounds

How your blood works

The science behind the miraculous fluid that feeds, heals and fights for your life

The heart pumps your blood around your cardiovascular system

Platelet
When activated, these sticky cell fragments are essential to the clotting process. Platelets adhere to a wound opening to stem the flow of blood, then they team with a protein called fibrinogen to weave tiny threads that trap blood cells.

Red blood cell
Known as erythrocytes, red blood cells are the body's delivery service, shuttling oxygen from the lungs to living cells throughout the body and returning carbon dioxide as waste.

Blood vessel wall
Arteries and veins are composed of three tissue layers, a combination of elastic tissue, connective tissue and smooth muscle fibres that contract under signals from the sympathetic nervous system.

Granulocyte
The most numerous type of white blood cell, granulocytes patrol the bloodstream destroying invading bacteria by engulfing and digesting them, often dying in the process.

FIRST CLUES

1. Discovery of veins and arteries
In 300 BC, Greek anatomist Herophilus of Chalcedon figured out that arteries and veins not only carry blood, but are distinct pathways.

FIRST SEMI-SUCCESS

2. First blood transfusion
After a century of animal-human blood transfusions, James Blundell performed the first recorded human-to-human transfusion in 1818.

MOST SIGNIFICANT

3. Discovery of blood types
In 1901, Austrian physician Karl Landsteiner was the first to identify three basic blood groups, revolutionising the success of blood transfusions.

DID YOU KNOW? If you took all of the blood vessels out of your body and laid them end to end, they would stretch for 160,000km

White blood cells
White blood cells, or leukocytes, are the immune system's best weapon, searching out and destroying bacteria and producing antibodies against viruses. There are five different types of white blood cells, all with distinct functions.

Monocyte
The largest type of white blood cell, monocytes are born in bone marrow, then circulate through the blood stream before maturing into macrophages, predatory immune system cells that live in organ tissue and bone.

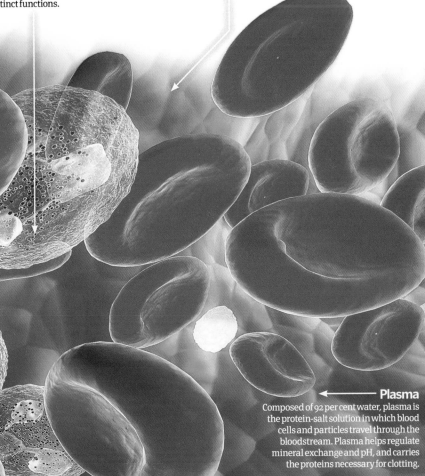

Plasma
Composed of 92 per cent water, plasma is the protein-salt solution in which blood cells and particles travel through the bloodstream. Plasma helps regulate mineral exchange and pH, and carries the proteins necessary for clotting.

Components of blood

Blood is a mix of solids and liquids, a blend of highly specialised cells and particles suspended in a protein-rich fluid called plasma. Red blood cells dominate the mix, carrying oxygen to living tissue and returning carbon dioxide to the lungs. For every 600 red blood cells there is a single white blood cell, of which there are five different kinds. Cell fragments called platelets use their irregular surface to cling to vessel walls and initiate the clotting process.

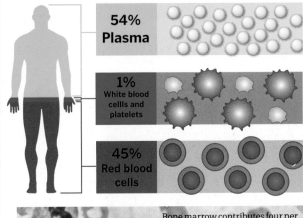

54% Plasma

1% White blood cells and platelets

45% Red blood cells

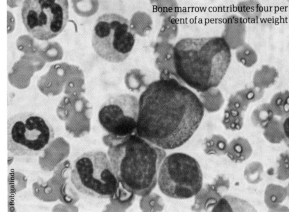

Bone marrow contributes four per cent of a person's total weight

©Bobjgalindo

"Red blood cells are so numerous because they perform the most essential function of blood"

Blood is the river of life. It feeds oxygen and essential nutrients to living cells and carries away waste. It transports the foot soldiers of the immune system, white blood cells, which seek out and destroy invading bacteria and parasites. And it speeds platelets to the site of injury or tissue damage, triggering the body's miraculous process of self-repair.

Blood looks like a thick, homogenous fluid, but it's more like a watery current of plasma – a straw-coloured, protein-rich fluid – carrying billions of microscopic solids consisting of red blood cells, white blood cells and cell fragments called platelets. The distribution is far from equal. Over half of blood is plasma, 45 per cent is red blood cells and a tiny fragment, less than one per cent, is composed of white blood cells and platelets.

Red blood cells are so numerous because they perform the most essential function of blood, which is to deliver oxygen to every cell in the body and carry away carbon dioxide. As an adult, all of your red blood cells are produced in red bone marrow, the spongy tissue in the bulbous ends of long bones and at the centre of flat bones like hips and ribs. In the marrow, red blood cells start out as undifferentiated stem cells called haemocytoblasts. If the body detects a minuscule drop in oxygen carrying capacity, a hormone is released from the kidneys that triggers the stem cells to become red blood cells. Because red blood cells only live 120 days, the supply must be continuously replenished; roughly 2 million red blood cells are born every second.

A mature red blood cell has no nucleus. The nucleus is spit out during the final stages of the cell's two-day development before taking on the shape of a concave, doughnut-like disc. Like all cells, red blood cells are mostly water, but 97 per cent of their solid matter is haemoglobin, a complex protein that carries four atoms of iron. Those iron atoms have ▶

"Platelets weave a mesh of fibrin that stems blood loss"

A look inside your blood

Waste product of blood cell

6. Reuse and recycle
As for the globin and other cellular membranes, everything is converted back into basic amino acids, some of which will be used to create more red blood cells.

1. Born in the bones
When the body detects a low oxygen carrying capacity, hormones released from the kidney trigger the production of new red blood cells inside red bone marrow.

2. One life to live
Mature red blood cells, also known as erythrocytes, are stripped of their nucleus in the final stages of development, meaning they can't divide to replicate.

Waste excreted from body

Life cycle of red blood cells

Every second, roughly 2 million red blood cells decay and die. The body is keenly sensitive to blood hypoxia – reduced oxygen carrying capacity – and triggers the kidney to release a hormone called erythropoietin. The hormone stimulates the production of more red blood cells in bone marrow. Red blood cells enter the bloodstream and circulate for 120 days before they begin to degenerate and are swallowed up by roving macrophages in the liver, spleen and lymph nodes. The macrophages extract iron from the haemoglobin in the red blood cells and release it back into the bloodstream, where it binds to a protein that carries it back to the bone marrow, ready to be recycled in fresh red blood cells.

5. Iron ions
In the belly of Kupffer cells, haemoglobin molecules are split into haem and globin. Haem is broken down further into bile and iron ions, some of which are carried back and stored in bone marrow.

4. Ingestion
Specialised white blood cells in the liver and spleen called Kupffer cells prey on dying red blood cells, ingesting them whole and breaking them down into reusable components.

3. In circulation
Red blood cells pass from the bone marrow into the bloodstream, where they circulate for around 120 days.

▶ the ability to form loose, reversible bonds with both oxygen and carbon dioxide – think of them as weak magnets – making red blood cells such an effective transport system for respiratory gases. The haemoglobin, which turns bright red when oxygenated, is what gives blood its characteristic colour.

To provide oxygen to every living cell, red blood cells must be pumped through the body's circulatory system. The right side of the heart pumps CO_2-heavy blood into the lungs, where it releases its waste gases and picks up oxygen. The left side of the heart then pumps the freshly oxygenated blood out into the body through a system of arteries and capillaries, some as narrow as a single cell. As the red blood

cells release their oxygen, they pick up carbon dioxide molecules, then course through the veins back toward the heart, where they are pumped back into the lungs to 'exhale' the excess CO_2 and collect some more precious O_2.

White blood cells are greatly outnumbered by red blood cells, but they are critical to the function of the immune system. Most white blood cells are also produced in red bone marrow, but white blood cells – unlike red blood cells – come in five different varieties, each with its own specialised immune function. The first three varieties, collectively called granulocytes, engulf and digest bacteria and parasites, and play a role in allergic reactions. Lymphocytes, another type of white blood cell, produce anti-bodies that

build up our immunity to repeat intruders. And monocytes, the largest of the white blood cells, enter organ tissue and become macrophages, microbes that ingest bad bacteria and help break down dead red blood cells into reusable parts.

Platelets aren't cells at all, but fragments of much larger stem cells found in bone marrow. In their resting state, they look like smooth oval plates, but when activated to form a clot they take on an irregular form with many protruding arms called pseudopods. This shape helps them stick to blood vessel walls and to each other, forming a physical barrier around wound sites. With the help of proteins and clotting factors found in plasma, platelets weave a mesh of fibrin that stems blood

loss and triggers the formation of new collagen and skin cells.

But even these three functions of blood – oxygen supplier, immune system defender and wound healer – only begin to scratch the surface of the critical role of blood in each and every bodily process. When blood circulates through the small intestine, it absorbs sugars from digested food, which are transported to the liver to be stored as energy. When blood passes through the kidneys, it is scrubbed of excess urea and salts, waste that will leave the body as urine. The proteins in plasma transport vitamins, hormones, enzymes, sugar and electrolytes. Pause for a second to listen to your pumping heart and be thankful for the river of life coursing through your veins. ✿

THE STATS
BLOOD

BLOOD PERCENTAGE OF BODY WEIGHT	7%	BLOOD PUMPED BY HEART PER DAY	7,000 litres
BLOOD IN HUMAN BODY	5 litres	RED BLOOD CELLS MADE EVERY SECOND	2 million

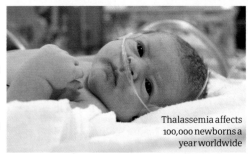

DID YOU KNOW? Until the 23rd week of foetal development, red blood cells are produced in the liver, not red bone marrow

Haemophilia

This rare genetic blood disorder severely inhibits the clotting mechanism of blood, causing excessive bleeding, internal bruising and joint problems. Platelets are essential to the clotting and healing process, producing threads of fibrin with help from proteins in the bloodstream called clotting factors. People who suffer from haemophilia – almost exclusively males – are missing one of those clotting factors, making it difficult to seal off blood vessels after even minor injuries.

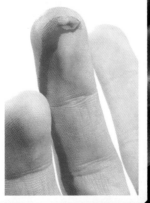

Thalassemia

Another rare blood disorder affecting 100,000 newborns worldwide each year, thalassemia inhibits the production of haemoglobin, leading to severe anaemia. People who are born with the most serious form of the disease, also called Cooley's anaemia, suffer from enlarged hearts, livers and spleens, and brittle bones. The most effective treatment is frequent blood transfusions, although a few lucky patients have been cured through bone marrow transplants from perfectly matching donors.

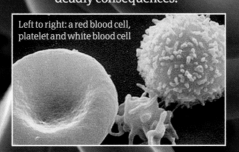

Thalassemia affects 100,000 newborns a year worldwide

Sickle cell anaemia

Anaemia is the name for any blood disorder that results in a dangerously low red blood cell count. In sickle cell anaemia, which afflicts one out of every 625 children of African descent, red blood cells elongate into a sickle shape after releasing their oxygen. The sickle-shaped cells die prematurely, leading to anaemia, or sometimes lodge in blood vessels, causing terrible pain and even organ damage. Interestingly, people who carry only one gene for sickle cell anaemia are immune to malaria.

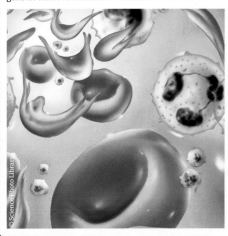

© Science Photo Library

Blood disorders

Blood is a delicate balancing act, with the body constantly regulating oxygen flow, iron content and clotting ability. Unfortunately, there are several genetic conditions and chronic illnesses that can disturb the balance, sometimes with deadly consequences.

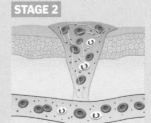

Left to right: a red blood cell, platelet and white blood cell

Haemochromatosis

One of the most common genetic blood disorders, haemochromatosis is the medical term for "iron overload," in which your body absorbs and stores too much iron from food. Severity varies wildly, and many people experience few symptoms, but others suffer serious liver damage or scarring (cirrhosis), irregular heartbeat, diabetes and even heart failure. Symptoms can be aggravated by taking too much vitamin C.

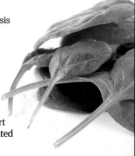

Deep vein thrombosis

Thrombosis is the medical term for any blood clot that is large enough to block a blood vessel. When a blood clot forms in the large, deep veins of the upper thigh, it's called deep vein thrombosis. If such a clot breaks free, it can circulate through the bloodstream, pass through the heart and become lodged in arteries in the lung, causing a pulmonary embolism. Such a blockage can severely damage portions of the lungs, and multiple embolisms can even be fatal.

Blood and healing

More than a one-trick pony, your blood is a vital cog in the healing process

Think of blood as the body's emergency response team to an injury. Platelets emit signals that encourage blood vessels to contract, stemming blood loss. The platelets then collect around the wound, reacting with a protein in plasma to form fibrin, a tissue that weaves into a mesh. Blood flow returns and white blood cells begin their hunt for bacteria. Fibroblasts create beds of fresh collagen and capillaries to fuel skin cell growth. The scab begins to contract, pulling the growing skin cells closer together until damaged tissue is replaced.

STAGE 1

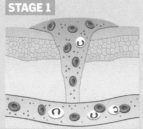

INJURY
When the skin surface is cut, torn or scraped deeply enough, blood seeps from broken blood vessels to fill the wound. To stem the flow of bleeding, the blood vessels around the wound constrict.

STAGE 2

HAEMOSTASIS
Activated platelets aggregate around the surface of the wound, stimulating vasoconstriction. Platelets react with a protein in plasma to form fibrin, a web-like mesh of stringy tissue.

STAGE 3

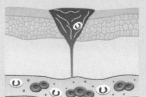

INFLAMMATORY STAGE
Once the wound is capped with a drying clot, blood vessels open up again, releasing plasma and white blood cells into the damaged tissue. Macrophages digest harmful bacteria and dead cells.

STAGE 4

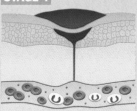

PROLIFERATIVE STAGE
Fibroblasts lay fresh layers of collagen inside the wound and capillaries begin to supply blood for the forming of new skin cells. Fibrin strands and collagen pull the sides of the wound together.

The biological structures that are so versatile they enable us to eat a varied diet

All about teeth

The trouble with teeth

Tooth decay, also often known as dental caries, affects the enamel and dentine of a tooth, breaking down tissue and creating fissures in the enamel. Two types of bacteria – namely Streptococcus mutans and Lactobacillus – are responsible for tooth decay.

Tooth decay occurs after repeated contact with acid-producing bacteria. Environmental factors also have a strong effect on dental health. Sucrose, fructose and glucose create large problems within the mouth, and diet can be an important factor in maintaining good oral health.

The mouth contains an enormous variety of bacteria, which collects around the teeth and gums. This is visible in the form of a sticky white substance called plaque. Plaque is known as a biofilm. After eating, the bacteria in the mouth metabolises sugar, which subsequently attacks the areas around the teeth.

Medication can also affect oral health, reducing the production of saliva, which offers natural protection and works against acidic matter. Various treatments can be applied to teeth that are damaged or decayed, these include extraction, filling or the replacement of teeth in the form of either dentures and implants.

The primary function of teeth is to crunch and chew food. For this reason, teeth are made of strong substances – namely calcium, phosphorus and various mineral salts. The main structure of the tooth is dentine, this itself is enclosed in a shiny substance called enamel. This strong white coating is the hardest material found in the human body.

Humans have different types of teeth that function in various ways. Incisors tear at food, such as the residue found on bones, while bicuspids have long sharp structures that are also used for ripping. Bicuspids tear and crush while molars, which have a flatter surface, grind the food before swallowing. This aids digestion. Because humans have a varied array of teeth (called collective dentition) we are able to eat a complex diet of both meat and vegetables. Other species, such as grazing animals, have specific types of teeth. Cows, for example, have large flat teeth, which restricts them to a simple diet.

Teeth have many functions, in some cases they aid hunting but they also have strong psychological connotations. Both animals and humans bare their teeth when faced with an aggressive situation. Teeth are the most enduring features of the human body. Mammals are described as diphyodont, which means they develop two sets of teeth. In humans

the teeth first appear at six months old and are replaced by secondary teeth after six or seven years. Some animals develop only one set of teeth, while sharks, for instance, grow a new set of teeth every two weeks.

With humans, tooth loss can occur through accident, gum disease or old age.

From ancient times healers have sought to treat and replace the teeth with false ones. Examples of this practice can be seen from ancient Egyptian times and today, we see revolutionary new techniques in the form of dental implants, which are secured deep within the bone of the jaw.

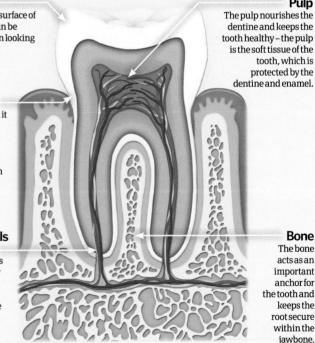

Enamel
The white, outer surface of the tooth. This can be clearly seen when looking in the mouth.

Pulp
The pulp nourishes the dentine and keeps the tooth healthy – the pulp is the soft tissue of the tooth, which is protected by the dentine and enamel.

Cementum
The root coating, it protects the root canal and the nerves. It is connected to the jawbone through collagen fibres.

Blood vessels and nerves
The blood vessels and nerves carry important nourishment to the tooth and are sensitive to pressure and temperature.

Bone
The bone acts as an important anchor for the tooth and keeps the root secure within the jawbone.

Head to Head
ANIMAL TEETH

1. Hippopotamus
A hippopotamus has an enormous mouth that can measure up to 1.2 metres wide. They are equipped with a pair of huge and very dangerous incisors.
© Artur
BIG

SMALL
2. Piranha
Piranha teeth are very small but can be extremely sharp and are often used by the local populations of South America to create a variety of tools and weapons.
© Andrewself 68

SHARP
3. Hamster
A member of the rodent family, the hamster has teeth that grow continuously. They therefore need to grind their teeth on a hard substance to prevent overgrowth.
© Keith Pomakis

DID YOU KNOW? The ancient Egyptians had severe problems with their teeth. They invented the world's first dental bridge

Inside your mouth

The upper and lower areas of the mouth are known as the maxilla and the mandible. The upper area of the mouth is attached to the skull bone and is often called the upper arch of the mouth, while the mandible is the v-shaped bone that carries the lower set of teeth.

Canine teeth
Long, pointed teeth that are used for holding and tearing at the food within the mouth.

Wisdom teeth
Usually appear between the ages of 17 and 25, and often erupt in a group of four.

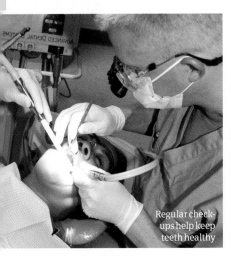
Regular check-ups help keep teeth healthy

Tooth anatomy

The tooth is a complex structure. The enamel at the surface of the tooth is highly visible while the dentine is a hard but porous tissue found under the enamel. The gums provide a secure hold for the tooth, while the root is anchored right into the jawbone. In the centre of the tooth there is a substance called pulp which contains nerves and blood vessels, the pulp nourishes the dentine and keeps the tooth healthy.

Tooth formation begins before birth. Normally there are 20 primary teeth (human baby teeth) and later, 28 to 32 permanent teeth, which includes the wisdom teeth. Of the primary teeth, ten are found in the maxilla (the upper jaw) and ten in the mandible (lower jaw), while the mature adult has 16 permanent teeth in the maxilla and 16 in the mandible.

Maxilla
A layout of the upper area of your mouth

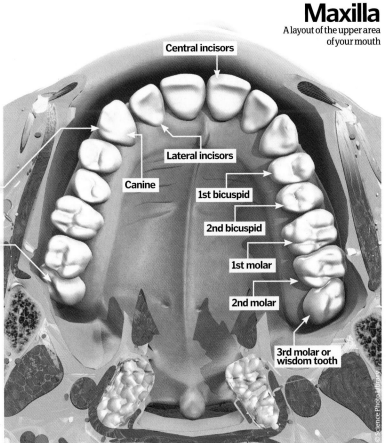

Central incisors
Lateral incisors
Canine
1st bicuspid
2nd bicuspid
1st molar
2nd molar
3rd molar or wisdom tooth
© Science Photo Library

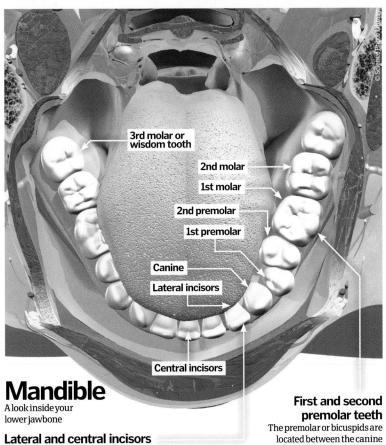

3rd molar or wisdom tooth
2nd molar
1st molar
2nd premolar
1st premolar
Canine
Lateral incisors
Central incisors
© Science Photo Library

Mandible
A look inside your lower jawbone

Lateral and central incisors
Incisor comes from the Latin word 'to cut', they are used to grip and bite.

First and second premolar teeth
The premolar or bicuspids are located between the canine and molar teeth. They are used for chewing.

Adult teeth start coming through early on

Eruption of teeth
The approximate ages at which the permanent teeth begin to erupt

Age 6
First molar

Age 7
Central incisor

Age 9
First premolar

Age 10
Second premolar

Age 11
Canine

Age 12
Second molar

Age 17 to 21 or not at all
Third molar (wisdom teeth)

 Learn more

For further reading, why not check out *Teeth Are Not For Biting* (2003), Elizabeth Verdick, Free Spirit Publishing; or *DIY Dentistry: And Other Alarming Inventions* (2008), Andy Riley, New English Library.

111

Why is there no cure for the common cold?

A general term for over 200 different viruses, why is the common cold so 'incurable'?

The common cold is a viral infection that attacks the upper respiratory tract, including the nasal cavity, the pharynx (back of the mouth) and the larynx (voice box). Every child can get up to 12 colds a year, and in adulthood we continue to get them on a regular basis. The symptoms of a cold are sneezing, a runny nose, sore throat and nasal congestion. Young children can also run a high temperature. In the first three days, the cold is highly contagious and is spread to anyone who inhales or touches anything contaminated by the virus. A cold lasts about a week, although a cough can persist for several days afterwards.

Rhinoviruses, coronaviruses, coxsackieviruses and adenoviruses are just some of the many different types of cold viruses. These viruses stick to the cells of the adenoids at the back of your throat. They quickly reproduce and rupture from the cells to spread to cells in the rest of the upper respiratory tract.

While we can treat the symptoms of a cold, we cannot find a single cure as there are so many types of virus and they mutate rapidly. Therefore, in the time it takes to develop a vaccine, it is no longer useful. ✲

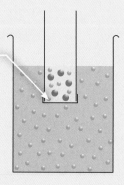

A heavy cold (sometimes referred to as man flu) can be debilitating

What is a virus?

Unlike bacteria, which have a cellular structure, viruses are much smaller and must replicate within other cells – for example, within the cells that line the inside of the nose.

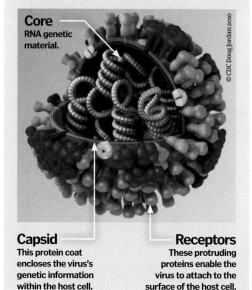

Core
RNA genetic material.

© CDC Doug Jordan 2010

Capsid
This protein coat encloses the virus's genetic information within the host cell.

Receptors
These protruding proteins enable the virus to attach to the surface of the host cell.

How does osmosis work?
How and why molecules move through a permeable membrane

Osmosis is the movement of a solvent, such as water, across a membrane (divider) from a region of high concentration to low concentration. The motion of molecules in an enclosed volume will always see them try to spread out equally, such as when perfume is sprayed into a room and the smell gradually dissipates as the molecules move. Osmosis is this same effect but across a membrane, which acts as a barrier. The membrane allows some molecules to pass through, but blocks the passage of others. Osmosis is frequently seen in animal and plant cells, where it allows the intake of useful nutrients and expels waste products. The process ceases when the molecular concentration on either side of the membrane is uniform, a state which is referred to as isotonic.

Substances high in protein, such as eggs and milk, are less likely to undergo the process of osmosis when an animal ingests them, because the large protein molecules block the way and prevent water molecules reaching the cell membrane. This is why eating protein-rich foods keeps your energy levels up; water is unable to leave your body, meaning cells and organs remain hydrated and functioning. ✲

© Science Photo Library

A cell can become flaccid or turgid, depending on the rate of osmosis

Osmotic pressure

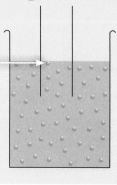

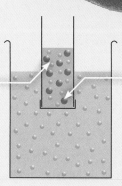

Uniform
Initially, the liquid in the tube and that outside of it are both level, before a semi-permeable membrane and solvent solution are added.

Membrane
The tube is then sealed with a semi-permeable membrane, and a salty solution is added. The membrane allows for the passage of water, but not salt molecules.

Osmosis
Water molecules permeate into the tube, pushing the liquid up. This 'osmotic pressure' makes the liquid rise above the level of surrounding liquid.

Solute
There is a higher concentration of water outside the tube than inside in the salty solution, but the salt cannot pass through the membrane.

HIGH DENSITY  © Alan Pennington, 2005	**1. Otters** Otters have the densest level of follicles (up to 1 million hairs per square inch in places), which helps them to keep warm in the cold north Pacific Ocean.
HIGHEST DENSITY (HUMAN) 	**2. Blondes** Blonde humans actually have more hair than other hair types. The average human has 100,000 follicles, but blondes have an average of 146,000.
LOW DENSITY 	**3. Elephants** Elephants have one of the lowest densities of hair per square inch, following a trend of larger animals generally displaying a lower density of hair on their body.

DID YOU KNOW? Hair doesn't continue to grow after death, it just appears that way as the body dehydrates and skin shrinks

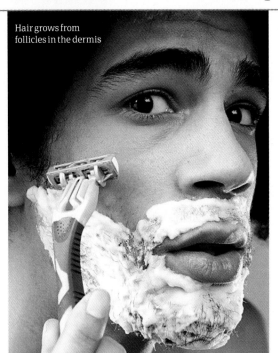

Hair grows from follicles in the dermis

Epidermis
This is the top layer of skin through which the hair penetrates.

Dermis
The dermis is the layer of skin below the epidermis, in which the hair follicles, blood vessels and sweat glands are situated.

Hair follicle
The sac-like structure from which the hair grows.

Hair and the skin it's in

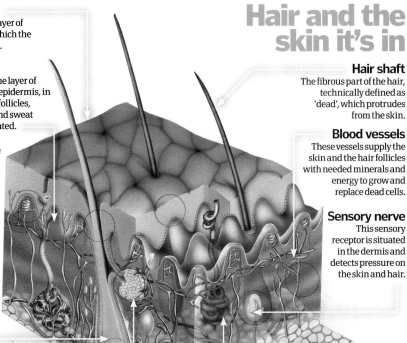

© Science Photo Library

Hair shaft
The fibrous part of the hair, technically defined as 'dead', which protrudes from the skin.

Blood vessels
These vessels supply the skin and the hair follicles with needed minerals and energy to grow and replace dead cells.

Sensory nerve
This sensory receptor is situated in the dermis and detects pressure on the skin and hair.

Sebaceous gland
These microscopic glands secrete an oily substance called sebum to lubricate the skin and hair.

Sweat gland
This gland, situated near to the hair follicle, releases sweat when the body is overheating to cool the body.

How does hair grow?

Hair is a key characteristic of mammals, but what is it made of?

Your hair is primarily made up of keratin, which is a form of protein. It grows from follicles situated in the dermis – a specific layer of the skin found below the epidermis but above the subcutaneous tissue – and is exclusive to mammals.

The human body is nearly entirely covered in hair, although some of it is so fine you cannot see it unless you look very closely. This fine hair is called vellus hair and the thicker, pigmented hair that is more visible is called either terminal or androgenic hair, dependent on location. Ratios of each will depend on the individual, heavily influenced by their sex.

The biology of both types of hair is quite similar, with each containing a cuticle, cortex and medula, which together form the shaft, bulb and follicle. The major difference between vellus and androgenic or terminal hair is the pigmentation, which is determined by melanin situated in the cortex, and thickness of the hair. There are two types of melanin – eumelanin and pheomelanin – and the levels of these types determine the colour of the hair. Although colour is primarily determined by genetics, grey hair results from a disappearance of melanin from the hair.

Hair can grow up to 5.5 metres long in some individuals that see high levels of hair growth in the active phase, but most hair reaches a set length and will then rest before shedding. The length of the phases differ depending on the type of hair, with head hair having a long growth period of around a year and body hair having a much shorter period of growth, but an extended resting period before shedding.

Whether hair is curly or straight is determined by the shape of the hair fibre – if it is circular it will be straight, but if it is oval it will be wavy or curly. The degree of curliness is determined by how stretched the oval shape is.

Functions of hair and fur in mammals are wide ranging, with thermoregulation being among the most important, alongside sensory function. As humans have evolved, we've seen a massive reduction in the thickness of hair covering our bodies, as we've found other ways to keep warm. The hair on our heads is retained to aid thermoregulation and in other areas, the functions of which are debated. ✿

Hair growth

Your hair grows in a cycle of growth and rest phases

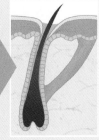

Growth phase (anagen)
This is the phase when hair grows out from the follicle. The length of this phase can vary quite dramatically, dependent on where the hair is growing and what type of hair it is. Vellus hair grows for a short period of time, whereas the terminal hair situated on the head can grow for up to a year and can grow up to 5.5 metres long.

Regeneration phase (catagen)
In this phase, the hair detaches from the follicle and the blood supply and is pushed up through the skin out of the follicle. The follicle renews itself in readiness for another new hair to grow once the present hair has shed from the skin.

Resting phase (telogen)
The hair rests for between one and four weeks before a new hair pushes the present hair out. This will happen all across the body and with all types of hair.

Hormones

How the human endocrine system develops and controls the human body

The glands in the endocrine system use chemicals called hormones to communicate with and control the cells and organs in our bodies. They are ductless glands that secrete different types of hormone directly into the bloodstream and target specific organs.

The target organs contain hormone receptors that respond to the chemical instructions supplied by the hormone. There are 50 different types of hormone in the body and they consist of three basic types: peptides, amines and steroids.

Steroids include the testosterone hormone. This is secreted by the cortex of the adrenal gland, the male and female reproductive organs and by the placenta in pregnant women. The majority of hormones are peptides that consist of short chains of amino acids. They are secreted by the pituitary and parathyroid glands. Amine hormones are secreted by the thyroid and adrenal medulla and are related to the fight or flight response.

The changes that are caused by the endocrine system act more slowly than the nervous system as they regulate growth, moods, metabolism, reproductive processes and a relatively constant stable internal environment for the body (homeostasis). The pituitary, thyroid and adrenal glands combine to form the major elements of the endocrine system along with other elements such as the male testes, the female ovaries and the pancreas. ✿

Excess testosterone can make you do some extreme things!

Hypothalamus
Releases hormones to the pituitary gland to promote its production and secretion of hormones to the rest of the body.

Pituitary gland
Releases hormones to the male and female reproductive organs and to the adrenal glands. Stimulates growth in childhood and maintains adult bone and muscle mass.

Pineal gland
Secretes melatonin, which controls sleep patterns and controls the production of hormones related to the reproductive organs.

The endocrine system

Thymus
Is part of the immune system. It produces thymosins that control the behaviour of white blood T-cells.

Adrenal glands
Controls the burning of protein and fat, and regulates blood pressure. The medulla secretes adrenaline to stimulate the fight or flight response.

© DK Images

Adrenal gland

We have two adrenal glands that are positioned on top of both kidneys. The triangular-shaped glands each consist of a two-centimetre thick outer cortex that produces steroid hormones, which include testosterone, cortisol and aldosterone.

The ellipsoid shaped, inner part of the gland is known as the medulla, which produces noradrenaline and adrenaline. These hormones increase the heart rate, and the body's levels of oxygen and glucose while reducing non-essential body functions.

The adrenal gland is known as the 'fight or flight' gland as it controls how we respond to stressful situations, and prepares the body for the demands of either fighting or running away as fast as you can. Prolonged stress over-loads this gland and causes illness.

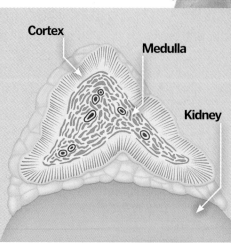

Cortex

Medulla

Kidney

Hormone replacement therapy (HRT)
At menopause, women no longer have ovarian follicles to secrete oestrogen. The reduction of oestrogen levels can cause insomnia, depression and more. HRT uses controlled doses of oestrogens and progesterone to help alleviate these symptoms.

DID YOU KNOW? When you are excited the hypothalamus and pituitary gland release opiate-like endorphins

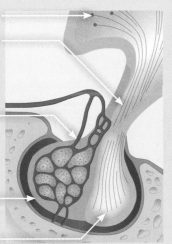

Hypothalamus

Hypothalamus neurons
These synthesise and send hormones to the posterior lobe.

Portal veins
Hormones from the hypothalamus are carried to the anterior lobe through these veins.

Anterior lobe

Posterior lobe

Pituitary gland

The pea-sized pituitary gland is a major endocrine gland that works under the control of the hypothalamus. The two organs inside the brain work in concert and mediate feedback loops in the endocrine system to maintain control and stability within the body.

The pituitary gland features an anterior (front) lobe and a posterior (rear) lobe. The anterior lobe secretes growth hormones that stimulate the development of the muscles and bones; it also stimulates the development of ovarian follicles in the female ovary. In males, it stimulates the production of sperm cells. The posterior lobe stores vasopressin and oxytocin that is supplied by the hypothalamus. Vasopressin allows the retention of water in the kidneys and suppresses the need to excrete urine. It also raises blood pressure by contracting the blood vessels in the heart and lungs.

Oxytocin influences the dilation of the cervix before giving birth and the contraction of the uterus after birth. The lactation of the mammary glands are stimulated by oxytocin when mothers begin to breastfeed.

Parathyroid
Works in combination with the thyroid to control levels of calcium.

Thyroid
Important for maintaining the metabolism of the body. It releases T3 and T4 hormones to control the breakdown of food and store it, or release it as energy.

Thyroid and parathyroids

Thyroid cartilage (Adam's apple)

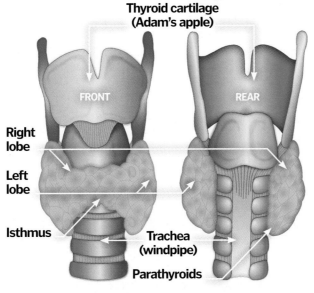

FRONT

REAR

Right lobe

Left lobe

Isthmus

Trachea (windpipe)

Parathyroids

The two lobes of the thyroid sit on each side of the windpipe and are linked together by the isthmus that runs in front of the windpipe. It stimulates the amount of body oxygen and energy consumption, thereby keeping the metabolic rate of the body at the current levels to keep you healthy and active.

The hypothalamus and the anterior pituitary gland are in overall control of the thyroid and they respond to changes in the body by either suppressing or increasing thyroid stimulating hormones. Overactive thyroids cause excessive sweating, weight loss and sensitivity to heat, whereas underactive thyroids cause sensitivity to hot and cold, baldness and weight gain. The thyroid can swell during puberty and pregnancy or due to viral infections or lack of iodine in a person's diet.

The four small parathyroids regulate the calcium levels in the body; it releases hormones when calcium levels are low. If the level of calcium is too high the thyroid releases calcitonin to reduce it. Therefore, the thyroid and parathyroids work in tandem.

Pancreas
Maintains healthy blood sugar levels in the blood stream.

Female ovaries
Are stimulated by hormones from the pituitary gland and control the menstrual cycle.

Male testes
These two glands produce testosterone that is responsible for sperm production, muscle and bone mass and sex drive.

Pancreatic cells

Islets of Langerhans

Red blood cells

Acinar cells
These secrete digestive enzymes to the intestine.

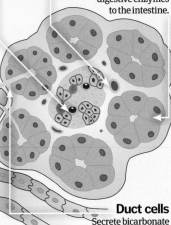

Duct cells
Secrete bicarbonate to the intestine.

The pancreas is positioned in the abdominal cavity above the small intestine. It consists of two types of cell, the exocrine cells that do not secrete their output into the bloodstream but the endocrine cells do.

The endocrine cells are contained in clusters called the islets of Langerhans. They number approximately 1 million cells and are only one or two per cent of the total number of cells in the pancreas. There are four types of endocrine cells in the pancreas. The beta cells secrete insulin and the alpha cells secrete glucagon, both of which stimulate the production of blood sugar (glucose) in the body. If the beta cells die or are destroyed it causes type 1 diabetes, which is fatal unless treated with insulin injections.

The other two cells are the gamma and delta cells. The former reduces appetite while the latter reduces the absorption of food in the intestine.

The power of MAGNETISM

This invisible force allows the production of super-powerful electromagnets and everyday items such as credit cards, but what does it mean to be magnetised?

Magnetism is the force of nature responsible not only for our ability to live on a rock floating through space, but also for major technological achievements that have advanced the human race like never before. Computers rely on them, our livelihood on Earth depends on their principles and our greatest science experiments use the most powerful magnets ever created by man. Were it not for magnetism we simply would not exist, and indeed without discovering the power of this fundamental force of nature, our life on Earth would bear no resemblance to what it is today.

Scientists over the years have employed magnetism in new and innovative ways, delving into realms of particle physics otherwise unexplored, but let's take a look at how basic magnets are made. It's fairly common knowledge that objects can be magnetised, making them stick to other magnetic objects, and we know that things such as a fridge or horseshoe magnet always have magnetism. To make permanent magnets like these, substances such as magnetite or neodymium are melted into an alloy and grounded into a powder. This powder can be moulded into any shape by compressing it with hundreds of pounds of pressure. A huge surge of electricity is then passed through it for a brief period of time to permanently magnetise it. Typically, a permanent magnet will lose about one per cent of its magnetism every ten years unless it is subjected to a strong magnetic or electric force, or heated to a high temperature.

Now let's take a look at the magnets themselves, and what's in and around them. Surrounding every magnet is a magnetised area known as a magnetic field that will exert a force, be it positive or negative, on an object placed within its influence. Every magnet also has two poles, a north and south. Two of the same poles will repel while opposite poles attract. Inside and outside a magnet there are closed loops known as magnetic field lines, which travel through and around the magnet from the north to south pole. The closer together the field lines of this magnetic field are, the stronger it will be. This is why unlike poles attract – the magnetic forces are moving in the same direction, so the field lines leaving the south of one magnet have an easy route into the north of another, creating one larger magnet. Conversely, like poles repel as the forces are moving in opposite directions, hitting one another and pushing away. It's the same effect as other forces. If

Magnetite

1 This iron oxide mineral, also known as lodestone (translated as 'course stone'), was once used as a primitive compass, as it can be found naturally magnetised.

Pyrrhotite

2 The most common naturally magnetic mineral after magnetite, some pyrrhotite specimens have a weak amount of magnetism, enough to attract a paper clip.

Haematite

3 Often considered to be non-magnetic, atoms within a haematite crystal are seen to align with one another very slightly, indicating a tiny magnetic force.

Earth

4 The Earth acts as a magnet due to electric currents in the core, similar to an electromagnet, but its magnetic field is 100 times weaker than a fridge magnet.

Magnetar

5 Often referred to as the most powerful magnet in the universe, if this rotating star came within 100,000 miles of Earth it would wipe every single one of our credit cards.

DID YOU KNOW? In 1997, Dutch and British researchers levitated a frog by placing it in a powerful magnetic field

Magnetic atom

So what's the difference between the atoms of magnetic and non-magnetic elements? Well, the main difference is the appearance of unpaired electrons. Atoms that have all their electrons in pairs can't be magnetised, as the magnetic fields cancel each other out. However, atoms that can be magnetised have several unpaired electrons. All electrons are essentially tiny magnets, so when they are unpaired they can exert their own force – known as a magnetic moment – on the atom. When they combine with electrons in the other atoms, the element as a whole gains a north and south pole and becomes magnetised.

Nucleus
Electrons of an atom orbit around the nucleus in the same way planets orbit the Sun, but this is due to the electromagnetic force and not gravity.

Paired electrons
Moving electrons create magnetism due to their electric charge, but in most atoms electrons are paired and there's no resultant magnetic force.

Unpaired electrons
Some atoms contain unpaired electrons, free to exert a magnetic moment (force) on the atom with a north and south pole.

Shells
Electrons travel round the nucleus in shells, moving in cloud-like orbits rather the common description of them as rigid circles.

INSIDE A MAGNET

An object that can become magnetic is full of magnetic domains, chunks of about one quadrillion atoms. When the object is magnetised, the domains line up to and point in the direction of the magnetic field now present. This is why a magnetic object is sometimes stroked with a magnet to magnetise it. It aligns the domains in one direction, so that a magnetic field can flow around the material.

Unmagnetised
With no magnetism, the object does not have a north and south pole, so there is no magnetic field present to align the domains.

Scattered
When a substance that can be magnetic is unmagnetised its domains go in random directions, cancelling each other out.

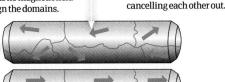

Magnetised
Introducing a magnet or electric current to the substance makes the domains all point in the same direction, with a magnetic field running from the north to south poles.

Aligned
When the domains are lined up, the substance as a whole becomes a magnet, with one end of it acting as a north pole and the other a south.

you push a revolving door while someone pushes from the other side, the door stays still and your forces repel. If you push in the same direction, however, the door swings round and you end up back at your starting point.

The defining feature of magnetic poles is that they always occur in pairs. Cut a bar magnet in half and a new north and south pole will instantly be created on each of the two new magnets. This is because each atom has its own north and south pole, which we will talk about later. However, the obvious question is why the poles are there in the first place. Why do magnets have to have these field lines moving from north to south? The answer involves magnetic domains. It is best to picture a magnet as smaller magnet chunks put together. Each chunk (or domain) has its own north and south pole and

again, as explained before, magnetic field lines travel from north to south. This means that all the domains stick together, with their forces concentrated in the same direction. They combine to make a larger magnet, exactly the same effect as when two magnets are stuck together. Each domain has about 1,000,000,000,000,000 (1 quadrillion) atoms, while 6,000 domains are approximately equivalent to the size of a pinhead. Domains within a

magnet are always aligned, but elements such as iron, which can become magnetic, initially have their domains pointing in random directions when the iron is unmagnetised. They cancel each other out until a magnetic field or current is introduced, making them point in the same direction and magnetising the iron, which creates its own new magnetic field.

To really understand magnets, though, we need to get into exactly ▶

An electronic motor relies on magnets

TYPES OF MAGNETISM

Ferromagnetism
The strongest magnet in this list, a ferromagnet will retain its magnetism unless heated to a temperature known as the Curie point. Cooling it again will return its ferromagnetic properties. Every atom in a ferromagnetic material aligns when a magnetic field is applied. Horseshoe magnets are ferromagnets.

© Gregory F. Maxwell

Ferrimagnetism
Ferrimagnets have a constant amount of magnetisation regardless of any applied magnetic field. Natural magnets like lodestones (magnetite) are ferrimagnets, containing iron and oxygen ions. Ferrimagnetism is caused by some of the atoms in a mineral aligning in parallel. It is different from ferromagnetism in that not every atom aligns.

© Ryan Somma

Antiferromagnetism
At low temps, the atoms in an antiferromagnet align in antiparallel. Applying a magnetic field to an antiferromagnet such as chromium will not magnetise it, as the atoms remain opposed. Heating to Néel temp (when paramagnetism can occur) will allow weak magnetism, but further heating will reverse this.

Paramagnetism
Paramagnets, such as magnesium and lithium, have a weak attraction to a magnetic field but don't retain any magnetism after. It's caused by at least one unpaired electron in the atoms of a material.

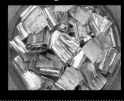

Diamagnetism
Gold, silver and many other elements in the periodic table are diamagnets. Their magnetic loops around the atoms oppose applied fields, so they repel magnets. All materials have some magnetism, but only those with a form of positive magnetism can cancel the negative effects caused by diamagnetism.

© Jeff Belmonte

"Electrons are just like tiny magnets, each with a north and south pole"

The laws of attraction revealed

what is happening inside these domains. For that, we need to get right down into the atom. Let's take an iron atom, for example. Electrons circle the nucleus of an atom in cloud-like orbitals, commonly described as rigid shells (although in actuality, their motion is much more random). Each atom has a particular number of shells depending on how many protons and neutrons it has, while within each shell electrons orbit in pairs. Electrons are just like tiny magnets, each one having its own north and south pole. In their pairs, the electrons cancel out one another so there is no overall magnetic force. In an atom such as that of iron, however, this is not the case. There are four electrons that are unpaired, which exert a magnetic force on the atom. When all the atoms are combined together and aligned, as we explained when talking about domains, the iron itself becomes magnetised and attracts other magnetic objects.

So we've snapped our magnet, broken it into chunks and subsequently examined the atoms of those tiny chunks. But can we go deeper? The answer to that is yes and

no, as we delve into the unknown areas of quantum physics. The underlying principle of magnetism is that in the universe there are four fundamental forces of nature, being gravity, electromagnetism, the weak force and the strong force. Even smaller than atoms and electrons are fundamental particles known as quarks and leptons, which are responsible for these forces. Any force – such as gravity, magnetism, nuclear decay or friction – results from these fundamental forces. A force such as magnetism at this level is 'thrown' between particles on what are known as force carrier particles, pushing or pulling the other particles around accordingly.

Unfortunately, however, at this level magnetism enters a completely different realm – that of theoretical physics, entering areas of quantum physics that have not yet been explored in as great detail as particle physics. For now, however, this standard model of physics explains magnetism to a level that can only actually be furthered when science can advance our understanding of quantum physics in the future.

EARTH'S MAGNETIC FIELD

It's best to imagine the Earth as a bar magnet 12,400 miles (20,000km) long. The magnetic fields move around us like they would in a fridge magnet, but they also protect us from the universe. Compass needles always point to a magnet's south pole, so the Earth's geographical north pole is actually magnetically south.

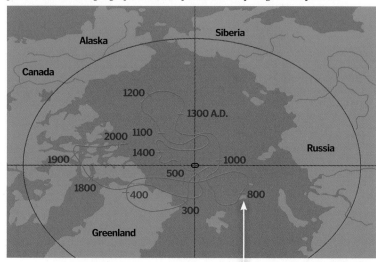

Key: ——→ wandering path of the magnetic north
⊖ rotational north pole

Effect
Charged particles from the Sun are deflected by the Earth's magnetic field, with some trapped in bands of radiation.

Tilt
The central 'bar magnet' of the Earth's magnetic field, the dipole, is tilted approximately 11° off the Earth's axis.

South is north
Magnetic fields always run from north to south, so when a compass points to the North Pole it is actually indicating southern magnetic polarity.

Magnetic movement
The North Magnetic Pole moves up to 1mm a second because of changes in the core. In 2005 it was pinpointed just off Ellesmere Island in Canada, but is now moving towards Russia.

Cause
The magnetic field of any planet, including Earth, is the result of the circulation of electrically conducting material in the core, in our case molten iron.

Off-centred
The magnetic north and south poles do not draw a straight line through the centre of the Earth. In fact, they miss by several hundred miles.

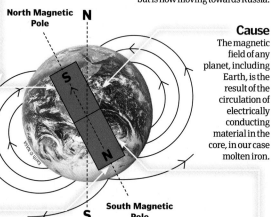

IRON FILINGS

Filings
By scattering tiny iron filings around a magnet on paper, it is possible to visibly see the magnetic field in action.

Field
By tapping the paper, the magnetic filings will align along the magnetic field lines of the magnet that run from its north to south pole.

Electromagnets

One of the four fundamental forces in the universe, electromagnetism results from the interaction of electrically charged particles. Physicist Michael Faraday deduced that a changing magnetic field produces an electric field, while James Maxwell discovered that the reverse is also true: a changing electric field produces a magnetic field. This is the basis of how an electromagnet works.

Electric fields
A wire wrapped around a magnetic core, such as iron, produces electric fields when a current runs through it, in turn creating a magnetic field.

Coil
The number of coils will increase the strength of the electromagnet because there is more current flowing in one direction, magnifying the force proportionally.

Core
As discussed on the previous page, the domains within the core are unaligned until a magnetic field is introduced, created by a moving current in the coil.

Magnetic field
The wire's magnetic field combines with the field of the core to produce a stronger field, with a larger current aligning more domains and increasing its strength.

POWERFUL

1. 12 Tesla
The world's most powerful MRI scanner at Oregon Health and Science University helps to provide unprecedented insight into the human brain.

STRONGER

2. 45 Tesla hybrid
8 trillion times stronger than a fridge magnet, this electromagnet at Florida State Uni has the strongest continuous magnetic field.

RIDICULOUS

3. 100 Tesla
At a laboratory in Sarov, Russia in 1998, explosives helped to create a 2,800 Tesla magnetic field, instantly destroying the machine.

DID YOU KNOW? In Australia, blind magnetic termites use the Earth's magnetic field for guidance

MAGNETS IN YOUR HOME

You'll be surprised at the number of magnets that are under your roof...

Microwave
Inside a microwave oven is a magnetron, which contains magnets. Strong permanent magnets are mounted inside this tube. When electricity passes through the magnetron, the resultant electric and magnetic fields produce electromagnetic energy in the form of microwaves.

Vacuum cleaner
Electromagnetism is used here to produce the desired effect. A magnetically conducting material is inside the motor of the vacuum cleaner. When an electric current is introduced to a coil around the material, repulsive forces make the motor spin. The material loses its magnetism when the vacuum is turned off.

Doorbell
For a buzzer-style doorbell, pressing the button moves and releases a contact from an electromagnet to break and complete a circuit. A chiming doorbell, meanwhile, moves an iron core through an electromagnet coil and back when the button is pressed, hitting two chime bars in sequence.

Computer
Like credit cards, the storage disks inside computers are coated with bits of iron. By changing the magnetic orientation of the iron, a pattern can be created to store a particular set of data. This pattern can be read by the computer and replicate the data on screen. The monitor itself uses magnets in the same way as an old cathode ray tube TV (see television).

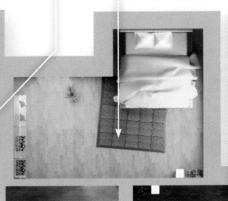

Speakers
Using electromagnetism, most speakers contain a stationary magnet and a wire coil inside a semi-rigid membrane. When a current runs through the coil, the membrane rotates in and out because of the force between coil and magnet, creating vibrations that produce sound. Phone speakers use this same mechanism, only smaller.

Credit card
All credit cards have a black strip on them, known as a magnetic stripe. Inside, minuscule bits of iron are held in a plastic film. These can be magnetised in a north or south direction to store important data. When you swipe the card through a machine, the line of tiny magnets is read and information is obtained.

Television
Most modern LCD or plasma TVs don't use magnets. However, older models use a cathode ray tube to fire electrons against the back of the screen. Coated in phosphor, parts of the screen glow when struck by the beam. Coils produce magnetic fields that move the beams horizontally and vertically to produce the desired picture.

EMP

An Electromagnetic Pulse (EMP) works by overwhelming electric circuits with an intense electromagnetic field. A non-nuclear EMP explodes a metal cylinder full of explosives inside a coil of wire, pushing out magnetic and electric fields that fry electric circuits. A nuclear EMP would explode a nuclear bomb in the atmosphere. The resultant gamma radiation would take in positive air molecules but push out negative electrons, sending a large electromagnetic field in all directions. A 10-megaton device detonated 200 miles (320km) above the centre of the United States would destroy every electronic device in the country but leave structures and life intact.

Buildings would survive; electronics wouldn't

Solar blackout 2013?

Could the geomagnetic storm of 1859 be repeated?

In 1859, a great geomagnetic storm wiped out transmission cables and set fire to telegraph offices when the Sun went through a period of intense solar activity. Scientists at NASA have warned that a similar storm could occur in 2013. The Sun's magnetic cycle peaks every 22 years, while every 11 years the number of sunspots and solar flares hits a maximum. If we were to experience a geomagnetic superstorm on the same scale as that in 1859, our many electronic devices would be damaged. Networks would go offline, aircraft couldn't fly, satellites would be destroyed.

"A strong acid has a high concentration of H+ ions"

Acids and bases

Discover the differences between acids and bases, and find out why they act the way they do

It is widely known that lemons taste sour due to their acid content, soil needs the optimum pH level for plants to grow properly and acid rain can wipe out entire ecosystems. But what really makes one thing acidic and the other one basic (alkaline)? Why can they be so corrosive? And why does litmus paper turn different colours when dipped in acid or a base?

Acids and bases can be defined in terms of their concentration of hydrogen ions. Normally an atom of hydrogen consists of one proton and one electron giving it a balanced electrical charge – protons being positively charged and electrons being negatively charged. Take away the electron and you are left with an ion of hydrogen, or a single proton, or 'H+', as it is often written. The thing about ions is they are very reactive, as they no longer have a balanced charge. They are constantly seeking ions of the opposite charge – an atom or molecule with an unequal number of electrons than protons, with which to react.

A strong acid has a high concentration of H+ ions and is defined by its ability to 'donate' hydrogen ions to a solution, whereas a base, also know as an alkali, has a much lower concentration of H+ ions and is defined by its ability to 'accept' hydrogen ions in a solution. Therefore, acids mixed with bases become less acidic and bases mixed with acids become less basic, or less alkaline.

Certain concentrated bases, like some concentrated acids, can attack living tissue and cause severe burns due to the ions reacting with the skin. However, the process of bases reacting with the skin, and other materials, is different to that of acids. That's why we call some concentrated acids 'corrosive', whereas reactive concentrated bases are 'caustic'. ⚙

Acids and bases have many uses, but stronger ones can be harmful

The power of hydrogen

The letters pH stand for 'power of hydrogen', as the scale refers to the concentration of hydrogen (H+) ions in the solution. It measures the acidity or basicity of a solution, with pH values ranging from 0-14, 0 being really acidic and 14 being really basic. A substance in the middle of the scale with a pH of 7 is classed as neutral, as it contains equal numbers of oppositely charged ions.

| pH0 | pH1 | pH2 | pH3 | pH4 | pH5 | pH6 |

Acid

A compound which 'donates' hydrogen ions when placed in an aqueous solution. The higher the concentration of hydrogen ions released, the stronger the acid.

Some natural boiling acid springs have a pH of about 1, similar to battery acid

© Allison Choppick

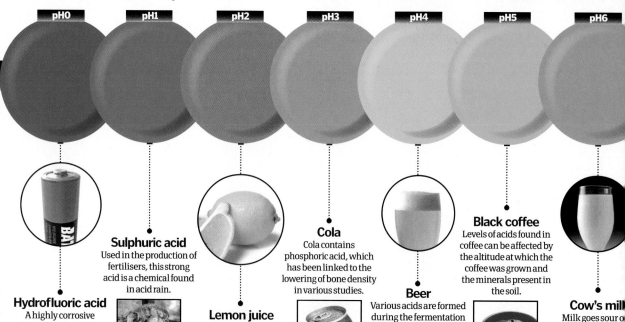

Hydrofluoric acid
A highly corrosive substance which as a gas is a severe poison and acts a catalyst in oil refining.

Sulphuric acid
Used in the production of fertilisers, this strong acid is a chemical found in acid rain.

Lemon juice
Lemon juice is about 5% citric acid – a weak organic acid that gives lemons their sour taste.

Cola
Cola contains phosphoric acid, which has been linked to the lowering of bone density in various studies.

Beer
Various acids are formed during the fermentation process in beer production. The addition of CO_2 also causes the pH to lower slightly.

Black coffee
Levels of acids found in coffee can be affected by the altitude at which the coffee was grown and the minerals present in the soil.

Cow's milk
Milk goes sour over time due to the bacteria produc lactic acid as part fermentation pro

MOST CORROSIVE

1. Sodium hydroxide
This is a highly caustic base that in high concentrations can be severely damaging to living tissue.

MORE CORROSIVE

2. Hydrofluoric acid
Hydrofluoric acid is highly corrosive, and it has the ability to dissolve most oxides including glass.

CORROSIVE

3. Sulphuric acid
Sulphuric acid releases heat upon contact with water, used in the steel industry to remove rust and oxidisation.

DID YOU KNOW? Carborane superacids are a million times stronger than sulphuric acid, yet can be entirely non-corrosive

The litmus test

We can test the acidity or alkalinity of a substance using litmus paper. Litmus paper is that which has been treated with a mixture of 10-15 natural dyes obtained from lichens. The dyes work as indicators, whereby upon exposure to acids (a pH less than 7) the paper turns red and upon exposure to bases (a pH more than 7) the paper turns blue. When the pH is neutral (pH equal to 7), the dyes cause the paper to turn purple.

Red cabbage juice can also be used to distinguish between acids and bases, as it contains a natural pH indicator called 'flavin'. Upon exposure to acid, flavin turns a red colour, neutral solutions appear a purple colour and basic solutions result in a greenish-yellow colour.

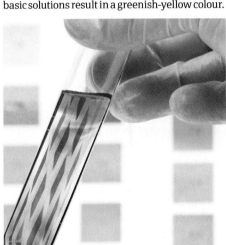

Neutralisation

A neutralisation reaction is the combination of an acid and base that results in a salt and, usually, water. In strong bases and acids, neutralisation is the result of the exchange of hydrogen and hydroxide ions, H+ and H- respectively, which produces water. With weak acids and bases, neutralisation is simply the transfer of protons from an acid to a base. The production of water, with a neutral pH of 7, indicates the neutralisation of the acid and base, while the resultant salt will often have a pH that is also neutral.

Neutralisation has a variety of practical uses. For example, as most plants grow best at neutral pH7,

Wasp stings are alkaline, so an acid-like vinegar will neutralise them

acidic or alkaline soil can be treated with chemicals to change its pH. In the case of acidic soil this is often calcium carbonate (chalk) or calcium oxide (quicklime). Another example is the human stomach, which contains hydrochloric acid. However, too much can lead to indigestion, so the acid can be neutralised with a base such as an indigestion tablet.

How do an acid and base react to produce salt, water and heat?

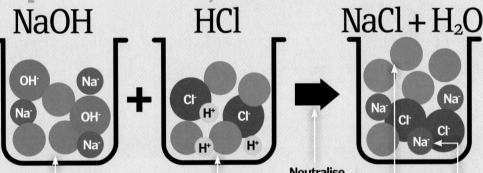

$$NaOH + HCl \rightarrow NaCl + H_2O$$

Sodium hydroxide
This strong alkali (a base soluble in water) has a pH of 13 or 14.

Hydrochloric acid
With a pH of 1 or 2, the H+ ions of this strong acid are removed by the alkali.

Neutralise
By removing the H+ ions, the alkali neutralises the acid and turns the ions into water.

Water
Neutral water of pH7 is produced.

NaCl
Neutral sodium chloride, or table salt, is also produced.

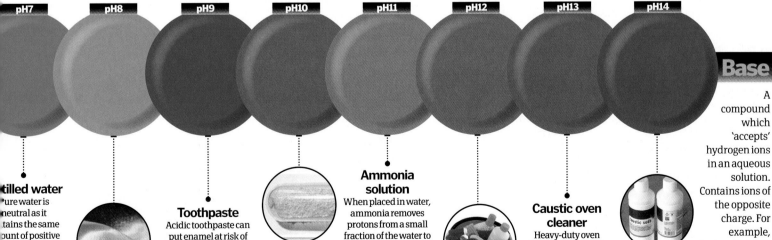

pH7 | **pH8** | **pH9** | **pH10** | **pH11** | **pH12** | **pH13** | **pH14**

Base

...tilled water
Pure water is neutral as it contains the same amount of positive ions as negative ions, though most water isn't pure in this sense.

Baking soda
A slightly salty substance used as a base in foods to regulate the pH if something is too acidic.

Toothpaste
Acidic toothpaste can put enamel at risk of decay, so a weak base such as sodium hydroxide is added in order to regulate the pH.

Milk of magnesia
A weak base of magnesium hydroxide in water, used to ease stomach aches caused by too much acid.

Ammonia solution
When placed in water, ammonia removes protons from a small fraction of the water to form ammonium and hydroxide. It is used in many cleaning products for its basic properties.

Bleach
Can contain sodium hypochlorite at different strengths, making it a strong caustic base.

Caustic oven cleaner
Heavy-duty oven cleaners can be really caustic and corrosive, helping to break down fat and grease.

Caustic soda
Chemically known as sodium hydroxide, in its purest form it is a white solid and can cause severe burns due to its high alkalinity.

A compound which 'accepts' hydrogen ions in an aqueous solution. Contains ions of the opposite charge. For example, hydroxide (OH-) which is naturally found in water and is negatively charged.

Cellulite affects 90 per cent of post-adolescent women but is rarely seen in men due to their thicker skin

Toothache

What causes this excruciating pain in our mouths?

Bacteria and acid in food and drink erodes the hard, white enamel coating on top of your teeth. Once this enamel has been eroded, the dentin below will also start to decay until it exposes the tooth's pulp. Pulp consists of blood vessels and nerve endings, which allow us to feel pain. When the pulp is exposed to water and saliva, hot, cold, sweet and sour substances activate the nerves and cause pain. Further tooth decay will uncover more of the pulp cavity, intensifying the ache.

Sometimes the pain from a tooth is so intense that the nerves send the wrong signals to the brain, and a healthy tooth on the other side of the jaw may incorrectly seem to ache. ✿

Dentin
Located between the pulp and the enamel, dentin decays from bacteria and acid, exposing the pulp cavity inside.

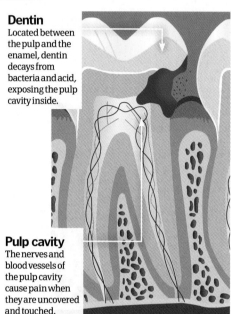

Pulp cavity
The nerves and blood vessels of the pulp cavity cause pain when they are uncovered and touched.

What is rust?

Learn why some objects turn a reddish brown when exposed to oxygen

The technical term for rust is oxidisation, when oxygen comes into contact with an object and creates a new compound. The red rust colour is caused by the oxidisation of iron. Only objects that contain iron – such as an iron alloy like steel – are capable of producing rust.

When an object containing iron comes into contact with water, the latter will combine with carbon dioxide in the air to form a weak acid. Some of the iron subsequently dissolves and the water separates into hydrogen and oxygen. The free oxygen bonds with the dissolved iron, creating iron oxide, which has a red hue. Rust is crumbly and brittle because the bonds within the iron oxide atoms are much weaker than those of regular iron. ✿

Rust is a chemical reaction that occurs between iron, oxygen and water

Cellulite dimples

Epidermis

Dermis

Fat cells

Septae

Muscle

Cellulite

What is the cause of this bump and dimple effect on the skin?

Cellulite is a skin condition resembling orange peel where pockets of fat are trapped and result in dimpling of the skin occurring. Cellulite occurs beneath the surface of the skin (the epidermis) in the subcutaneous level. Here, fat cells are arranged in segments and are surrounded by septae, a connective tissue that attaches from the muscle to the dermis (the layer below the epidermis) and allow the skin to flex. The fat cells expand and stretch the septae as they retain water, but over time waste products and toxins may cause the septae to harden. When this happens, the section of skin attached to a specific septae is no longer flexible, holding the skin down. The fat continues to expand in other areas, bulging the skin out and giving a lumpy appearance on the surface of the skin known as cellulite. ✿

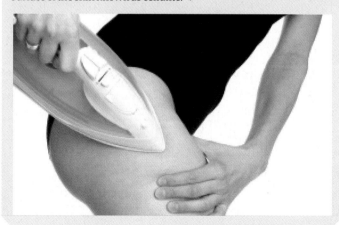

5 TOP FACTS
ITEMS IN A FREEDIVER KIT

First aid trained buddy
1 Due to the complications that can occur with freediving, every sensible freediver has a first aid trained buddy ready at the surface. They can help them if they get into trouble.

Snorkel and mask
2 A snorkel is often used by the diver to aid release of air. The mask is crucial so the diver can see which way they are swimming and the surface when they are ascending.

Weights
3 Weights help the diver descend, and in various freediving disciplines (such as variable weight apnea), weights are used to speed up the process.

Flippers (fins)
4 Sometimes used, and sometimes not. They are used in the disciplines of freediving when distances are key, such as the dynamic apnea with fins discipline.

Wetsuit
5 A good wetsuit will help the individual retain heat in the colder water of the deep, and also smoothes the body surface of the diver to reduce drag during descent.

DID YOU KNOW? Humans can't normally hold their breath for more than a minute – brain damage can occur after three minutes

DEEPEST DIVES

Which creatures can dive to the deep, dark depths of the ocean and survive?

0m

DAVE MULLINS
Freediver, dynamic apnea without fins
218m (715ft)

1,000m

PASCALE BERNABE
Scuba diver
330m (1,080ft)

2,000m

SPERM WHALE
Deepest diving mammal
Approx 2,500m (8,200ft)

3,000m

4,000m

ALVIN
Submersible capable of taking people within
4,500m (14,760ft)

5,000m

6,000m

7,000m

SNAILFISH
These tiny fish actually live 7,000m down in deep ocean trenches, areas thought to be devoid of life until 2008
Approx 7,000m (23,000ft)

8,000m

9,000m

TRIESTE
Machine-operated submarine
10,916m (35,813ft)

10,000m

11,000m

Monofin
This Russian invention increases a freediver's efficiency and mobility.

Wetsuits
Tiny bubbles sealed within the neoprene rubber of a freediver's wetsuit compress when under pressure, reducing buoyancy.

Freediving explained

How can a human hold their breath under water for over 11 minutes and dive to depths of over 200m unaided?

Freediving is classified as the sport of individuals descending underwater while holding their breath. There are various competitive and non-competitive classifications of this sport, and national competitions are held across the world every year. The current record for static apnea (individuals just holding their breath while submerged, normally in a pool) is 11 minutes 35 seconds for a man (Stephane Mifsud) and 8 minutes 23 seconds for a woman (Natalia Molchanova). But how do they do this?

The technical term for holding your breath is apnea; the body will actually make physiological adaptations to the lack of oxygen while underwater. These are caused by the mammalian diving reflex and involve lowering the heart rate and restricting blood flow to areas of the body, among other adaptations. Individuals can also actually develop their ability to hold their breath for longer periods of time through various forms of training.

One form of training is to perform an 'apnea walk'. This is where an individual holds their breath at rest for a minute, and then walks as far as they can without needing to take a breath. This activity can help to prepare the body for the anaerobic conditions it will experience in freediving. Also, prior to freediving, individuals will sometimes hyperventilate to lower carbon dioxide levels in their blood, which will ultimately slightly delay signals travelling to the brain that warn of asphyxiation. ✿

Weight belts
Weighted belts can be worn to counteract the effects of buoyancy.

Guide line
A guide rope leads the way down when deep freediving.

Mammalian diving reflex
A trait we share with dolphins

There are four primary adaptations that the human body makes during freediving. The first is a drop in heart rate, which ultimately slows body functions and causes the body to use less oxygen. Alongside this, vasoconstriction occurs and the spleen releases extra red blood cells – the latter ensures oxygen levels rise slightly and the former ensures oxygen is delivered to the vital organs as opposed to the limbs. Large muscles constrict to aid this process. Also, dependent on the depth, blood plasma will fill blood vessels in the lungs to reduce volume, which will stop damage occurring when the body is exposed to pressure created by diving to depths greater than 30m. Dolphins and seals display these same traits and archaeologists have seen evidence of individuals using freediving to source food and resources from as early as the 5th Century BCE.

Memory and retaining information

We take it for granted, but how do we retain and utilise information from our environment?

Memory is the capacity to store and retain information, then recall it for use when needed. It is used by most organisms to operate in the most successful manner they possibly can in their unique environment. There are three main types of memory: sensory, short-term and long-term, although long-term is often split into different types of memory. Sensory memory is a very short-term type of memory, which is evoked through the senses. It lasts for a few seconds at most and is not stored. Short-term memory is a slightly longer-lasting form, sitting at around 20 secs. It's the recording of memories currently being used – ie, remembering a number to dial in the next 30 seconds. If the information is repeated, however, it causes pathways to form between neurons in the brain and a phrenological loop to be formed, causing a memory to be stored as a long-term memory. Unless this repeated firing of the neurons occurs, forced by repeating of the information, a memory will be lost.

When we cannot remember something, it's generally not because of suddenly developing a degenerating brain disease like Alzheimer's – it's far more likely to be that the correct stimuli have not been presented to prompt retrieval of the memory, or that you did not register or retain the original information properly. For example, if you cannot remember where you put your shoes when you took them off the night before, it may be that you were not paying attention when you put them down and consequently not transferred the memory from short-term to long-term in the first place, rather than having forgotten. As long as you have registered and retained the event, correct stimuli would cause a refiring of the neurons fired when creating the original memory, allowing successful retrieval of the information required. Dependent on its type, a memory is stored in different areas of the brain. This helps people to store related information more easily, as it can be linked to previously stored related material. ✿

Areas in the brain that are used in memory

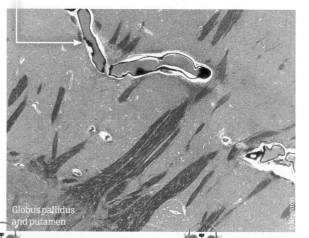

Frontal lobe (including the pre-frontal cortex)
The frontal lobe plays a crucial role in storing long-term memories, in particular those related to behavioural and social norms and expectations.

Putamen
This area of the brain is very important in movement, therefore it is an important area for procedural long-term memory.

Amygdala
These groups of nuclei play a very important role in the forming of emotional memory, such as reaction to fear.

Globus pallidus and putamen

Temporal lobe
This lobe of the brain primarily stores and processes auditory information, and therefore plays a particularly important role in speech and language. The hippocampus sits within the temporal lobe.

Hippocampus
The hippocampus is one of the crucial parts of the brain for the transferal of short-term memories into the long-term. Damage to this area will hinder an individual's ability to make new memories.

How do we form and store long-term memories?
The time it takes for a memory to really stick

Attention — 0.2 secs
If something grabs our attention, we're far more likely to remember it. Neurons fire as we continue to focus, ensuring memory moves from short-term to long-term. The thalamus plays a big role in directing attention.

Emotion — 0.25 secs
Events or things that cause an emotional response are more likely to be remembered because they activate raised levels of activity in the amygdala, and this arousal means more information is taken in and processed.

Sensation — 0.2-0.5 secs
Sensory memory is based on receiving information from our senses – ie sight, smell, touch. The lingering feeling you have after someone touches your arm is the sensory memory fading, and this first information from the senses is the starting point for any memo

Autistic skills

1 Individuals with autism often have skills such as fantastic mathematical ability. Some individuals such as Stephen Williams can draw entire landscapes from memory.

Sleep helps memory

2 Sleep is important to memory. Although scientists don't know exactly how it affects the brain, it has been seen that sleep aids storage and retrieval of long-term memories.

Memory and age

3 Our memory doesn't decrease very much with age. The memory loss we see in older people is generally because we tend to exercise our brains less as we age.

Complex = memorable

4 The more you have to try to work out a problem, the more likely you are to recall it. Initially your brain has to work harder, making stronger links between the active neurons.

False memories

5 People can 'remember' events that haven't happened. Often if they're led to believe something, their brain will then gather any relevant info to form a false memory.

DID YOU KNOW? *Contrary to popular belief, goldfish actually have a memory of about three months – not just a few seconds*

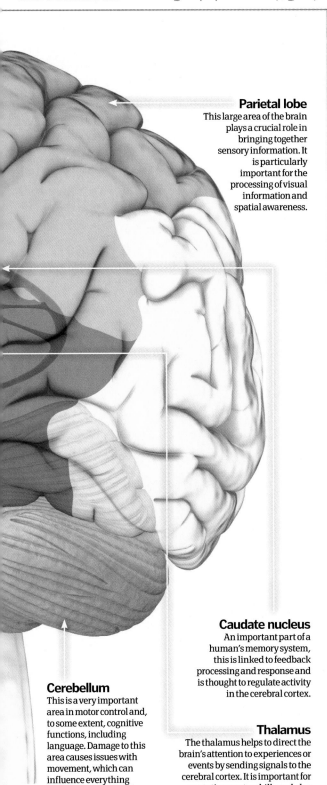

Parietal lobe
This large area of the brain plays a crucial role in bringing together sensory information. It is particularly important for the processing of visual information and spatial awareness.

Cerebellum
This is a very important area in motor control and, to some extent, cognitive functions, including language. Damage to this area causes issues with movement, which can influence everything from balance to speaking and walking.

Caudate nucleus
An important part of a human's memory system, this is linked to feedback processing and response and is thought to regulate activity in the cerebral cortex.

Thalamus
The thalamus helps to direct the brain's attention to experiences or events by sending signals to the cerebral cortex. It is important for sensation, motor skills and also helps to regulate sleep.

Motor skills – or 'body memories'

How do we store memories?

Memories are formed in our brains through electronic pulses passing between neurons. As neurons fire more than once, the pathway and link between the neurons strengthens; if the first neuron is triggered in the future, it is more likely that the others will too. Memories are stored in different areas of the brain, depending on what they are and what they are used for.

Input
The stimulus for a memory can be nearly anything. It can be related or unrelated. For example, if you see a letterbox, you may remember you had a letter to post, therefore stimulating a memory through a related input. However, some people use unrelated stimuli, like a piece of string tied to their finger, which they have formed an unrelated link to something else with.

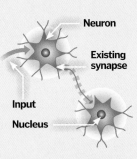

Neuron

Existing synapse

Input

Nucleus

Circuit formation
As a memory is being formed, certain neurons will link together in a circuit to store this memory. It will link related memories and repetition of this circuit firing will strengthen the memory. This is called a phrenological oop.

Forged new link

Input

Increased activity

New synapse

Increasing activity
Repeated firing of the neurons involved in the first memory formation (repetition to remember) will strengthen the memory, as the neuron pathway becomes stronger and the memory can be retrieved and utilised faster.

New link established

Regular input

Facilitated synapse

Types of memory

The complex ways we remember...

Sensory memory
Sensory memory is evoked through the senses and is the initial perception of something. This is a fleeting memory, and will not be transferred into short- or long-term unless we focus on remembering the event.

Short-term
This type of memory is stored temporarily for up to 20 seconds. It can, however, be confused with working memory, a separate type of memory that allows an individual to retain information only for long enough to, say, complete a sum. Unless information is repeated several times to establish a pathway between neurons, it will decay and be lost.

Long-term – procedural (implicit)
This kind of long-term memory is how we remember to do things such as ride a bike. It is where we store our 'body' memories – our motor skills.

Long-term – declarative (explicit)
This type of memory is how we store facts for retrieval, and consists of things such as names and dates.

Long-term – episodic
This is where we store event-related memories and link them together. For example, if you went to a dinner party you wouldn't remember every moment, but you would recall a collection of events, smells and sounds which link together when you think of the overall event.

0.5 secs - 10 mins

Working memory
Working memory is when information is briefly stored in order to be used in the immediate future. It lasts for a few seconds or so, but if repetition occurs, refreshing the time limit in which it can survive, it will be retained and can move into short- or long-term.

10 mins - 2 years

Hippocampal processing
If we need to retain a piece of information, or it particularly strikes us, it will travel from the short-term memory, based in the pre-frontal cortex, and travel to the hippocampus where it is processed and can move into the long-term memory.

2 years +

Consolidation
If you use a piece of information repeatedly, the links between the neurons remain strong. These are likely to stay in place for a long time. Although the pathways between neurons are changing as we receive, process and retain new information, repetition and reuse can cause the pathways to remain and the memory to stay in the brain.

How cloning works

From Dolly the sheep to stem cell farms, we explore the myths and reality of cloning

Inside the nucleus of every living cell is DNA, the genetic blueprint that makes each living creature unique. In rare cases, a fertilised egg will divide and separate inside the womb, forming two embryos with the same DNA. The resulting identical twins, which make up a scant 0.2 per cent of the world's population, are nature's perfect clones.

When we think of artificial cloning, most of us tend to fall back on bad science-fiction movies where teams of evil scientists replicate humans with giant photocopiers or grow armies of clone babies in glass-walled tanks. The reality of artificial cloning is much closer to Mother Nature's model.

When scientists set out to artificially (or asexually) clone an organism, they take their cues from natural (or sexual) reproduction. In sexual reproduction, the sperm and egg cells each carry a single set of chromosomes containing exactly half of each parent's genes. When the sperm fertilises the egg, the two halves of the genetic map combine to form a full set of chromosomes that is unique from either parent.

A fertilised egg is called a zygote. As the zygote divides and develops into an embryo, the same copy of DNA is passed along to every cell in the organism, whether it's a liver cell, eye cell or brain cell. The cells ultimately look and behave differently because different genes along the DNA strand are expressed to perform different cell functions.

The earliest artificial cloning efforts in the late-Seventies were quite basic. In a procedure called artificial embryo twinning, scientists mimicked the natural twinning process by physically dividing an early embryo into individual cells that had yet to specialise. After a day or two in a petri dish, the developing identical embryos were implanted into a surrogate mother and brought to term.

But the most effective artificial cloning method to date – the one that brought us Dolly the sheep in 1996 – is called somatic cell nuclear transfer. Somatic cells are 'body' cells like skin or liver cells that carry a full copy of DNA. To create a clone using this method, scientists extract the nucleus of an adult somatic cell and insert it into an 'enucleated' egg cell from a second animal, ie an egg whose nucleus and original genetic material has been destroyed or removed. Lab technicians execute these manoeuvres with pipette needles 2/10,000th of an inch wide.

5 TOP FACTS
CLONING

Baby clones?
1 Despite several high-profile claims in the past, there is no scientific evidence that anyone has successfully delivered an artificially cloned human being.

Stem cell research
2 Researchers can apply for a licence to clone human embryos for stem cell research. It is illegal, however, for any of those embryos to be implanted in a surrogate mother.

Human-animal hybrids
3 In 2008, the Human Fertilisation and Embryology Authority approved research into 'cytoplasmic' hybrids, the transfer of human genetic material into a cow egg cell.

Photocopy clones
4 There is no known technology that can create an instant copy of a living organism. Experiments are intergenerational, meaning the clone will be younger than the original.

Clones or twins?
5 Twins are clones – two organisms that share the same genetic material – but not all clones are twins. If the cloned organisms are born at the same time, then they're twins.

DID YOU KNOW? The success rate of cloning by somatic cell nuclear transfer is only between one and four per cent

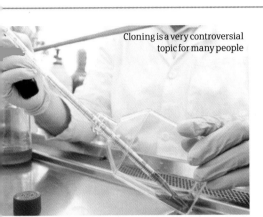

Cloning is a very controversial topic for many people

Father
Sperm collected from bull

Mother
Cows are treated with hormones to ensure egg production

The science of cloning

1. Sexual reproduction
The original embryo carries exactly half of the mother's chromosomes and half of the father's, creating an organism with unique DNA.

Early embryo

Artificial embryo twinning

Identical twins are a fluke. When the fertilised egg is only days old, it spontaneously and inexplicably splits into two equal clusters of stem cells, each carrying the exact same genetic blueprint. Researchers can mimic this process in the lab by physically separating individual stem cells during the earliest moments of cell division and implanting the identical embryos into surrogate mothers.

5. Herd of clones
The genetic makeup of the surrogate mothers has no effect on the offspring. Each calf carries the same exact combination of the original parents' DNA, resulting in identical physical traits.

2. Separation
In the earliest days of cell division, researchers can physically divide the embryonic cell cluster into individual stem cells. Each cell carries the organism's full genetic record.

New embryo

3. Growing embryos
The isolated stem cells are placed in culture where they are stimulated with chemicals to restart cell division. In a few days, a new cluster of embryonic stem cells has formed.

Stem cells

4. Transplantation
Each cloned embryo is implanted into a surrogate mother, who will carry the growing fetus to term.

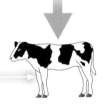
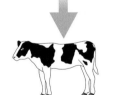
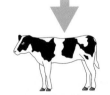
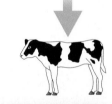

Scientists then use a precision jolt of electricity or a chemical trigger to stimulate cell division in the transplanted egg. Instead of generating more specialised somatic cells – as you might expect DNA from an 'adult' cell to do – the transplanted DNA reboots to its original orders and starts to create an embryo. The resulting foetus, implanted into a surrogate mother, grows to become an exact genetic clone of the animal that donated the somatic cell.

Somatic cell transfer is often used for reproductive cloning – making copies of organisms with highly desirable genetic traits. For example, the same researchers who cloned Dolly have also cloned a genetically modified sheep named Polly whose milk contains a protein that aids blood clotting in haemophiliacs. By producing thousands of clones of Polly,

scientists can isolate more and more of the protein to manufacture blood-clotting drugs.

Cattle, sheep, pigs and other animals have been bred by farmers for millennia to produce leaner, protein-rich meat and more flavourful milk. But conventional breeding still allows for a genetic roll of the dice, occasionally resulting in small, sickly offspring. Successful reproductive cloning, some say, would ensure a steady supply of only the fittest animals.

In 2008, the US Food and Drug Administration approved the sale of foods containing milk and meat from cloned animals, although the prohibitive cost of cloning has kept cloned food off the shelves so far. The European Union has made no such approvals, although breeders throughout Europe are already using ▶

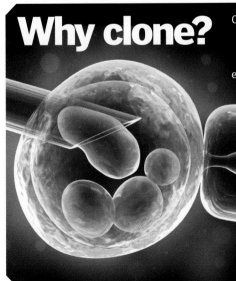

Why clone?

Cloning takes the risk out of reproduction. In nature, the unpredictability of sexual reproduction ensures biological diversity and is the engine behind evolution. But for research scientists, that diversity is not nearly as desirable as control. If you're developing a drug to treat pancreatic cancer, you want to test hundreds of different treatments on identical samples of pancreatic cells. You won't find that in nature, but you could create that in a lab through cloning.

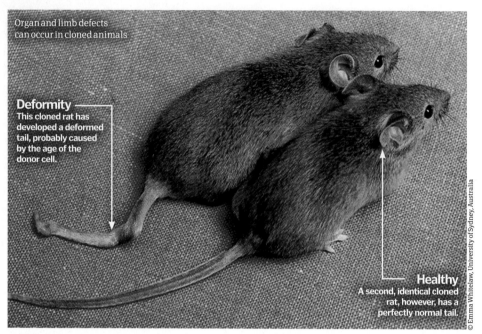

Organ and limb defects can occur in cloned animals

Deformity
This cloned rat has developed a deformed tail, probably caused by the age of the donor cell.

Healthy
A second, identical cloned rat, however, has a perfectly normal tail.

© Emma Whitelaw, University of Sydney, Australia

Dolly the sheep

A remarkable breakthrough that changed the world of cloning

Dolly the sheep was the celebrity of the cloning world. Back in 1996, after 276 failed attempts, researchers at the Roslin Institute in Scotland became the first scientists to successfully clone a mammal. The method was somatic cell nuclear transfer, in which the nucleus of an egg cell is sucked out and replaced with the nucleus of a normal body cell (or 'somatic' cell) from an adult sheep. Using electrical impulses, the egg is induced to divide, growing into an embryo that shares the identical genetic material as the somatic cell donor. This requires sensitive manipulations of cellular material at the microscopic level, explaining the low success rate. Dolly's life in the spotlight was relatively short-lived and she died at age six. One drawback of somatic nuclear transfer is that the age of the donor cell seems to affect the longevity of the cloned organism.

Dolly – the most famous sheep in the world

▶ imported semen and embryos from cloned animals bred in the States.

Scientists have also used reproductive cloning to bring endangered species back from the brink of extinction. In 2001, researchers used somatic cell nuclear transfer to clone an endangered guar ox, but the animal died soon after birth from an infection. Since then, another ox and three African wildcats have been successfully cloned to repopulate their species.

The first cloned cat was born in 2001 and a firm in South Korea produced the first cloned canine in 2005. Since then, passionate pet owners have paid as much as £600 a year to preserve their beloved cat or dog's tissue for post-mortem cloning, a process that runs to nearly £100,000.

Not all cloning experiments have been for the sake of reproduction, though. With therapeutic cloning, the goal of researchers is to isolate and replicate stem cells in order to study their potentially life-saving applications. Stem cells are undifferentiated cells that carry a full copy of an organism's DNA, but have yet to express any of their genes as skin cells, bone cells, sperm cells or any other adult cell. Researchers can program stem cells to grow specific organ tissue, like healthy brain cells to treat Alzheimer's sufferers or replacement bone marrow cells for cancer patients.

Therapeutic cloning also relies on the somatic cell nuclear transfer method. In 2007, researchers harvested stem cells from cloned rhesus monkey embryos. It takes about five days for a cloned embryo to reach the blastocyst phase, when the total cell count has grown to around 100. At this size, stem cells can be extracted and placed in a nutrient-rich culture medium where they grow into complete stem cell 'lines'. ✿

1. In vitro fertilisation
Egg cells are surgically removed from a female and mixed with sperm cells in a laboratory culture that's conducive to fertilisation.

2. Blastocyst
Once the egg is fertilised, it becomes a zygote and begins to divide and multiply. Five days later, a cluster of 100 cells has formed, called a blastocyst.

© Science Photo Library

3. Locating stem cells
The inner ring of the blastocyst is composed primarily of undifferentiated stem cells, the 'blank slates' that will become organ cells, nerve cells, bone cells and reproductive cells.

4. Harvesting stem cells
Researchers remove the stem cells from the blastocyst and place them in a nutrient-filled culture medium to stimulate growth.

From stem cell to body part

Embryonic stem cells are 'pluripotent', meaning they can grow to become any specialised cell in the body. Nature has its own complex mechanisms for differentiating stem cells into brain, muscle or bone, involving both genetic and environmental markers. In the lab, researchers can isolate embryonic stem cells in culture and provide the right chemical triggers to grow fresh skin cells and even organs.

5. Differentiation
Batches of stem cells are transferred to other culture dishes where they are stimulated with chemicals, and even segments of genes to grow into specialised cells.

6. Organ formation
In recent years, researchers have found success growing bladder and skin cells on prefab scaffolds that mould the cells into the shape of the desired body part.

1. Star Wars: Attack Of The Clones
The evil Count Dooku attempts to generate a massive army of clones based on the DNA of intergalactic bounty hunter Jango Fett.

HIGHLY IMPROBABLE

2. Jurassic Park
Dinosaurs are replicated using DNA found in mosquitoes fossilised in amber. The odds of finding undamaged DNA in fossilised remains are extremely (extremely) low.

PURE SCIENCE FICTION

3. The Sixth Day
Arnold Schwarzenegger's character is cloned by implanting a copy of his DNA into an adult-sized 'blank' human along with a 'recording' of his brain.

DID YOU KNOW? Cloned animals don't always look identical. The first cloned cat had a different coloured coat than its match

How to make a sheep

1. The donor
Researchers chose a six-year-old Finn Dorset ewe as the donor animal, since its pure white coat and white face would be easily distinguishable from other breeds.

5. Enucleation
Using a miniature drilling pipette mounted on a specialised microscope, the scientists bored through the cell wall and sucked out the egg cell's nucleus.

4. Donor egg
Meanwhile, researchers removed a batch of eggs from an adult Scottish Blackface ewe, easily distinguishable by her dark facial markings.

9. Implantation
The embryo was then implanted into another Scottish Blackface ewe and carried to term in the surrogate mother.

10. Birth of Dolly
Dolly entered the world on 5 July 1996, sharing the identical white coat and white face of the mammary tissue donor and none of the markings of either the egg donor or surrogate mother.

2. Somatic cells
Researchers removed a small amount of somatic cells from the mammary tissue of the ewe. Yes, Dolly the sheep is named after Dolly Parton.

7. Fertilisation
Using another jolt of electricity, researchers induced proteins in the cytoplasm of the egg cell to 'reprogram' the genes of the somatic cell to grow an embryo, not more mammary tissue.

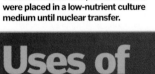

3. Low-nutrient culture
To inhibit cell division, the donor cells were placed in a low-nutrient culture medium until nuclear transfer.

6. Electroporation
The enucleated egg cells and somatic cells are placed in together and zapped with an electric field, causing cells to fuse and share a nucleus.

8. Embryo formation
Placed in a nutrient-rich culture medium, the egg cell began to divide and grow until it formed a blastocyst.

Uses of stem cells

Brain tissue
Stem cells are the body's repair kit. Researchers believe that stem cells could help repair and regrow brain tissue damaged by Alzheimer's and Parkinson's disease.

Heart disease
Researchers can extract adult stem cells from heart muscle tissue – or use similar cells taken from bone marrow – and inject them into damaged heart tissue to induce the formation of new capillaries and improve heart function.

Skin grafts
Today's artificial skin grafts can trick skin cells to regenerate, but the replacement skin can't sweat or grow hair. Researchers hope that by isolating skin stem cells, they can grow cultured tissue that preserves full skin function.

Diabetes
For sufferers of type-one diabetes, their immune system kills beta cells in the pancreas that produce insulin. Researchers hope to grow beta cells from stem cell cultures and implant them into diabetes patients.

Bone marrow
Currently, patients undergoing chemotherapy for leukaemia and lymphoma are injected with adult stem cells that help replenish depleted marrow supplies.

The risks of cloning

Cloning is far from an exact science. Dolly was the 277th cloned embryo and the first to survive. But even Dolly only lived to six years old, half the average life span of her species. Several genetic abnormalities have surfaced in cloned animals, including high birth weight, organ defects and premature ageing. The culprit, many believe, is the age of the somatic donor cell. Chromosomes get shorter over time as they divide and multiply. At some point, the chromosome becomes too short to divide and the cell dies. It appears that a somatic cell's chromosomal clock is not fully reset when it's implanted into an egg, resulting in shorter life spans and sudden organ failure.

Evaporation and steam

How do these processes work, and is there a difference between them?

The change of state from a solid or a liquid to a vapour is known as 'evaporation'. This change of state occurs from the amount of energy the molecules have. Apart from at absolute zero (-273.15 °C), when molecules are said to have zero energy, molecules are in constant motion and, as temperature increases, they gain more and more energy. This in turn increases their movement and, the faster they move, the more likely they are to collide with one another. When these collisions occur, a molecule can gain enough energy – and subsequently heat – to rise up into the atmosphere, because as we know hot air rises.

However, there is a difference between evaporation of vapour and steam. While vapour can be said to be any substance in a gaseous state at the same temperature as its environment, steam is specifically vapour from water that is hotter than the surrounding environment, commonly seen when boiling. There is no difference in chemical composition of the two. The steam we actually observe is the vapour cooling and condensing as it leaves the hot water and enters the cooler surrounding air. ✿

Boiling water

Steam
As the vapour cools and condenses, it produces visible steam.

Vapour pressure
Evaporation occurs when the vapour pressure reaches that of the surrounding air.

Boil
When water boils at 100°C (212°F), vapour pressure increases.

© Science Photo Library

The science of skateboarding

Kick, twist and grab your way through the physics of half pipes

In a halfpipe a skateboarder will typically start at one end (deck), then roll down into the flat of the halfpipe. They carry enough speed and momentum to shoot up the other side, gaining 'air' to perform tricks before landing again in the bowl of the halfpipe. ✿

A skateboarder's energy is constantly being transferred

1. Potential energy
At the deck of the halfpipe, before the skateboarder jumps into the halfpipe, they have a certain amount of potential energy, the result of gravity pulling them down.

2. Potential to kinetic
As a skateboarder travels down the slope of one side, the potential energy becomes kinetic energy, giving them forward momentum.

4. Kinetic to potential
As the rider travels up the opposite slope, kinetic energy turns back to potential as they move against the force of gravity, slowing them down.

5. All potential
When in the air, all the energy is now potential energy again. If the skateboarder makes the landing, he can use that energy to reach the other side again.

7. Pumping
The skateboarder crouches on entry to the flat and rises as they go upwards, tightening their radius of travel in the 'circle' and increasing their linear momentum.

3. All kinetic
At the flat bottom of the halfpipe, all of the rider's energy is kinetic energy, so they are at their maximum speed.

6. Work
If a skateboarder wants to go higher at one end, they need to do some work as they travel through the pipe.

Energy in a halfpipe

Sonic boom

Contrary to popular belief, a sonic boom is not created only at the exact moment when something such as a plane breaks the sound barrier. Any object moving faster than the speed of sound will constantly emit a sonic boom to observers at different places.

What is a shock wave?

The science of breaking the sound barrier

Shock waves are large amplitude pressure waves produced by an object moving faster than the speed of sound like a boat or plane, or other things such as an explosion, lightning or even a moving piston.

When a source moves faster than the waves it produces, no waves will form in front of the source but will pile up behind and become compressed. The waves protruding are confined to a cone that narrows as the speed of the source increases and the waves bunch up, creating high-pressure regions outside the compressed waves. This border from inside to outside is the shock wave. The strength of a shock wave dissipates greatly with distance, much more so than a regular wave, as heat and other energy are more quickly transferred into the surrounding environment. Once enough energy has dissipated, the shock wave will become a regular wave such as a sound wave. ✿

In this image, the USS Iowa is firing shells from its cannon, which travel about twice the speed of sound. While the shells themselves will likely produce their own shock waves as they travel through the air, it is the shock wave caused by the explosion of the cannons that is visible on the water

Explosions
As the cannons fire their projectiles they produce large explosions, which send spherical shock waves travelling outwards.

Expansion
The expanding gases, caused by the shock waves protruding from the explosions of the cannons as they fire, can be seen travelling across the water.

"An atom represents the smallest part of an element that can exist by itself"

Atoms

Up and atom with our look at these particles inside all matter in the universe

At the centre of every atom is a nucleus containing protons and neutrons. Together, protons and neutrons are known as nucleons. Around this core of the atom, a certain number of electrons orbit in shells. The nucleus and electrons are referred to as subatomic particles. The electrons orbit around the centre of the atom, which is due to the charges present; protons have a positive charge, neutrons are neutral and electrons have a negative charge. It is the electromagnetic force that keeps the electrons in orbit due to these charges, one of the four fundamental forces of nature. It acts between charged objects – such as inside a battery – by the interaction of photons, which are the basic units of light.

An atom is about one tenth of a nanometre in diameter. 43 million iron atoms lined up side by side would produce a line only one millimetre in length. However, most of an atom is empty space. The nucleus of the atom accounts for only a 10,000th of the overall size of the atom, despite containing almost all of the atom's mass. Protons and neutrons have about 2,000 times more mass than an electron, making the electrons orbit the nucleus at a large distance.

An atom represents the smallest part of an element that can exist by itself. Each element's atoms have a different structure. The number of protons inside a specific element is unique. For example, carbon has six protons whereas gold has 79. However, some elements have more than one form. The other forms – known as isotopes – of an atom will have the same number of protons but a totally different number of neutrons. For example, hydrogen has three forms which all have one proton; tritium has two neutrons, deuterium has one neutron and hydrogen itself has none.

As different atoms have different numbers of protons and neutrons, they also have different masses, which determine the properties of an element. The larger the mass of an atom the smaller its size, as the electrons orbit more closely to the nucleus due to a stronger electromagnetic force. For example an atom of sulphur, which has 16 protons and 16 neutrons, has the same mass as 32 hydrogen atoms, which each have one proton and no neutrons. ✿

Shell
Each shell can hold a different number of electrons. The first can hold 2, then 8, 18, 32 and so on.

Inside the atom
Dissecting what makes up an atom

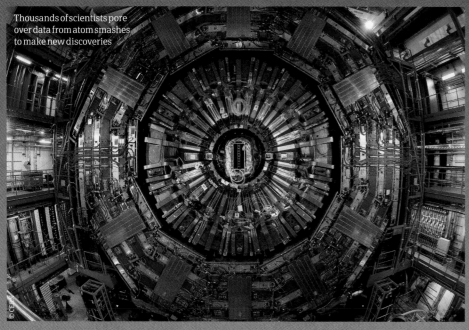

Thousands of scientists pore over data from atom smashes to make new discoveries

© Science photo library

Protons
A stable elementary particle with a positive charge equal to the negative charge of an electron. A proton can exist without a neutron, but not vice versa.

Quantum jump
An electron releases or absorbs a certain amount of energy when it jumps from one shell to another, known as a quantum leap.

5 TOP FACTS
ATOMS

Open the atom
1 Parts of atoms are smashed together to break them up into smaller particles, which allows scientists to discover what the particles are actually made of.

Collision
2 Subatomic particles, such as nuclei and electrons, are smashed together at almost the speed of light inside a giant collider to break them apart.

Quark
3 Protons and neutrons are broken into quarks, which are one of the fundamental particles of nature. Quarks cannot be broken down into smaller pieces.

CERN
4 The European Organization for Nuclear Research, or CERN is the world's largest particle physics laboratory. It carries out many high-energy physics experiments.

Large Hadron Collider
5 The LHC is the world's biggest and most powerful particle accelerator. It is a 17-mile ring of superconducting magnets, which are used to smash particles together.

DID YOU KNOW? If you took all the empty space out of every atom, the human race would fit into the size of sugar cube

Electron
An elementary particle (one of the basic particles of matter), an electron has almost no mass and a negative charge.

Nucleus
Held together by the strong nuclear force, the strongest force in nature, the nucleus is tightly bound and holds the protons and neutrons.

Neutrons
An elementary particle with a neutral charge and the same mass as a proton. The number of neutrons defines the other forms of an element.

Analysing an atom smash can provide a whole range of useful information
© CERN

No, this isn't the world's longest water slide, it's the Large Hadron Collider

© CERN

Power of the atom

Atomic bombs are notorious for their devastating power. By harnessing the energy in the nucleus of an atom, atomic bombs are one of the most powerful man-made weapons. In 1939, Albert Einstein and several other scientists told the USA of a process of purifying uranium, which could create a giant explosion known as an atomic bomb. This used a method known as atomic fission to 'split' atoms and release a huge amount of energy.

The only two bombs to ever be used in warfare were a uranium bomb on Hiroshima and a plutonium bomb on Nagasaki in 1945 at the end of World War II. The effects were frighteningly powerful, and since then no atomic bomb has ever been used as a weapon.

Early atomic bomb tests showed the raw power of the atom

Size of an atom

If the solar system were shrunk to the size of a gold atom, the distance from the Sun to Pluto would be half the distance from the nucleus of the gold atom to its furthest electron. One unit here is defined as the width of a gold atom.

Earth → **Moon – 0.3 units away**

Sun → **Pluto – 5,000 units away**

Gold atom → **Furthest electron – 10,000 units away**

Moon / Pluto / background © NASA

DIETS

Understand the value of eating a balanced diet and maintaining a healthy weight and you'll discover that opting for a quick-fix crash diet is not the answer to losing weight and staying fit long-term

Many people think that the primary reason an individual may choose to diet is to lose weight. However, there are several reasons why people might undertake particular diets. For instance, going on a detox diet has become popular. The emphasis on this diet is to remove all toxins and harmful substances to cleanse the body by only drinking water and eating fruits and vegetables to flush out the body. Weight loss is a potential side effect here, rather than the main purpose.

Diets work in differing ways, dependent on what they are being used to do. A standard, weight-loss or control diet will normally focus on lowering the individual's caloric intake to an appropriate level below the body's daily requirement. This will force the body to use its fat stores, bringing the individual's weight down. A specific diet tailored to, say, a patient with a history of heart attacks will be carefully planned to ensure cholesterol and fat levels are low to reduce risk of further medical issues.

5 TOP FACTS
FREAKY EATING

Pie's the limit
1 Every year since 1992, the World Pie-Eating Championships have been held in Wigan. Today emphasis is on speed not quantity.

Festival La Tomatina
2 This event occurs in August, in Bunol, near Valencia, Spain. Having started as a riot in 1944, people now turn up, with tomatoes, and just starting throwing.

Wood eating (xylophagia)
3 This is a relatively common condition where individuals like to eat a variety of wood products, such as paper, pencils and even tree bark! Just imagine the splinters...

12 grapes on New Year
4 Started back in 1909, the tradition of eating a grape every second for the last 12 seconds of the New Year is supposed to bring good luck. It is practised across Spain.

Insect eating (entomophagy)
5 Many societies across the world still eat insects – they are a fantastic source of protein. The western world has even started selling ants in chocolate now.

DID YOU KNOW? *Because men have a higher muscle-to-fat ratio, males have faster metabolisms than females*

The problem with a lot of crash diets and popular fad diets is that they often ignore the tried-and-trusted fact that we humans must eat a balanced diet that contains all the food groups in moderation in order to function in every department. Intelligent eating and this 'balance' or 'moderation' of food groups is crucial to ensuring you get the best from your body. This is how we obtain the energy for optimum body operation as well as the minerals and vitamins crucial for body maintenance and cell regeneration. If an individual is not consuming a balanced diet – and is instead missing out vital food groups, or not receiving enough of a particular vitamin – they may suffer a whole host of illnesses. A lack of vitamin C, for example, can cause scurvy – an illness you might consider old-fashioned because historically it was common in sailors who had no access to fruit and vegetables for weeks on end. And although now extremely rare in developed countries, cases of scurvy do still arise. Likewise, extreme dieters who cut entire food groups from their diets can often be at risk of deficiencies if they do not get their intake of all the necessary nutrients. In developing countries, for example, a deficiency in protein can result in a disease called kwashiorkor, which, if displayed during growth, can actually affect intelligence of the individual.

So which foods are 'bad'? Highly processed, high sugar foods are generally considered the worst as they are high in fat and sugars and low in both vitamins and minerals. These foods are often the cheapest to produce, which is one reason why we're seeing a growing trend in obesity in a number of developing countries. Also, these food stuffs tend not to 'fill you up' in the way 'good foods' such as brown bread and fruit do, and consequently people then snack and eat more, even though it is probable that they will have exceeded their daily recommended calorie intake.

Our sedentary work lives, combined with all our household appliances and gadgets that make our life easier in our homes, also mean that our average daily energy needs are significantly lower than those of our parents' and grandparents' generations. For instance, housewives back in the Sixties are thought to have burned over 1,000 calories a day just by doing housework.

So we understand that to maintain a healthy weight demands a balance of all ▶

Why we get hungry

Hunger is a sensation created by hormones across the body, causing you to respond and find food. The hypothalamus situated in the brain is the keen receptor for hunger signals and it will pick up on hormonal secretions, which indicate when the stomach is empty or full. Some cases of obesity are caused by problems with the hypothalamus development.

So once you feel the hunger, how much food do you actually need? Your energy requirements depend on your activity levels, sex, size and stage of life. By not exceeding these calorie intake recommendations you should be able to maintain a healthy weight.

How much food energy do we need?

	KCAL PER DAY
Child 8 years:	1,853 kcal (7,760 kj)
Girl 15 years:	2,207 kcal (9,240 kj)
Boy 15 years:	2,875 kcal (12,035 kj)
Woman inactive:	1,917 kcal (8,025 kj)
Woman active:	2,150 kcal (9,000 kj)
Man inactive:	2,515 kcal (10,530 kj)
Man active:	3,000 kcal (12,560 kj)

Why we gain weight

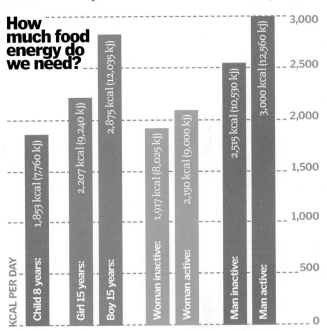

Fat storage occurs when calorie intake exceeds calorie output. Although there are other factors that can make us gain weight – including hormones that can affect our metabolism (the rate at which we burn the calories we take in) – usually it comes down to consuming more calories/energy than your body requires in order to function. So if you're doing less exercise than you might normally, your calorie intake should be reduced, and vice versa. All calories surplus to requirements are then stored in fat cells mostly in our subcutaneous fat just under the skin. Other fat gets stored undesirably around the vital organs.

Obesity is medically defined as having a body mass index (BMI) of over 30 (a healthy person should have a BMI of 18.5-24.9) and this condition can increase the likelihood of such life-threatening illnesses as heart disease, cancer and osteoarthritis. It is also likely to prompt the development of type 2 diabetes. A reported one in four people in the UK are technically obese.

"It just makes you have the best fats, carbohydrates and proteins to offer a balanced diet with no cravings" GI diet

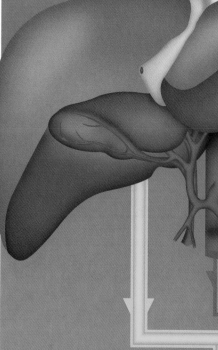

▶ good foods and even a spot of housework. We also know that we should not consume more calories than we require for our bodies to function. And yet in their droves people keen to lose weight quickly turn to so-called crash diets. These eating plans tend to promise quick and easy weight loss, either by eliminating a certain food group (such as carbohydrates) or by highlighting specific foods (such as cabbage soup).

While some do indeed have their good points such as encouraging you to eliminate excess sugar and saturated fats from your diet, many suggest cutting out healthy nutrients such as complex carbohydrates (oats, brown rice) and essential fatty acids. And as we all know, a balanced diet is key to ensuring the body functions.

So what's wrong with dieting? Well, not only does a crash diet fail to address the ultimate problem – the fact that weight was gained in the first place – but also, by definition, they are quick-fix remedies that do little to promote long-term healthy eating and a sustainable diet. Initially you may lose some weight, but this is often in the form of fluid, not fat. This is because low-calorie diets make the body burn excess glycogen – the glucose that absorbs excess body fluids. This 'water weight' will be put straight back on again as soon as the diet is over.

Once they've lost a bit of weight, some dieters reach a plateau – when the weight loss stops – and often they'll actually regain weight. The metabolism – or the rate at which the body burns calories – is linked to what's known as the yo-yo effect. The body realises it's receiving fewer calories than usual, and automatically adjusts the metabolic rate to burn fewer calories in order for the body to function. A slower metabolism means you'll burn calories slower and gain weight easier. So next time you're thinking of going on a crash diet to lose some weight, you might want to think twice as you may actually end up packing the pounds on even quicker. ☼

Digestion explained

Your diet must contain the vital nutrients for your organs to function. Find out how the body processes food

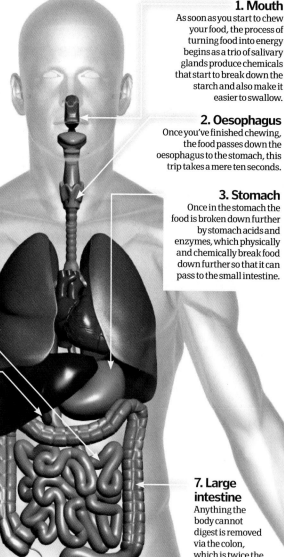

4. Small intestine
The very long and very coiled small intestine takes up most of the space in your abdomen where digestion is completed. The small intestine's many folds offer a massive surface area, ideal for absorbing nutrients into the bloodstream.

5. Gall bladder/pancreas
The gall bladder and pancreas both produce secretions for food breakdown in the early section of the small intestine.

6. Liver
Nutrients are stored in the liver, which also regulates the level of nutrients in the blood to ensure cells get all the goodness they require. This large organ carries out many metabolic functions, which ensure the blood's composition is regulated.

1. Mouth
As soon as you start to chew your food, the process of turning food into energy begins as a trio of salivary glands produce chemicals that start to break down the starch and also make it easier to swallow.

2. Oesophagus
Once you've finished chewing, the food passes down the oesophagus to the stomach, this trip takes a mere ten seconds.

3. Stomach
Once in the stomach the food is broken down further by stomach acids and enzymes, which physically and chemically break food down further so that it can pass to the small intestine.

7. Large intestine
Anything the body cannot digest is removed via the colon, which is twice the width of the small intestine, but only a quarter of the length. Waste material passes to the rectum and out of the body in the form of faeces.

Growth and repair
Cells need to multiply for growth and cell replacement and amino acids band together to facilitate this. Other fatty acids broken down by the liver power cells and help form cell membranes.

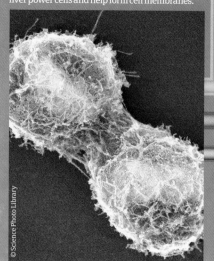

© Science Photo Library

How villi absorb nutrients in the small intestine
Humans need energy to function, yet the food we consume is not readily accessible for use by cells. We must first process our food, and break it down into much smaller molecules before it can be properly absorbed and utilised. The process where food is broken into smaller pieces until the molecules and nutrients we need can pass through the intestinal walls is called digestion. Absorption occurs within the small intestine, which has a huge surface area due to the presence of villi.

DID YOU KNOW? Canned or frozen veg can be just as vitamin rich as fresh as they're packaged within hours of being picked

How the liver turns your food into nutrients

The liver is one of the key organs involved in breaking down the food we eat into useable nutrient molecules for the body to release. These vital nutrients are then distributed around the body via the bloodstream to be utilised for growth, cell repair and movement. Excess energy can be stored around the body in fat cells or in glycogen granules and then broken down at a later date when necessary. If you're on a diet that eliminates certain foods, your body will be nutritionally unbalanced, which can lead to long-term poor health.

Metabolism
The liver is the place where nutrients are stored, changed and then distributed to cells across the body. The cells then metabolise these nutrients insuring that bloodstream nutrient levels are consistent.

Energy release
All cells need energy to operate, the same as any living organism. Most cells primarily use glucose, but some types of cells (such as muscle cells) also use fatty acids. During starvation, cells can also break down amino acids for energy to continue operating.

Glucose

Fatty acids

Amino acids

Key
- Usable glucose leaves the liver
- Glucose released from storage
- Fatty acids leave the liver for storage
- Fatty acids released from storage
- Amino acids leave liver to be used

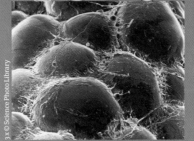

Fat cells
Fatty acids are stored within fat cells, alongside excess glucose, and these are broken down as and when needed and released in the bloodstream.

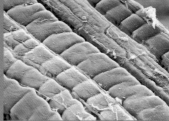

Muscle cells
Muscle cells are some of the highest consumers of energy and they also store energy (glucose) as glycogen. They then release this for muscle contraction.

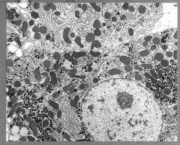

Liver cells
Liver cells can store surplus glucose as glycogen granules and mitochondria convert these granules into energy needed for the cell to operate.

3 x © Science Photo Library

1. Lacteal
Situated in the centre of each villi, there is a structure called the lymphatic capillary which absorbs fats.

2. Blood capillaries
These sit underneath the microvilli cells which line the villi's external surface. They quickly absorb nutrients and transfer them into the bloodstream immediately.

3. Blood vessels
These blood vessels lie beneath the villi, and allow for the capillaries that are situated within the villi to transport nutrients around the body with speed.

4. Epithelium
This one cell layer covers the whole external surface villi and allows for quick absorption of nutrients into the blood stream.

5. Nutrients
These are molecules which are absorbed from the stomach after being broken down. They travel through the epithelium and then enter the bloodstream via the capillaries.

How enzymes work

Enzymes are crucial in our processing of food. Many enzymes are present in saliva and they start the breakdown process of nutrients such as sugars and starches (carbohydrates) before food reaches the stomach. However, most of the breakdown occurs in the stomach, and three enzymes secreted by the pancreas and intestinal wall are crucial in this process; amylase, protease and lipase. Amylase is primarily used to break down starches and sugars, and will bind to them to do so. Protease works with proteins, breaking the large protein molecules down into amino acids. Lipase breaks down fat in smaller molecules so it can pass through into the lymphatic vessels and be transported to fat storage sites around the body via the blood.

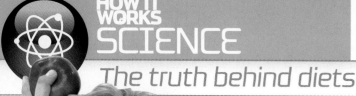

Types of diets

Do they work, or are they just dangerous?

The type of diet an individual goes on depends on the aim of the diet and how quickly they want results. It may also depend on what is popular at the time. Recent 'food fad' the Atkins diet was all the rage in the early-2000s, mainly due to celebrity endorsement. However, such extreme crash diets do not work because they ignore the real issue, which is the reason for the weight gain in the first place. Another reason why they fail to produce results long-term is that they are either too difficult to maintain or simply too dangerous to keep up for extended periods.

CABBAGE SOUP DIET

People looking to shift up to 10lbs in a week often turn to this diet. This regime involves eating just one food – cabbage soup – for seven days.

What you can eat: As much cabbage soup as desired.
What you can't eat: Everything else.
What are the benefits? A quick fix.
What are the risks? There is no balance to this diet – no protein, no carbohydrate. Despite being able to eat unlimited amounts of cabbage soup, the dieter will feel very hungry and, if continued for more than a week or so, the body will start lacking essential vitamins and minerals that are needed for operation.
How does it work? This diet is low in fat and calories, and because of this the weight does fall

CABBAGE SOUP DIET

off. However, this weight is lost mainly in the form of water and will be regained as soon as the dieter resumes their normal eating habits.
Does it work?
In the short term this will work, but it doesn't promote a healthy attitude towards dieting.

LOW CALORIE

Calorie counting (or point counting) can be very successful. However, individuals must have a reasonable idea of their previous intake and actual daily calorie demands from their body to make this work.

What you can eat: Fruit, vegetables, fish, chicken, rice.
What you can't eat: Cakes, sweets, chocolate, fats, alcohol.
What are the benefits? An effective way to analyse energy intake and restructure diet. A good way to slowly lose weight.
What are the risks? Significant cuts in calories can result in lethargy, hunger and tiredness and if the calories are not cut from the right food groups, fat intake may still be too high and weight will not be lost. Diet must also be balanced to ensure individuals get all necessary vitamins and minerals.
How does it work? Exceeding the recommended daily calorie intake causes the body to store the excess as fat, so adhering to this daily allowance means weight should not be gained through calorie intake.

Does it work?
Although calorie counting can work, individuals must still be aware of their fat intake as well as ensuring they stay active.

LOW CARB

This diet's been engineered to work by removing the more complex starches and sugars from your diet. You are encouraged to eat more fats on this diet (but only 'good' fats), but you are more likely to feel hungry as you do not have the steady-releasing carbohydrates in your diet.

What you can eat: Red meat, eggs, olive oil, cheese, poultry.
What you can't eat: Fruit, pasta, rice, bread, soft drinks.
What are the benefits? You're allowed to eat meats, cheese, fats – everything that is normally rationed in a diet!
What are the risks? Main risks are increased blood pressure, and lack of vitamins due to a reduced intake of vegetables and fruit.
How does it work? Removing the complex starches and sugars from your diet means that food taken into the body is immediately broken down and used.
Does it work?
Well, yes. However, there are several risks associated and due to the strict nature of what you are allowed, it is not healthy to follow long term.

VEGETARIAN/VEGAN

There are many health benefits to cutting all meat (and all animal products if vegan) out of your diet. However, vegetarians should endeavour to ensure that they obtain the nutrients found in meat and fish by eating protein-rich foods such as soy beans.

What you can eat: Bread, rice, pasta, vegetables, fruit, tofu.
What you can't eat: Beef, chicken, pork, game (vegan – no dairy).
What are the benefits? Increased vitamin intake, lower fat content.
What are the risks? Major risk is that individual will not eat enough protein – diet must be carefully planned to ensure it is balanced.

"Turning vegetarian may help you lose weight and be much healthier" Vegetarian diet

How does it work? Eliminating meat (and all animal products if vegan) reduces the intake of fat, resulting in an overall calorie reduction.
Does it work?
Individuals are far more likely to eat lower fat diets, with higher levels of vegetables and carbs. They are likely to get higher doses of vitamins and more fibre than a meat eater. Overall, turning vegetarian may help you lose weight and be much healthier.

Cut it out

Fat is the most caloric of all foods, and close behind is alcohol, so one of the simplest ways to lose weight is to reduce the amount of fat and alcohol in your diet. We do still need some fat in our diet for cell health and hormone production, for example. It's tough to lead a fat-free existence as even fruit and vegetables contain small amounts of fat.

DID YOU KNOW? 'Diet' foods labelled as 'low fat' can be misleading as this often means they are high in sugar instead

GI DIET

Milk is on the menu if you're following the GI diet

GI DIET

This diet doesn't cut out any one food group – it makes you have the best fats, proteins and carbs to offer a balanced diet with no cravings.

What you can eat: All-Bran, wholegrain bread, peanuts, carrots, milk.
What you can't eat: Doughnuts, white bread, potatoes, dates, syrup.
What are the benefits? Great for lowering sugar – recommended for diabetics. It is the diet you are supposedly least likely to feel hungry on! Will improve and steady your energy levels.
What are the risks? No real risks, but GI is hard to track so the individual must know all contents of a meal before being able to work out GI.
How does it work? The aim of the diet is to stabilise calorie intake while also encouraging healthier eating. It works by encouraging the participant to eat 'good' foods which have a more consistent, steady release of energy throughout the day and to avoid high sugar foods.
Does it work?
It is recommended for individuals who need to lose weight over a long term basis, and for individuals looking to maintain their weight.

DETOX DIET

This diet is supposed to cut all 'bad' foods and 'cleanse' the body of unwanted chemicals or toxins that accumulate in our systems through food additives, caffeine, poor diet and so on. The supposed side effects of such toxins are weight gain, cellulite, headaches, bad skin, bloating, and generally feeling unwell.

What you can eat: Usually water, fresh vegetables and fruit.
What you can't eat: Alcohol, chocolates, preserved foods, fried/greasy foods.
What are the benefits? The individual who partakes in a diet such as this is likely to feel refreshed and 'cleansed' at the end of the diet. Weight may be lost.
What are the risks? Main risk is lack of balance to the diet, and the extreme nature can mean the

"A dramatic and extreme diet which can have negative results" Detox diet

body is shocked and goes into starvation mode. Therefore, if weight loss is the aim, this may not occur. Also, for the first few days/week, outbreaks of spots and lethargy have been reported.
How does it work? Due to the associated low calorie intake of a detox diet, weight loss is indeed a likely outcome of such a diet.
Does it work?
Yes and no. The weight loss will vary depending on how strict the detox is, but it is often a dramatic and extreme diet which can have negative results.

LOW FAT

The low-fat diet is well known for promoting a healthy heart and reducing the amount of fat – especially saturated fats and cholesterol – in the diet instantly lowers your calorie intake.

What you can eat: Fruit, vegetables, oily fish (oily fish is high in fat, but guidelines recommend eating one portion per week to prevent blood from being sticky, thereby reducing the risk of heart attack).
What you can't eat: Processed or takeaway foods, fatty meats, full-fat dairy products, diet food (although diet snacks may claim to be low-fat, many are in fact very high in sugar).
What are the benefits? Reducing saturated fats can lower the cholesterol linked to heart diseases.
What are the risks? A healthy diet requires some fat to insulate the body's major organs. Also, some essential vitamins are soluble in fat so cutting out fat completely isn't ideal.
How does it work?
Because fat contains more calories than almost any type of other food, it seems only sensible to watch the amount of fat in the diet and ensure the daily calorie intake doesn't exceed the recommended allowance.
Does it work?
Experts confirm that a diet low in fat but high in fibre will aid weight loss and help it stay off.

One portion of oily fish a week is recommended

LOW FAT DIET

LOW CARB DIET

Eggs are a great source of protein, but don't have them fried!

MEAL REPLACEMENT

Meal replacement plans claim to offer a way of controlling calorie intake by removing the need to count the calories of two of your three daily meals – usually breakfast and lunch are supplemented with shakes, bars, and soups.

What you can eat: "A shake for breakfast, a shake for lunch, and then a proper dinner," two to three 100-calorie snacks per day (most plans also recommend drinking plenty of water or low-calorie drinks), a 600-calorie healthy meal.
What you can't eat: High-calorie snacks, processed foods, sweets.
What are the benefits? By law the meal supplement must contain the recommended daily nutrients for a healthy diet (including calories, proteins, vitamins and minerals). A convenient way to live by a calorie-controlled diet without the need to get your calculator out.
What are the risks? This type of diet does little to instill the values of healthy eating and without the plan, there's a chance the individual will be unable to maintain a balanced diet.
How does it work? Much like the low-calorie diet, the meal replacement plan is aimed at carefully controlling calorie intake so the dieter takes in fewer calories than the body needs and so draws on their fat stores for the extra energy required for the body to function properly.
Does it work?
Sticking to a reduced-calorie diet should shift the weight. However, it depends on the number of calories consumed and the physical activity taken up. Generally, an intake of 1,200 to 1,400 calories per day results in a loss of 1-2lb per week.

"This diet does very little to instill the values of healthy eating" Meal replacement diet

categories
explained

Exploration Solar System The Universe Astronomy General

HOW IT
WORKS
SPACE

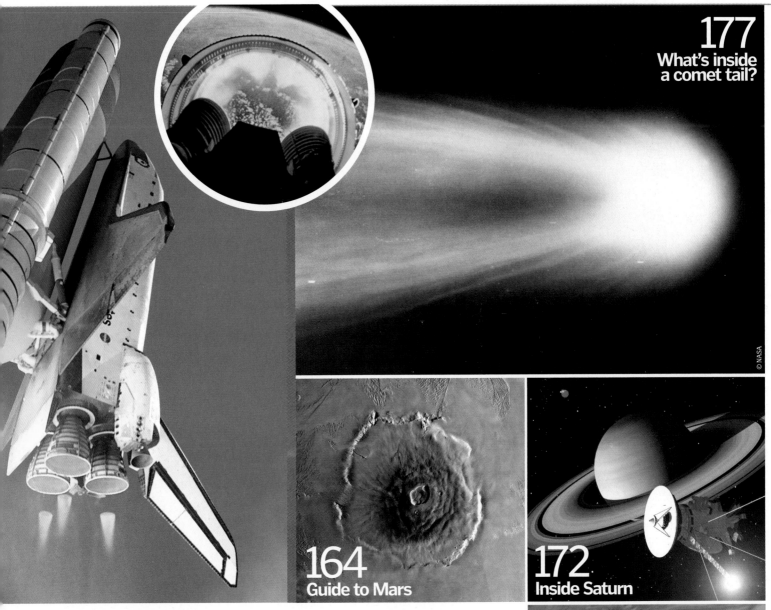

© NASA

Planet killers

Remnants of failed planets, asteroids are dry, dusty and atmosphereless rocks drifting through space

 Asteroids are the most numerous bodies in our solar system, with hundreds of thousands of them orbiting around the Sun in both belts and as individuals. They far outnumber our well-documented planets (and dwarf planets, to that matter) and are being studied by space agencies world wide, each of which are trying to shed some light on what historically were written off as simple floating rocks. However, asteroids are unique in the fact that they tell us much about the conditions of the universe post-big bang, how astrophysics effect space phenomena and how planets are formed, granting the scientific community great insight into our solar system's origins and workings.

Head to Head
ASTEROID FILMS

FAIL
1. Asteroid
The city of Dallas, Texas, is going to be destroyed by an asteroid. The American government fires huge lasers to destroy it but only succeed in breaking it into small pieces that still go on to destroy the city.

BIG FAIL
2. Armageddon
Another asteroid is on course to destroy the world. The American government hatches a plan to plant a bomb in its core to split it in two so it will miss Earth. However, an earlier meteorite destroys Shanghai, China.

EPIC FAIL
3. Deep Impact
Yet another asteroid is on a collision course with the Earth. The American government detonates nuclear bombs to destroy it but only succeed in splitting it in two pieces, one of which destroys quarter of the planet.

DID YOU KNOW? The first probe dedicated to studying asteroids was the NEAR Shoemaker, launched by NASA in 1997

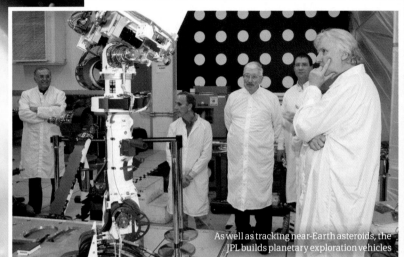

As well as tracking near-Earth asteroids, the JPL builds planetary exploration vehicles

© Science Photo Library

Structures

There are three types of asteroid: carbonaceous (C-type), siliceous (S-type) and metallic (M-type) variants, each corresponding to the composition of an asteroid, be that stony, stony-iron or iron. The composition of an asteroid – be that shape or material – is dependent on when and what it was formed from, as well as if it has undergone reconstruction post-collision.

Initially, at the dawn of the solar system, most asteroids were much larger than those now commonly found by astronomers, with sizes more consistent with a planet such as Mars and shapes varying wildly. However, the radioactive decay of elements within the asteroid rock melted these larger bodies, and during their fluid stage, gravity pulled them into spherical shapes before they cooled. At this point, though, many smaller asteroids – which cooled more efficiently than their larger brethren – did not reach melting point and retained their uniform rocky-metallic composition and their initial irregular shape.

This process of asteroid formation can be seen vividly when contrasting many of the asteroids that modern scientists and astronomers are currently studying. Take the asteroid Ceres (Ceres was the first asteroid to be discovered and is now considered by some astronomers as a dwarf planet) for example – this is a large asteroid (it has an equatorial radius of 487km) and, in turn, is both spherical in structure and carbonaceous composition (C-class), as it was pulled apart easily and cooled slowly. However, if you compare Ceres to Ida, for example, which is a small asteroid (it has a mean radius of 15.7km), you find the latter is both irregular in shape (funnily, it looks like a potato) and heavily composed of iron and magnesium-silicates (S-class).

Orbits

The majority of asteroids in our solar system are found in a concentration known as the main belt, which lies between Mars and Jupiter. This belt contains thousands of asteroids and takes roughly four and a half years to orbit the Sun on a slightly elliptical course and low inclination. Despite the fact that they all orbit in the same direction, collisions do occur at low velocities (for such large objects) and these cause the asteroids to be continuously broken up into smaller variants. Of this main belt, certain groups have been captured into peculiar orbits, such as the Trojan group of asteroids that follow Jupiter's orbit, or the Amor or Apollo groups, which cross the paths of Earth and Mars respectively and the Aten group, which sits inside Earth's own orbit.

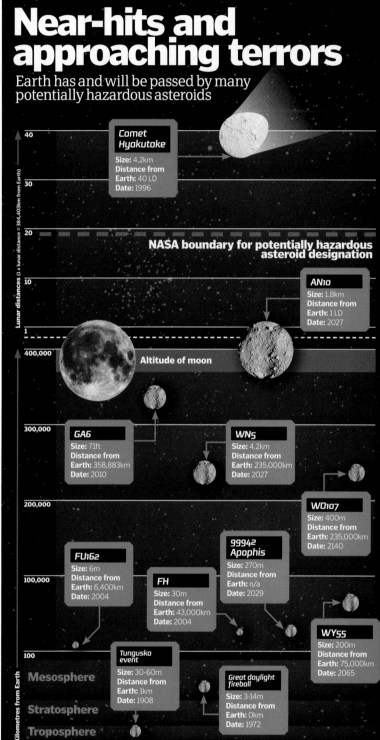

Near-hits and approaching terrors
Earth has and will be passed by many potentially hazardous asteroids

Lunar distances (1 x lunar distance = 384,403km from Earth)

Kilometres from Earth

Comet Hyakutake
Size: 4.2km
Distance from Earth: 40 LD
Date: 1996

NASA boundary for potentially hazardous asteroid designation

AN10
Size: 1.8km
Distance from Earth: 1 LD
Date: 2027

Altitude of moon

GA6
Size: 71ft
Distance from Earth: 358,883km
Date: 2010

WN5
Size: 4.2km
Distance from Earth: 235,000km
Date: 2027

WO107
Size: 400m
Distance from Earth: 235,000km
Date: 2140

FU162
Size: 6m
Distance from Earth: 6,400km
Date: 2004

FH
Size: 30m
Distance from Earth: 43,000km
Date: 2004

99942 Apophis
Size: 270m
Distance from Earth: n/a
Date: 2029

WY55
Size: 200m
Distance from Earth: 75,000km
Date: 2065

Mesosphere

Tunguska event
Size: 30-60m
Distance from Earth: 1km
Date: 1908

Great daylight fireball
Size: 3-14m
Distance from Earth: 0km
Date: 1972

Stratosphere

Troposphere

"The composition of an asteroid is dependent on when and what it was formed from"

Asteroids in our solar system

Most of the asteroids in our solar system are positioned between the orbits of Mars and Jupiter, clustered in massive belts. However, some come close to Earth on their individual orbits and these are referred to as near-Earth asteroids. We take a look at some of the most notable...

A gravity map of the asteroid Eros. Blue indicates a low gravity slope, red a high slope

Saturn's orbit

Jupiter's orbit

Earth's o

Main belt

Mars's orbit

Direction of orbits

Eros

Dimension: 16.84km
Aphelion: 266.762Gm (1.783 AU)
Perihelion: 169.548Gm (1.133 AU)
Orbital period: 643.219 days
Escape velocity: 0.0103km/s
Temperature: ~227K
Spectral type: S

With a one-in-ten chance of hitting either Earth or Mars in the next million years, Eros is one of the largest and well-studied near-Earth asteroids. In fact, Eros is one of a few asteroids to actually be landed upon by an Earth probe, and as such we have a wealth of information on it.

Ceres as imaged by the Hubble Space Telescope

Ceres

Dimension: 590 miles   **Aphelion:** 446,669,320km (2.9858 AU)   **Perihelion:** 380,995,855km (2.5468 AU)   **Orbital period:** 1,680.5 days   **Escape velocity:** 0.51km/s
Temperature: ~167K   **Spectral type:** C

Technically classed as a dwarf planet, Ceres – named after the Roman goddess of growing plants and the harvest – is by far the most massive body in the asteroid belt. Indeed, it is so big compared to its neighbouring asteroids that it contains 32 per cent of the belt's total mass.

Icarus

Dimension: 1.4km   **Aphelion:** 294.590Gm (1.969 AU)
Perihelion: 27.923Gm (0.187 AU)   **Orbital period:** 408.778 days   **Escape velocity:** 0.000 74 km/s
Temperature: ~242K   **Spectral type:** U

Icarus is from the Apollo asteroid sub-class of near-Earth asteroids and has the unusual characteristic that at its perihelion it is closer to the Sun than Mercury. Named after the Icarus of Greek mythology, the asteroid passes by Earth at gaps of nine, 19 and 38 years.

How to deflect an impact...

1. Nuclear explosions
This method involves firing a nuclear bomb into the asteroid. Problems may occur if the explosion just splits the asteroid into smaller pieces.

Nuclear explosion

2. Multiple explosions
Detonating multiple nuclear bombs close to impact would push the asteroid to one side and onto another, non-Earth destroying trajectory.

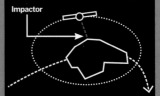

Impactor

3. Kinetic impactor
Similar to the last option, this method would involve firing a solid projectile into an asteroid in order to alter its momentum and change its course.

5 TOP FACTS
ASTEROIDS

Naked
1 The only asteroid in the main belt visible to the naked eye is Vesta, which has a mean diameter of 530km and contains nine per cent of the entire asteroid belt's mass.

Coma
2 The way comets and asteroids are distinguished relies on visual appearance, with comets displaying a perceptible coma behind them while asteroids have none.

Naming
3 An asteroid can only be named under the consultation of the International Astronomical Union, who will approve or disapprove the proposition.

Photo
4 The first true asteroids to be photographed close up were Gaspra in 1991 and Ida in 1993. They were imaged by the Galileo space probe en route to Jupiter.

New
5 The latest asteroid to be landed on is Itokawa, an S-type asteroid that crosses the path of Mars. The Hayabusa probe returned to Earth with a surface sample.

DID YOU KNOW? The asteroid Ida has its own moon, Dactyl, which orbits at a distance of 56 miles

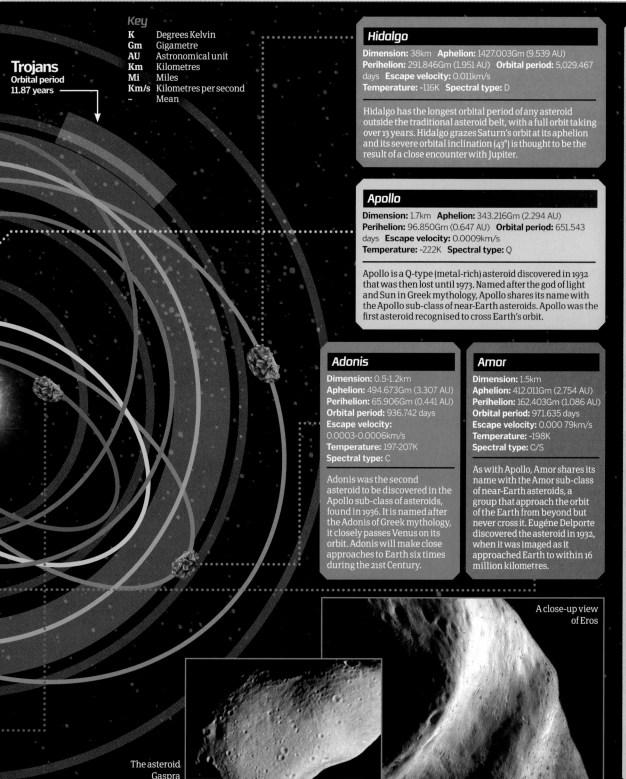

Key
K	Degrees Kelvin
Gm	Gigametre
AU	Astronomical unit
Km	Kilometres
Mi	Miles
Km/s	Kilometres per second
~	Mean

Trojans
Orbital period 11.87 years

The asteroid Gaspra

Hidalgo
Dimension: 38km **Aphelion:** 1427.003Gm (9.539 AU)
Perihelion: 291.846Gm (1.951 AU) **Orbital period:** 5,029.467 days **Escape velocity:** 0.011km/s
Temperature: ~116K **Spectral type:** D

Hidalgo has the longest orbital period of any asteroid outside the traditional asteroid belt, with a full orbit taking over 13 years. Hidalgo grazes Saturn's orbit at its aphelion and its severe orbital inclination (43°) is thought to be the result of a close encounter with Jupiter.

Apollo
Dimension: 1.7km **Aphelion:** 343.216Gm (2.294 AU)
Perihelion: 96.850Gm (0.647 AU) **Orbital period:** 651.543 days **Escape velocity:** 0.0009km/s
Temperature: ~222K **Spectral type:** Q

Apollo is a Q-type (metal-rich) asteroid discovered in 1932 that was then lost until 1973. Named after the god of light and Sun in Greek mythology, Apollo shares its name with the Apollo sub-class of near-Earth asteroids. Apollo was the first asteroid recognised to cross Earth's orbit.

Adonis
Dimension: 0.5-1.2km
Aphelion: 494.673Gm (3.307 AU)
Perihelion: 65.906Gm (0.441 AU)
Orbital period: 936.742 days
Escape velocity: 0.0003-0.0006km/s
Temperature: 197-207K
Spectral type: C

Adonis was the second asteroid to be discovered in the Apollo sub-class of asteroids, found in 1936. It is named after the Adonis of Greek mythology, it closely passes Venus on its orbit. Adonis will make close approaches to Earth six times during the 21st Century.

Amor
Dimension: 1.5km
Aphelion: 412.011Gm (2.754 AU)
Perihelion: 162.403Gm (1.086 AU)
Orbital period: 971.635 days
Escape velocity: 0.000 79km/s
Temperature: ~198K
Spectral type: C/S

As with Apollo, Amor shares its name with the Amor sub-class of near-Earth asteroids, a group that approach the orbit of the Earth from beyond but never cross it. Eugéne Delporte discovered the asteroid in 1932, when it was imaged as it approached Earth to within 16 million kilometres.

A close-up view of Eros

Filling the gap

Franz Xaver von Zach (1754-1832), astronomer and leader of the Seeberg Observatory, Germany, believed that there was a missing planet orbiting the Sun between Mars and Jupiter. To prove his theory von Zach organised a group of 24 astronomers and gave them each a part of the celestial zodiac to search in an attempt to track down his errant planet. Unfortunately, despite such a large team, von Zach was beaten to the discovery by the Italian Catholic priest and mathematician Giuseppe Piazzi, who accidentally discovered the asteroid Ceres in 1801.

Franz Xaver Von Zach

Giuseppe Piazzi

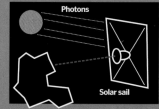
4. Solar sail
This method would involve attaching a 5,000km-wide sail to an asteroid. The constant pressure of sunlight over a large area would slowly alter its course.
Photons / Solar sail

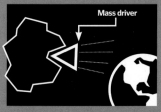
5. Mass driver
A huge space drill would be fired into the asteroid, and drill out the innards before firing them into space, altering its mass and changing the course.
Mass driver

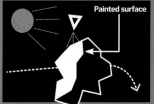
6. Paint
By coating parts of the asteroid in paint, the amounts of thermal radiation emitted by the asteroid's Sun-facing side could be increased, altering its path.
Painted surface

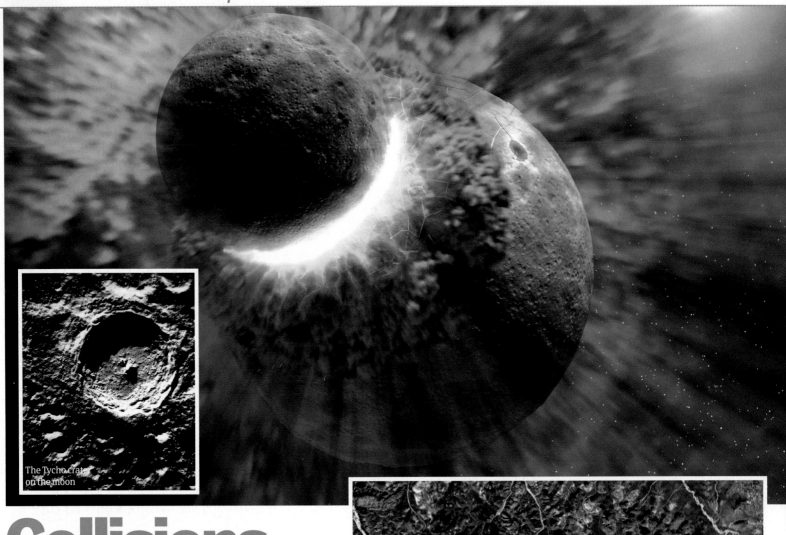

The Tycho crater on the moon

Collisions and craters

Evidence of collisions can be found everywhere

When asteroids collide with each other there are three main outcomes, each of which depends on the size of the impacting asteroid. If the incoming asteroid is 1/50,000th the size of the larger body then it will merely create a large crater, sending small fragments out into space. If the impactor is roughly 1/50,000th the size of the impacted, then the latter will fracture before breaking into rock and dust, before being pulled back together into a ball of rubble by gravity. Finally, if the incoming asteroid is larger than 1/50,000th the size of the other, larger asteroid, then it will immediately shatter into pieces and form a mini belt of smaller asteroids.

Very rarely, asteroids collide with the Earth, the most notable of which in the past 100 million years was the instigator of the Cretaceous-Tertiary extinction event that wiped out the majority of the dinosaurs 65.5 million years ago. However, there is evidence across the world of many other lesser-sized asteroids impacting the Earth, with their craters remaining a testament to their size. Importantly, their size is not directly represented by the size of the crater, which is roughly ten times the size of the impacting body. These impacts are postulated to have occurred infrequently over the Earth's 4 billion year life span.

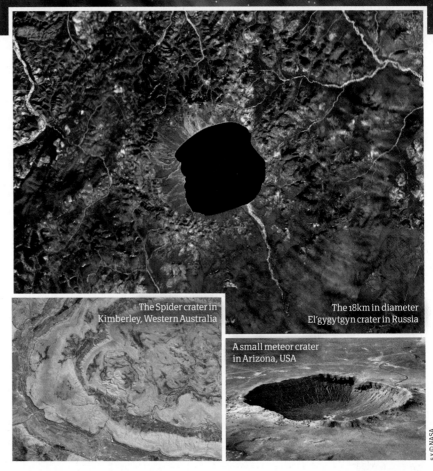

The Spider crater in Kimberley, Western Australia

The 18km in diameter El'gygytgyn crater in Russia

A small meteor crater in Arizona, USA

5 x © NASA

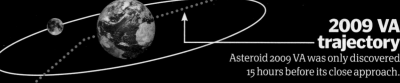

Meteor

Asteroids vs meteoroids vs comets

Despite common misconceptions, these space phenomena are different from each other. An asteroid is a small solar system body in orbit around the Sun, which are sometimes referred to or classed as minor planets. A meteoroid, however, is a sand-to-boulder-sized particle of debris drifting through space in orbit around the Sun or other bodies. They are smaller than asteroids and tend to travel at higher speeds; their composition ranging from iron to ice. Crucially, though, meteoroids differ from meteors and meteorites, although they are all part of the same body. A meteor is the visible streak of light that occurs when a meteoroid enters the Earth's atmosphere, while a meteorite is the remaining part of the meteoroid that impacts Earth.

Finally, comets are ice-based small solar system bodies that when close to the Sun display a visible coma (a nebulous temporary atmosphere) and tail of ice, dust and rock particles. Comets, unlike asteroids, generally originate in the outer solar system.

Comet

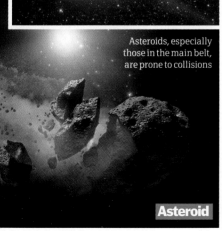

Asteroids, especially those in the main belt, are prone to collisions

Asteroid

6 x © NASA

Blast off
The Near Earth Asteroid Rendezvous (NEAR) space probe Shoemaker is launched.

JPL engineers work on the Dawn space probe pre-launch

On its trail
A chart from the JPL tracking the movement of an asteroid through space.

The asteroid finders

The Near Earth Asteroid Tracking (NEAT) program run at NASA's Jet Propulsion Laboratory has one sole purpose, to find, explore and track near-Earth asteroids

The Near Earth Asteroid Tracking program based at NASA's Jet Propulsion Laboratory has discovered thousands of asteroids during its life span, both from its range of ground-based telescopes – a good example is the GEODSS (Ground-based Electro-Optical Deep Space Surveillance) telescope located on Haleakala, Maui, Hawaii – to its deep space probes, scanning space for new asteroids and other space phenomenon. Its greatest achievement, however, has been its successful insertion of the NEAR (Near Earth Asteroid Rendezvous) Shoemaker space probe into orbit around the asteroid Eros in 2001, as well as landing upon its surface. This made it the first ever spacecraft to complete a soft-land (a landing where the probe is functional afterwards) on any asteroid.

The mission to Eros was primarily to return data on its composition, mineralogy, morphology, internal mass distribution and magnetic field. However, considering its success and time spent orbiting the asteroid, it was possible to also study its regolith properties (the loose material scattered over its surface), interactions with solar winds and spin rate. This information was garnered with the spacecraft's equipped x-ray/gamma ray spectrometer (used to measure the intensity of gamma radiation), near-infrared imaging spectrograph (used to measure and image the light properties of the near-infrared end of the electromagnetic spectrum), multi-spectral camera fitted with CCD imaging detector, laser rangefinder and

magnetometer (measures the strength and/or direction of a magnetic field). Indeed, thanks to this wealth of information, we now have more first-hand data on Eros than any other asteroid.

NASA's Jet Propulsion Laboratory in California

"Olbers' Paradox suggested that the night sky should be uniformly bright, not dark"

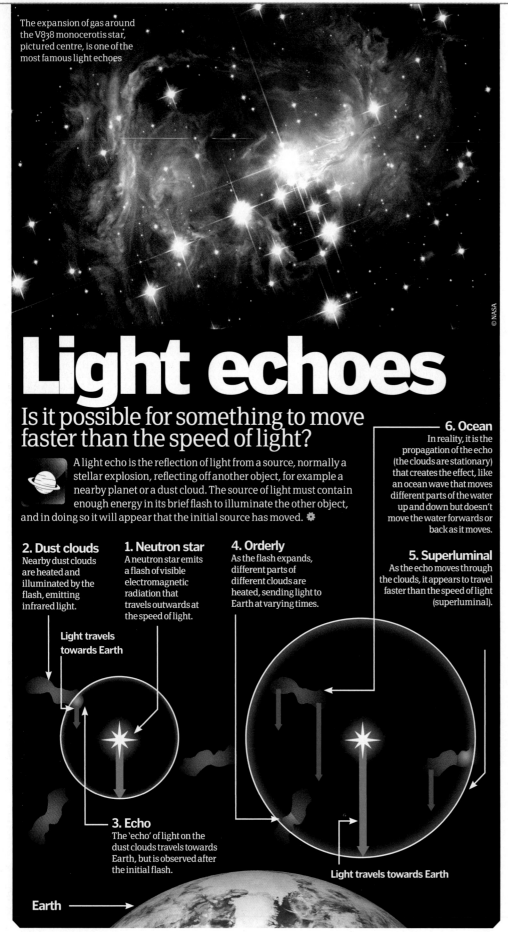

The expansion of gas around the V838 monocerotis star, pictured centre, is one of the most famous light echoes

© NASA

Light echoes

Is it possible for something to move faster than the speed of light?

A light echo is the reflection of light from a source, normally a stellar explosion, reflecting off another object, for example a nearby planet or a dust cloud. The source of light must contain enough energy in its brief flash to illuminate the other object, and in doing so it will appear that the initial source has moved. ⚙

2. Dust clouds
Nearby dust clouds are heated and illuminated by the flash, emitting infrared light.

1. Neutron star
A neutron star emits a flash of visible electromagnetic radiation that travels outwards at the speed of light.

4. Orderly
As the flash expands, different parts of different clouds are heated, sending light to Earth at varying times.

6. Ocean
In reality, it is the propagation of the echo (the clouds are stationary) that creates the effect, like an ocean wave that moves different parts of the water up and down but doesn't move the water forwards or back as it moves.

5. Superluminal
As the echo moves through the clouds, it appears to travel faster than the speed of light (superluminal).

Light travels towards Earth

3. Echo
The 'echo' of light on the dust clouds travels towards Earth, but is observed after the initial flash.

Light travels towards Earth

Earth →

Why is the night sky black?
To find out, we need to understand Olbers' Paradox

In the early-20th Century, astronomers had a problem. It was largely believed that, in both space and time, the universe was infinite and non-moving. Under Newton's law of gravitation, this was the only way the universe could be seen to be stable. However, a German astronomer called Heinrich Wilhelm Olbers had come up with a problem in 1823 that seemed unsolvable. If stars and galaxies were randomly spread throughout an infinite, static universe that had been around forever, then at every point in the night sky we should see a star emitting light. Known as Olbers' Paradox, this conundrum suggested that the night sky should be uniformly bright, not dark.

Astronomers started observing stars and galaxies and, instead of them being static, they realised that everything was actually moving away from one another. They measured this by noting the redshift of stars, the movement of light towards one end of the spectrum as a source moves away (like a police siren moving away from you that spreads out its sound waves and appears to lower in pitch). They realised that the universe was expanding from a Big Bang, and thus Olbers' Paradox was satisfied. With a finite, non-static universe, it was deduced that not only had the light from every star not reached Earth – as they each had a finite lifetime – but also there was almost certainly not a star in every direction, meaning the night sky should appear black. ⚙

Should there be a bright star in every direction?

© NASA

5 TOP FACTS
PLANETARY NEBULAE

Formation
1 Small-to-medium sized stars, such as our Sun, form these stunning nebulae at the end of their stellar lifetime when they have exhausted their nuclear fuel.

Life and size
2 These nebulae survive for 25,000 to 100,000 years, a short life by astronomical standards, and expand at approximately 16 kilometres per second.

Red giant
3 The dying stars that eject planetary nebulae – red giants – are not massive enough to become supernovae as they have previously shed some mass.

The Sun
4 It is estimated that in 5 billion years our Sun will also become a planetary nebulae, following a rapid expansion that will consume the Earth.

Not so planetary
5 William Herschel incorrectly described these nebulae as "planetary" in 1764 when he mistook the star at the centre for a planet. Despite the error, the name stuck.

DID YOU KNOW? *The Cat's Eye Nebula was discovered by William Herschel on 15 February 1786*

The Cat's Eye Nebula

A dying star's last breath has produced unprecedented insight into nebula formation

Throwing off glowing gas in concentric shells, the Cat's Eye Nebula is one of the most complex and interesting known planetary phase nebulae and is located about three thousand light years from Earth in the Draco constellation. This image, captured by the Hubble Space Telescope in 2004, has led scientists to believe the complicated and intricate structures on display may be the cause of a binary star system in the centre of the nebula because of the unique shell formation.

In astronomical terms the nebula is very young – at only about a thousand years old – forming after a sudden change in mass of the central star (or stars). The reason for this change in mass is still unknown, but the lighter rings of gas around the edges are known to have been produced in bursts in the latter stages of stellar evolution before the inner nebula formed. Observations over the past 20 years indicate the nebula is still expanding. ⚙

The bright central star is surrounded by a multi-million-degree gas cloud

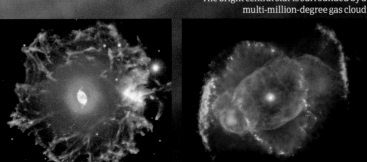

This processed image reveals the concentric rings

All images © NASA

"Enceladus reflects nearly all the sunlight that reaches it"

Enceladus

Enceladus is Saturn's sixth-largest moon and orbits within the E ring, the planet's outermost ring

Although Enceladus is the sixth largest moon of Saturn, it's still on the small side. This flattened ellipsoid is one-seventh the size of Earth's moon and about the size of Great Britain, with a mean diameter of 505km (314mi). One of the brightest bodies in the solar system, Enceladus is icy and reflects nearly all of the sunlight that reaches it. This keeps the moon at about -201°C.

Enceladus is one of five Saturnian moons known to orbit within the E ring. It orbits about 240,000km (150,000mi) from Saturn, with an orbital period of 32 hours.

The moon's rotational period is the same as its orbit, so the same side is always facing Saturn. Enceladus is also in a 2:1 orbital resonance with the nearby moon Dione. For every orbit of Saturn completed by Dione, Enceladus completes two orbits, and each moon exerts a gravitational force on the other. This relationship helps to keep Enceladus's orbital path stable.

Enceladus's place within the E ring may explain how the ring stays in existence, as astronomers believe that otherwise this wide, diffuse ring – comprising ice and dust particles – would have broken apart. The moon's cryovolcanism may have

caused it to form in the first place and may well be replenishing the ring. There's a chance it could also be replenished by dust particles that rise when meteors strike Enceladus's surface, as well as the surface of other moons nearby.

Although Enceladus was first observed in 1789, little was known about this icy moon until NASA's Voyager flybys in the early-Eighties. The Cassini spacecraft revealed much more about Enceladus in 2005, but there's still a lot to learn. A joint NASA/ESA mission to return to several of Saturn's moons has been proposed but may not take place until 2020. ⚙

Enceladus could easily fit in the length of the UK

Shear heating on Enceladus

The moon was once thought to be entirely composed of ice. However, the water vapour on Enceladus was found to contain high levels of salt, which pointed to a sub-surface ocean. This liquid means that Enceladus must have an internal heat source. It may come from both radioactive decay or shear heating, also known as tidal friction. As the moon orbits Saturn, the planet's tides cause Enceladus to be alternately compressed and pulled apart. Faults on Enceladus rub against each other and the subsequent friction melts ice and forces water, vapour and other gases out of vents.

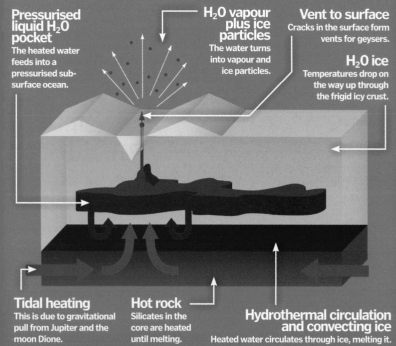

Pressurised liquid H_2O pocket
The heated water feeds into a pressurised sub-surface ocean.

H_2O vapour plus ice particles
The water turns into vapour and ice particles.

Vent to surface
Cracks in the surface form vents for geysers.

H_2O ice
Temperatures drop on the way up through the frigid icy crust.

Tidal heating
This is due to gravitational pull from Jupiter and the moon Dione.

Hot rock
Silicates in the core are heated until melting.

Hydrothermal circulation and convecting ice
Heated water circulates through ice, melting it.

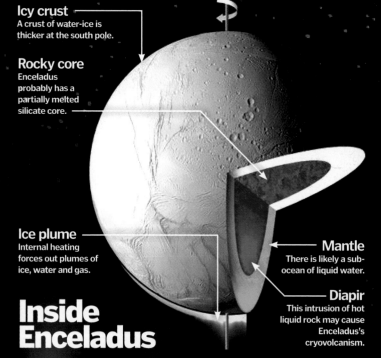

Icy crust
A crust of water-ice is thicker at the south pole.

Rocky core
Enceladus probably has a partially melted silicate core.

Ice plume
Internal heating forces out plumes of ice, water and gas.

Mantle
There is likely a sub-ocean of liquid water.

Diapir
This intrusion of hot liquid rock may cause Enceladus's cryovolcanism.

Inside Enceladus

Plumes of ice, water and gas are expelled from the surface

BIG

1. Iapetus
At 1,436 km (892 miles) in diameter, Iapetus is Saturn's third largest moon. Its equatorial ridge and half-dark, half-light appearance make it unique.

BIGGER

2. Rhea
Discovered back in 1672, Rhea is about 100 kilometres (62 miles) wider in diameter than Iapetus. It is heavily cratered and has a wispy terrain.

BIGGEST

3. Titan
Titan is Jupiter's largest moon by far, at more than 5,150km (3,200 miles) in diameter. It also has a thick atmosphere. It was discovered by Christiaan Huygens in 1655.

DID YOU KNOW? The geological features on Enceladus are named after characters and locations in the book *Arabian Nights*

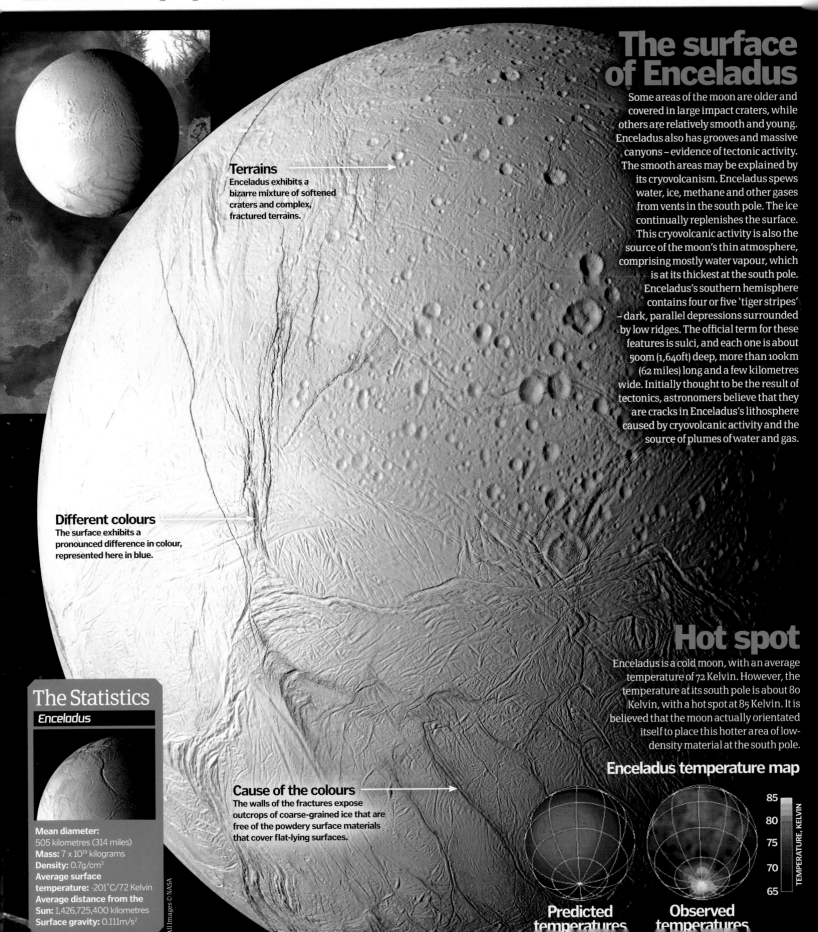

The surface of Enceladus

Some areas of the moon are older and covered in large impact craters, while others are relatively smooth and young. Enceladus also has grooves and massive canyons – evidence of tectonic activity. The smooth areas may be explained by its cryovolcanism. Enceladus spews water, ice, methane and other gases from vents in the south pole. The ice continually replenishes the surface. This cryovolcanic activity is also the source of the moon's thin atmosphere, comprising mostly water vapour, which is at its thickest at the south pole. Enceladus's southern hemisphere contains four or five 'tiger stripes' – dark, parallel depressions surrounded by low ridges. The official term for these features is sulci, and each one is about 500m (1,640ft) deep, more than 100km (62 miles) long and a few kilometres wide. Initially thought to be the result of tectonics, astronomers believe that they are cracks in Enceladus's lithosphere caused by cryovolcanic activity and the source of plumes of water and gas.

Terrains
Enceladus exhibits a bizarre mixture of softened craters and complex, fractured terrains.

Different colours
The surface exhibits a pronounced difference in colour, represented here in blue.

Hot spot

Enceladus is a cold moon, with an average temperature of 72 Kelvin. However, the temperature at its south pole is about 80 Kelvin, with a hot spot at 85 Kelvin. It is believed that the moon actually orientated itself to place this hotter area of low-density material at the south pole.

Enceladus temperature map

85
80
75
70
65

TEMPERATURE, KELVIN

Predicted temperatures

Observed temperatures

Cause of the colours
The walls of the fractures expose outcrops of coarse-grained ice that are free of the powdery surface materials that cover flat-lying surfaces.

The Statistics
Enceladus

Mean diameter: 505 kilometres (314 miles)
Mass: 7 x 10¹⁹ kilograms
Density: 0.7g/cm³
Average surface temperature: -201°C/72 Kelvin
Average distance from the Sun: 1,426,725,400 kilometres
Surface gravity: 0.111m/s²

Finding your bearings in the event of reversal

Greater complexity
During transition, the field, though depleted and 'tangled', is unlikely to disappear entirely.

Geographic poles
These are fixed: it is the polarity not the continental land mass that shifts 180° during reversal.

Confusing directions
What we know as the current magnetic north pole is actually a southern polarity.

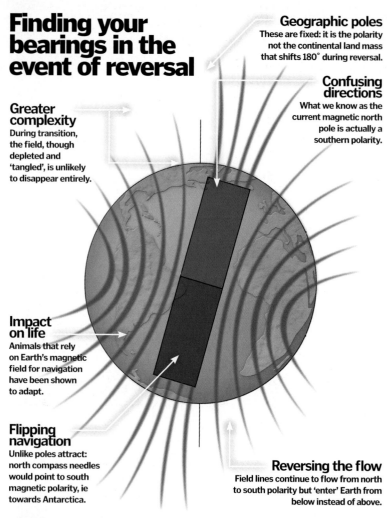

Impact on life
Animals that rely on Earth's magnetic field for navigation have been shown to adapt.

Flipping navigation
Unlike poles attract: north compass needles would point to south magnetic polarity, ie towards Antarctica.

Reversing the flow
Field lines continue to flow from north to south polarity but 'enter' Earth from below instead of above.

Geomagnetic reversal

Every 300,000 years the Earth's magnetic poles switch places and we're overdue a change! So just what causes this to happen...

A geomagnetic reversal is a change in the orientation of Earth's magnetic field where magnetic north and south become interchanged. This occurs as Earth's magnetic field derives from the fluid motion in its outer-core, with heat from the inner-core causing this 'fluid' to rise. It is the currents that flow in this electrically conductive iron-rich fluid that generate the magnetic field, so when these change, so does the field's direction.

On average, every 300,000 years Earth's magnetic poles switch places; a

process historically described and dated by the orientation of magnetite crystals set in place by cooling volcanic rocks. It is thought, though, that every few thousand years or so the fluid outer-core attempts to reverse, but that the solid inner-core can only change by diffusion and, because of this, acts as a braking mechanism. When it does actually occur, lengthy falls in field intensity tend to precede a reversal.

Interestingly, while current field strength is relatively high, it has continued to fall for approximately the past 2,000 years. ✿

Red dwarf

At 7.5 per cent the mass of the sun, these slow-burning stars create a less than white-hot profile

The red dwarf represents the most common star-type in the known universe. It is so-named after its distinct spectral class and diminutive size: at less than half the mass of the Sun. Sufficient gravitational pressure at the core of a star sparks hydrogen fusion: a process whereby hydrogen nuclei collide to form helium. It is this energy that gives off heat and causes the star to shine.

With increasing size and weight, core pressure builds, raising the temperature and speeding up fusion. At 7.5 per cent the mass of the Sun, the smallest red dwarfs barely possess enough mass to sustain this process, often slow-burning at 1/10,000th the intensity, forging a less than white-hot profile.

Despite appearances, this is an advantage; a red dwarf can consume energy at much lower levels, helping extend its life. It may take 10 trillion years to exhaust its store of hydrogen fuel, easily outdoing the age of the universe. ✿

Small but perfectly formed

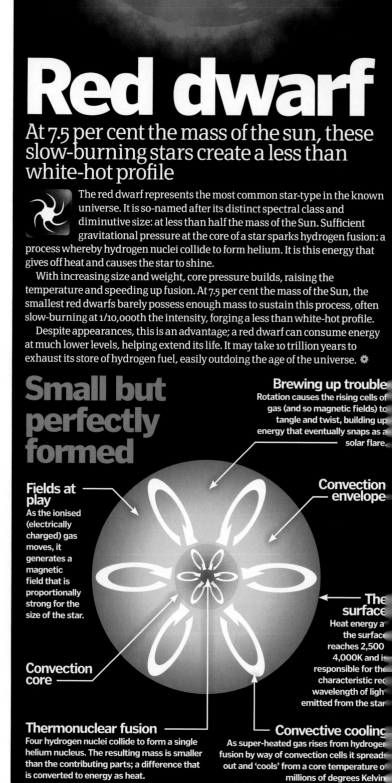

Brewing up trouble
Rotation causes the rising cells of gas (and so magnetic fields) to tangle and twist, building up energy that eventually snaps as a solar flare.

Fields at play
As the ionised (electrically charged) gas moves, it generates a magnetic field that is proportionally strong for the size of the star.

Convection envelope

The surface
Heat energy at the surface reaches 2,500 - 4,000K and is responsible for the characteristic red wavelength of light emitted from the star.

Convection core

Thermonuclear fusion
Four hydrogen nuclei collide to form a single helium nucleus. The resulting mass is smaller than the contributing parts; a difference that is converted to energy as heat.

Convective cooling
As super-heated gas rises from hydrogen fusion by way of convection cells it spreads out and 'cools' from a core temperature of millions of degrees Kelvin.

Head to Head
COMET VISITS

RARE

1. Hale-Bopp
Before 1997, the last time Hale-Bopp flew near Earth – approximately 4,200 years ago – the Great Pyramids of Egypt had only recently been built.
© NASA

OCCASIONAL

2. Halley
We see Halley's comet enter our inner solar system every 76 years, with the last visit in 1986. The next predicted visit date is 28 July 2061.
© NASA

FREQUENT

3. Tempel 1
This comet orbits the Sun every 5.5 years and was the subject of the Deep Impact space mission, which retrieved samples from it.
© NASA

DID YOU KNOW? 39 people of the Heaven's Gate cult committed suicide in 1997, thinking aliens were following Hale-Bopp

Hale-Bopp comet

The Great Comet of 1997 grabbed headlines when it lit up the night sky

Often cited as the most observed comet of all time, Hale-Bopp was visible in the night sky for 18 months during its flyby of Earth in 1997. It was the first comet to be discovered by a small amateur telescope. Hale-Bopp is roughly 40 kilometres (25 miles) in diameter. It is mainly because of its large size that it appears so bright. Its solid centre – the nucleus – is a frozen and dusty wasteland mostly composed of ice that reflects a large amount of sunlight. The nucleus is surrounded by a combination of gases and dust – known as the coma – such as a metal-rich silicate mineral.

The light coming out of the comet is a product of ice evaporating and disintegrating into a cloud of particles. Hale-Bopp provided an abundance of information on the physical and chemical nature of comets, including the presence of a third tail made of sodium trailing the comet in addition to a dust and gas tail. ✿

Hale-Bopp passed closest to Earth back in March 1997

© E. Kolmhofer, H. Raab; Johannes-Kepler-Observatory, Linz, Austria

Sunspots

What are these dark areas that appear on the surface of the Sun?

Sunspots appear on the Sun's photosphere, which is the layer of gases that make up its visible surface. It is hundreds of miles deep until it reaches the core of the Sun where heat and energy are produced. As the Sun is mostly made of highly magnetic plasma it has a very strong magnetic field, which constantly shifts. The power of the magnetic field is such that the lines of magnetism can become twisted and pierce the photosphere of the Sun, forming a sunspot. They are a few thousand degrees cooler than the surface of the Sun, which is about 5,500°C, and therefore have a darker and dimmer appearance.

Magnetic field lines form loops around an object, so sunspots actually appear in pairs where the loop goes into and back out of the Sun. Sunspots are usually created as the result of a magnetic storm on the Sun, and are often accompanied by a solar flare shock wave. The number of sunspots varies across the 11-year solar cycle, from many in the solar maximum to almost none in the solar minimum. These are the periods of greatest and lowest activity of the Sun respectively. ✿

Umbra
The magnetic field lines are perpendicular to the surface of the Sun at the centre of the sunspot, the umbra.

Penumbra
As the magnetic lines curve in a loop, the edge of the sunspot (the penumbra) has a weaker magnetic force acting on it.

© NASA

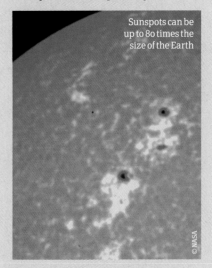

Sunspots can be up to 80 times the size of the Earth

© NASA

Understanding
ROCKET
SCIENCE

Modern rocket science was used in entertainment and weaponry, long before the realms of space travel

Rocket science has been around since the 280s BCE, when ancient Chinese alchemists invented gunpowder. Initially used in fireworks, gunpowder was soon put to use in weaponry as fire-arrows and bombs among other things. Throughout the centuries, rockets continued to be used as weapons until the early-20th Century. In 1912, Robert Goddard built the first liquid-fuel rocket (previous rockets were solid-fuel) and began the age of modern rocketry. To date, there have been somewhere in the region of 500 rocket launches from NASA's Cape

Canaveral, and more than five thousand satellites launched by rockets from spaceports throughout the rest of the world.

While the term 'rocket' can be used to describe everything from cars to jet packs, most of us think space travel when we see rocket. Most rockets follow the same basic design. Typically they are tube-like, with stacks of components. Rockets carry propellants (a fuel and an oxidiser), one or more engines, stabilisation devices, and a nozzle to accelerate and expand gases. However, there's a lot of variation among those basic elements.

There are two main types of rockets: solid-fuel and liquid-fuel. The former have some similarities to those early gunpowder rockets. For space applications, solid-fuel rockets are often used as boosters to lower the amount of needed liquid fuel and reduce the overall mass of the vehicle as a whole. A common type of solid propellant, used in the solid rocket boosters on the NASA space shuttles, is a composite made of ammonium percholate, aluminium, iron oxide and a polymer to bind it. The propellant is packed into a casing. Solid-fuel rockets are used alone sometimes to launch lighter objects

Liquid-fuel rocket

1 Robert Goddard built and launched the first liquid-fuel rocket on 26 March 1926. It was fuelled by gasoline and liquid oxygen, the flight lasted 2.5 seconds.

True rocket

2 In 1232 BCE, the Chinese used rocket-arrows propelled by burning gunpowder in their war with the Mongols. They were likely a frightening sight.

Launch into Earth orbit

3 On 4 October 1957, the R-7 ICBM was the first rocket to launch an artificial satellite – Sputnik 1 – into orbit. This sparked the space race between the US and USSR.

Launch into space

4 Germany launched the first rocket capable of reaching space, the V-2 rocket, in 1942. The missile was launched at sites in England and Belgium.

Private launch, Earth orbit

5 Commercial space travel company Space X launched Falcon 9 in December 2010. With an unmanned capsule, it orbited Earth twice before landing in the Pacific.

DID YOU KNOW? Advances in gunnery left rockets forgotten until an Indian prince used them in the Mysore Wars (late-1700s)

into low-Earth orbit, but they cannot provide the type of overall thrust needed to propel a very heavy object into Earth orbit or into space. They can be difficult to control once ignited.

The difficulty in getting off the ground is due to the strength of Earth's gravity. This is why thrust – a rocket's strength – is measured in pounds or Newtons. One pound of thrust is the amount of force that it takes to keep a one-pound object at rest against Earth's gravity. A rocket carries fuel that weighs much more than the object that it's trying to move (its payload – a spacecraft or satellite). To understand why, think about what happens when you blow up a balloon and then release it. The balloon flies around the room because of the force exerted by the air molecules escaping

from it. This is Newton's third law in action (see The three laws of motion on page 156). But the balloon is only propelling itself; rockets need to generate thrust greater than their mass, which includes the weight of the fuel. For example, the space shuttle in total weighs about 4.4 million pounds, with a possible payload of about 230,000 pounds. To lift this, rocket boosters provided 3.3 million pounds of thrust each, while three engines on the main tank each provided 375,000 pounds of thrust.

Liquid-fuel rockets have the benefit of losing mass over time as their propellant is used up, which in turn increases the rate of acceleration. They have a higher energy content than solid-fuel rockets. Typically they consist of a fuel and an oxidiser in

separate tanks, mixed in a combustion chamber. Guidance systems control the amount of propellants that enter, depending on the thrust needed. Liquid-fuel rockets can be stopped and started.

Launch location can also help rockets become more efficient. European Space Agency member country France chose to build a spaceport in French Guiana not only for its location near water, but also its location near the equator. Launching a rocket near the equator, in an easterly direction, makes use of energy created by the Earth's rotation speed of 465m per second. This also means that putting a rocket into geosynchronous orbit is easier, because few corrections have to be made to its trajectory. ❀

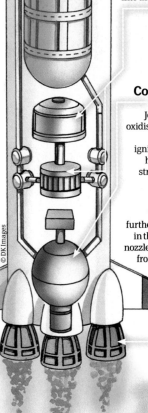

Liquid-fuel rocket

The components of a liquid fuel rocket and how they work

Fuel
Common fuels used today include kerosene (RP-1), liquid hydrogen and hydrazine.

Oxidiser
The oxidiser may be liquid hydrogen, or in the case of hydrazine, nitrogen tetroxide.

Pumps
These pumps move the fuel and oxidiser into the combustion chamber.

Combustion chamber
Jets of fuel and oxidiser meet here, where their ignition creates a high-pressure stream of gases.

Nozzle
The gases are further accelerated in the throat. The nozzle directs them from the engine.

© DK Images

Escape velocity How rockets break free of Earth's gravity

Throw an apple into the air and it will keep travelling away from Earth until gravity overcomes the force of your throw. At this point the apple will fall back down to the ground. If,

however, you launched that apple from a cannon at a speed of 40,000km/h (25,000mph) – that's a nippy 11km (7 miles) per second – the apple will reach what's known as

escape velocity. At this speed, the force of gravity will never be stronger than the force causing the apple to move away from Earth, and so the apple will escape Earth's gravity.

Escaping other bodies

Escape velocity depends on the mass of the planet or moon, meaning that each planet's escape velocity is different

Ceres
Mass (Earth = 1):
0.00015
Escape velocity:
2,301km/h (1,430mph)

The moon
Mass (Earth = 1):
0.012
Escape velocity:
8,561km/h (5,320mph)

Earth
Mass (Earth = 1):
1
Escape velocity:
40,000km/h (25,038mph)

The Sun
Mass (Earth = 1):
333,000
Escape velocity:
2,223,469km/h (1,381,600mph)

1. Gravity
An object fired from a cannon is returned to Earth by gravity, in the direction of Earth's core.

2. Mid-range
The greater the object's speed, the further it travels before returning to Earth (falls at the same rate of acceleration).

3. Long-range
With enough velocity, the object reaches the horizon, at which point the ground 'falls away' (due to Earth's curve) and the object travels further before landing.

5. Orbital velocity
At this speed the object's gravitational fall is balanced with the curvature of the Earth.

6. Circular orbit
The object travels so fast it falls all the way around the world. It is now in orbit.

7. Elliptical orbit
Object speed is greater than orbital velocity but less than escape velocity. The object continues to circle the Earth.

8. Escape velocity
At escape velocity, the object will break free of Earth's gravitational pull.

Newton's cannon
How an object's velocity helps it escape Earth's gravitational pull

4. Half orbit
Earth's surface falls away from the object nearly equal to gravity's rate of acceleration.

The three laws of motion

Rockets have been around for thousands of years, but the science behind them wasn't understood until Isaac Newton's 1687 book *Philosophiae Naturalis Principia Mathematica*. In it, Newton explained three laws that govern motion of all objects, now known as Newton's Laws of Motion. Knowing these laws have made modern rocketry possible.

FIRST LAW

The first law states that objects that are at rest will stay at rest, while objects that are in motion will stay in motion unless an external, unbalanced force acts upon it. A rocket is at rest until thrust unbalances it; it will then stay in motion until it encounters another unbalanced force.

SECOND LAW

Force = mass x acceleration. Force is the pressure from the explosions. It accelerates the rocket's mass in one direction and the mass of the expelled gases in the other. Mass decreases as it burns up propellants, while acceleration increases.

THIRD LAW

The third law states that for every action, there is an equal and opposite reaction. When a rocket launches, the action is the gas expelling from its engine. The rocket moves in the opposite direction, which is the reaction. To lift off, the thrust must be greater than the rocket's mass.

Saturn V: The biggest and most powerful

Rockets like Saturn V, the one used to launch NASA's Apollo and Skylab programs, are multi-stage liquid-fuelled boosters. The Saturn V is considered to be the biggest, most powerful and most successful rocket ever built. It was 110.6m tall, 10.1m in diameter and had a payload of 119,000kg to low-Earth orbit.

There were three stages, followed by an instrument unit and the payload (spacecraft). The total mission time for this rocket was about 20 mins. The centre engine was ignited first, then engines on either side ignited. The first stage lifted the rocket to about 70km and burned for 2.5 mins. When sensors in the tanks sensed that the propellant was low, motors detached the first stage. The second stage continued the trajectory to 176km and burned for six mins. About halfway through this stage's ignition, the instrument unit took control of calculating the trajectory.

Second stage complete, solid-fuel rockets fired it away from the third stage. The third stage burned for two minutes and 30 seconds and stayed attached to the spacecraft while it orbited the Earth, at an altitude of 191.2km. It continued to thrust and vent hydrogen before ramping up and burning for six more minutes, so the spacecraft could reach a high enough velocity to escape Earth's gravity.

Launch Umbilical Tower
Built as part of the MLP (but removed and installed permanently at the launch site for the shuttle missions), the Launch Umbilical Tower contains swing arms to access the rocket, a crane and a water suppression system.

Payload
The Saturn V payload was either Apollo spacecraft or the Skylab space station. With the former, it carried both the Command Service Module (CSM) and the Lunar Module (LM).

Instrument unit
The instrument unit, containing telemetry and guidance systems, controlled the rocket's operations until the ejection of the third stage.

© DK Images

Third stage
The third stage is S-IVB. It only had one engine but also used liquid hydrogen and liquid oxygen. Fully fuelled, it weighed 119,000 kilograms.

Second stage
The second stage, or S-II, also contained five engines and was nearly identical to the first stage. However, it was powered by liquid hydrogen and liquid oxygen and weighed 480,000 kilograms.

First stage
The first stage was also known as S-IC. It contained a central engine, four outer engines, RP-1 fuel (kerosene) and liquid oxygen as the oxidiser. Fully fuelled, it weighed 2.3 million kilograms.

Crawler Transporter
This tracked vehicle moved spacecraft from the Assembly Building to the launch complex along a path called the Crawlerway, and then moved the empty MLP back to the VAB.

Mobile Launcher Platform (MLP)
A three-storey platform designed to support and launch the Saturn V (and later, the space shuttle). Spacecraft are built vertically, in a ready-for-launch configuration, in the Vehicle Assembly Building (VAB).

THE STATS ROCKETS

SPEED NEEDED TO ESCAPE EARTH'S GRAVITY	**11.3km/s**	GALLONS OF FUEL ON BOARD **500,000**
TIME IT TAKES TO REACH SPACE	**8 mins**	SPEED NEEDED TO STAY IN EARTH ORBIT **28,000km/h**

DID YOU KNOW? In 100 BCE the Greek inventor Hero created the aeolipile, a rocket-like jet engine that ran on steam

6. Payload launched
Ariane's payload, a satellite, is released by steel springs. The rocket is also capable of carrying and launching dual satellites and also delivered a spacecraft to the International Space Station.

4. Third stage
This third stage is known as the storable propellant stage. It contains two propellant tanks of nitrogen tetroxide and hydrazine, which feed an engine that provides the energy to release the payload.

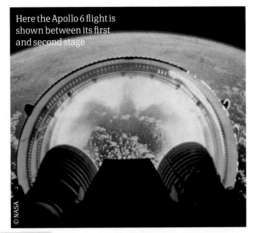
Here the Apollo 6 flight is shown between its first and second stage

© NASA

5. Fairing
The fairing protects the upper stages and payload from thermodynamic and acoustic pressure during launch. It falls off about three minutes after liftoff, at an altitude of about 100km.

3. Main stage
Ariane's main, or second stage comprises two separate compartments, containing liquid oxygen and liquid hydrogen. These power an engine that burns for ten minutes until the stage separates, at an altitude of 145km.

2. Solid rocket boosters
These solid rocket boosters provide 110 tons of thrust. At an altitude of 60km, about 130 seconds after liftoff, the boosters are spent and detach from the main stage.

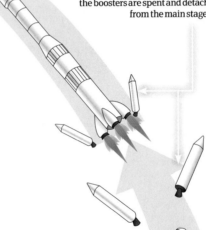

Multi-stage rockets

Multi-stage rockets are essentially multiple rockets (each with their own engines and fuel systems) stacked on top or beside each other. Sometimes this assembly is known as a launch vehicle. As the fuel burns, the container holding it becomes dead weight. When a stage separates from the main body, the next stage is capable of generating more acceleration. The downside of a multi-stage rocket is that they're more complex and time-consuming to build, and there are multiple potential failure points. However, the fuel savings are worth the risk. This example shows the ESA's Ariane rocket launching a satellite in Earth orbit.

1 Payload packed
Any external features of a payload (such as solar panels) will remain folded up until it reaches orbit.

THE FINAL COUNT DOWN
Liquid-propellant rockets have come a long way since their inception...

1981
STS
NASA's Space Transportation System took the shuttle into orbit for 135 space missions, the last of which was 8 July 2011.

1967
Saturn V
The most powerful space rocket to date, Saturn V was taller than a 36-storey building and launched every Apollo moon mission.

1957
Sputnik
The Soviet Union's Sputnik Rocket launched the world's first satellite, Sputnik 1, a major landmark at the start of the space race with the USA.

1944
V-2 Rocket
Developed by Germany for use at the end of WWII, the V-2 was the first rocket to achieve sub-orbital spaceflight.

1926
The first modern rocket
American Robert Goddard built the first successful liquid-propellant rocket. It climbed 12.5 metres before landing in a nearby cabbage patch.

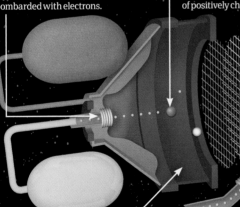

Propellant injection
Ion engines use a propellant fuel, which is injected into a discharge chamber and bombarded with electrons.

Collision
The collision of propellant atoms and electrons results in the release of positively charged ions.

Ion engine propulsion

Multi-aperture grids
This series of grids extracts the positively charged ions and electrically accelerates them into ion jets, generating thrust.

Cathode
A hollow cathode injects negatively charged electrons into the positively charged ion beam to render it neutral.

Magnetic field
Magnetic rings generate a magnetic field that facilitates the ionisation process.

Both solid-fuel and liquid-fuel rocket engines generate thrust through chemical reactions, but in the future, rockets may be powered by ion engines while in space. An ion engine uses either electromagnetic or electrostatic force to accelerate ions, atoms with a net positive or negative charge. While the amount of thrust generated is comparatively low, the engine is more efficient and can last for a very long time.

"Skylab required only one unmanned launch to be complete"

Skylab

How NASA's first space station provided the groundwork for the ISS

Following on from the success of the Apollo missions, and using the same equipment, NASA launched its Skylab space station in 1973 to observe the effects on a human during a prolonged period in orbit around the Earth. It was also intended to provide more astronomical information than could be provided from Earth-based observations. It was operational until 1979, completing more than 300 experiments in the process with three different three-man crews inhabiting the station. Unlike the ISS, which has taken over 12 years to build and is still ongoing, Skylab required only one unmanned launch to be complete and needed no assembly in space.

The shell of Skylab was a modified Saturn V rocket used to go to the moon. It was also initially launched on top of a Saturn V, but the later manned missions used a Saturn 1B rocket. An Apollo spacecraft transported the crew to the station and returned them to Earth. The success of Skylab missions proved that humans could be a positive asset when working in space, demonstrating excellent mobility and limited space-related problems barring a few bouts of space sickness. Skylab also, for the first time, showed that the resupply of space vehicles was indeed possible.

The crew were able to produce unprecedented data on the Earth and the Sun using the equipment on board like the Apollo Telescope Mount (ATM), which acted as a solar observatory, giving views of the Sun and stars with no atmospheric interference. The crew exceeded all expectations, performing unplanned experiments such as observing a nearby comet. The station also famously had two spiders on board, which showed that they could build a near-perfect – if slightly irregular – web in space.

Although a successful six-year mission, the station did encounter problems on launch when its meteoroid shield ripped off and damaged the station's solar protection. When astronauts first arrived the station was a rather sweltering 52°C. A sun-parasol had to be deployed to lower the temperature. ✿

Inside Skylab
Discover the layout of this groundbreaking space station

Apollo Telescope Mount
Housing a number of solar telescopes used primarily in attempting to observe solar flares, which were of great interest to NASA. It was successful on several occasions.

© NASA

Multiple Docking Adaptor
Provided a primary and secondary docking port for the Apollo spacecraft. Also contained control panels for the Apollo Telescope Mount.

Command and service module
Used as a workstation, the crews also used this module to travel to and from the station. The last crew, knowing the space station might not survive, packed it with valuable equipment that would have been lost.

Some experiments were attached to the outside of Skylab and collected by astronauts

© NASA

LONG

1. Skylab
Three crews manned the station (although not continuously) for 171 days and 13 hours, a record at the time. The longest stay was 84 days.

LONGER

2. ISS
Broke Mir's record for uninterrupted human presence in space (3,644 days) on 23 October 2010, and could remain operational for at least another ten years.

LONGEST

3. Mir
Occupied for 4,592 days (not continuously) from 1986 to 2001. Mir was one of the Soviet Union's major achievements in space.

DID YOU KNOW? A story written by Edward Everett Hale in 1869 pioneered the idea of placing a manned space station into orbit

Airlock
Allowed crews on board to perform spacewalks outside the station, which consisted largely of repair work. The first crew had to deploy a sun-shield through the airlock to protect the station from the Sun's rays.

Solar panels
These were folded against the station for launch and extended in space, providing power for the station. They were initially damaged and later repaired by astronauts.

Workshop
The upper part of this housed the workstation for experiments, and the lower had the living quarters including a kitchen, dining room (known as the ward room) and bedroom.

Micrometeoroid shield
Protected the workshop from micrometeoroids moving through space, and provided shade from the rays of the Sun. It broke on take-off, damaging the station.

The lower level experiment area provided equipment for human biology experiments

Size comparison

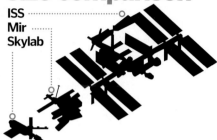

ISS
Mir
Skylab

Crashing to Earth

NASA originally had plans to dock a shuttle with Skylab in 1979 to push it into a higher orbit where it would not be dragged into Earth's atmosphere. However, in late-1978 the National Oceanographic and Atmospheric Administration (NOAA) warned that an increase in solar activity would move Skylab into the atmosphere within a year.

With the shuttle program delayed until 1981, Skylab became the subject of a huge media storm when NASA announced it would be re-entering Earth's atmosphere on 11 July 1979. Controllers at the Johnson Space Center attempted to manoeuvre the station to ensure it disintegrated upon re-entry, but some of it survived and its remains were found near Perth, Australia. *The San Francisco Examiner* gave £5,000 ($8,000) to a groundkeeper in Western Australia for winning a competition to deliver a piece of debris to its office, and The Shire of Esperance in Australia fined the US £250 ($400) for littering.

The statistics...

A solar sunshade is sewn to be deployed on Skylab

Skylab

Weight: 91,000kg

Height: 36 metres (118 feet)

Diameter: 6.7 metres (22 feet)

Living space: 283m³ (9,994ft³)

Altitude: 435 km (270 miles)

Orbital period: 93 minutes

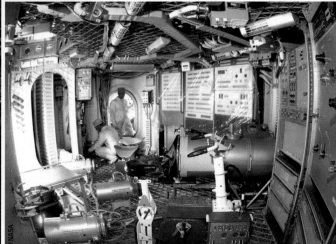

© NASA

"The Oort cloud was created during the formation of the solar system"

The Oort cloud

What is this comet-filled cloud in our solar system?

The Oort cloud is a giant sphere of icy cometary nuclei that surrounds our solar system. Its maximum distance is 1.9 light years away from the Sun, which is as far as the Sun's gravitational influence extends.

In 1950, Dutch astronomer Jan Oort developed the concept of this cloud as the origin of comets. It was created during the formation of the solar system, when planetesimal bodies gathered to form planets or moons. The gravitational influence of Uranus and Neptune sent some of these planetesimals outwards to form the Oort cloud.

Over time the gravitational effects of the Sun, planets in the solar system and even nearby stars have caused objects to actually leave the Oort cloud. They then either turn up in the form of comets in the inner solar system, or they are sent completely out of our system's influence altogether. Just as objects are lost from the cloud, new ones from outside the solar system can also be attracted into it. ✿

The Oort cloud's population

1. Elliptical plane
This is where the Oort Cloud is most dense.

2. Long period comets
These can take thousands of years to orbit the Sun. Their orbits do not conform to the ecliptic plane and they can travel round the Sun in a clockwise or anticlockwise direction.

3. Transformation
Over time the influence of gravity can cause long period comets to become short period comets. Halley's comet is thought to have originated from the Oort cloud as a long period comet.

4. Short period comet
These orbit in the same direction as the planets on the ecliptic plane. Their orbit is relatively short, such as Halley's comet, which takes 76 years to orbit the Sun.

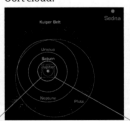

Sedna

Evidence of the Oort cloud's existence is supported by the discovery on 14 November 2003 of the furthest object in the solar system. Named Sedna, it is currently 13 billion kilometres away from Earth. Its highly elliptical orbit around the Sun takes 11,250 years and to a maximum distance of 130 billion kilometres.

Sedna has a diameter of between 1,180 to 1,800 kilometres, making it larger than an asteroid but smaller than a planet. It is the second reddest object in the solar system after Mars, and its surface temperature is a rather cold -240°C.

A sticking point is that it is much closer than the predicted position of the Oort cloud. One suggestion is that millions of years ago a rogue star passed by, causing comets and bodies like Sedna to form an inner Oort cloud.

Survival training
1 NASA's first manned space programmes involved landing space capsules in the ocean. Astronauts were trained for surviving on the ocean and also had jungle training.

Centrifuges
2 To gain experience of high g-forces experienced from high levels of acceleration, trainee astronauts are spun on the end of a long arm that rotates at high speed.

Fitness
3 Astronauts have to be fit and healthy. Fitness programmes in the early days of space exploration were intensive and involved training in oxygen-deprived environments.

Floating
4 Astronauts are given the sensation of working in spacesuits in giant water tanks. NASA uses the world's largest indoor pool-holding shuttle and station mock-ups.

Simulators
5 Astronauts train for their mission in mock-ups and simulators. These give a realistic impression of the tasks that they will carry out and the living conditions.

DID YOU KNOW? NASA has operated 100,000 parabolic zero-gravity flights to support all of its manned space programmes

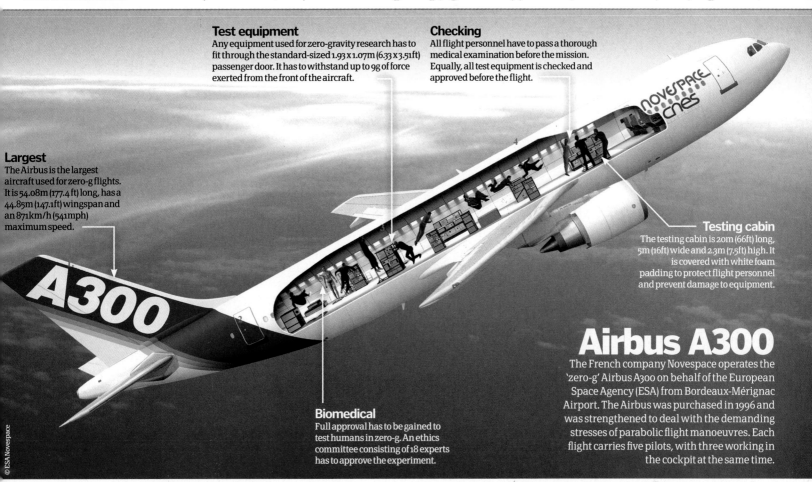

Test equipment
Any equipment used for zero-gravity research has to fit through the standard-sized 1.93 x 1.07m (6.33 x 3.51ft) passenger door. It has to withstand up to 9g of force exerted from the front of the aircraft.

Checking
All flight personnel have to pass a thorough medical examination before the mission. Equally, all test equipment is checked and approved before the flight.

Largest
The Airbus is the largest aircraft used for zero-g flights. It is 54.08m (177.4 ft) long, has a 44.85m (147.1ft) wingspan and an 871km/h (541mph) maximum speed.

Testing cabin
The testing cabin is 20m (66ft) long, 5m (16ft) wide and 2.3m (7.5ft) high. It is covered with white foam padding to protect flight personnel and prevent damage to equipment.

Biomedical
Full approval has to be gained to test humans in zero-g. An ethics committee consisting of 18 experts has to approve the experiment.

© ESA Novespace

Airbus A300

The French company Novespace operates the 'zero-g' Airbus A300 on behalf of the European Space Agency (ESA) from Bordeaux-Mérignac Airport. The Airbus was purchased in 1996 and was strengthened to deal with the demanding stresses of parabolic flight manoeuvres. Each flight carries five pilots, with three working in the cockpit at the same time.

How a vomit comet trains astronauts

Find out how fixed-wing aircraft can simulate zero-gravity conditions for astronaut training

 When an aircraft follows a parabolic flight path, it creates a weightless period for several seconds. This is ideal for providing astronauts with the sensation of zero gravity and testing equipment for use in outer space. A typical three-hour training mission makes at least 30 parabolic flights. They can simulate zero-g for 25 seconds, one-sixth g (lunar-g) for 30 seconds or one-third g (martian-g) for 40 seconds.

In 1959, NASA used a Convair C-131 Samaritan aircraft to train the Mercury programme astronauts. It was quickly nicknamed the 'vomit comet', as one in three passengers became violently sick.

Most aircraft used for such flights are adapted versions of transport or commercial passenger aircraft. NASA currently uses a McDonnell Douglas C-9 and the European Space Agency uses an Airbus A300.

Since 2004, commercial companies started offering such flights to the public, and NASA offers a scheme for students to design and fly micro-gravity missions. ✿

The parabolic flight manoeuvre

1. Entry pull-up phase
Flying at an altitude of 5km (16,404ft) at a speed of 825km/h (513mph), the aircraft ascends at 47 degrees. Up to 2g is experienced.

2. Injection point
In 20 secs, at an altitude of 7km (22,966ft), the aircraft reaches the injection point. Engine thrust is reduced and in five secs enters the zero-g phase. Speed drops from 570km/h (354mph) to 370km/h (230mph).

3. Zero-gravity phase
At the microgravity phase, lasting 20 secs, zero-g is experienced. Using a video link, pilots can control the aircraft to keep objects free-floating in the testing cabin.

4. Pull-out phase
The free-falling aircraft is pulled out of the zero-g phase, and in 20 secs it descends at 42 degrees to its original cruising speed and altitude.

5. Repeat
After returning to normal-level flight for two mins, the parabolic manoeuvre is repeated. 30 can be done in a three-hour flight.

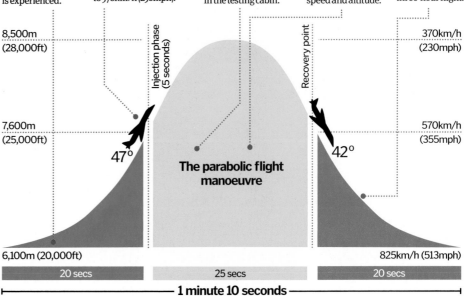

8,500m (28,000ft)

7,600m (25,000ft)

6,100m (20,000ft)

Injection phase (5 seconds)

Recovery point

370km/h (230mph)

570km/h (355mph)

825km/h (513mph)

47°

42°

The parabolic flight manoeuvre

| 20 secs | 25 secs | 20 secs |

— 1 minute 10 seconds —

"One teaspoon of mass would weigh up to a billion tons"

Neutron stars

These remnants of supernovae are some of the most massive objects in the universe

A star with a mass of less than 1.5 solar masses (the mass of the Sun) forms a white dwarf at the end of its lifetime, owing to its gravity being too weak to collapse it further. If the mass of a star is greater than five solar masses, the forces will be so intense that the star collapses past the point of a neutron star and becomes a black hole. However, between these two extremes a neutron star will form as the result of a supernova, although only approximately one in a thousand stars will become one.

As a star runs out of fuel it will eventually collapse in upon itself. In the formation of a neutron star, the protons and electrons within every atom are forced together, forming neutrons. Material that is falling to the centre of the star is then crushed by the intense gravitational forces in the star and forms this same neutron material.

Like the Earth, magnetic fields surround neutron stars and are tipped at the axis of rotation, namely the north and south poles. However, interestingly, the magnetic field of a neutron star is more than a trillion times stronger than that of Earth's.

The gravitational forces in a neutron star are also incredibly strong. The matter is so densely packed together into a radius of 20 kilometres (12 miles) that one teaspoon of mass would weigh up to a billion tons, about the same as a mountain. They also spin up to 600 times per second, gradually slowing down as they age.

Oddly enough, as a neutron star becomes heavier it also becomes smaller. This is because a greater mass means a greater force of gravitational attraction, and therefore the neutrons are squeezed more densely together. In fact, if you were able to drop an object from a height of one metre on the surface of a neutron star, it would hit the ground at about 2,000 kilometres (1,200 miles) per second.

A neutron star sits at the centre of the Crab Nebula

© NASA

Supernovae can leave neutron stars as remnants

© NASA

Magnetar
A neutron star with an extraordinarily large magnetic field is known as a magnetar. Small 'glitches' in the magnetic field of a magnetar can cause giant stellar quakes, one of the largest known explosions in the universe.

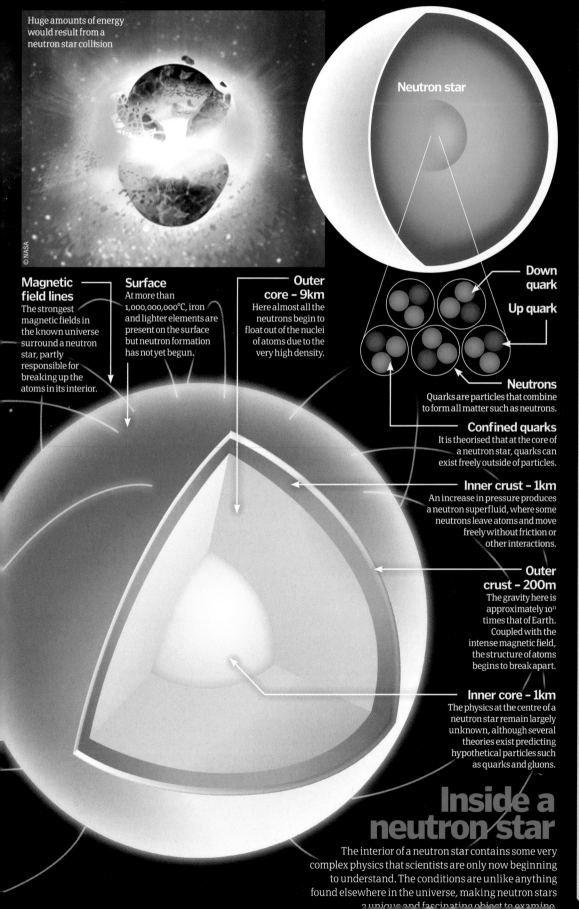

Huge amounts of energy would result from a neutron star collision

© NASA

Neutron star

Down quark

Up quark

Neutrons
Quarks are particles that combine to form all matter such as neutrons.

Magnetic field lines
The strongest magnetic fields in the known universe surround a neutron star, partly responsible for breaking up the atoms in its interior.

Surface
At more than 1,000,000,000°C, iron and lighter elements are present on the surface but neutron formation has not yet begun.

Outer core – 9km
Here almost all the neutrons begin to float out of the nuclei of atoms due to the very high density.

Confined quarks
It is theorised that at the core of a neutron star, quarks can exist freely outside of particles.

Inner crust – 1km
An increase in pressure produces a neutron superfluid, where some neutrons leave atoms and move freely without friction or other interactions.

Outer crust – 200m
The gravity here is approximately 10^{11} times that of Earth. Coupled with the intense magnetic field, the structure of atoms begins to break apart.

Inner core – 1km
The physics at the centre of a neutron star remain largely unknown, although several theories exist predicting hypothetical particles such as quarks and gluons.

Inside a neutron star
The interior of a neutron star contains some very complex physics that scientists are only now beginning to understand. The conditions are unlike anything found elsewhere in the universe, making neutron stars a unique and fascinating object to examine.

Radiation
Pulsars emit beams of radiation that sweep through our line of sight.

Rotating pulsars
Most neutron stars begin life as a rapidly rotating pulsar with strong magnetic fields.

Pulses
Pulses of high energy are caused by the rotation and magnetic axis being out of line.

© Science Photo Library

Pulsars
A rapidly rotating neutron star that emits jets of particles and a large amount of electromagnetic energy (such as x-rays and light) is known as a pulsar. All neutron stars begin life as a pulsar, but as they age and lose rotational energy they are no longer considered a pulsar. The jets of electromagnetic radiation are fired out from the north and south poles of the pulsar. The gravitational force of a pulsar is so strong that apart from at the poles, matter and even light are not able to escape from its surface.

Pulsars can rotate up to 1,000 times per second, although some spin much faster. Their rate of rotation is so regular that they are the most accurate record of time in the universe; no clock on Earth can replicate their accuracy. We observe pulsars as their emitted radiation sweeps through our line of sight. Their high rotation speeds are due to a misalignment of their rotation and magnetic axis, sending them into an uncontrollable but regular spin.

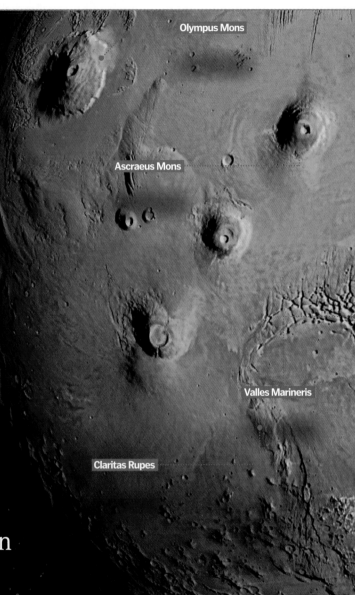

Olympus Mons

Ascraeus Mons

Valles Marineris

Claritas Rupes

The Red Planet

Though man has yet to set foot on the surface of another planet, our fascination with learning about Mars is endless...

To date there have been 42 missions to Mars, with exactly half of them being complete failures. Other than the Earth it is the most studied planet in the solar system, and for centuries it has been at the heart of wild speculation and groundbreaking scientific discoveries. Observations of Mars have not only revealed otherwise unknown secrets but also posed new and exciting questions, and it is for these reasons that it has become the most intriguing planetary body of our time.

Named after the Roman god of war, Mars has fascinated astronomers since Nicolaus Copernicus first realised Mars was another planet orbiting the Sun in 1543. Its notable features such as huge impact craters, gullies and dormant volcanoes suggest it was once more geologically active than it is now, leading scientists to speculate on whether it supported water and life in the past, or indeed if it still does today. Astronomers in the 19th Century falsely believed they could see large oceans, and there were several reports of people receiving 'communications' from Martians in the form of bursts of light when they observed the planet

through a telescope. Of course, we now have a better understanding of the planet, but we are still yet to unlock some of its most puzzling mysteries.

Mars sits 227 million km (141 million miles) from the Sun and takes 687 Earth days to orbit. As its orbital path is not in sync with Earth's it goes through a 26-month cycle of being closest (known as opposition) and furthest (conjunction) from us, located at a distance of 56 million km (35 million miles) and 401 million km (249 million miles) respectively. This change in distance means spacecraft destined for Mars are sent in a launch window every 26 months, when Mars is closest to Earth. The next will be in November 2011, when NASA plans to launch its new Mars rover, Curiosity. The journey time is upwards of six months, so Mars will actually be closest on 3 March 2012.

Like all of the planets in our solar system, it is believed that Mars formed about 4.5 billion years ago inside a solar nebula, when dust particles clumped together to form the planet. At just under half the size of Earth Mars is actually quite a small planet, which is apparently due to the fact Jupiter formed first. The gravitational forces of Jupiter – a

gas giant – consumed available material that would have otherwise contributed to Mars's growth, while Jupiter's gravity prevented another planet forming between Mars and Jupiter and instead left us with the asteroid belt. The northern hemisphere of Mars is significantly younger and lower in elevation than the southern hemisphere, which suggests that the planet was struck by a Pluto-sized object some time early in its lifetime.

Mars is often referred to as something of a dead planet. Indeed, its lack of folded mountains – like those we have here on Earth – shows that it has no currently active plate tectonics, meaning that carbon dioxide cannot be recycled into the atmosphere to create a greenhouse effect. For this

5 TOP FACTS
DISCOVERY OF MARS

1,500BC
1 Egyptians refer to Mars as 'Horus of the Hawk', a god with the head of a hawk. They note its retrograde motion, when it moves backwards in its orbit relative to Earth.

350BC
2 Aristotle proposes that Mars orbits at a further distance than the moon when he notes that the moon passes in front of Mars in his observations.

1609
3 Galileo Galilei uses a telescope to become the first to observe Mars. He's later vilified by the Vatican for saying that the planets orbit the Sun and not Earth.

1666
4 Astronomer Giovanni Cassini calculates the length of a Martian day, notes the polar ice caps and even calculates its distance from Earth.

1840
5 Astronomers Wilhelm Beer and Johann Heinrich Mädler study Mars through a 3.75-inch telescope and produce the first sketched map of its surface.

DID YOU KNOW? Of the nine 21st Century missions to Mars only Beagle 2 has failed

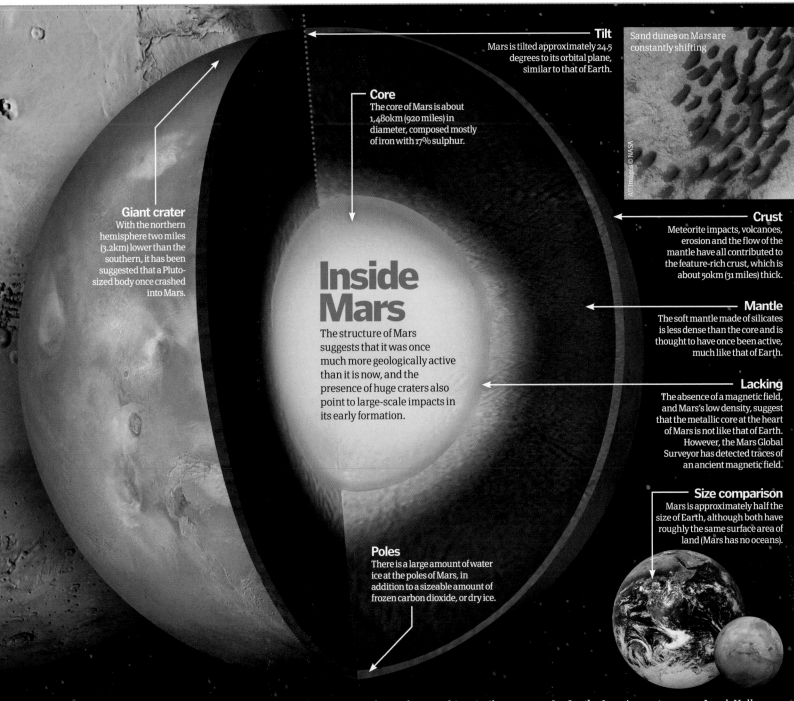

Tilt
Mars is tilted approximately 24.5 degrees to its orbital plane, similar to that of Earth.

Sand dunes on Mars are constantly shifting

All images © NASA

Core
The core of Mars is about 1,480km (920 miles) in diameter, composed mostly of iron with 17% sulphur.

Giant crater
With the northern hemisphere two miles (3.2km) lower than the southern, it has been suggested that a Pluto-sized body once crashed into Mars.

Inside Mars

The structure of Mars suggests that it was once much more geologically active than it is now, and the presence of huge craters also point to large-scale impacts in its early formation.

Crust
Meteorite impacts, volcanoes, erosion and the flow of the mantle have all contributed to the feature-rich crust, which is about 50km (31 miles) thick.

Mantle
The soft mantle made of silicates is less dense than the core and is thought to have once been active, much like that of Earth.

Lacking
The absence of a magnetic field, and Mars's low density, suggest that the metallic core at the heart of Mars is not like that of Earth. However, the Mars Global Surveyor has detected traces of an ancient magnetic field.

Size comparison
Mars is approximately half the size of Earth, although both have roughly the same surface area of land (Mars has no oceans).

Poles
There is a large amount of water ice at the poles of Mars, in addition to a sizeable amount of frozen carbon dioxide, or dry ice.

surface temperature as low as -133°C at the poles in the winter, rising to 27°C on the day side of the planet during the summer.

Despite this, the atmosphere of Mars offers conclusive evidence that it was once geographically active. The outer planets in the solar system have atmospheres composed of predominantly hydrogen and helium, but that of Mars contains 95.3% carbon dioxide, 2.7% nitrogen and 1.6% argon, with minimal traces of oxygen and water. This strongly suggests that volcanoes once erupted across its surface and spewed out carbon dioxide, further evidenced by giant mountains, such as Olympus Mons, which appear to be dormant volcanoes.

It might not be geologically active, but Mars does play host to some extreme weather conditions, most

tornadoes, ten times larger than anything similar on Earth, can be several miles high and hundreds of metres wide, creating miniature lightning bolts as the dust and sand within become electrically charged. The wind inside one of these, though, is almost unnoticeable, as the atmospheric pressure on Mars is so low. Interestingly, one of the reasons for the long survival rate of NASA's Mars rovers is that these dust devils have been cleaning their solar panels, allowing them to absorb more sunlight.

Mars's gravity is about 38% that of Earth, with just 10% of the mass. The surface pressure is just over 100 times weaker than ours at sea level, meaning that a human standing on the surface would see their blood instantly boil. The red colour on Mars's surface is the result of rusting, due to iron present in the rocks and

In 1877 the American astronomer Asaph Hall, urged on by his wife, discovered that Mars had two moons orbiting so close that they were within the glare of the planet. They were named Phobos and Deimos, after the attendants of Ares in the Iliad. Interestingly, the moons are not spherical like most other moons; they are almost potato-shaped and only about ten miles wide at their longest axis, indicating that they are the fragments of the collision of larger objects near Mars billions of years ago. Phobos orbits Mars more than three times a day, while Deimos takes 30 hours. Phobos is gradually moving closer to Mars and will crash into the planet within 50 million years, a blink of an eye in astronomical terms. The moons have both been touted as a possible base, from which humans could

"Mars's gravity is about 38% of that of Earth, with just 10% of the mass"

THE SURFACE OF MARS
Take a virtual stroll around the red planet...

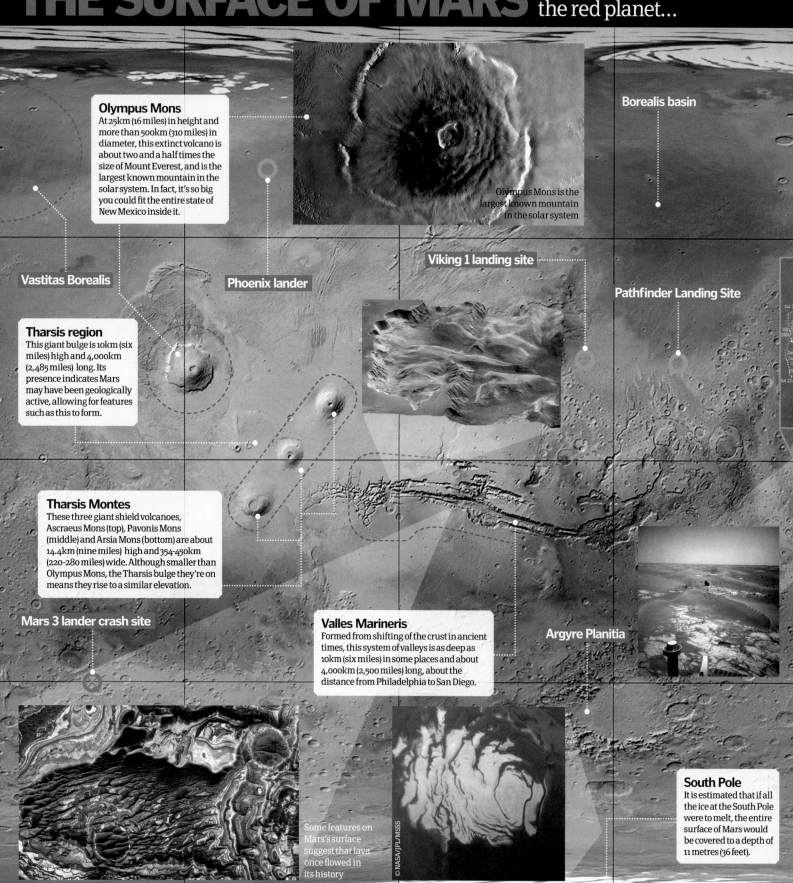

Olympus Mons
At 25km (16 miles) in height and more than 500km (310 miles) in diameter, this extinct volcano is about two and a half times the size of Mount Everest, and is the largest known mountain in the solar system. In fact, it's so big you could fit the entire state of New Mexico inside it.

Olympus Mons is the largest known mountain in the solar system

Borealis basin

Viking 1 landing site

Vastitas Borealis

Phoenix lander

Pathfinder Landing Site

Tharsis region
This giant bulge is 10km (six miles) high and 4,000km (2,485 miles) long. Its presence indicates Mars may have been geologically active, allowing for features such as this to form.

Tharsis Montes
These three giant shield volcanoes, Ascraeus Mons (top), Pavonis Mons (middle) and Arsia Mons (bottom) are about 14.4km (nine miles) high and 354-450km (220-280 miles) wide. Although smaller than Olympus Mons, the Tharsis bulge they're on means they rise to a similar elevation.

Mars 3 lander crash site

Valles Marineris
Formed from shifting of the crust in ancient times, this system of valleys is as deep as 10km (six miles) in some places and about 4,000km (2,500 miles) long, about the distance from Philadelphia to San Diego.

Argyre Planitia

Some features on Mars's surface suggest that lava once flowed in its history

© NASA/JPL/MSSS

South Pole
It is estimated that if all the ice at the South Pole were to melt, the entire surface of Mars would be covered to a depth of 11 metres (36 feet).

DID YOU KNOW? *11 artificial objects are currently on Mars, although only one – the Opportunity rover – is still active*

○ Proposed landing site for Curiosity   ○ Successful landing   ⊗ Crash landing

Capturing this image
This map of Mars was created by reconstructing data from NASA's Mars Global Surveyor, the Mars Orbiter Laser Altimeter and observations by its Viking spacecraft

NASA's rovers have returned thousands of images

The ice cap on Mars's North Pole is about 1,100km (680 miles) wide

North Pole
There is about 1.6 million cubic km (1 million cubic miles) of ice at the North Pole of Mars – that's just over half the amount of ice in the Greenland ice sheet on Earth.

Viking 2 landing site

Elysium Planitia

Santa Maria

Spirit rover
Landing on 4 January 2004, NASA's first Mars Exploration Rover explored various regions before becoming stuck in soil as it travelled round an area known as the Home Plate. However, since 22 March 2010 all communication with the rover has been lost, and during May 2011 Spirit was finally declared dead.

Beagle 2 crash site

Opportunity rover
Landing exactly three weeks after its sister rover Spirit at Meridiani Planum, Opportunity is the longest-serving artificial object on Mars. It has provided unprecedented views of the Victoria crater, and is on its way to the Endeavour crater.

OSU Mapping and GIS Laboratory

No this isn't Tatooine, it's the sunset over the Gusev crater on Mars

All uncredited images © NASA

Gullies on Mars show evidence of water flow

Hellas Planitia

Mars Polar Lander crash site

"If there is liquid water on Mars, that means there could be life as well"

Evidence of water

The cold temperature and low atmospheric pressure on Mars means that finding liquid water on its surface is highly improbable, as it would immediately freeze and then evaporate. While ice has been discovered at the poles, it is the search for liquid water that is the most important. Scientists have found life on Earth in many different environments, but none has been discovered in the absence of water. If there is liquid water on Mars, that means there could be life as well.

In 2008, NASA's Phoenix Mars lander provided proof that there was water beneath the surface when it dug a trench and observed that some material subsequently disappeared, suggesting that underground water was being vaporised as it was exposed to the air. NASA's Spirit rover gleaned one of the most conclusive pieces of evidence for water on Mars, after becoming stuck in soil in early 2009. Attempts to move the rover disturbed the ground and brought subsurface soil up to the surface, which suggested that water had moved downwards through the surface.

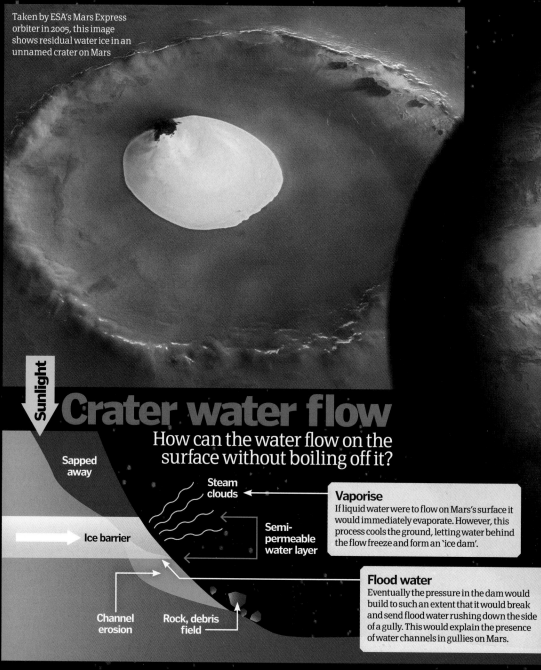

Taken by ESA's Mars Express orbiter in 2005, this image shows residual water ice in an unnamed crater on Mars

Subsurface soil uncovered by NASA's Spirit rover revealed the water-soluble mineral ferric sulphate, a sign of downward-flowing water

Crater water flow

How can the water flow on the surface without boiling off it?

Sunlight

Sapped away

Ice barrier

Steam clouds

Semi-permeable water layer

Channel erosion

Rock, debris field

Vaporise
If liquid water were to flow on Mars's surface it would immediately evaporate. However, this process cools the ground, letting water behind the flow freeze and form an 'ice dam'.

Flood water
Eventually the pressure in the dam would build to such an extent that it would break and send flood water rushing down the side of a gully. This would explain the presence of water channels in gullies on Mars.

Eight key missions to Mars

With the window for launch to Mars occurring just once every two years, and with a journey time of about six months, ensuring the success of a mission is vital. Take a look at eight of the most important successful and failed

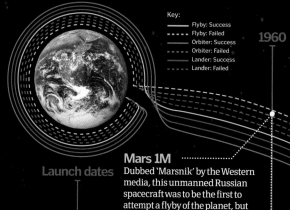

Key:
— Flyby: Success
--- Flyby: Failed
— Orbiter: Success
--- Orbiter: Failed
— Lander: Success
--- Lander: Failed

Launch dates

1960

Mars 1M
Dubbed 'Marsnik' by the Western media, this unmanned Russian spacecraft was to be the first to attempt a flyby of the planet, but experienced a launch failure in 1960.

Mariner 4
This NASA spacecraft was the first to ever visit the Mars when it flew by in 1965, returning 22 close-up images.

1970

FACES

1. Smart life
The Viking 1 orbiter imaged an optical illusion that looked remarkably like a human face, many believing that it was an alien artefact.

© NASA

ALIENS

2. Spirit rover
This image of a vaguely human-shaped rock taken by the Spirit rover in 2008 had many touting the discovery of alien life on Mars.

© NASA

GHOSTS

3. Mars failures
As half of all missions to Mars have failed, a long-running joke within NASA claims a 'Galactic Ghoul' eats spacecraft.

© NASA/JPL-Caltech/
S.Carey (Caltech)

DID YOU KNOW? NASA's Opportunity rover has functioned 25 times longer than it was expected to

Artist's impression
This shows how Mars might look like if it was terraformed. Features such as Valles Marineris are clearly visible.

NASA hopes to use its Orion spacecraft to reach Mars by the 2030s

Why haven't we set foot on Mars?

One of the problems with any manned mission to Mars is the region of space the crew must traverse. To get to Mars with current technology would take about six months, and a human spacecraft would also need enough fuel to take off and return to Earth. Another problem is the amount of solar radiation the crew would be subjected to. Outside Earth's magnetosphere (and with Mars not having one), there is a high chance of potentially fatal damage caused by the Sun. There is the also the added mental strain of travelling such a long distance. The Mars-500 mission at the Russian Academy of Sciences is currently performing an experiment where a crew of volunteers have been placed inside a mock-up potential Mars spacecraft for 640 days to simulate such a mission. All communications outside the enclosed environment have been given a 20-minute delay, similar to what humans would experience if they were to travel to Mars.

Currently, NASA and private enterprises are stepping up efforts to get humans to Mars by the 2030s. NASA's space shuttle replacement, the Orion spacecraft, has provisionally been tasked with taking humans to Mars by 2035, while private companies such as SpaceX (with its Dragon capsule) also hope to eventually reach Mars at a similar time.

Greenhouse effect
A large volume of liquid water could theoretically allow its atmosphere to resemble the greenhouse effect on Earth.

Mars Reconnaissance Orbiter
Launched in 2005 and still in operation today, NASA's MRO has been imaging the planet from orbit to search for evidence of water on the surface.

Opportunity
NASA's Opportunity rover has remained in operation since it landed on Mars on 25 January 2004, the longest surviving lander.

Mars 2 & 3 1980
These two identical spacecraft, consisting of an orbiter and lander, were launched a few days apart by the USSR in 1971. However, both landers lost contact on the surface.

Viking 1 1990
In 1976, NASA's Viking 1 became the first spacecraft to land on Mars and return images of its surface.

2000

Beagle 2
Contact was lost with the British lander six days after it separated from the ESA's Mars Express orbiter in 2003.

Mars Polar lander
It was launched to return data from the South Pole, but comms were lost when it failed to slow its descent in 1999.

2010

One of the two modified Boeing 747s used to transport the space shuttles between the landing site and the launch complex

©NASA

The shuttle's main parts

At launch, the space shuttle system, or 'stack' comprises three main components: a black-and-white orbital vehicle (OV) containing payload and crew, as well as the space shuttle main engines (SSMEs) and orbital manoeuvring engines (OMEs), two white solid rocket boosters (SRBs) and an orange external tank (ET) carrying liquid fuel oxidiser and liquid hydrogen.

Orbiter
The orbiter is the only part of the space shuttle system that actually goes into space. It transports a crew of up to seven astronauts as well as payloads, including satellites, ISS components and experiments.

Fuel tank
The external fuel tank stores fuel for the orbiter's main engines. It contains more than 700,000 kilograms of liquid oxygen and liquid hydrogen, separated into two separate tanks. The tank is insulated with foam to shield the fuels from heat.

How the space shuttle works

April 2011 marked 30 years since NASA's main spacecraft's first mission. July 2011 marked its retirement. Take a look at this marvellous space machine and discover how it works

In January 1972, the US president Richard Nixon announced a plan to create the first reusable spacecraft. Ten years later, on the 20th anniversary of the first human space flight, NASA had its first successful mission with the orbiter Columbia. This flight demonstrated that the space transportation system (STS) was viable. The space transportation system was designed by Maxime Faget, the same American engineer who designed all of NASA's previous spacecraft systems. Since then the program had 135 launches, experiencing some significant successes, not to mention some devastating losses and setbacks.

Although we think of the winged, plane-like spacecraft as the shuttle, it is actually the orbiting part of the entire space shuttle system. The spacecraft's design came about in part because of the need for a large payload capacity, from which satellites could be deployed. Its unique design means that it launches and flies like a rocket, but lands like a plane. The orbiter and solid rocket

boosters are recovered and reused, making it more efficient than the previous spacecraft systems.

Originally the first orbiter was going to be named the Constitution, but fans of the cult television show *Star Trek* staged a write-in campaign and convinced NASA to change its name to that of the sci-fi show's spaceship, the Enterprise. This orbiter was not designed to fly into space, but NASA intended to upgrade it to do so as needed after testing. However, enough significant design changes were made between test flights and the first fully functional launch to require the building of a new orbiter, the Columbia. The Enterprise is still on display at the United States National Air and Space Museum in Washington DC.

NASA's space shuttle programme ended in July 2011. Potential replacement spacecraft, such as NASA's Orion, are in progress with targets of completing a lunar mission by the early-2020s. However, with funding always a concern, there could still be a gap of several years before the US is fully re-engaged in space travel and exploration. ✿

©NASA

Rocket boosters
The solid rocket boosters provide nearly 75 per cent of the thrust required to lift the rest of the shuttle system off the launch pad. They have a jointed structure and contain solid rocket fuel, a catalyst, instruments, a parachute and explosive charges.

Crawler transporters
NASA uses these tracked vehicles to move the space shuttle from the assembly building to the shuttle launch pad. They travel on a special pathway called the 'crawlerway' and have been in use since 1965. Each crawler transporter weighs nearly 3,000 tons.

THE STATS SHUTTLE

HEIGHT 56m	**DIAMETER** 9m	**MASS** 2,030metric tons	
RE-ENTRY SPEED 28,000km/h		**ROCKET BOOSTER THRUST** 15 meganewtons	

DID YOU KNOW? *The complexly built shuttle contains more than 375km of wire and more than 2.5 million individual parts*

Launching the space shuttle

The space shuttle launch is a multi-step process that begins on the launch pad at the Kennedy Space Center in Cape Canaveral, Florida

The first step of the launch is controlled by computers on the orbiter. They ignite the space shuttle main engines (SSME) one at a time, then fire the solid rocket boosters (SRB). As the shuttle begins its ascent, it rolls 180° to the right. Once the shuttle reaches about 45km (28 miles), the SRBs then separate. They deploy parachutes and fall into the ocean for retrieval by ships. The space shuttle continues travelling horizontally towards Earth orbit.

About five minutes into the flight, the SSMEs are turned off and the external tank is released. It typically burns up upon re-entry into the atmosphere, although small pieces may reach the ocean. Then the shuttle fires its orbital manoeuvring engines (OMEs) to orient it vertically and provide the final push into low Earth orbit. They fire again to get into orbit 400km (250 miles) above the Earth. The orbiter typically flies upside down and nose first.

© NASA

On the way down

Before the orbiter can land, its crew must perform several operations for a safe and smooth re-entry

When the orbiter ends a mission, the first step is to close the payload bay doors. Then the RCS thrusters are fired to turn the orbiter so that it is tail first. The pilot slows the orbiter down by firing the OMEs, then fires more RCS thrusters to orient it in a nose-first position with its underside facing the atmosphere at an attitude of 40°. The forward RCS thrusters are fired to burn off any excess fuel, since the front of the orbiter encounters the most heat.

Once it is inside Earth's atmosphere, the orbiter flies like an aeroplane via computer controls, making S-shaped turns to help slow it down as it approaches the runway. When the orbiter is about 40 kilometres (25 miles) from the runway and 600 metres (2,000ft) from the ground, the commander lines it up and pulls up the nose. He deploys the landing gear and a parachute to cause drag and eventually stop the orbiter.

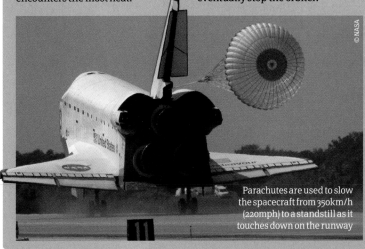

© NASA

Parachutes are used to slow the spacecraft from 350km/h (220mph) to a standstill as it touches down on the runway

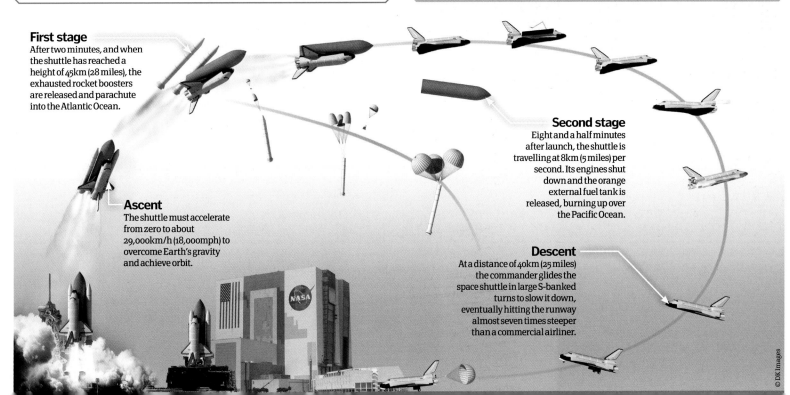

First stage
After two minutes, and when the shuttle has reached a height of 45km (28 miles), the exhausted rocket boosters are released and parachute into the Atlantic Ocean.

Ascent
The shuttle must accelerate from zero to about 29,000km/h (18,000mph) to overcome Earth's gravity and achieve orbit.

Second stage
Eight and a half minutes after launch, the shuttle is travelling at 8km (5 miles) per second. Its engines shut down and the orange external fuel tank is released, burning up over the Pacific Ocean.

Descent
At a distance of 40km (25 miles) the commander glides the space shuttle in large S-banked turns to slow it down, eventually hitting the runway almost seven times steeper than a commercial airliner.

© DK Images

Wave-like structures in the clouds can be seen in Saturn's atmosphere

Inside Saturn

Saturn is believed to have a small rocky core with a temperature of more than 11,000°C. It is surrounded by a layer of gases and water, followed by a metallic liquid hydrogen and a viscous layer of liquid helium and hydrogen. Near the surface, the hydrogen and helium become gaseous. Saturn has no solid surface.

Inner layer
This thickest layer surrounding the core is liquid hydrogen and helium.

Saturn

Only Jupiter is larger than this gas giant, best known for its ring system

We've been viewing Saturn with the naked eye since prehistoric times, but the planet's most unique feature – its ring system – wasn't discovered until 1610. Each ring contains billions of chunks of dust and water-ice. Saturn has about 14 major ring divisions, but there are also satellites and other structures within some of the rings and gaps. Saturn's rings are believed to have come from the remains of moons, comets or other bodies that broke up in the planet's atmosphere.

The rings aren't the only fascinating thing about Saturn, however. This gas giant is less dense than any other planet in our solar system and has a mostly fluid structure. It radiates a massive amount of energy, thought to be the result of slow gravitational compression. Saturn takes about 29.5 years to revolve around the Sun, and its rotation is a bit more complex – different probes have estimated different times, the latest estimate is ten hours, 32 minutes and 35 seconds. The variations probably have something to do with irregularities in the planet's radio waves, due to the similarities between its magnetic axis and its rotational axis.

Saturn has a cold atmosphere comprising layered clouds of both water-ice and ammonia-ice. It also has winds of up to 1,800 kilometres per second. Occasionally Saturn has storms on its surface, similar to those of Jupiter. One such storm is the Great White Spot, a massive storm in the planet's northern hemisphere that has been observed about once every Saturnian year since 1876. ✿

Outer layer
The outer layer is gaseous hydrogen and helium, blending with its atmosphere.

Rings in view

Saturn takes 29.5 years to orbit the Sun, and it has an elliptical orbit like most planets. The closest Saturn comes to the Sun is 1.35 billion kilometres, while at its furthest, Saturn is 1.5 billion kilometres away. Saturn has a tilt of 26.7 degrees relative to the orbital plane. During half of its orbital period, the northern hemisphere is facing the Sun, while the southern hemisphere faces the Sun during the other half. When viewing Saturn from Earth, this impacts whether we can see the rings full-on or as a thin line.

North pole tilt
The northern hemisphere is visible with the rings appearing below.

Both hemispheres
Both hemispheres are visible with the rings appearing as a thin line.

Orbit
Saturn has an elliptical orbit of 29.5 years

South pole tilt
The southern hemisphere is visible from Earth with the rings above

DID YOU KNOW?

Discovering the rings

Galileo thought that he was seeing moons orbiting Saturn instead of rings because his telescope was not powerful enough. Astronomer Christiaan Huygens observed the rings in 1655, but thought they were a single ring.

DID YOU KNOW? *Images from the Cassini probe show that Saturn has a bright blue northern atmosphere*

The Statistics
Saturn

Diameter: 120,535 km
Mass: 5.6851×10^{26} kg
Density: 0.687 grams per cm³
Average surface temperature: -139°C
Core temperature: 11,000°C
Moons: 62
Average distance from the Sun: 1,426,725,400km
Surface gravity: 10.44 metres per second squared

Inner core
The inner core is likely very small and contains silicate rock, much like Jupiter's core.

Outer core
Saturn's outer core is much thicker than its inner core, containing metallic liquid hydrogen.

Extreme bulge

Saturn is an extreme example of an oblate spheroid – the difference between the radius of the planet at its poles and at its circumference is about ten per cent. This is due to its very short rotational period of just over ten hours.

Cassini probe
The first spacecraft to ever orbit Saturn, the Cassini probe has provided incredible images of the planet and its ring system.

Float that planet

If we had a big enough pond, we could float Saturn on its surface. Although Saturn is the second-largest planet as well as the second-most massive, it's the least-dense planet in our solar system. Its density is just 0.687 grams per cubic centimetre, about one-tenth as dense as our planet and two-thirds as dense as water.

Saturn's southern storm

In 2004, the Cassini space probe discovered a massive, oddly shaped convective thunderstorm in Saturn's southern atmosphere. Dubbed the Dragon Storm, this weather feature emitted strong radio waves. Like storms on Earth, the Dragon Storm emits flashes of lightning that appear as white plumes. Scientists believe it exists deep in the atmosphere and can occasionally flare up.

An artist's impression of Saturn's ring particles

Rings
Saturn's rings comprise particles of ice and dust that range from microscopic to several thousand kilometres in diameter.

NASA's Hubble Space Telescope took this image of the Antennae galaxies, which began colliding a few hundred million years ago

© ESA / NASA

Galaxy collisions
What happens when two galaxies collide?

When two galaxies cross paths, the chance of any stars colliding is almost zero. In fact, if the Milky Way collided with the nearby Andromeda galaxy, we would barely notice a thing on Earth. Instead, the multitude of dust and gas in each galaxy interacts and creates the characteristic spectacle. As the material in the stars interacts gravitationally, newly formed gas clouds give birth to stars. Friction between the gases can cause numerous shock waves, which also become instrumental in the formation of new stars.

Colliding galaxies usually take millions or even billions of years to merge. As they collide, tidal gravitational forces will rip the smaller of the two galaxies apart, scattering dust and stars. The inner core of the collision will heat up and radiate strongly, creating one of the brightest infrared objects in space. In this instance the larger galaxy will swallow the smaller one, but on some occasions the galaxies may pass through each other and emerge almost unharmed.

Joining forces
How galaxy collisions work, step by step

1. First contact
The first signs of a galaxy collision will be a bridge of matter between the two, caused by gravitational forces.

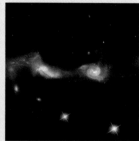

2. Tidal tails
Long streams of gas and dust known as tidal tails spiral out of the collision as the material is thrown out.

3. Ripped apart
Gravitational forces pull the matter in all directions, creating shock waves throughout the cloud of gas.

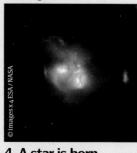

© images x 4 ESA / NASA

4. A star is born
The core of the collision is subjected to intense frictional and gravitational forces, resulting in the formation of massive stars.

BIG

1. Supernova
Over the course of just a few weeks a supernova will emit as much energy as the Sun in its 10 billion year lifetime.

BIGGER

2. Stellar quake
Stellar quakes more than 10,000 times weaker than a gamma-ray burst are described as soft gamma-ray emissions.

BIGGEST

3. Gamma-ray burst
As a star goes supernova, a gamma-ray burst releases as much energy in a second as the Sun in its entire lifetime.

DID YOU KNOW? Stellar quakes are also known as starquakes

Stellar quakes

What causes these giant explosions that rock the universe?

At the heart of a stellar quake is a neutron star, which has a highly dense mass of protons and electrons that have been forced together to form neutrons. Neutron stars have up to five times the mass of the Sun but are only about 20 kilometres (12.4 miles) in diameter. They spin on average at 400 rotations per second, but their strong magnetic fields cause them to slow down over time. The highest observed spin speed of a neutron star is 1,122 rotations per second.

As they rotate, the incredibly strong gravitational force of the star counteracts the spin of the star. The former attempts to draw in the equator, while the centrifugal forces resulting from the spin of the star try to push the equator out. This changes its shape from an oblong to a sphere, cracking the rigid iron crust. Mountains only a few centimetres tall begin to appear across the surface as the tension builds.

Eventually, the tension in the surface reaches such a level that the crust 'snaps' and a huge number of gamma-rays and x-rays are released as a stellar quake. As the geometry of the star readjusts, the strong magnetic fields temporarily drop to a lower energy level. Combined with the energy released from inside the star, this creates one of the largest known flashes of x-rays in the universe. ✿

27 December 2004 saw a neutron star flare up so brightly it blinded all the x-ray satellites in space for an instant

Cassiopeia A, a supernova remnant in the constellation Cassiopeia

An image taken by the Chandra Observatory of a giant eruption

Magnetars

Recent evidence suggests the primary causes of the largest stellar quakes are magnetars, large neutron stars with an incredibly powerful magnetic field. At twice the size of a regular neutron star, a magnetar can have up to 30 times more mass than the Sun, despite the Sun being 46,000 times larger. A tablespoon of mass from a magnetar would weigh the same as 274 Empire State buildings. The magnetic field of a magnetar is several trillion times stronger than that of Earth while its rigid crust is 10 billion times stronger than steel and 1.5km (0.9 miles) thick.

ALMA telescope

How this array will give us our best view of the universe from Earth

ALMA will be used to study stars and galaxies that are billions of years old

High in the Chilean Andes on the Chajnantor plain, 5,000m (16,400ft) above sea level, an array of radio telescopes known as the Atacama Large Millimeter Array (ALMA) is under construction, which will provide us with one of the clearest views of the universe yet. Once completed there will be 66 antennas trained at the sky, working in tandem with one another to observe the cosmos, the largest and most expensive ground-based telescope in history.

The truly remarkable aspect of this $1.3bn telescope group – a partnership between scientific teams across the world – is that a giant vehicle known as the ALMA Transporter can individually move each 12-metre wide antenna. This means the spread of the telescopes can range from just 150m to more than 18km (492ft to 11 miles), providing varying levels of resolution to observe different parts of the universe. Once completed in 2013, ALMA will be ten times more powerful than the Hubble Space Telescope. Normally, ground-based telescopes cannot compare to space telescopes, the latter of which do not have their view obstructed by the Earth's atmosphere. However, the huge scale of the ALMA array, coupled with its height above sea level where the atmosphere is thinner, will allow ground-based telescopes to match their space-faring brothers. ✿

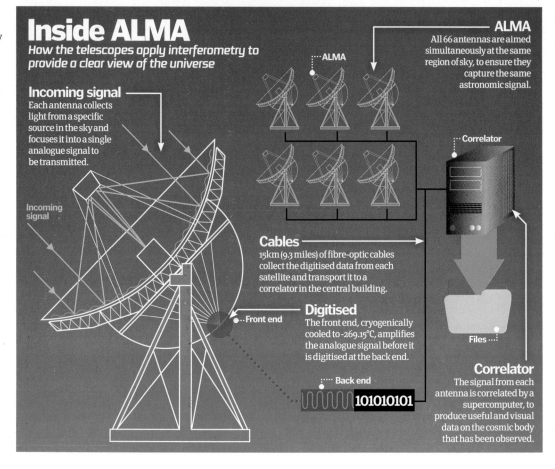

Inside ALMA
How the telescopes apply interferometry to provide a clear view of the universe

Incoming signal
Each antenna collects light from a specific source in the sky and focuses it into a single analogue signal to be transmitted.

Incoming signal

ALMA

ALMA
All 66 antennas are aimed simultaneously at the same region of sky, to ensure they capture the same astronomic signal.

Correlator

Cables
15km (9.3 miles) of fibre-optic cables collect the digitised data from each satellite and transport it to a correlator in the central building.

Front end

Digitised
The front end, cryogenically cooled to -269.15°C, amplifies the analogue signal before it is digitised at the back end.

Back end
101010101

Files

Correlator
The signal from each antenna is correlated by a supercomputer, to produce useful and visual data on the cosmic body that has been observed.

Three's a crowd

Hale-Bopp is the only comet observed to have a third tail, made of sodium. This faint tail extends 50 million km (31 million miles) behind the comet in between the dust and ion tail, yet the cause of it is unknown.

DID YOU KNOW? NASA's Stardust spacecraft is the only craft to ever collect samples from a comet's coma

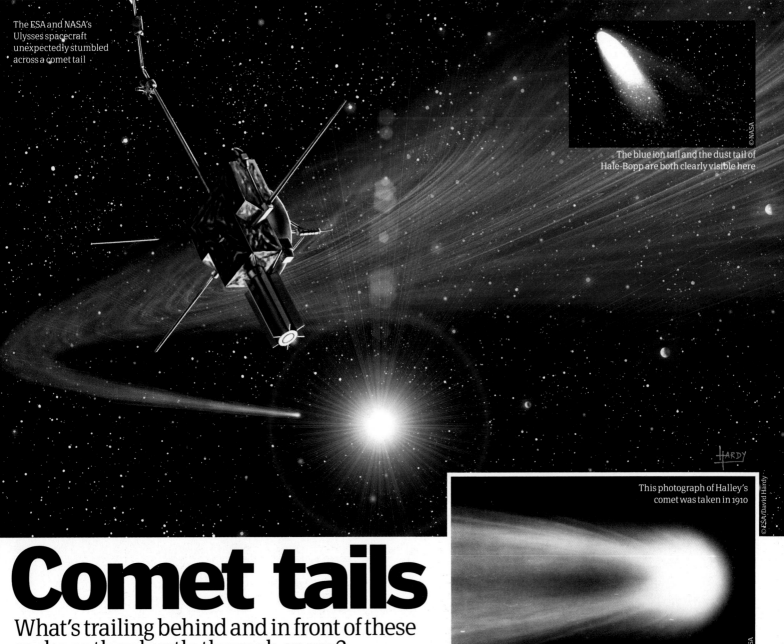

The ESA and NASA's Ulysses spacecraft unexpectedly stumbled across a comet tail

The blue ion tail and the dust tail of Hale-Bopp are both clearly visible here

©NASA

HARDY

This photograph of Halley's comet was taken in 1910

©ESA/David Hardy

Comet tails

What's trailing behind and in front of these rocks as they hurtle through space?

Comets are small, icy bodies in orbit around the Sun surrounded by a gaseous coma that consists of water, carbon dioxide and other gases. The most noticeable features of a comet are its tails, with most having two, a dust and ion tail. Both tails point away from the Sun at varying angles due to the solar wind, regardless of the comet's directions.

The dust tail of a comet appears whitish-yellow, because its microscopic dust particles reflect sunlight. It is anywhere from 1 to 10 million km (600,000 to 6 million miles) in length, pushed out from the comet by the solar wind and curving slightly because of the comet's orbit around the Sun. The other tail, known as the plasma or ion tail, is composed of charged gases (ions) such as carbon monoxide, and stretches as far as 160 million km (100 million miles) from the comet. The solar wind also pushes this tail away, but it is largely unaffected by the comet's orbit. This means that when the comet approaches the Sun the tail runs behind it, but when the comet moves away from the Sun, the ion tail leads in front of the comet. ✿

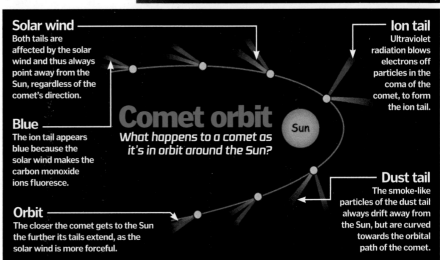

Solar wind
Both tails are affected by the solar wind and thus always point away from the Sun, regardless of the comet's direction.

Ion tail
Ultraviolet radiation blows electrons off particles in the coma of the comet, to form the ion tail.

Blue
The ion tail appears blue because the solar wind makes the carbon monoxide ions fluoresce.

Comet orbit
What happens to a comet as it's in orbit around the Sun?

Sun

Dust tail
The smoke-like particles of the dust tail always drift away from the Sun, but are curved towards the orbital path of the comet.

Orbit
The closer the comet gets to the Sun the further its tails extend, as the solar wind is more forceful.

"*50 moons to date are known to orbit the gas giant*"

Inside Jupiter

We take a look inside the most massive planet in our solar system

When Galileo Galilei discovered Jupiter in 1610, it is doubtful that he was aware of the impact this giant planet had on the surrounding solar system. From altering the evolution of Mars to preventing the formation of a ninth planet, the size and mass of Jupiter has seen it exert an influence on its neighbours second only to the Sun.

Jupiter's mass and composition almost more closely resemble a star than a planet, and in fact if it was 80 times more massive it would be classified as the former. It can virtually be regarded as being the centre of its own miniature solar system: 50 moons to date are known to orbit this gas giant, with the four largest (Io, Europa, Ganymede and Callisto, the Galilean satellites) each surpassing Pluto in size.

The comparison of Jupiter to a star owes a lot to the fact that it is composed almost entirely of gas. It has a large number of ammonia-based clouds floating above water vapour, with strong east-west winds in the upper atmosphere pulling these climate features into dark and light stripes. The majority of its atmosphere, however, is made up of hydrogen and helium.

The strength of Jupiter's gravity is such that it is held responsible for much of the development of nearby celestial bodies. The gravitational force of the gas giant is believed to have stunted the growth of Mars, consuming material that would have contributed to its size. It also prevented a new planet forming between these two and instead gave rise to the asteroid belt.

Much of our knowledge of Jupiter comes from seven spacecraft missions to visit the planet, starting with NASA's Pioneer 10 in 1973. The only man-made object to orbit the planet is the Galileo spacecraft, which studied the planet from 1995 until 2003, when it was sent crashing into Jupiter so as not to contaminate its moons with the debris. ✿

NASA's Jupiter orbiter Juno will embark on a five-year journey

All Images © NASA

Jupiter's diameter is 11 times that of Earth, and 318 times the mass

DID YOU KNOW? The Greeks and later the Romans named the gas giant after their most important deities – Zeus and Jupiter

Jupiter's anatomy

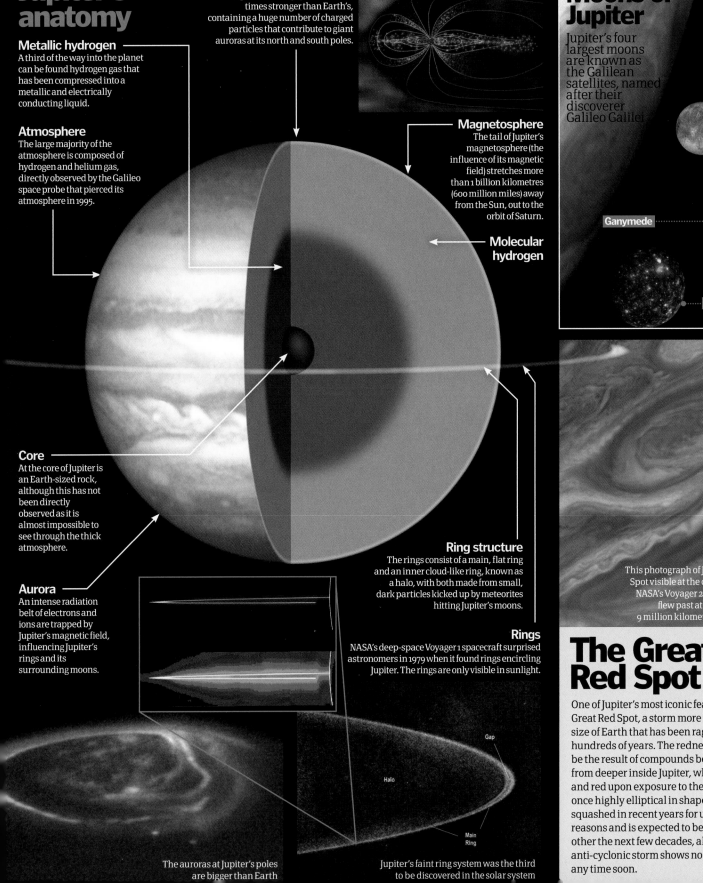

Metallic hydrogen
A third of the way into the planet can be found hydrogen gas that has been compressed into a metallic and electrically conducting liquid.

Atmosphere
The large majority of the atmosphere is composed of hydrogen and helium gas, directly observed by the Galileo space probe that pierced its atmosphere in 1995.

Magnetic field
The magnetic field of Jupiter is 20,000 times stronger than Earth's, containing a huge number of charged particles that contribute to giant auroras at its north and south poles.

Magnetosphere
The tail of Jupiter's magnetosphere (the influence of its magnetic field) stretches more than 1 billion kilometres (600 million miles) away from the Sun, out to the orbit of Saturn.

Molecular hydrogen

Core
At the core of Jupiter is an Earth-sized rock, although this has not been directly observed as it is almost impossible to see through the thick atmosphere.

Aurora
An intense radiation belt of electrons and ions are trapped by Jupiter's magnetic field, influencing Jupiter's rings and its surrounding moons.

Ring structure
The rings consist of a main, flat ring and an inner cloud-like ring, known as a halo, with both made from small, dark particles kicked up by meteorites hitting Jupiter's moons.

Rings
NASA's deep-space Voyager 1 spacecraft surprised astronomers in 1979 when it found rings encircling Jupiter. The rings are only visible in sunlight.

The auroras at Jupiter's poles are bigger than Earth

Gap

Halo

Main Ring

Jupiter's faint ring system was the third to be discovered in the solar system

Moons of Jupiter
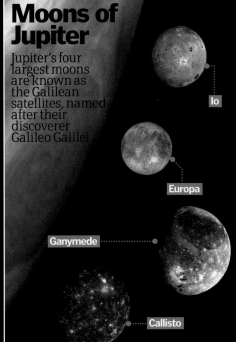
Jupiter's four largest moons are known as the Galilean satellites, named after their discoverer Galileo Galilei

Io

Europa

Ganymede

Callisto

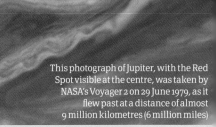
This photograph of Jupiter, with the Red Spot visible at the centre, was taken by NASA's Voyager 2 on 29 June 1979, as it flew past at a distance of almost 9 million kilometres (6 million miles)

The Great Red Spot
One of Jupiter's most iconic features is the Great Red Spot, a storm more than twice the size of Earth that has been raging for hundreds of years. The redness is believed to be the result of compounds being brought up from deeper inside Jupiter, which turn brown and red upon exposure to the Sun. Although once highly elliptical in shape, it has become squashed in recent years for unknown reasons and is expected to become circular other the next few decades, although this anti-cyclonic storm shows no sign of dying out any time soon.

Explore the miracle of

THE GALAXY

It's one of about 100 billion other galaxies in the universe, but it's our home – join us as we explore the Milky Way

THE STATS
MILKY WAY

DIAMETER 100,000 light years   **OLDEST STAR** **13.2 billion yrs**

THICKNESS **1,000 light years**   **STARS** **>200,000 billion**

DID YOU KNOW? *According to Greek mythology, the Milky Way was formed when Hera spilt milk while breastfeeding Heracles*

The Milky Way is our galaxy, home to our solar system. It formed a little more than 13 billion years ago, just a few billion years after the Big Bang. The galaxy is estimated to be about 100,000 light years in diameter and 1,000 light years thick. It is part of a system of 50 galaxies known as the Local Group, which is part of the Virgo Supercluster. Containing as many as 50 billion planets and 400 billion stars, the Milky Way is a spiral galaxy. It has a centre known as a 'bulge', surrounded by a flat disk comprising several loose arms that contain stars and their orbiting bodies, as well as gases and dust. The centre contains a massive black hole and a complex radio source known as 'Sagittarius A'. Around the outside of the Milky Way there is a halo containing dark matter and a very small percentage of the galaxy's total number of stars. Some astronomers believe that the Milky Way is actually a special type of spiral galaxy called a barred spiral, meaning that it has a bar-shaped distribution of stars running across its centre.

Aristotle first wrote of the Milky Way in the mid-300s BCE. He broke with other Greek philosophers, who believed that the milky streak in the sky might be stars. Aristotle thought that it was a sort of fiery emission coming from a cluster of very large stars, and that it resided in the Earth's atmosphere. Astronomers continued to speculate about the true nature of the Milky Way, until Galileo determined in 1610 that it comprised a massive number of stars. In 1755 Immanuel Kant realised that the Milky Way rotated and was held together by gravity. 30 years later, William Herschel attempted to depict the shape of the Milky Way and the Sun's location in it by counting and recording the position of visible stars. Finally Edwin Hubble determined in the Twenties that there were nebulae beyond the Milky Way, proving ▶

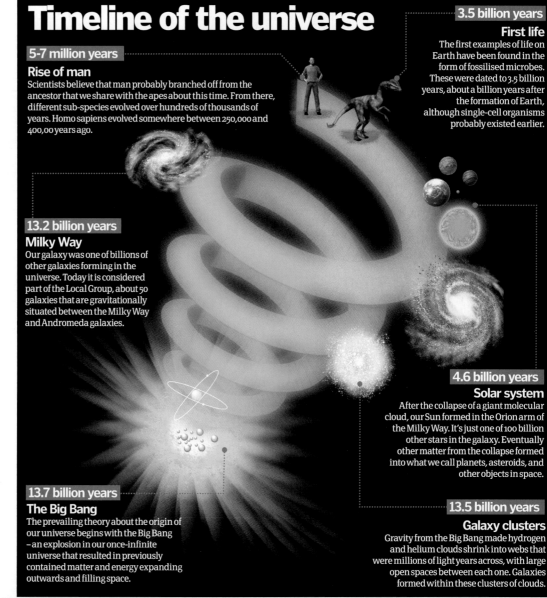

Timeline of the universe

5-7 million years
Rise of man
Scientists believe that man probably branched off from the ancestor that we share with the apes about this time. From there, different sub-species evolved over hundreds of thousands of years. Homo sapiens evolved somewhere between 250,000 and 400,00 years ago.

3.5 billion years
First life
The first examples of life on Earth have been found in the form of fossilised microbes. These were dated to 3.5 billion years, about a billion years after the formation of Earth, although single-cell organisms probably existed earlier.

13.2 billion years
Milky Way
Our galaxy was one of billions of other galaxies forming in the universe. Today it is considered part of the Local Group, about 50 galaxies that are gravitationally situated between the Milky Way and Andromeda galaxies.

4.6 billion years
Solar system
After the collapse of a giant molecular cloud, our Sun formed in the Orion arm of the Milky Way. It's just one of 100 billion other stars in the galaxy. Eventually other matter from the collapse formed into what we call planets, asteroids, and other objects in space.

13.7 billion years
The Big Bang
The prevailing theory about the origin of our universe begins with the Big Bang – an explosion in our once-infinite universe that resulted in previously contained matter and energy expanding outwards and filling space.

13.5 billion years
Galaxy clusters
Gravity from the Big Bang made hydrogen and helium clouds shrink into webs that were millions of light years across, with large open spaces between each one. Galaxies formed within these clusters of clouds.

Structure of the Milky Way

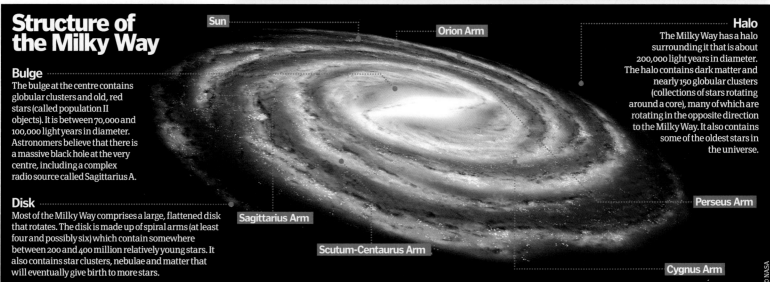

Sun   **Orion Arm**   **Halo**

Sagittarius Arm   **Scutum-Centaurus Arm**   **Perseus Arm**   **Cygnus Arm**

Bulge
The bulge at the centre contains globular clusters and old, red stars (called population II objects). It is between 70,000 and 100,000 light years in diameter. Astronomers believe that there is a massive black hole at the very centre, including a complex radio source called Sagittarius A.

Disk
Most of the Milky Way comprises a large, flattened disk that rotates. The disk is made up of spiral arms (at least four and possibly six) which contain somewhere between 200 and 400 million relatively young stars. It also contains star clusters, nebulae and matter that will eventually give birth to more stars.

Halo
The Milky Way has a halo surrounding it that is about 200,000 light years in diameter. The halo contains dark matter and nearly 150 globular clusters (collections of stars rotating around a core), many of which are rotating in the opposite direction to the Milky Way. It also contains some of the oldest stars in the universe.

© NASA

that there were other galaxies in the universe. Hubble is also responsible for coming up with the classification system for galaxies that we use today, which includes spiral, elliptical and irregular galaxies.

For all our observations, the Milky Way is still mysterious. Determining its actual size and our location in it has been difficult; Herschel and astronomers before him believed that our solar system was in its centre because of the apparently equal distribution of stars in our sky, for example. Several different indirect methods have been used to calculate the actual size of the Milky Way. This includes using the period-luminosity relation of certain stars. The luminosity, or brightness of some stars pulse in a predictable pattern, which can be measured along with its apparent magnitude to estimate distance. In the early-20th Century, an astronomer named Harlow Shapley used some of these measurements to extrapolate the distances of globular clusters outside the Milky Way. This showed that the Sun was not at the centre of the galaxy and provided a rough (although inaccurate) estimate of the Milky Way's diameter. Today we can map the galaxy using telescopes that pick up light and radio waves emitted by gases and molecules floating in space.

The Milky Way isn't a static object – the arms rotate about the centre, and it is also moving in the direction of a large gravitational anomaly known as the Great Attractor. Our galaxy also has its own orbiting galaxies. The two largest of these galaxies, the Small Magellanic Cloud and the Large Magellanic Cloud, create a vibrational warp in the Milky Way's disk as they orbit, due to the presence of dark matter.

Because of light and other types of atmospheric pollution, it's difficult to view the Milky Way from Earth with the naked eye – indeed, it's best viewed in very rural areas under clear skies – and it also looks like a faint milky band of clouds stretching across the night sky. Light pollution maps are available online, and local astronomy clubs can help locate the best place to go.

A trip through the Milky Way

To take a journey from Earth out beyond the edge of the Milky Way would be to travel a distance of thousands of light years

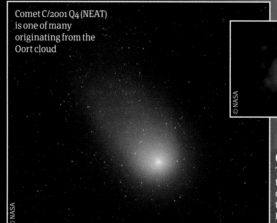

Comet C/2001 Q4 (NEAT) is one of many originating from the Oort cloud

4.22 light years
Nearest stars
Aside from the Sun, the nearest star to Earth is the red dwarf Proxima Centauri. Part of the three-star Alpha Centauri system, it's slightly closer to Earth than the more visible Alpha Centauri A and B. Sirius, the brightest star in the night sky, is 8.6 light years.

6 billion kilometres
Oort Cloud and Kuiper Belt
The next major objects are the Oort Cloud and the Kuiper Belt. The Oort Cloud is a cloud of comets believed to be the source of many of the comets in our solar system. The Kuiper Belt is an area of the solar system containing dwarf planets and other small astral bodies.

40 million kilometres
Other planets and Sun
We'll have to travel tens of millions of kilometres before coming upon the other planets that share our solar system. At nearly 40 million kilometres away at the closest point in its orbit, Venus is our nearest neighbour. Once we reach the furthest planet from Earth, Neptune, we're about 4.4 billion kilometres away.

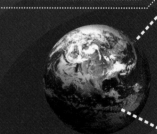

644,000 km (400,000 mi)

A digital composite of the Milky Way's disk over Tenerife

643,737 kilometres
Near-Earth asteroids
Our first stop past the moon would be a visit to our near-Earth asteroids. There are at least 7,000 of these small rocky, metallic objects. They can be up to 32 kilometres in diameter. Compared to the lifetime of other objects in the galaxy, these asteroids have life spans of just a few million years.

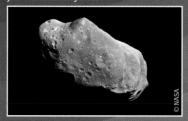

BIG

1. Irregular galaxies
The smallest types of galaxies are irregular, including compact dwarf irregulars that are as small as 200 light years across.

BIGGER

2. Spiral galaxies
Our Milky Way is an average-sized spiral, but others such as UGC 2885 can be more than 800,000 light years across.

© NASA

BIGGEST

3. Elliptical galaxies
The biggest galaxies, ellipticals can be up to 10 kiloparsecs across and form when two smaller galaxies collide.

© NASA

DID YOU KNOW? The name 'Milky Way' comes from Latin and Greek astronomers, who observed the stars' milky appearance

GALACTIC OBJECTS

300 light years
Neighbour stars
Once we get 100 light years away from the Earth, we're nearing the outer edges of the Milky Way. Some of the better-known stars past this distance include Canopus at more than 300 light years away and Betelgeuse at about 640 light years away.

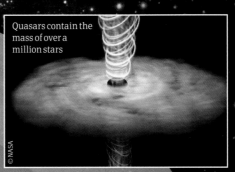

Quasars contain the mass of over a million stars

© NASA

3 billion light years
Distant quasars and galaxies
Quasars are the most distant visible objects in the universe; the closest one is about 3 billion light years away and the furthest is nearly 13 billion light years away. That means that on Earth we see this distant quasar, named CFHQS J2329-0301, less than 1 billion years after the Big Bang.

300 million light years
Galaxy groups and galaxy clusters
The further we get, the greater the leaps in distance. Now we encounter groups of galaxies and other massive structures. The Great, or Coma Wall, is a super-structure filling large spatial voids in the universe. It contains superclusters of galaxies and has dimensions of more than 500 million light years long and 300 million light years wide.

© NASA

25,000 light years
Nearby galaxies
Now we're beyond the Milky Way, visiting other galaxies. There's a dwarf galaxy known as Canis Major being consumed by the Milky Way right now, 25,000 light years away. The closest galaxy outside the Milky Way is the Sagittarius Dwarf elliptical galaxy, 70,000 light years from Earth.

© NASA

1,000 light years
Milky Way
The edge of the Milky Way is about 1,000 light years away from Earth. Keep in mind that our solar system is already on the outer edges of the Milky Way itself, about 28,000 light years from its centre.

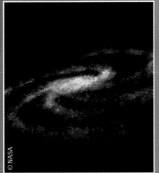

© NASA

DISTANCE

6.4 trillion km (4 trillion miles)

10 light years

1,000 light years

100,000 light years

10 million light years

1 billion light years

11-15 billion light years

Galaxy on the move

The spinning galaxy rotates differentially (the closer to the centre an object is, the less time it takes to complete an orbit). The Sun travels around the galactic centre at 800,000km/h (500,000mph), taking 225 million years to make one orbit.

The galaxy rotates differentially, which means that objects closer to its core orbit the core faster than the stars in the arms of the galaxy. The Milky Way rotates at about 170km per second. Our solar system, located around 30,000 light years away from the galactic core, completes an orbit once every 225 million years. The Milky Way is also moving through space at about 630km per second, relative to the cosmic background radiation – the Big Bang's remnants. It moves in the direction of a gravitational anomaly in the universe, known as the Great Attractor.

When galaxies collide

Astronomers are predicting that in about 3 to 5 billion years, the Andromeda galaxy may collide with the Milky Way. The violent crash will result in a blob-like elliptical galaxy, dubbed 'Milkomeda'. Currently Andromeda is about 2.5 million light years from the Milky Way, but it is moving towards our galaxy at 120km per second. The possibility of stars and planets within the galaxies actually colliding is highly unlikely, but the different gravitational fields will jostle them out of their current locations. Our solar system could even be ejected during the collision, but that probably wouldn't affect the planets much. By the time of the proposed collision, Earth will probably already be devoid of life due to the Sun's increasing heat.

Galaxy collisions can be less dramatic than they sound

© NASA

TRANSPORT
Explaining road, rail, sea and air

186
300mph supercars

190
Canal locks

© Tanarus

192
Helicopters

194
Superbikes

categories explained

Extreme vehicles

Air

Rail

Road

Sea

Future vehicles

General

HOW IT WORKS
TRANSPORT

216
Aerobatic displays

204
Battle tanks

222
Hovercraft

224
How to land a plane

300mph hypercars

Get the inside line on three of the fastest road cars in the world – the tech, the design and those all-important top speeds

For some, only the most extreme will do. Hypercars are for these people. A hypercar may never even travel at half its ultimate speed – but the knowledge that it can do it is enough. The trick for the makers is to make sure they *can* do it… and get a place in the record books to prove it.

Such cars cannot be developed like normal models. Road cars have a diverse set of requirements, and even fast Ferraris must also carry luggage, have long service intervals and be easy to drive in city centres. Not so for hypercars. There, the main focus is top speed, with every engineering decision being made with this in mind.

It's why the cars are so very different to all others – and this is what people are so keen to buy into. Every component, every suspension change, even

the spec of the glass in the windows has been made to help achieve that top speed.

Cars are usually built by smaller companies, often highly specialised unknowns. The market for these models is limited and big-brand makers struggle to make a business case for them. The compromises that very high top speeds impose make the models less useable in daily conditions than the more rounded supercars – hypercars really are just that.

15 years ago, 200mph was a massive, headline-grabbing deal. Today, well in excess of 250 miles per hour is a prerequisite. Future cars must have 300mph as a target. Such a high speed will require big developments in technologies such as tyres and brakes, driveshafts and wheel bearings, even body materials that have to deal with such aerodynamic loads. But relentless progress means they'll come.

Visually, hypercars are unmistakable. They contrast with cars built for handling, which generate downforce to keep them stuck to the ground in corners. This is why Formula 1 cars have huge rear wings, for example. If speed is a priority, these wings become surplus: getting a low aerodynamic drag factor is vital. This is the coefficient of drag (Cd). As such, hypercars generally have smooth surfaces and gently rounded edges for good Cd figures: picture the profile of a water drop. This is also why they often have long but sharply cut-off tails: the 'wake' of air must be as small as physically possible.

Similarly, the frontal area should be minimised, which means getting it low to the ground. The air drag index is actually a function of Cd and frontal area: if both are low, the car will be very aerodynamic – but even a low and lean front end

5 TOP FACTS
AWESOME HYPERCARS

McLaren F1
240mph/627hp

1 To protect the carbon fibre body of the McLaren F1, the engine bay is actually lined in gold foil, as it's the best reflector of heat...

Ferrari F40
200mph/471hp

2 This Eighties supercar remains a legend over 20 years since its launch. The F40 held the road car world top speed record between 1987-1989.

AC Cobra
186mph/485hp

3 Legend has it, the AC achieved this serious speed in 1964 – on the M1 motorway. It's said that this led to the introduction of UK speed limits...

Bloodhound SSC
1,000mph/>130,000hp

4 The jet-and-rocket engined land speed world record challenger is aiming for 1,000mph. Trial runs are due either late-2011/early-2012.

Koenigsegg CCR
241mph/896hp

4 This Swedish supercar broke the production car world speed record set by the McLaren F1 thanks to a supercharged V8 engine.

DID YOU KNOW? *The material of choice for hypercars, carbon fibre was invented in 1958*

won't make a car sleek if the rest of it hasn't been thought through properly.

Impressive power is essential. Whereas road cars have power figures in the hundreds, hypercars measure output in the thousands. It is virtually a prerequisite for a 250mph car to have more than 1,000 horsepower: so quickly do loads rise at speed, big increases in output are needed for apparently minor jumps in top speed.

Hyper top speeds are actually a function of three variables – engine power, air resistance and rolling resistance. This is why many land speed record cars have such skinny tyres. These are completely unrealistic for road use, where cars also have to corner – hence the focus on power and aerodynamics.

Tyres carry huge loads: bespoke land speed tyres must be fitted, as roadgoing tyres simply can't cope. Pressures are often very high – a Bugatti Veyron Super Sport has inflation pressures of 43psi, compared with 30psi of a Ford Fiesta.

Official rules for the ultimate world land speed record state a fixed length course must be used. Two runs must be made, in opposite directions, within an hour. The speed is taken as the average of the two.

No such official test exists for production cars, though. Some claims are therefore dubious: the most valid are claims verified by independent testers such as Guinness World Records. Along with German independent body TUV, it verified the Bugatti Super Sport top speed, from an average of three runs. ✿

SSC Ultimate Aero

SSC is an American company that has long punched well above its weight. Despite being a relative unknown, it has taken on allcomers in the hypercar arena – and, until recently, won through. Till the Bugatti Veyron Super Sport beat it, the Ultimate Aero was officially the world's fastest car.

Its shape was developed and tested in NASA's full-size wind tunnel at Langley, Virginia. This was to ensure the car would be aerodynamically stable at high speeds before they were actually reached. Six NASA scientists worked with the SSC team to hone the Ultimate Aero's surfaces: the challenge was to make it smooth through the air, without creating dangerous lift at either end of the vehicle.

Braking from high speed is helped by an AeroBrake rear spoiler. This pops up by up to eight inches, depending on how hard the brake pedal is pushed, but remains tucked away when not needed to minimise drag.

The follow-up Ultimate Aero II has one-piece carbon fibre wheels. SSC engineers say these are half the weight of regular forged alloy wheels, and are stiffer too. Reduced unsprung masses improves handling and stability, particularly at high speed where the

already-loaded suspension can be less unsettled by sudden road impacts.

The V8 engine is made from a single piece of billet aluminium. This is stronger than cast aluminium so it can be tuned more strongly. It also helps produce more power because the cylinders are 'truer' – there is a better ring seal with such tight tolerances, meaning less leakage of combustion gases and a bigger 'bang' transmitted to the road wheels.

Because the Ultimate Aero is sold in the United States, it requires road car legislation certificates, including emissions. SSC has even achieved California Smog Certification, which is an extremely strict test that places tight limits on exhaust gas emissions.

On-board diagnostics are provided by an Azentek PC-based monitor. This keeps track of the car's systems and also provides the full capability of a PC, meaning it is flexible and adaptable by laptop-wielding car technicians.

The statistics...

Ultimate Aero

Manufacturer: SSC

Dimensions:
Length: 4,470mm, width: 2,080mm, height: 1,090mm

Weight: 1,292kg

0-60 speed: 2.78secs

Top speed: 257.41mph (273mph projected)

Horse power: 1,287

Unit price: £350,000 (est)

Status: Available now

NO.1 CHALLENGER

The Ultimate Aero was officially the fastest car in the world

It's named Ultimate for a reason

Chip off the block
The engine block is made from a forged billet of aluminium, instead of cast aluminium. Tensile strength improves by a third, yield strength by two thirds – *and* it's lighter as well.

Monster gearing
A six-speed gearbox and a 272mph top speed means huge speed in other gears: 81mph in 2nd, 117mph in 3rd, 155mph in 4th – and more than 200mph in 5th.

Ultimate tyres
Michelin PS2 tyres are rated for ultra-high top speeds. They are also used on the Bugatti Veyron and other hypercars.

Carbon fibre cool
Additional carbon fibre louvers on the side of the latest Aero improve airflow to radiators by 20 per cent. This provides adequate cooling to the engine.

Big brakes
Incredible speed needs incredible brakes. The SSC has 14-inch vented discs, with slots, grabbed by eight-piston callipers up front. Normal cars have two-piston callipers.

The Aero's carbon fibre road wheels are strong and lightweight

A mile in half a minute
From a standing start, the Aero can cover a quarter-mile in just 9.9 seconds. It will then be covering 144mph, illustrating just how fast it is.

More than its weight
Around a constant circle, the SSC generates up to 1.05g in cornering force. So it weighs more in hard cornering than it does at rest.

5 x © Shelby Super Cars

> "Whereas road cars have power figures in the hundreds, hypercars measure output in the thousands"

Million-pound miracle

Adjustable wing
The angle of the rear wing adjusts according to use. For top speed it's three degrees, rising to 55 degrees to brake for maximum retardation.

Suspension descends
Height-adjusting suspension runs 115mm front and rear in normal use. For top speed, this reduces to 65mm at the front and 70mm at the rear.

© Bugatti

CURRENT WORLD RECORD HOLDER

0.1-second gearchanges
The seven-speed gearbox uses twin clutches, to which alternate gear sets are connected. This ensures no breaks in gearchanges.

High-tech carbon
Bugatti introduced a new carbon fibre structure for the Super Sport monocoque. This is more rigid, safe, and light.

Veyron Super Sport

The Bugatti Veyron Super Sport is the car *Top Gear* proved to be the world's fastest. Presenter James May flew to a test track in Germany and drove it 253mph. Earlier, a Bugatti test driver took it up to 268mph – independently verified and therefore creating a new land speed world record. Allegedly, the record-breaking top speed took even the engineers by surprise – they were expecting 264mph. So how did it do it? Mainly thanks to a lot more power.

The Super Sport puts out 1,200bhp thanks to four larger turbochargers than the standard model, fed by four larger intercoolers. They supply charged air to an 8.0-litre mid-mounted W16 engine. As it is – on a basic level, two V8 engines paired together – it is relatively compact for such a large 16-cylinder engine: it's 710mm long and 767mm wide.

The engine is fed air from two NACA ducts located in the roof. These are named after the National Advisory Committee for Aeronautics, and are low drag due to the exremely smooth shape. They generate tiny vortices, which deflect the boundary layer of slow-moving air clinging to the car's body –

this allows in the faster-moving air, so a far greater quantity of air is ingested.

Aerodynamics have been revised. The front intakes have been reshaped and there's a double diffuser at the rear: exhausts are central for rear-end stability. The body is smoother – the NACA ducts sit flush, instead of the standard Veyron's stick-up intake ducts, so there's less drag and air disturbance. The car weighs over 1.8 tons, but weight is not vital to top speed. But it is for acceleration: imagine how quick off the line the Bugatti would be if it were lighter.

HYPERCAR SHOWDOWN
AND A FIESTA!

Here are the best of the best – some of the fastest road cars money can buy. For rich record-seekers, buying one of these models is the 'quickest' way to hypercar honours. To illustrate just how hyper they are, we've included a mainstream Ford Fiesta 1.25…

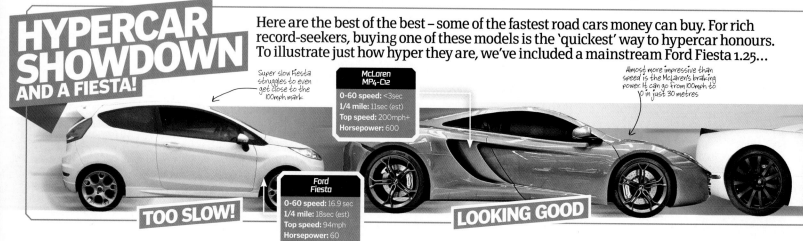

Super slow Fiesta struggles to even get close to the 100mph mark

Almost more impressive than speed is the McLaren's braking power. It can go from 100mph to 0 in just 30 metres

McLaren MP4-12
0-60 speed: <3sec
1/4 mile: 11sec (est)
Top speed: 200mph+
Horsepower: 600

Ford Fiesta
0-60 speed: 16.9 sec
1/4 mile: 18sec (est)
Top speed: 94mph
Horsepower: 60

TOO SLOW!

LOOKING GOOD

200 MPH

1. McLaren MP4-12C
The MP4-12C uses an F1-style carbon fibre tub that weighs just 80kg around which the high-tech car is constructed.

220MPH

2. Aston Martin One-77
The One-77 is an all-carbon fibre monocoque model powered by a 7.3-litre V12 engine producing 750bhp. Max speed over 220 mph.

230MPH

3. Pagani Huayra
6.0-litre V12 Mercedes twin-turbo engine put out 730bhp, and clever aerodynamics give it a top speed of 230mph.

DID YOU KNOW? Jaguar's C-X75 supercar concept uses electric drive with Li-ion batteries recharged by gas micro-turbines

Limited top speed
Bugatti limits the road car top speed to 257mph to protect the tyres. The Super Sport available to buy will otherwise be identical to the 268mph record breaker.

Speedy
Accelerating from a standing start, the Veyron will cover a whole mile just 23.6 seconds later.

The statistics...

Veyron 16.4 Super Sport

Manufacturer:	Bugatti
Dimensions:	Length: 4,462mm, width: 1,998mm, height: 1,190mm
Weight:	1,838kg
0-60 speed:	2.5sec
Top speed:	268mph
Horse power:	1,200
Unit price:	£1.5m
Status:	Available now

Dagger GT

The Dagger designers are not using the latest technology to achieve awesome top speeds. Instead, they're using proven engineering solutions and decades of land speed and NASA experience. Five versions of the Dagger are available. The 300mph car will be a bespoke Dagger GT-LS version, with a one-inch ride height, roll cage, drag chutes and 450kg of front ballast (for high-speed safety, it will keep the front of the GT-LS on the ground). The engine will be so highly tuned, it won't be suitable for road use.

Horsepower is key to high top speeds – that, and good aerodynamics. TranStar used a NASA aerodynamicist, who discovered that the shape of the GT, including 1.95m² frontal area and 0.28 Cd, will allow 300mph... if it also has 2,000bhp. So, that's what it has, via a petrol-methanol, twin-turbo 572 cubic inch V8 engine. There are dual fuel injectors for each cylinder – at 300mph, the dual fuel tanks will empty in six minutes. TranStar says that, for 'a little insurance', it can offer up to 2,500bhp. A special custom-made six-speed gearbox has also been designed to deal with such high horsepower.

TranStar says there are good aerodynamic reasons why supercars have not exceeded 300mph: "This is the danger zone and you must take precautions before attempting these speeds. We have the horsepower, aerodynamics and the engineering know-how. It can be done mathematically, on paper. And we have the guys who can make it reality."

POTENTIAL TO BREAK 300MPH!

546 cubic inches...
The US firm measures engine capacity in cubic inches – 572. In European terms, it's 9,376cc, or a 9.3-litre engine.

Super-smooth shape
Aerodynamics are as vital as power for best top speed: the Dagger's Cd is 0.28.

The statistics...

Dagger GT

Manufacturer:	TranStar Racing
Dimensions:	Length: 4,876mm, width: 2,133mm, height: 1,117mm
Weight:	1,350kg
0-60 speed:	1.5secs
Top speed:	300mph-plus (est)
Horse power:	2,000-plus
Unit price:	£350,000
Status:	In production 2011

Deploy the chute
It's common practice for world speed record cars to have a rear parachute for rapid braking.

Big bore engine
Each cylinder in the engine is 'square' in dimensions – 114mm bore and 114mm stroke.

Quarter mile hurricane
The benchmark quarter-mile from a standing start is estimated to take 6.6 seconds.

Clutch can cope
The huge clutch is made up of three friction plate discs. It is rated to 2,500bhp.

Dagger sticks it in

All torque
TranStar is aiming for 2,000lb-ft of torque from the engine. Such pulling power will provide massive response to the throttle.

SSC Ultimate Aero
0-60 speed:	2.7sec
1/4 mile:	9.9sec
Top speed:	257mph
Horsepower:	1,183

The Ultimate Aero is the closest to the Veyron at present, but will the Ultimate Aero II take pole position?

Bugatti Veyron 16.4 Super Sport
0-60 speed:	2.78sec
1/4 mile:	7.2sec
Top speed:	268mph
Horsepower:	1,287

Current, fastest production car in the world, but still can't catch the Dagger GT.

TranStar Racing Dagger GT
0-60 speed:	1.5sec
1/4 mile:	6.7sec
Top speed:	314mph
Horsepower:	2,000

First past the line, already passing 314mph!

FINISH LINE
1/4 mile mark

3RD PLACE

2ND PLACE

WINNER!

189

Gate
Made of oak or steel, gates are made watertight by using a mitre joint. The two gates fit together at an angle – and the height difference by the two water levels pushes them tight together. Only a small difference is needed to seal them.

Chamber
This is the area of water that raises or lowers the boat. It is completely sealed by gates at either end. Some 'super' chambers can lift a boat six metres, this distance is called the 'rise'.

Paddle
This is the valve used to fill and empty chambers. There are gate paddles, which are holes in the lower gate that water flows out of, and ground paddles, which flows water underground through a culvert. There can be several paddles in a lock.

Canal locks

Canal locks have been around for centuries, and are both elegant yet ingenious

In the early days of canals, locks were not necessary. Engineers built them on flat land; gradients were not an issue. However, canals are man-made structures originally designed for work, not pleasure. To make best use of them, they needed to go where the factories were – hills and all.

Locks were invented to let boats travel up and down gradients on water. They work like an 'aqua lift'; the boat is enclosed in a chamber, which is either filled with or emptied of water. This commonly carries the boat up or down a height change of several metres.

Where there is a steep gradient to climb, there are numerous locks spaced across the gradient. These can either be individual locks separated by a lock-free waterway, or a 'staircase' – these are faster as the 'upper' gate of one lock is the 'lower' gate of another.

Each lock cycle involves the transfer of many tens of thousands of gallons of water. On artificial canals, it is important this water flow is managed to ensure the canal does not run dry. Luckily, the historic engineers considered this too, ensuring even Victorian lock systems work as well today as they always have. ❁

© DK Images

Balance beam
The most famous visual aspect of a lock. Made from heavy timber, the beam 'balances' the gate and ensures it does not drag on the ground, so can be moved easily. It also provides leverage to swing the heavy gates open and closed.

Winding gear
This is what opens the paddle valve that fills and empties a lock. An operator turns a windlass, which lifts the sliding panel covering the valve; it looks like a mere wooden stub but is actually the 'control panel' of the lock.

Ship stabilisers

How do they help keep ships level in rough waters?

Ship stabilisers come in three main categories: bilge keels, ship stabilisers and gyroscopic ship stabilisers. Bilge keels are long thin strips of metal that run in a 'V' shape along the length of a ship at the turn of the bilge (the area on the outer surface of a ship's hull where the bottom curves meet the vertical sides). Bilge keels work by dampening a ship's roll capability by counteracting roll pressure with physical hydrodynamic resistance. Bilge keels are one of the simplest and cheapest ways to stabilise a ship and mitigate roll.

Ship stabilisers differ to bilge keels in shape and positioning, resembling fins rather than gills and are often positioned in pairs at the stern and bow

of a ship. They do, however, work in the same way and are usually positioned on the bilge in line with the ship's bilge keel. Due to their larger size and protrusion, ship stabilisers offer greater resistance to ship roll but negatively affect its manoeuvrability and increase its hull clearances when docking.

Finally, gyroscopic ship stabilisers – which are the stabiliser of choice on most modern, large-scale vessels – are complex fin systems that cannot only be incrementally adjusted in their angle of attack (a vector representing the relative motion between lifting body and the fluid through which it is moving) to counteract roll, but also brought in and out of the hull at will thanks to specially tailored hydraulic mechanisms. ❁

Main control
Dictating orders, the elements of the fin system are enacted and disseminated here.

Bridge control
The position and equipment used by the officers to issue commands.

Local control
This unit controls the movement of individual fins and their machinery.

Oil header tank

Stabiliser unit
This helps to maintain fin positioning and ship stability while moving.

Pump motor starter

Hydraulic unit
The power to move the massive fins and bring them in and out of the ship comes from hydraulics.

Fin
The part of the system that can be extended out of the body, used to prevent roll and achieve an accurate and efficient tracking course.

Improving efficiency

Modern piezoelectric fuel injectors use piezo wafers that, when charged, expand and control the nozzle. Their key benefit is immense speed of reaction; they can deliver multiple injections of fuel for every combustion cycle – this helps reduce noise and emissions, and increase power.

© BMW AG

Fuel injection

The electrically powered, computer-controlled syringe that injects more power into an engine

Fuel injection systems are the delivery agents that help a car move. They spray fuel into the combustion chamber, where it mixes with air before being ignited. Fuel injection is a totally computer-controlled process that is fully responsive – the very millisecond any parameters change, so too will the amount of fuel injected.

Fuel injection has replaced old-fashioned carburettors. Electronic systems were first fitted into cars in the Seventies – mechanical setups existed before this, but they were far less reliable. Today, emissions legislations mean every car on sale must be fitted with fuel injection. The latest solenoid injector is a highly precise 'syringe' that sprays just the right amount of fuel into a cylinder. The injector is powered by electricity, its default mode is closed but electric power to the solenoid opens it for a microsecond. The duration of this 'open' period is called the pulse width.

Fuel is delivered from a pump in the fuel tank – this means it is injected under pressure. This atomises the fuel, enabling it to mix more fully with the air. This is called stoichiometric, or 'complete', combustion. The latest fuel injectors can deliver fuel under thousands of bar pressure.

Fuel tube
This high-pressure tube feeds off from the fuel rail and supplies the injector with a constant stream of fuel. Forces involved are immense, yet intricately controlled.

Fuel injector
Fuel is injected into the combustion chamber via a solenoid or piezoelectric injector; some diesel injectors can fire six or seven 'bursts' for each combustion cycle!

Atomised fuel
Such is the immense force of the fuel injection, it actually forms a fine mist – this allows more 'complete' combustion, helping reduce emissions.

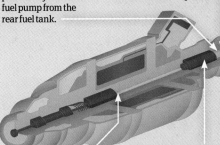

© BMW AG

Common rail
Fuel is constantly pressurised, up to several thousand bar in diesels; this is key to the overall efficiency of common rail fuel injection.

High-precision tech atop each cylinder

Fuel injectors are precise and expensive technology. There is one for every cylinder in a car's engine. The amount of fuel injected is calculated by an ECU (electronic control unit), which measures parameters from oxygen, mass air flow, outside temperature, throttle position and crank position sensors. A solenoid coil acts on a plunger when charged to initiate injection.

STAGE ONE
Solenoid off

Fuel delivered
Fuel is delivered to each injector under pressure by an electric fuel pump from the rear fuel tank.

Fuel pressurised
A spring keeps the injector sealed by forcing the needle in the 'closed' position.

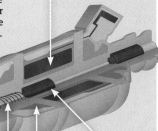

Fuel waits
Fuel waits in the injector to be injected into the engine with the opening of the solenoid.

Fuel filtered
To ensure no debris can enter the precise injector, a filter cleanses all fuel before it enters.

STAGE TWO
Solenoid on

Fuel mist
A spray tip can have many holes, further helping atomise the fuel into a fine mist.

Solenoid control
The solenoid surrounds the plunger; it is this that presses on the valve spring to keep the injector shut.

Fuel fed in a flash
As the valve spring lifts, pressurised fuel is squirted through the spray tip; when the solenoid is turned off, the plunger snaps back and closes the valve.

Solenoid action
When charged, the solenoid lifts the plunger. This releases pressure on the valve spring.

Fuel precision
It is a closed loop feedback system; sensors feed a computer that calculates individual fuel injection quantity.

Injecting accuracy

Carburettors were far less accurate than injectors. They could not achieve the pressure of an injector, so fuel was injected in drops rather than a fine mist. This was more difficult to fully combust, which led to wasted fuel and higher emissions. Carburettors did not allow computer control so operated as an open loop with no feedback from sensors. Therefore they were very slow in responding to transient conditions.

Modern legislation demands such tight control of exhaust emissions, a carburettor simply would not achieve the required standard – particularly in very hot or cold conditions. Fuel injection also provides more flexibility for engine designers, who don't have to consider the inflexible placement of a carburettor. This helps packaging for modern front-end crash tests.

© Arno McNemo

> "Unlike fixed-wing aircraft such as planes, the flight principles of helicopters differ markedly"

The Dauphin: essential on a treacherous rescue mission

© Tanarus

The statistics...

Sea King HAS.5

Crew: 2-4

Length: 17m (56ft)

Height: 5.13m (16ft)

Weight: 6,387kg

Rotor diameter: 18.90m (62ft)

Range: 1,230km (764 mi)

Powerplant: 2x Rolls-Royce Gnome H1400-2 turboshafts (1,660shp each)

Max speed: 207kph (129mph)

Service ceiling: 3,050m

Rate of climb: 10.3m/s

Helicopters

Arguably the most versatile vehicles used on Earth, helicopters are used for military, civil and industrial purposes, offering unrivalled flight dynamism

Helicopters consist of a large airfoil (a rotating blade assembly) mounted via a hinged shaft to an aircraft fuselage, engine and flight controls. Unlike fixed-wing aircraft such as planes, however, the flight principles of helicopters differ markedly, with their power emanating from the rotating motion of the airfoil instead of from the plane's fixed wings and turbofan jet engines. Indeed, the fact that helicopters obtain lift from this cyclical motion complicates things massively, as it is directly affected by the horizontal or vertical movement of the vehicle at all times.

For example, in a plane the flight path of a wing is fixed in relation to its forward flight, while in a helicopter the flight path advances both forward and backwards through the circulation process of the rotors, with generated thrust parallel and in the opposite direction to it at 90 degrees. Therefore, when a helicopter is hovering in a stationary position, the plane of rotor rotation is directly parallel to the ground, balancing the helicopter's weight and drag with its generated perpendicular thrust/lift. In order to move forward, backwards or side to side, the helicopter therefore tilts the plane of rotor rotation (ie, the opposite direction to that of produced thrust) in that direction.

Complicating this process, however, are the effects of the rotor's opposite torque reaction, which due to the high rpm speed rotates the helicopter's fuselage in the opposite direction to that of the spinning blades. This is controlled by the addition of the helicopter's tail rotor, which is manually controlled by the pilot with the anti-torque pedals located in the cockpit (see 'How to fly a helicopter'). By adjusting these pedals the pilot can increase, decrease or neutralise torque dependent on the required manoeuvre.

In addition to variable rotation planes and torque reactions, helicopters are also subject to a 'gyroscopic precession' effect, a dissymmetry of lift caused by its forward movement. This occurs because as the rotor rotates while the helicopter is moving, the blades at the fore of any single cycle combine both their own velocity with that of the movement, while those at the rear of any cycle hold the difference between their velocity and the movement. This, in simple terms, means that the blades at the front move quicker than those at the back, producing more lift. If left unchecked, the helicopter would roll, so this is counteracted by altering the blade's individual angle of attack (the angle between the helicopter's lifting plane and oncoming flow of the atmosphere), decreasing that of those advancing and increasing those retreating to generate equilibrium. ✿

Rotors

With a diameter of 18.9m and constructed with a steel rotor head along with five interchangeable composite blades, the Sea King's rotors grant it supreme lifting power, able to carry multi-ton loads. The rotors are designed to be immune to notches and corrosion, as well as being impact-resistant and foldable.

A helicopter being used for rescue training operations in Iceland

5 TOP FACTS
HELICOPTERS

Screwed
1 The first reference to a rotor system is credited to Leonardo da Vinci, who designed an 'aerial screw' in 1480. No full-scale variant was made during his lifetime.

Steamed
2 The word 'helicopter' was coined by French inventor Gustave de Ponton d'Amécourt, who used it to name his small, steam-powered rotorcraft.

Untethered
3 The first helicopter to achieve untethered flight was the Cornu of 1907, which managed to hover one foot above the ground for 20 seconds.

Fastest
4 The record for the fastest helicopter in the world is held by the Sikorsky X2 which, during a flyby over Florida, United States, clocked 416km/h (258mph).

Phileas
5 The current world record speed for an eastbound round-the-world helicopter trip is 136km/h (220mph) set by Edward Kasprowicz in an Augusta A109S Grand.

DID YOU KNOW? *The first fully functional helicopter was the 1936 Focke-Wulf Fw 61*

Westland Sea King HAS.5

How It Works looks inside the Westland Sea King, one of the foremost utility helicopters in the world…

Powerplant

The Westland Sea King is fitted with two Rolls-Royce Gnome H1400-2 turboshafts, each capable of delivering 1,660shp. Both engines are governed by Westland's comprehensive avionics suite, a selection of systems designed to handle automatic functions such as start-up and on-the-fly maintenance.

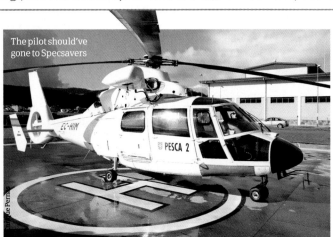

The pilot should've gone to Specsavers

Utilities

Utilities on the Sea King include a multi-band homing system, satellite navigation suite, search radar, video/infrared detection pod, electric generator for medical equipment (such as incubators) and a hydraulically operated rescue hoist. Night vision goggles are also available for crew members when operating at night.

Instrumentation

The cockpit of the Sea King is fitted with a gyro-horizon, altimeter, airspeed indicator, dual torquemeter, engine temperature indicator, voltmeter, ammeter and triple tachometer. Many of these instruments are directly accessible through multifunctional displays.

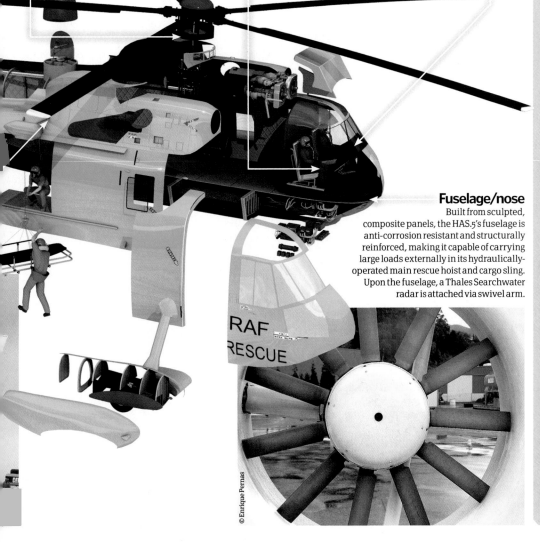

Fuselage/nose

Built from sculpted, composite panels, the HAS.5's fuselage is anti-corrosion resistant and structurally reinforced, making it capable of carrying large loads externally in its hydraulically-operated main rescue hoist and cargo sling. Upon the fuselage, a Thales Searchwater radar is attached via swivel arm.

RAF RESCUE

© Enrique Pernas

How to fly a helicopter

Think flying a plane would be hard? This is even harder…

Flying a helicopter is significantly harder than piloting a plane, due to the increased number of control inputs that need to be co-ordinated. There are four flight control inputs: the cyclic and collective controls, as well as the anti-torque pedals and throttle. The cyclic control – the joystick that sits between the pilot's legs – alters the pitch of the helicopter's rotor blades cyclically, allowing the pilot to change the rotor's thrust direction and overall vehicle tilt. For example, if a pilot pushes the cyclic stick forward then the rotor disc does also, creating forward thrust. The collective control is positioned to the left-hand side of the pilot (in a handbreak-type position) and when risen changes the pitch angle of all main rotor blades collectively, independent of their position, increasing or decreasing altitude.

Anti-torque pedals are positioned at the pilot's feet and control the direction of the helicopter's nose when pushed. These work by adjusting the pitch of the tail rotor blades, increasing yaw (rotation around a vertical axis) either to the left or right, dependent on which pedal is pressed. Finally, the throttle control – which is usually positioned as a twist grip on the collective control – affects the amount of power produced by the helicopter's engine, directly affecting the rpm speed of its rotors. Professional pilots must be trained to utilise these four controls in unison.

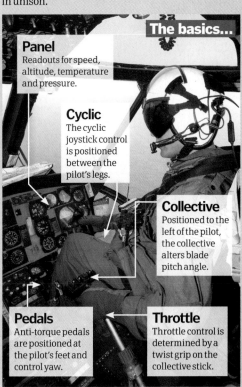

The basics…

Panel
Readouts for speed, altitude, temperature and pressure.

Cyclic
The cyclic joystick control is positioned between the pilot's legs.

Collective
Positioned to the left of the pilot, the collective alters blade pitch angle.

Pedals
Anti-torque pedals are positioned at the pilot's feet and control yaw.

Throttle
Throttle control is determined by a twist grip on the collective stick.

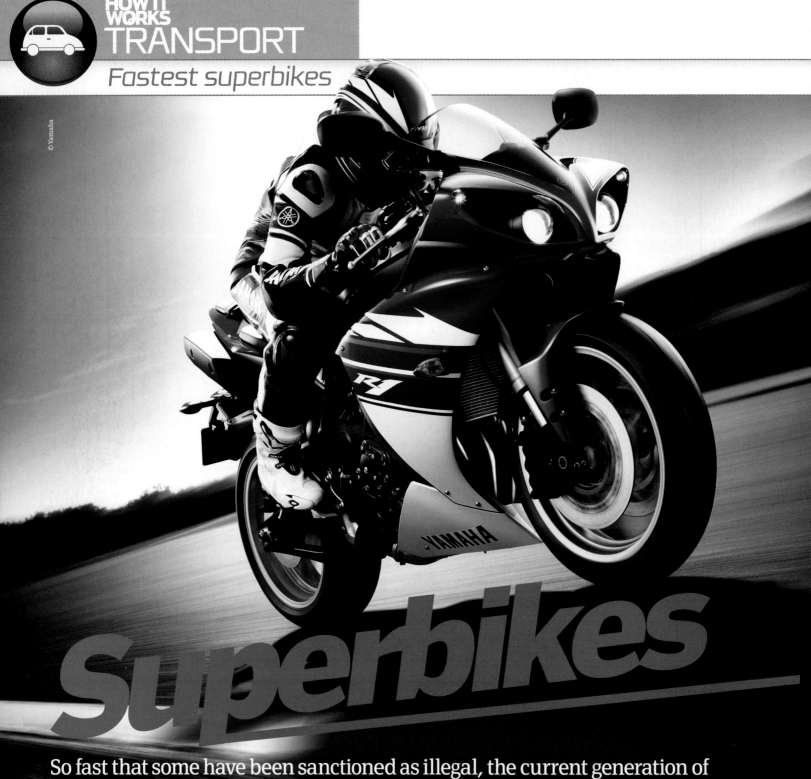

© Yamaha

Superbikes

So fast that some have been sanctioned as illegal, the current generation of superbikes are changing the nature of two-wheeled transport. Take a look at some of the most notable and the advanced technologies they employ

Optimised for some extreme acceleration, mad braking and unthinkable cornering, superbikes are aggressive, mass-centred machines designed with one thing in mind – pure speed. And it is a steadfast mission of which nothing can stand in the way. There is no compromise. Comfort? Forgotten. Fuel economy? Laughable. Legality? Deeply questionable.

Superbikes are completely transforming the levels of speed at which a human being is capable of travelling on two wheels, pushing the boundaries of

performance that few hypercars can better – and, indeed, for a fraction of the cost. Driven by the blurring of the lines between professional MotoGP superbikes and those available to the public – as well as the collapse of a gentleman's agreement between bike manufacturers to limit their vehicles to maximum top speeds of 200 miles per hour – today's superbikes are breaking loose from traditional constraints with the help of some very nifty next-generation technology.

Fundamentally the superbike works by adopting the traditional design elements of a motorcycle and

refining it and evolving it to maximise speed and performance. First and foremost, engine power is increased – often well over one litre (1,000cc) – and encased within an aluminium alloy frame to reduce weight. The engine is also rebuilt from scratch from lightweight composite materials (see 'Inside a superbike engine' boxout) and repositioned to maximise weight distribution, structural integrity and crucially, chassis rigidity. The latter is important as it affects dynamism and stability when accelerating, braking and cornering. The motorcycle's geometry is also completely

5 TOP FACTS
SUPERBIKES

Champ
1 The Superbike World Championship was founded in 1988 and allows modified versions of road-legal superbike models to be raced against each other.

Moto
2 In contrast, the Road Racing World Championship was first organised in 1949. This competition is split into three main categories, with MotoGP being the fastest.

Speedus Maximus
3 The highest speed achieved on a MotoGP motorcycle is 217.037mph. This record was set by Dani Pedrosa on a Repsol Honda RC212V 800cc superbike in 2009.

RR
4 The world's fastest street legal superbike as of 2010 is the Ducati Desmosedici RR, which has a rated top speed of 199mph. Ducati claims it is capable of over 200mph.

Tomahawk
5 The world's fastest street illegal superbike is the Dodge Tomahawk, which has a top speed of over 400mph. Only ten were ever built. They cost $550,000.

DID YOU KNOW? The Suzuki Hayabusa was the fastest road-legal superbike to be built in the 20th Century

Hayabusa GSX1300R

Engine
The Hayabusa GSX1300R is equipped with a 1,340cc, in-line, liquid-cooled engine with 16 valves.

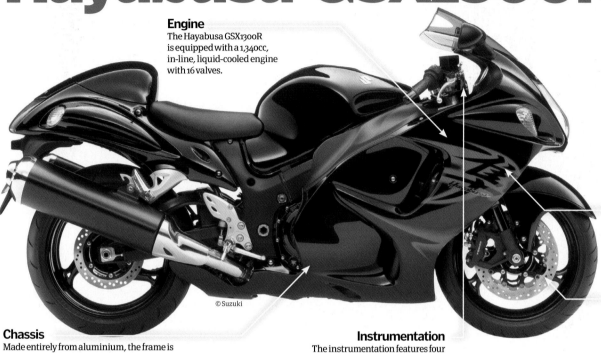
© Suzuki

The statistics...
Hayabusa GSX1300R

Length: 2,190mm

Width: 724mm

Height: 1,166mm

Wheelbase: 1,481mm

Mass: 260kg

Engine: Four-stroke, liquid-cooled, DOHC

Power: 145 kW @ 9,500rpm

Torque: 155N.m @ 7,200rpm

Clutch: Wet multi-plate

Transmission: Six-speed constant mesh

Gearshift: One-down, five-up

Transmission
The GSX1300R is kitted out with an optimised six-speed transmission. Oil is automatically sprayed to the 4th, 5th and 6th gears to reduce wear and mechanical noise.

Brakes
Radial-mount front brake callipers allow the GSX1300R to be fitted with smaller 310mm front brake rotors to reduce unsprung weight and improve handling. A single piston rear brake calliper works in conjunction with a 260mm rear brake disc.

Chassis
Made entirely from aluminium, the frame is designed to maximise strength while minimising weight. This is evident in the bike's bridged aluminium swingarm.

Instrumentation
The instrumentation features four analogue meters for the bike's speedometer, tachometer, fuel gauge and water temperature.

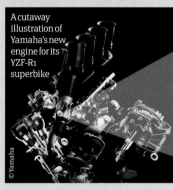
The Hayabusa GSX1300R features an optimied six-speed transmission
© Suzuki

Inside a superbike engine

Why do they have such explosive performance?

Almost all modern superbikes have extensive liquid-cooling systems and smart composite materials to improve cooling and heat transfer while in operation. Further, many components are made from lightweight aluminium alloys and are covered with chrome-nitride coatings to reduce friction. Combustion efficiency is achieved by employing iridium spark plugs in conjunction with refined fuel injection systems. In addition, advanced engine firing systems are used to improve the smoothness of energy transfer to the road, as demonstrated in the crossplane crankshaft installed on the Yamaha YZF-R1. Here the YZF-R1's crankshaft is designed to fire unevenly in order to produce combustion rather then inertial torque. This improves power, smoothness and rider feel when riding at speed.

rewritten in order to ensure correct front-to-rear weight distribution and rider positioning for high speed riding. These design alterations include a smoothing of the bike's chassis to increase aerodynamic performance and reduce drag, as well as the repositioning of instrumentation and controls – such as higher foot pegs and lower handlebars – to ensure optimised rider positioning.

Superbikes also feature a significant number of advanced and upgraded components and technologies. In terms of braking, thicker high-grade brake pads are used in conjunction with larger iron, carbon or ceramic-matrix disc brakes, which in turn are fitted with multi-piston callipers clamped onto oversized vented rotors. Suspension systems are multi-adjustable at both the front and rear – which allows adjustment for road conditions and riding style – and wheel forks are fitted with independent left and right cushioning to improve damping

A cutaway illustration of Yamaha's new engine for its YZF-R1 superbike

The crossplane crankshaft from the YZF-R1
© Yamaha

performance (the reduction of friction and oscillation at high velocity). Engine crankshafts (the part of the engine that translates the reciprocating linear piston motion of the power stroke into rotational motion) are also custom built to ensure a smoother combustion process. On top of this, each superbike's transmission is modified to use with dual wet, multiplate clutches (see 'Superbike transmission explained' boxout) for lightning-fast and super-smooth gear changes. Both front and rear tyre sizes are also dramatically increased in order to increase traction and maximum riding angle.

And finally, superbikes come fully equipped with numerous smart electronic systems in order to help the rider control the extreme power and speed at which they are travelling. These can range from traditional tachometers, speedometers and rev-counters through to automatic systems to control intake performance across the superbike's rpm range and throttle-valve opening timings for responsive and smooth power. Quite simply, these machines represent the pinnacle of vehicular progress. ✿

Kawasaki Ninja ZX-10R

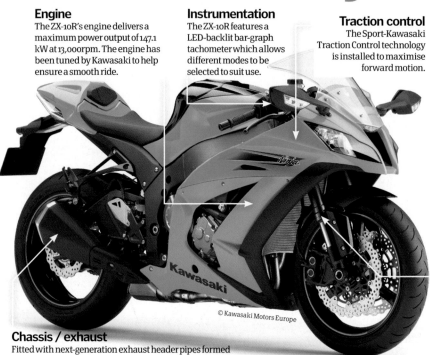

Engine
The ZX-10R's engine delivers a maximum power output of 147.1 kW at 13,000rpm. The engine has been tuned by Kawasaki to help ensure a smooth ride.

Instrumentation
The ZX-10R features a LED-backlit bar-graph tachometer which allows different modes to be selected to suit use.

Traction control
The Sport-Kawasaki Traction Control technology is installed to maximise forward motion.

© Kawasaki Motors Europe

Chassis / exhaust
Fitted with next-generation exhaust header pipes formed from heat-resistant titanium alloy and sporting a new curved chassis to increase aerodynamic performance.

The statistics...

Kawasaki Ninja ZX-10R

Length: 2,075mm
Width: 714mm
Height: 1,115mm
Wheelbase: 1,425mm
Mass: 201kg
Engine: Four-stroke, liquid-cooled, in-line four
Power: 147.1 kW @ 13,000rpm
Torque: 112N.m @ 11,500rpm
Clutch: Wet multi-plate
Transmission: Six-speed return
Gearshift: One-down, five-up

Suspension
The ZX-10R sports horizontal back-link rear suspension above the bike's swingarm. This arrangement increases road holding in the final third of the engine's stroke range and increased stability when cornering.

Superbike transmission explained

Because it takes two to transmission

Modern superbikes use dual-clutch transmissions for maximum performance. These work by having two clutches instead of the usual one sharing the gearbox, with each clutch attached to half the number of total gears. In essence this means that when the bike is in a certain gear the next gear is also selected by the second clutch. Consequently, when the rider changes up a gear and the first clutch is disengaged, the second clutch can instantly engage the next gear, providing a super-fast response time.

Due to the compact, advanced design of the superbike dual-clutch transmission, most systems on the market use wet multi-plate clutches. Wet clutches involve submerging the clutch components in lubricating fluid to reduce friction and limit the production of excess heat. This is due to the fact that wet multi-plate clutches use hydraulic pressure to drive the superbike's gears. This works as when the clutch engages, hydraulic pressure from its internal piston forces its series of stacked plates and toothed friction discs against a fixed pressure plate. In turn, the friction discs mesh with the splines on the inside of the clutch drum and the force is transferred from drum to gearset.

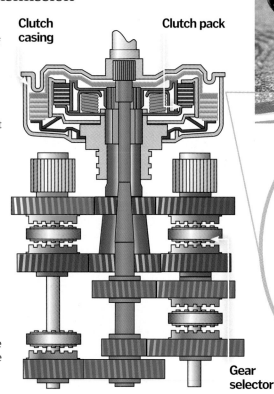

Clutch casing

Clutch pack

Gear selector

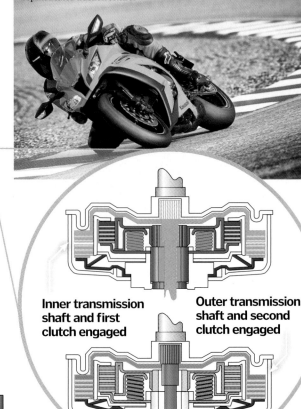

The Kawasaki Ninja ZX-10R boasts sophisticated traction control

© Kawasaki Motors Europe

Inner transmission shaft and first clutch engaged

Outer transmission shaft and second clutch engaged

Yamaha YZF-R1

Engine
The YZF-R1's engine is a four-stroke, liquid-cooled variant. It delivers a maximum power output of 133.9 kW at 12,500 rpm.

Electronics
Yamaha's YCC-I (Yamaha Chip-Controlled Intake) adjusts the length of the four intake funnels of the YZF-R1 for accurate and balanced performance across the rpm range.

The wheelbase on the YZF-R1 offers extreme control

© Yamaha

The statistics...

Yamaha YZF-R1

Length:	2,070mm
Width:	714mm
Height:	1,130mm
Wheelbase:	1,415mm
Mass:	205kg
Engine:	Four-stroke, liquid-cooled, DOHC, forward inclined
Power:	133.9 kW @ 12,500rpm
Torque:	115.5 Nm @ 10,000rpm
Clutch:	Wet, multiple-disc coil spring
Transmission:	Six-speed, constant mesh
Gearshift:	One-down, five-up

Suspension
The YZF-R1 features multi-adjustable front and rear suspension that can be varied depending on riding style and road conditions.

Crankshaft
The YZF-R1 is the first production bike with a crossplane crankshaft. This grants the rider extra control and feel as the crossplane produces combustion rather than inertial torque.

Wheelbase
Imported directly from Yahama's MotoGP bikes, the YZF-R1 sports a short wheelbase and long swingarm frame which helps deliver maximum traction and control.

Dodge Tomahawk
When $500 million meets 500bhp

Costing over $500 million and sporting the 500bhp, 8.3-litre V10 that can be found in the Dodge Viper supercar, the Dodge Tomahawk is the world's fastest superbike. Indeed, it is so powerful – think 0-60 in 2.5 seconds and a top speed of over 400mph – that it has been banned for legal use on public roads. Despite this, however, Dodge has sold more than ten Tomahawks for private collectors for use on racetracks and private estates.

The Tomahawk is constructed from a 356-T6 aluminium alloy block with cast-iron liners and a series of aluminium alloy cylinder heads. The bike is cooled by twin aluminium radiators mounted atop its engine intake manifolds as well as a force-fed belt-driven turbine fan. Braking is

handled by 20-inch perimeter-mounted drilled and machined stainless rotors, partnered with multiple four piston fixed aluminium callipers.

Clearly Bruce Wayne is a fan

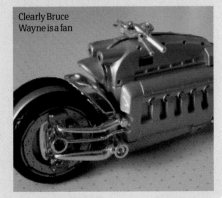

How It Works
fantasy race
How long will it take these two-wheelers to get from Alaska to Argentina, assuming they travel at top speed all the way?

Distance:
9,681 miles

START (Alaska)

21 days

Push bike
Top speed: 20mph

7 days

Scooter
Top speed: 50mph

3.3 days

Motorbike
Top speed: 120mph

2.2 days

Superbike
Top speed: 186mph

Tomahawk
Top speed: 400mph

1 day

FINISH (Argentina)

Bike images © Khaosaming, Falcon Motorcycles, Suzuki

197

"The cement hopper is fitted with vibrators to stop blockages"

Concrete mixers

These vehicles are vital to construction projects of every scale, but how do they get the job done so quickly and efficiently?

The need for different types of concrete – in bulk quantities – has led to demands for adaptable, variable concrete mixers. The key to successful concrete mixing is to use the correct amounts of each ingredient. At the heart of the Nurock concrete mixer is a conveyer belt that carries sand and stone, stored in the main hopper, out to a continuous mixing screw. The proportions of sand and stone are controlled using electric flow control gates to vary the proportions. Here, the mixer lets gravity do some of the work. Its hopper is angled at 45 degrees on the bottom to encourage the material to flow effectively. The hoppers are even rigged with vibrators to ensure that any blockage is quickly shaken apart.

Water stored at the front of the mixer is fed, via a hydraulic pump, into the continuous mixing screw at a specified speed for the type of concrete, all monitored by an advanced mixer computer system for accountability and accuracy.

Finally, the cement itself is held in a rear hopper. Once added, the completed material is mixed using a variable-speed, continuous mixing screw. This produces a uniform flow of freshly mixed concrete from the rear of the mixer, it can be stopped and started at will, with no waste. The mixer can be rotated through 180 degrees and extra delivery chutes can be added allowing up to 20ft discharge from the rear of the mixer allowing the concrete to be placed on the construction site. ✻

The glue that holds it all together

Making the mixture
A lot of work goes into creating a steady flow of concrete

1. Hydraulic oil tank
Situated next to the water tank, ensuring heat from it dissipates out through the water.

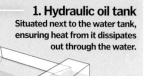

2. Water tank
The water flow into the mixer can be controlled by the operator.

3. Aggregate hopper
Angled at the bottom to keep the flow of the mixture smooth, it also vibrates, breaking up any blockages.

4. Cement feed
Again, these can be controlled, ensuring the correct ratio of sand and stone is added.

5. Continuous mixing screw
A variable speed – and reversible – hydraulic screw, this ensures the cement flows steadily.

Cement flow through the Nurock mixer
The parts and processes that create perfect concrete every time

6. Cement hopper
The hopper holds the bulk of the cement, with a water-tight door allowing for easy loading.

4. Stone hopper
On the opposite side of the mixer, the stone hopper can also have its flow modified, ensuring the correct mixture is achieved.

5. Cement feed
The feed system ensures a constant delivery of cement meeting the exact tolerances needed to produce any strength of concrete required.

2. Water tank
Water is pumped into the mixer screw at a constant speed as required and eliminates pressure variance from the tank.

1. Conveyer belt
Vital to the proportioning process, the conveyor belt carries the unmixed sand and stone to the mixing screw.

3. Sand hopper
The Nurock is designed to hold sand and stone separately if needed.

The Nurock mixer makes light work of concrete production

A building site's best friend

All Images © Nurock

5 TOP FACTS
TRANSMISSION TECHNOLOGIES

Fuzzy logic
1 In the Nineties, automatic transmissions gained computer control – this enabled them to 'learn' each driver's style, and adjust the gear change profiles to suit.

Dual-clutch
2 A dual-clutch gearbox has two clutches, onto which 'odd' and 'even' gears are mounted. These are pre-selected, with alternate gears engaged by swapping drive to the clutches.

Automated manual
3 In an automated manual, a conventional manual gearbox is controlled hydraulically by electronic actuators. These shift gear ratios and also operate the clutch.

Satnav profiling
4 Cutting-edge cars link the auto gearbox to the satnav system. This means the gearbox can 'see' when bends in the road are coming up, and profile gear changes to suit.

CVT
5 A Continuously Variable Transmission has an infinite number of gear ratios, by adjusting the sections of two pulleys on which a belt or metal band runs.

DID YOU KNOW? *Sometimes, thanks to computer trickery and carefully programmed shift patterns, a full auto is more efficient*

Automatic transmission

Since the Thirties auto transmissions have provided convenience for drivers, and still play a part in development

An automatic transmission makes a car easier to drive. Most executive cars have automatic gearboxes, and while there are various types of 'self-shifting' transmissions on the market, the most well-established is the conventional torque converter automatic.

The key component is the torque converter itself. This provides the coupling between the engine and the transmission, converting engine motion into vehicular movement. This is not a direct connection, though – instead, it is a hydraulic connection. Automatic cars are said to use a hydraulic coupling or fluid coupling.

There are three main components in a torque converter – the impeller, turbine and stator. The impeller and turbine face one another in a round metal case that looks like a doughnut: the impeller is connected to the engine and the turbine is connected to the transmission. The case is sealed and filled with transmission fluid, and both impeller and turbine are fitted with blades that catch the fluid when rotated.

When the engine rotates, the impeller begins to circulate. As this also swirls the transmission fluid, the turbine thus begins to move in the same direction – this is how engine drive is sent to the transmission. Due to centrifugal force, the fluid is forced to the outside edge of the blades. The stator redirects this back to the side of the turbine – this flow of fluid is what multiplies the engine power.

The torque converter is connected to a planetary gear set. This consists of a central sun gear, around which several planetary gears and an outside ring gear can rotate. Ratios are altered by locking and unlocking different combinations of gears. Most automatic transmissions consist of compound planetary gears, where two gear sets are connected in series. ✿

The eco-friendly BMW ActiveHybrid 7 comes with eight-speed auto transmission

© BMW AG

Understanding the automatic gears in your vehicle

Park
In this mode, the output shaft is locked by a device called a 'parking pawl': a pin locks the output shaft to the transmission casing. It is the first position on all automatic transmission shift patterns: the ordering layout was standardised in the Sixties.

Reverse
The planetary gear set is locked, so it can't move. Power is applied to the ring gear, which causes the sun gear to turn in the opposite direction. This enables the vehicle to move backwards. Most gearboxes have a shift lock, so you have to press a button on the shifter to engage reverse: electronic computers mean it doesn't engage when you're going forwards.

Neutral
This mode disengages the transmission from the road wheels – it enables the car to be pushed freely without disturbing the gearbox. Most cars cannot be started unless they are either in 'N' or 'P'.

Drive
In this mode, the transmission can engage the full set of gear ratios automatically. The torque converter allows the vehicle to stop with the transmission in gear, with the engine still running. All the driver does is engage the 'D' setting and drive.

Inside an automatic

Auto efficiency
A torque converter is a fluid connection, so there is always a small percentage of slippage. This is why automatic gearboxes are less fuel-efficient than manual units.

Clutch straw
The torque converter takes the place of the clutch in a manual transmission car. It can also replicate the 'direct' connection of a clutch. A torque converter clutch locks the turbine to the impeller, bypassing the torque converter, usually at higher vehicle speeds.

Hold the ratio
Hydraulic servos actuate the bands and clutches within the planetary gear set, holding individual elements of the planetary gear set stationary to create the different ratios.

Stator boost
The torque converter provides a degree of torque multiplication, which gives the car an extra 'boost' away from the line. This is thanks to the stator harnessing the kinetic energy of the rotating transmission fluid.

Hydraulic control
The pump is housed between the torque converter and the planetary gear set: the input is connected to the torque converter housing and, thus, the engine flywheel.

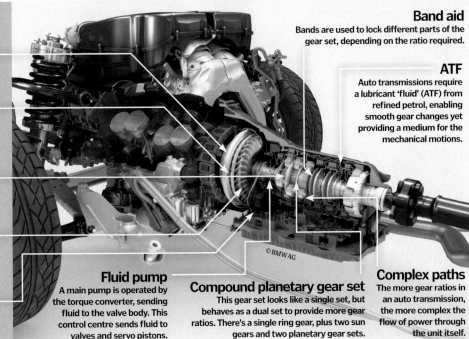

Band aid
Bands are used to lock different parts of the gear set, depending on the ratio required.

ATF
Auto transmissions require a lubricant 'fluid' (ATF) from refined petrol, enabling smooth gear changes yet providing a medium for the mechanical motions.

© BMW AG

Fluid pump
A main pump is operated by the torque converter, sending fluid to the valve body. This control centre sends fluid to valves and servo pistons.

Compound planetary gear set
This gear set looks like a single set, but behaves as a dual set to provide more gear ratios. There's a single ring gear, plus two sun gears and two planetary gear sets.

Complex paths
The more gear ratios in an auto transmission, the more complex the flow of power through the unit itself.

Car steering

The ability to steer is crucial to a car's operation, but how does it work?

Rack and pinion is by far the most common type of steering system. Picture a flat rack with teeth cut in, connected to the road wheels. This is moved left or right by a pinion gear to which the steering shaft is connected. This turns the rotation of the steering wheel into linear road wheel input.

Recirculating ball car steering is less common nowadays but is still seen on heavier vehicles such as buses. It is a block with a threaded hole within, and gear teeth cut into the outside. The steering rod connects to the block – turning the steering wheel turns the entire 'block', moving the gear and turning the road wheels.

Power steering lightens the load on the steering wheel by adding an extra set of muscles. Traditionally, a hydraulic pump was used, driven by the engine via a belt. A piston is connected to the rack, with pressurised fluid either side. The pump supplies higher-pressure fluid to one side of the piston, which forces it to the other side.

When turning a corner, the 'inside' wheel to the curve has to turn a smaller radius than the outside. If designers didn't allow for this, one of the wheels would 'scrub' on the road surface as the difference in distance was absorbed. Ackermann steering geometry is a way of setting up systems to avoid this.

Ackermann geometry is created by moving steering pivot points inwards, which means the front wheels turn at increasing differences of angle as the steering is rotated. It means all wheels turn about the same 'turning circle' if lines were drawn from their centres. If there were no difference in front wheel angles, there would be different turning circles for each wheel. ⚙

London's new cab drivers are much cheaper to employ

Turning X into Y

1. Basic principles
The basic aim of a steering system is to turn the rotational instructions of the driver into linear reactions at the front wheel.

10. Fixed at the back
The rear wheels in the pictured example drive the car: they are fixed and cannot steer. They form the basis of the turning circle.

8. Steering ratio
This is how far you turn the steering wheel compared to how far the wheels turn. If one complete steering wheel turn results in a 17 degree wheel change, the steering ratio is 21:1 (360/17=21).

5. Driver initiation
The driver turns the steering wheel, which is directly connected to a steering column. This in turn rotates the pinion, which is attached to the steering rack.

3. Steering leverage
The wheels receive steering torque through a short lever-arm – the steering arm.

9. Sporting focus
Lower ratio steering racks are fitted to sportier cars. More front wheel movement is generated from any given steering input, which enthusiasts prefer because it is more direct.

4. Output path
The steering arm is connected to swivel pin ball joints, to which the tie rods are also attached. These feed the outputs from the steering rack itself.

7. Steering rack
The steering rack is encased within a tube for protection. Tie rods attach to either end.

6. Lock to lock limit
The pinion is fixed but the rack is free to move within a defined 'lock range' usually three full rotations of the steering wheel.

2. Scientific definition
A car's steering system is an example of a linear actuator. This is the creation of linear motion when driven by non-linear motion.

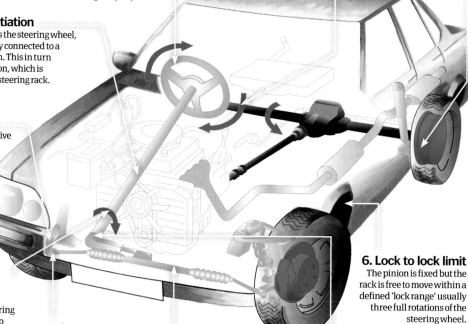

The Ackermann effect

3. Alter the angle
Ackermann allows for this difference in angle by allowing the suspension geometry to alter when the wheel is turned. It allows the inside wheel to adopt a greater angle than the outside.

1. Straight and narrow
In a straight line, all wheels sit parallel. What's more, in corners, the rear wheels remain parallel. All the work has to be done by the front wheels (which is why front suspension is more complicated than rear suspension).

4. Perfect Ackermann
The Ackermann effect can be seen on cars parked with the wheels turned. One wheel will appear to 'lean over' much more than the other. In extremes, the difference in angle between them can be ten degrees or more.

2. Inside line
The inside wheel travels on a tighter radius than the outside wheel. Therefore it has to be turned in more to compensate, else it would scrub on the ground.

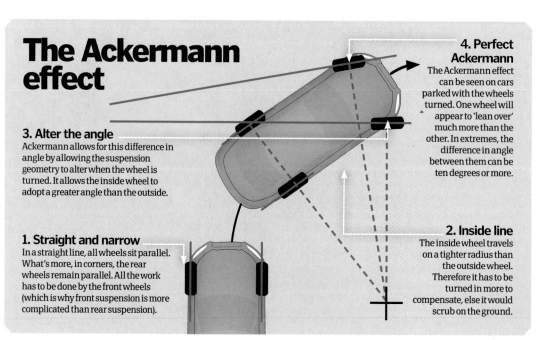

5 TOP FACTS
TRANSMISSION TECHNOLOGIES

Fuzzy logic
1 In the Nineties, automatic transmissions gained computer control – this enabled them to 'learn' each driver's style, and adjust the gear change profiles to suit.

Dual-clutch
2 A dual-clutch gearbox has two clutches, onto which 'odd' and 'even' gears are mounted. These are pre-selected, with alternate gears engaged by swapping drive to the clutches.

Automated manual
3 In an automated manual, a conventional manual gearbox is controlled hydraulically by electronic actuators. These shift gear ratios and also operate the clutch.

Satnav profiling
4 Cutting-edge cars link the auto gearbox to the satnav system. This means the gearbox can 'see' when bends in the road are coming up, and profile gear changes to suit.

CVT
5 A Continuously Variable Transmission has an infinite number of gear ratios, by adjusting the sections of two pulleys on which a belt or metal band runs.

DID YOU KNOW? *Sometimes, thanks to computer trickery and carefully programmed shift patterns, a full auto is more efficient*

Automatic transmission

Since the Thirties auto transmissions have provided convenience for drivers, and still play a part in development

An automatic transmission makes a car easier to drive. Most executive cars have automatic gearboxes, and while there are various types of 'self-shifting' transmissions on the market, the most well-established is the conventional torque converter automatic.

The key component is the torque converter itself. This provides the coupling between the engine and the transmission, converting engine motion into vehicular movement. This is not a direct connection, though – instead, it is a hydraulic connection. Automatic cars are said to use a hydraulic coupling or fluid coupling.

There are three main components in a torque converter – the impeller, turbine and stator. The impeller and turbine face one another in a round metal case that looks like a doughnut: the impeller is connected to the engine and the turbine is connected to the transmission. The case is sealed and filled with transmission fluid, and both impeller and turbine are fitted with blades that catch the fluid when rotated.

When the engine rotates, the impeller begins to circulate. As this also swirls the transmission fluid, the turbine thus begins to move in the same direction – this is how engine drive is sent to the transmission. Due to centrifugal force, the fluid is forced to the outside edge of the blades. The stator redirects this back to the side of the turbine – this flow of fluid is what multiplies the engine power.

The torque converter is connected to a planetary gear set. This consists of a central sun gear, around which several planetary gears and an outside ring gear can rotate. Ratios are altered by locking and unlocking different combinations of gears. Most automatic transmissions consist of compound planetary gears, where two gear sets are connected in series.

The eco-friendly BMW ActiveHybrid 7 comes with eight-speed auto transmission

© BMW AG

Understanding the automatic gears in your vehicle

Park
In this mode, the output shaft is locked by a device called a 'parking pawl': a pin locks the output shaft to the transmission casing. It is the first position on all automatic transmission shift patterns: the ordering layout was standardised in the Sixties.

Reverse
The planetary gear set is locked, so it can't move. Power is applied to the ring gear, which causes the sun gear to turn in the opposite direction. This enables the vehicle to move backwards. Most gearboxes have a shift lock, so you have to press a button on the shifter to engage reverse: electronic computers mean it doesn't engage when you're going forwards.

Neutral
This mode disengages the transmission from the road wheels – it enables the car to be pushed freely without disturbing the gearbox. Most cars cannot be started unless they are either in 'N' or 'P'.

Drive
In this mode, the transmission can engage the full set of gear ratios automatically. The torque converter allows the vehicle to stop with the transmission in gear, with the engine still running. All the driver does is engage the 'D' setting and drive.

Inside an automatic

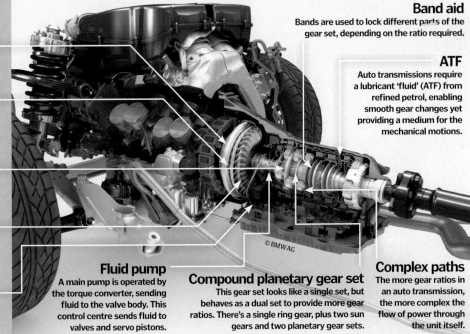

Auto efficiency
A torque converter is a fluid connection, so there is always a small percentage of slippage. This is why automatic gearboxes are less fuel-efficient than manual units.

Clutch straw
The torque converter takes the place of the clutch in a manual transmission car. It can also replicate the 'direct' connection of a clutch. A torque converter clutch locks the turbine to the impeller, bypassing the torque converter, usually at higher vehicle speeds.

Hold the ratio
Hydraulic servos actuate the bands and clutches within the planetary gear set, holding individual elements of the planetary gear set stationary to create the different ratios.

Stator boost
The torque converter provides a degree of torque multiplication, which gives the car an extra 'boost' away from the line. This is thanks to the stator harnessing the kinetic energy of the rotating transmission fluid.

Hydraulic control
The pump is housed between the torque converter and the planetary gear set: the input is connected to the torque converter housing and, thus, the engine flywheel.

Band aid
Bands are used to lock different parts of the gear set, depending on the ratio required.

ATF
Auto transmissions require a lubricant 'fluid' (ATF) from refined petrol, enabling smooth gear changes yet providing a medium for the mechanical motions.

Fluid pump
A main pump is operated by the torque converter, sending fluid to the valve body. This control centre sends fluid to valves and servo pistons.

Compound planetary gear set
This gear set looks like a single set, but behaves as a dual set to provide more gear ratios. There's a single ring gear, plus two sun gears and two planetary gear sets.

Complex paths
The more gear ratios in an auto transmission, the more complex the flow of power through the unit itself.

© BMW AG

"The front wheels turn at increasing differences of angle as the steering is rotated"

Car steering

The ability to steer is crucial to a car's operation, but how does it work?

Rack and pinion is by far the most common type of steering system. Picture a flat rack with teeth cut in, connected to the road wheels. This is moved left or right by a pinion gear to which the steering shaft is connected. This turns the rotation of the steering wheel into linear road wheel input.

Recirculating ball car steering is less common nowadays but is still seen on heavier vehicles such as buses. It is a block with a threaded hole within, and gear teeth cut into the outside. The steering rod connects to the block – turning the steering wheel turns the entire 'block', moving the gear and turning the road wheels.

Power steering lightens the load on the steering wheel by adding an extra set of muscles. Traditionally, a hydraulic pump was used, driven by the engine via a belt. A piston is connected to the rack, with pressurised fluid either side. The pump supplies higher-pressure fluid to one side of the piston, which forces it to the other side.

When turning a corner, the 'inside' wheel to the curve has to turn a smaller radius than the outside. If designers didn't allow for this, one of the wheels would 'scrub' on the road surface as the difference in distance was absorbed. Ackermann steering geometry is a way of setting up systems to avoid this.

Ackermann geometry is created by moving steering pivot points inwards, which means the front wheels turn at increasing differences of angle as the steering is rotated. It means all wheels turn about the same 'turning circle' if lines were drawn from their centres. If there were no difference in front wheel angles, there would be different turning circles for each wheel. ⚙

London's new cab drivers are much cheaper to employ

Turning X into Y

1. Basic principles
The basic aim of a steering system is to turn the rotational instructions of the driver into linear reactions at the front wheel.

10. Fixed at the back
The rear wheels in the pictured example drive the car: they are fixed and cannot steer. They form the basis of the turning circle.

8. Steering ratio
This is how far you turn the steering wheel compared to how far the wheels turn. If one complete steering wheel turn results in a 17 degree wheel change, the steering ratio is 21:1 (360/17=21).

5. Driver initiation
The driver turns the steering wheel, which is directly connected to a steering column. This in turn rotates the pinion, which is attached to the steering rack.

3. Steering leverage
The wheels receive steering torque through a short lever-arm – the steering arm.

9. Sporting focus
Lower ratio steering racks are fitted to sportier cars. More front wheel movement is generated from any given steering input, which enthusiasts prefer because it is more direct.

4. Output path
The steering arm is connected to swivel pin ball joints, to which the tie rods are also attached. These feed the outputs from the steering rack itself.

7. Steering rack
The steering rack is encased within a tube for protection. Tie rods attach to either end.

6. Lock to lock limit
The pinion is fixed but the rack is free to move within a defined 'lock range' usually three full rotations of the steering wheel.

2. Scientific definition
A car's steering system is an example of a linear actuator. This is the creation of linear motion when driven by non-linear motion.

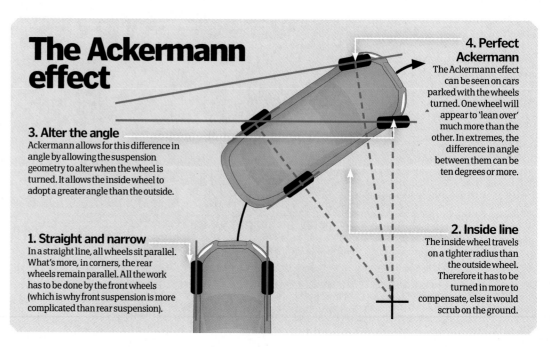

The Ackermann effect

3. Alter the angle
Ackermann allows for this difference in angle by allowing the suspension geometry to alter when the wheel is turned. It allows the inside wheel to adopt a greater angle than the outside.

1. Straight and narrow
In a straight line, all wheels sit parallel. What's more, in corners, the rear wheels remain parallel. All the work has to be done by the front wheels (which is why front suspension is more complicated than rear suspension).

4. Perfect Ackermann
The Ackermann effect can be seen on cars parked with the wheels turned. One wheel will appear to 'lean over' much more than the other. In extremes, the difference in angle between them can be ten degrees or more.

2. Inside line
The inside wheel travels on a tighter radius than the outside wheel. Therefore it has to be turned in more to compensate, else it would scrub on the ground.

TINY

1. Nano Air Vehicle
The hummingbird-like NAV is in development by AeroVironment, with the intention of using it as a flying robot spy.

© AeroVironment Inc
www.avinc.com

SOLAR POWER

2. Solar Eagle
By 2013 Boeing aims to launch the Solar Eagle, a solar-powered UAV that's designed to stay airborne for five years.

© Boeing

VERTICAL

3. Fire Scout
Northrop Grumman's MQ-8 Fire Scout is a 1,420kg unmanned helicopter, which is currently under evaluation by the US Army and Navy.

Credit Kurt Lengfield, US Navy

DID YOU KNOW? Early recon drones were used as decoys to fool enemy fighters and anti-aircraft guns

Recon drones
How do unmanned aerial vehicles work?

An unmanned aerial vehicle (UAV) is a military aircraft that is piloted either autonomously or by remote control, designed to observe or interfere with enemy targets from the air. With no crew on board, it is capable of remaining operational for a large period of time and provide continuous reconnaissance from remote areas that would otherwise be inaccessible.

Most recon drones such as the American MQ-1 Predator, which has been a pioneer for unmanned aircraft development since its first flight in 1994, employ a propeller driven by a piston engine to fly at about 130km/h (80mph) for up to 24 hours. They carry visible and infrared imaging equipment in addition to radar and, on occasion, air-to-ground missiles. A satellite relays ground-based commands to the aircraft and also transmits sensor outputs from the aircraft back to ground. Larger UAVs, such as the US RQ-4 Global Hawk, are powered by jets and can typically stay in flight for around 36 hours.

Predator vs Global Hawk
The Predator might be in wider use, but the Global Hawk dwarfs its brother in terms of size and capability

© US Air Force

VS

© US Air Force

Predator	Global Hawk
Length: 8m (26ft)	**Length:** 13.5m (44ft)
Wingspan: 12.5m (41ft)	**Wingspan:** 35.4m (116ft)
Height: 2.1m (7ft)	**Height:** 4.6m (15ft)
Endurance: 24 hours	**Endurance:** 36 hours
Cruise speed: 130km/h (80mph)	**Cruise speed:** 649km/h (403mph)
Altitude: 7,620m (25,000ft)	**Altitude:** 20,000m (65,600ft)

Engine
A 101-horsepower engine, commonly seen in snowmobiles, powers the drive shaft that rotates the twin-blade variable-pitch propeller.

Satellite
A communications satellite in geosynchronous (stationary) orbit relays signals between the ground station and the aircraft.

Altitude
The Predator typically operates at a height of 7,620 metres (25,000 feet) to allow it to view large portions of the ground below.

Composition
The Predator is made of a mixture of carbon and quartz fibres, together with Kevlar, while the carbon and glass frame provides insulation for the internal components.

Top speed
The aircraft can increase its speed from a cruising 130km/h to 217km/h if needed, by altering the pitch of its blades.

Steering
The slender V-shaped tail of the Predator provides stability, while a rudder beneath the propeller steers it.

Sensors
The laser-guided multi-spectral targeting system (MTS) locates, identifies and tracks ground targets and is used in conjunction with cameras or Hellfire missiles for imaging or attack runs.

Wings
The titanium wings of the Predator have tiny holes that seep out an ethylene glycol solution to break down ice.

Ground station
The aircraft is piloted remotely from a ground station, where commands are sent via a satellite link.

Some UAVs are so small that they can be launched by throwing them, like the FQM-151 Pointer/Raven

© US Army

© Nicolle R Fuller

201

Brown and green markings camouflaged the aircraft from above, while the black underside concealed it from the ground

Airfix: the fun is building

Merlin engines
The famous engine that powered the Spitfire also powered the Lancaster. There were four in total.

The model aircraft kits with an enduring heritage and unfailing fun

Since 1952, Airfix has been producing model kits for eager, nimble-fingered children to build and enjoy. Through the faithful reconstruction of countless planes and other vehicles, Airfix model kits have been capturing imaginations for generations. Though very few of us will ever get the chance to fly in a Spitfire, Lancaster or Red Arrow Hawk, by building these brilliant models youngsters from the age of eight can explore another world and – without even realising it – acquire skills such as planning, engineering, painting, history, dexterity and more. Building and creating with Airfix provides a 'three-dimensional' pastime that will last a lifetime.

Of course, Airfix isn't just about aircraft. There are also ships, cars, tanks, buildings, rockets and soldier figures in a variety of sizes. Plus there's a huge selection of standalone kits, starter sets and gift packages, complete with everything you need to get started. You can check out the range

on the Airfix website www.airfix.com, but it's also available to buy in hundreds of shops throughout the UK.

To enjoy the full Airfix experience, the best tools for the job – including paint shades, glues and other great accessories – are available from Humbrol, Airfix's sister company.

So if you're looking for something to keep you occupied during the summer holidays – and from just £5.99 too – what could be better than a lifetime of fun with Airfix? ✿

The origins of Airfix

Airfix was founded in 1939 by Nicholas Kove, a refugee from Hungary who originally manufactured rubber inflated toys. The name 'Airfix' was chosen because part of the process involved fixing air into products. Kove believed that all successful companies should have their names at the beginning of business directories, and consequently the name 'Airfix' was born. After the Second World War, he switched to producing plastic combs, and was the first manufacturer to introduce an injection-moulding machine.

Lancaster
1 Crowds in attendance at air shows throughout the UK will get the opportunity to see the only operational Lancaster as part of the Battle of Britain Memorial Flight.

Red Arrows Hawk
2 There are actually ten aircraft in the touring Red Arrows team, as they always take along a spare aircraft. The dedicated ground crew are called the Blues.

Vulcan
3 The delta-winged monster carried the UK's nuclear threat for many years and most famously went on a bombing run from the UK to the Falklands in 1982.

Battle of Britain
4 The iconic Lancaster, Spitfire and Hurricane embody the skill and sacrifices made by RAF crews during WWII. All three aircraft are among Airfix's best-selling subjects.

Try Airfix for free
5 You can try out Airfix modelling for free at many air shows across the UK in 2011. Just pop along to the Airfix marquee and the team there will let you have a go.

DID YOU KNOW? In 1952, a small-scale Golden Hind was the first ever Airfix kit sold

ADVERTORIAL

Lancaster bomber

The actual G-for-George Lancaster flew 90 combat missions over occupied Europe. Most operational Lancasters were shot down before they completed 20, and this particular aircraft had the distinction of bringing every crew member back home to the UK who flew aboard it. The Airfix kit comes with 126 pieces and brilliantly replicates this iconic aircraft.

Long range
The Lancaster's range was 2,700 nautical miles. Enough to fly across Germany and back again – as long as the crew stayed on course, which was almost impossible considering the defences they came upon.

Lucky seven
She carried seven crew: pilot, flight engineer, navigator, bomb aimer, wireless operator, mid-upper and rear gunners.

Bomb load
The Lancaster came with a maximum normal bomb load of 6,350 or 9,980kg (14,000 or 22,000lb), Grand Slam with modifications to the bomb bay. Airfix kits come with model bombs.

Though the smoke trails look pretty ace for spectators, their main purpose is actually safety. Pilots use them to judge wind speed and direction

BAe Systems Hawk

Though most famously flown by the Red Arrows display team, the iconic Hawk is also one of the main jet trainers for the RAF. Anyone can request a display or flypast by the Red Arrows, but the team don't choose where they perform; display allocation is controlled by the RAF Events Team.

Smoke
Diesel mixed with appropriately coloured dye is injected into the jet exhaust, to produce the colourful vapour trails for which the Red Arrows are famed.

Range
The Hawk has a maximum altitude of 14,630m (48,000ft) and fuel capacity gives a range of 1,000 nautical miles.

Engine
The Hawk's Rolls Royce Adour engine produces 2,358kg (5,200lbs) of thrust and can achieve a top speed of Mach 1.2.

Tanks

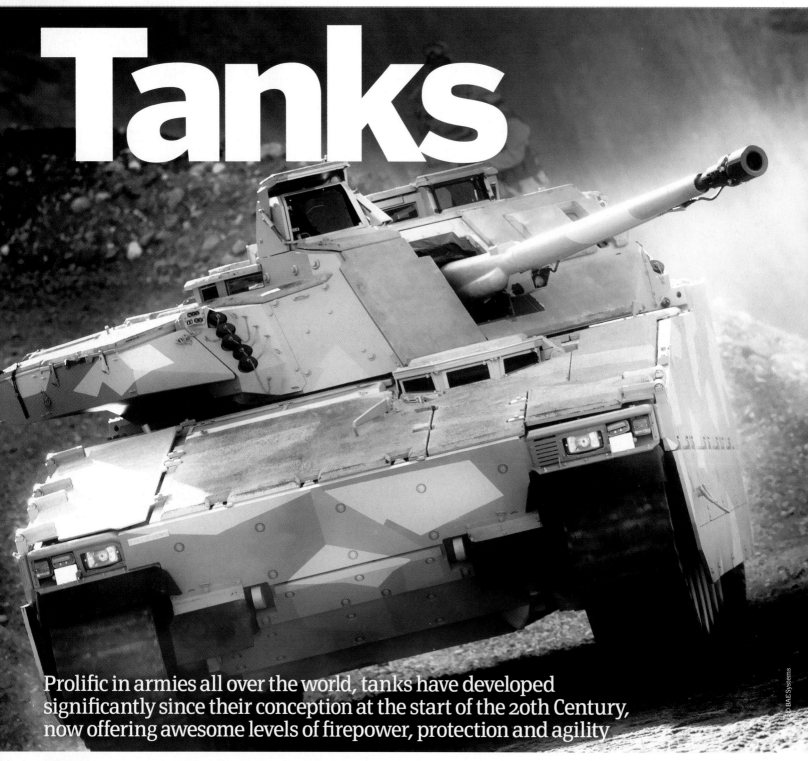

Prolific in armies all over the world, tanks have developed significantly since their conception at the start of the 20th Century, now offering awesome levels of firepower, protection and agility

Tanks work by providing an armoured, mobile platform upon which various weapons can be mounted, as well as a secure transport vehicle for soldiers in the theatre of war. Central to any tank's design are three key areas: armour, mobility and firepower, which are intrinsically linked at a fundamental level, with changes in each area directly affecting the others. For example, if a tank features super-thick armour plating, while excellent at protecting its mechanical components and crew, it reduces its acceleration, top speed and armament loadout.

Today, the absolute pinnacle of tank design worldwide is demonstrated in the main battle tank (MBT) category of tanks, a series of high-powered, heavily armoured vehicles whose role consists primarily of direct/indirect fire support on the battlefield. Featuring large primary cannons that are capable of firing a range of high-explosive and kinetic energy penetrator (ammunition that has no explosive charge but relies purely on kinetic energy to penetrate armour) rounds, as well as autocannons, GPS/laser-guided missiles and smart submunitions, MBTs specialise in large-scale

destruction of enemy vehicles and structures. Currently, arguably the pinnacle of the MBT category is the United States's M1A2, a juggernaut that is presently in use in the Iraq and Afghanistan wars.

Weighing in at 67.6 short tons, measuring in at 7.93 metres in length by 3.66 metres in width, fitted with a 1,500hp Honeywell AGT1500C turbine engine and packing a 120mm L44 M256 smoothbore cannon, the M1A2 typifies current tank design. It's fast – think a top speed of 45mph with a power-to-weight ratio of 24.5hp/metric ton – heavily armoured, and insanely well armed. Composite plates made from

5 TOP FACTS
TANKS

2050
1 Due to the prolificacy of the M1 Abrams – in service in Australia, Egypt, Iraq, Kuwait, Morocco, Saudi Arabia and the US – it is predicted to remain in service until 2050.

Horses
2 Tanks require engines capable of serious hp. The M1 Abrams' engine churns out over 1,500hp, exceeding the Bugatti Veyron, the world's fastest car.

Monster
3 The largest tank never to be built was approved by Hitler in 1942 but later cancelled. It was designed to use an 800mm Krupp cannon that could fire over 23 miles.

Water
4 The word 'tank' stems from its development, with all but the highest-profile members of government told they were designing a mobile water tank.

Periscope
5 Targets used to be identified by using a periscope and by opening the top hatch and using binoculars. Modern tanks use light intensification and thermal imaging equipment.

DID YOU KNOW? *The M1 Abrams has been deployed in the Gulf, Afghanistan and Iraq wars*

ASCOD SV

General Dynamics's latest armoured vehicle is introducing modular construction to tanks

Turret
The ASCOD's turret is built around a 1.7-metre race ring and can house both the vehicle's commander and gunner. The turret is installed with a dual-axis, stabilised, CTAI, 40mm case telescopic weapon system, which is capable of identifying targets through an infrared imaging sensor and laser rangefinder. This can be upgraded to a 120mm direct fire cannon if needed.

New technology on an age-old design

Modules
Thanks to the Core Infrastructure Distribution System (CIDS) – a special, super-strength, electronic base frame that is capable of handling systems control, security partitioning, power management and data transfer – the ASCOD SV can be installed quickly with additional modules dependent on mission parameters.

Armour
The ASCOD SV is fitted with sloping front armour, side skirts and passive plate panels. The armour is designed to withstand conventional blast, rocket-propelled grenades (RPGs) and armour-piercing rounds.

Chassis/hull
The SV is designed around a common base platform forged from lightweight steel. It features a concave hull floor, an integral composite frame and armour-plated, ceiling-mounted seats. The chassis and hull are specifically designed to mitigate the effects of improvised explosive devices (IEDs).

Tracks
Consisting of dual-rate suspension and double-pin track, the ASCOD's tracks and running gear are designed with high mobility in mind, with increased smoothness and comfortability when travelling at speed.

Electronics
Apart from featuring a fully digital transmission, the ASCOD features a suite of electronic countermeasure systems, including an active defence controller, laser warning system and obscurant discharges.

Engine
The ASCOD SV utilises a militarised Daimler Chrysler heavy truck engine, optimised for fuel efficiency and serviceability that produces 750hp. It is installed in the front centre of the SV to maximise protection and increase the vehicle's load-carrying capabilities. The engine allows the ASCOD to accelerate from 0-40mph in under 13 seconds.

© General Dynamics

layered ceramic tiles and forged metal matrixes are utilised by the M1A2 to mitigate the effects of shaped charges, while steel-encased depleted uranium mesh plating is used due to its high density to reinforce key impact zones, such as the hull front and turret. The L44 M256 smoothbore cannon, meanwhile, provides awesome range and round versatility – muzzle velocity lying at 1,750m/s and max range at over 8,000 metres.

Key, however, to the M1A2's success and prolificacy is its advanced electronic control and detection sensors, electronic countermeasures and modern communication systems. Light intensification and thermal imaging systems help the M1A2 detect enemies while at night, in smoke or in poor visibility conditions, while a fire-control computer collates information from the vehicle's laser rangefinder, ammunition payload and

lead angle to ensure an accurate shot. In addition to these three core factors, the fire-control computer also tracks and utilises data from the M1A2's crosswind sensor, pendulum static cant sensor, boresight alignment sensor, ammunition temperature sensor, air temperature sensor, barometric pressure sensor and target speed.

However, despite the current inclination for heavily armoured, well-weaponed, one-role tanks – such as the Abrams M1A2 and British-made Challenger 2 – cutting-edge tank design is seriously evolving, with increased versatility and greater mobility favoured due to the rapidly-moving nature of the modern-day war zone. Compromising a degree of protection and firepower to facilitate agility, tanks such as BAE's CV90120-T and General Dynamics UK's modular ASCOD SV are allowing nations to

The ASCOD SV adapts to its conditions

invest in multi-role vehicles, with a single-base chassis and hull, which is capable of being fitted with a variety of turrets, cranes, extendable bridges, med bays and earth movers dependent on the mission parameters and context. This way, no matter

whether the tank is deployed in the heart of a city or the open plains and hills of a rural environment, it can quickly be adapted to better suit conditions, maximising its operational efficiency – not to mention its performance. ✿

"The CV90120-T's 120mm cannon can fire 14 high-explosive rounds per minute"

Inside a war machine

Driving a tank

How tanks are controlled has evolved massively over the last 100 years

Originally, driving a tank required its own dedicated team. The WWI Mark I tank, for example, required four people just to make it accelerate, decelerate or turn. The primary driver was responsible for the clutch, hand throttle and primary gearbox, which when operated correctly delivered two speeds of forward acceleration and one in reverse. Sitting next to him at the fore of the tank was the commander, who dictated orders and operated the brakes. To the rear, two gearsmen then worked two secondary gearboxes that were responsible for the tank's individual track movements. These constituent controls had to be operated in unison – a feat that was made even harder due to the deafening noise and intense smoke inside the cabin – with every single change in movement requiring a controlled collaboration.

Driven by the complexity and crudeness of early systems and rapid advances in military technology, WWII tank controls received an overhaul, significantly reducing the amount of people required to make them move. Controls of this era (1940-1960) are typified by the T-34/M4 Sherman medium tanks. Here only one primary driver was needed, with acceleration, individual track controls and breaks all installed in the front cockpit. This system worked though a combination of twin steering sticks, five-forward one-back gearbox and manual clutch pedal.

Today, main battle tank controls have been simplified even further, with complex auto transmissions partnered with fly-by-wire joysticks. Here – as aptly shown by the Abrams M1A2 – the driver merely has to put the tank in drive mode and then can control speed and direction with a central joystick. Also, thanks to advanced multi-fuel turbine engines, noise, heat and the chances of stalling are significantly reduced.

An M1A1's gunner placing its main cannon on a target

The commander and driver of a Abrams M1A1 undertaking manoeuvres in Baghdad, Iraq

Abrams M1A1 undergoing a live firing test

© Bakur3
A cannon's rifling

High mobility is prized in tank design

© BAE Systems

© BAE Systems

Tank evolution

From its conception at the start of the 20th Century, the tank and its role on the battlefield have changed massively

1916
Mark I
Born out of the need to break the stranglehold of trench warfare, the Mark I was primitive and little more than an armoured, mobile bunker for soldiers to advance forward in.

BRITAIN

1. Challenger 2
Arguably the most armoured and best-protected tank in the world, featuring state-of-the-art second-gen composite Chobham armour, the details of which are classified.

©Andrew Skudder

RUSSIA

2. T-90
Packed with the largest cannon (125mm) currently on a battle tank, the T-90 can fire high-explosive and armour-piercing rounds capable of piercing up to 37 inches of steel.

AMERICA

3. Abrams M1A2
A vast suite of electronic defensive systems and countermeasures, with a 120mm main gun, laser-guided missiles and 50-cal heavy machine gun.

DID YOU KNOW? The T-90's 125mm cannon can penetrate 37 inches of steel armour plating

Smart weapons

Apart from traditional high-explosive rounds, modern tanks are fitted with smart missile and shell weaponry

From the M712 Copperhead laser-guided direct-fire round to the M982 Excalibur GPS guided missile, tanks now have various weapons systems available to them to destroy enemy targets. One of the most notable, however, is the SMArt 155, a recently released 155mm artillery round that delivers two autonomous, sensor-fused, fire-and-forget submunitions. Each submunition contains a high-penetration EFP warhead (a shaped charge designed to penetrate armour at a stand-off distance), that once separated from its carrier shell, descend downwards towards multiple targets, identifying their location through infrared sensor and millimetre wave radar.

A Copperhead laser-guided anti-tank missile about to destroy a dummy tank

1. The tank fires the SMArt-155 round.

2. Flying on a parabolic arc, the round progresses a set distance.

3. As the round approaches the target area, a timer fuse ignites a small ejector rocket, dragging the two submunitions out of the casing.

5. The submunitions then both deploy parachutes, independently corkscrewing downwards and scanning for targets.

6. Once a target has been located, the submunition detonates its payload to create an explosively formed projectile that penetrates the vehicle's weak top armour.

4. The submunitions free fall towards the ground.

Deploying a smart round

Tank design

Three factors must be addressed when designing a battle tank: firepower, protection and mobility

Firepower
Modern tanks now have large, smooth-bore cannons for traditional direct fire destruction, as well as GPS/laser-guided smart missiles for long-range, tactical strikes. However, the level of firepower is linked to a tank's armour and mobility levels, with an increase in cannon size leading to an increase in hull/chassis size to maintain stability and firing accuracy.

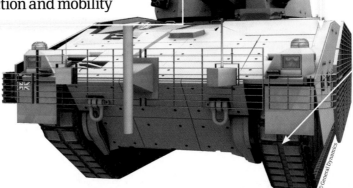

©General Dynamics

Protection
Armour is a critical factor. Blocking and deflecting incoming kinetic energy penetrators (non-explosive rounds) and high-explosive anti-tank shells is of foremost importance – factors that have led to the development of composite armours, which incorporate layers of ceramics, plastics and resin matrixes between steel plates.

Mobility
Mobility is increasingly important in battle tanks, driven by the rapidly moving nature of the modern battlefield. Tanks must be able to traverse a variety of obstacles and terrains, as well as remain active for lengthy periods, capable of great operational ranges. Mobility is compromised by the weight of the tank's armour and the size and number of its weapon's loadout.

A Challenger 2 in Iraq

1942
M4 Sherman
The primary tank used by Allied forces during WWII, the M4 Sherman was mass produced (with over 50,000 built) and delivered greater mobility and firepower than before.

1960
M60 Patton
A second-generation main battle tank, the M60 was one of a new breed of fighting vehicles that was highly versatile, with variants being used to clear mines and lay bridges.

1972
T72
The Russian counter to the M60, the T72 was the most commonly used tank until the collapse of the Soviet Union. It delivered a lightweight, small-framed unit with a massive 125mm cannon.

©Balcer

1980
M1 Abrams
The most famous third-generation main battle tank, the M1 Abrams replaced the M60 and brought a plethora of electronic and computer systems to tank design, including GPS and smart missile countermeasures.

"Cruise control systems control a vehicle in the same way that the pedals do"

How does cruise control work?

Why is it possible for some cars to regulate their own speed?

Cruise control allows your car to maintain or alter its speed without the manual compression of the pedals. It is usually controlled by buttons on a steering wheel. Cruise control systems control a vehicle in the same way that the pedals do, namely by adjusting the throttle position of the engine. A throttle valve controls how much air an engine takes in and ultimately its speed. Cruise control systems control this by using an actuator attached to a cable. This cable is attached to a pivot that controls the throttle valve and also the pedal of the car. As the speed is increased using the buttons, the actuator (powered by an engine vacuum) pulls the cable, which in turn releases more air into the engine by altering the pivot and also pulls the acceleration pedal towards the floor, as if you were pressing it with your foot. The opposite is true for deceleration. Cruise control systems adjust the throttle to accelerate towards the desired speed at a decelerating rate, so that it does not overshoot. ✪

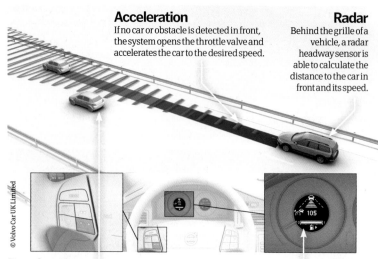

Acceleration
If no car or obstacle is detected in front, the system opens the throttle valve and accelerates the car to the desired speed.

Radar
Behind the grille of a vehicle, a radar headway sensor is able to calculate the distance to the car in front and its speed.

© Volvo Car UK Limited

Deceleration
If the car in front slows down, a signal is immediately sent to the engine to begin braking.

Distance
Intelligent cruise control can detect a car or obstacle up to 150m (492ft) away, and operates at speeds from 32-177km/h (20-110mph).

Electric bikes

Feeling too lazy to pedal? Why not let a motor do the legwork for you...

Anyone who's ever ridden a bicycle with a dynamo light should get an idea of how electric bikes work. With a dynamo light the kinetic energy of the spinning tyre turns the dynamo, transferring energy and ultimately powering the light. Electric bikes work oppositely. A dynamo of sorts, in this case a battery, produces energy that transfers to kinetic energy in the tyres and moves them forwards.

A typical battery in an electric bike will have approximately a quarter of the power of a toaster, 350-500W. The batteries need to be able to store as much power as possible, and for this reason lithium-ion batteries (like the ones in your mobile phone and computer) are most commonly used. They can often be taken out of the bike and recharged by being plugged into a standard mains plug socket, and most bikes will give upwards of 80km (50 miles) of battery-assisted riding. The battery powers the motor, which will normally increase the speed by about double what the rider is pedalling, up to a top speed of 32km/h (20mph). ✪

Inside the EBCO Eagle electric bike
A look at the key parts of this motor-driven bicycle

Battery
Giving a range of 16-64km (10-40 miles) and a top speed of 20mph, the battery is activated manually and supplies power to the motor.

Throttle
A throttle on the handlebar activates the battery, which in turn drives the motor that will assist in turning the wheels of the bike.

● ─ ─ ─ ● Transmission cable
● ─ ─ ─ ● Electric wire

© EBCO

Motor
The motor works oppositely to one you'd find in, say, an electric toothbrush. Instead of the bristles (hub) being turned, the toothbrush (wheel) is moved by the stationary bristles.

Spokes
The spokes of an electric bike are much sturdier than those of a regular bike, as they have to withstand the large turning force (torque) the motor creates.

Controller
A controller in the throttle system adjusts the power distribution to ensure a smooth ride. Without it you'd go from a standstill to top speed with nothing in else between.

Shock absorbers

How do these devices dissipate unwanted motion and improve a passenger's comfort?

 Shock absorbers are fitted to the majority of modern vehicles to control the unwanted motion inflicted upon their spring-mounted suspension. They achieve this by absorbing the vibrational energy stored in the springs when compressed or elongated through the medium of a hydraulic, fluid-filled cylinder. The shock absorber is attached to the vehicle's frame and axle by two eye-mounts, located at the top and bottom of its body. The top mount is directly connected to the shock's piston rod and head, meaning that any relative motion between the vehicle's frame and the axle causes the piston to act – moving either up or down – against the cylinder's internal hydraulic fluid. The piston's movement reduces the vibrational energy stored in the vehicle's springs – caused by the road's uneven layout – and equalises it through the resisting force generated by the pressurised hydraulic fluid. ✿

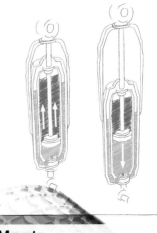

Piston
The piston moves up and down within the pressure tube. The piston head is perforated to allow small quantities of highly pressurised oil to filter through, slowing it down and dissipating the spring's vibrations.

Valve
The valve is positioned in the base of the pressure tube and controls the flow of hydraulic fluid between the pressure tube and reserve cylinder.

Pressure
The pressure tube is filled with hydraulic fluid, which, when compressed by the piston head, absorbs the spring's vibrational energy.

Mounts
Shock absorbers are connected to the vehicle at the top via the upper mount, and the wheel by the lower mount. Vibration from springs is transferred to the piston head through the upper mount.

Cylinder
The majority of shock absorbers feature a reserve cylinder exterior to the pressure tube. This stores excess hydraulic fluid.

How do traffic jams start?

Ever wondered why traffic jams seem to appear for no reason? Read on to find out what causes them

5. Ghost
By the time the traffic at the back of the shock wave reaches the point of the original incident, the causes of the jam are long gone.

4. Acceleration
The offending vehicle A has now completed its manoeuvre and left the motorway. However, acceleration is still hindered and slowed by traffic density and vehicle limitations.

3. Domino
This braking effect is then transferred to each following vehicle, the total speed of the cars decreasing the further back in the chain they are, until standstill is reached. Often the shock wave travels over 2km (1mi) to the rear, leaving drivers completely unaware of the cause of their deceleration.

2. Impact
The immediate impact of the error is that the vehicles behind cars A and B must break suddenly to 72km/h (45mph) to avoid crashing into them from the rear as they brake. This applies to vehicles in all three lanes, as car A crosses each of them to exit the motorway.

1. Error
The traffic shock wave begins when a vehicle, travelling at the road's stated speed of 96km/h (60mph), manoeuvres at the last minute. In this example, car A swerves across car B, causing the latter to break to 80km/h (50mph) in order to remain at a safe distance.

"If electricity is the power of the future, sourcing and managing solar energy will become key to this"

The Statistics
The Türanor

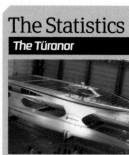

The propeller steers the Türanor forward

Length: 31m
Width: 15m
Height: 6.1m
Weight: 95 tons
Surface of solar panels: 536m²
Power from solar energy: 93.5kW
Solar panel efficiency: 18.8 per cent

Solar-powered vehicles

Discover the planes, boats and cars that run on Sun power

The Sun is a bounty of free energy, and harnessing its power has been a challenge occupying inventors for years. Now though, new machines are being developed that are powered by only energy from the Sun: the best are capable of some remarkable feats. It has long been the dream to utilise this democratic energy of the Sun. It costs nothing, is available to everyone across the planet, and makes consumers independent of fossil fuels. Unlike oil or gas, the Sun won't run out in our lifetime. This is why there is a growing determination to crack the solar code.

Vehicles are ideal objects to be powered by the Sun. They do not stay static in one location so they can avoid shade and even angle themselves for best solar capturing. They can also utilise other energy-generation methods such as kinetic regeneration to supplement solar power.

There is an obvious downside to solar power too, though. What do you do when it gets dark? Or if it's cloudy? The problem of managing motion when the Sun is in is the real challenge. Until now. Would you believe there is now a solar plane that can fly around the globe? Or solar cars that can travel from one end of Australia to the other?

If electricity is the power of the future, sourcing and managing solar energy will become a key part of this. Will these planes, boats and cars be shooting you round the globe in years to come? ✿

The Türanor

Sailing boats have always relied on 'free' power: the Türanor aims to replicate this with far less effort: let the Sun do the work

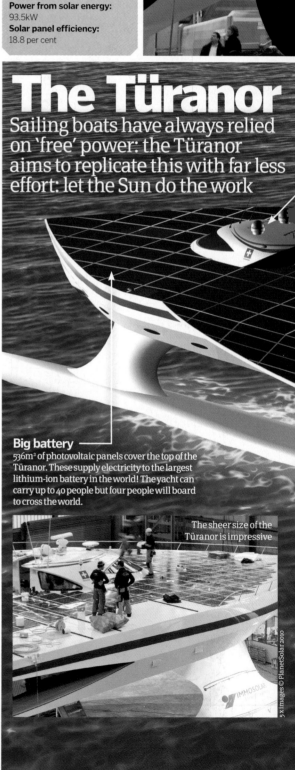

Big battery
536m² of photovoltaic panels cover the top of the Türanor. These supply electricity to the largest lithium-ion battery in the world! The yacht can carry up to 40 people but four people will board to cross the world.

The sheer size of the Türanor is impressive

5 x Images © PlanetSolar 2010

5 TOP FACTS
SOLAR CONCEPTS

Solar ferry
1 The only ferry allowed to carry people across London Hyde Park's Serpentine lake is the Solar Shuttle. Solar panels on the roof power a lead acid battery.

Auriga
2 Toyota cars are shipped across the globe using solar-assisted vessels. The Auriga has enough PV cells on its deck to supply 40kW of electricity.

Stanford Solar Car Project
3 A student-run organisation set up in 1989 to help members learn and develop solar car theories. On two-year cycles, students design and build solar cars.

Power of One
4 This Canadian one-seat electric car weighs 300kg, is 5m long and has a top speed of 75mph. It has set a distance record of 9,940 miles and is 'open source'.

Prius roof
5 Toyota's Prius Hybrid has a solar panel fitted on its roof. When the car is parked it powers the ventilation system, so the car remains cool inside on a hot day.

DID YOU KNOW? Space vehicles combine solar power and electrical propulsion (such as ion drives) for high exhaust velocity

The boat is covered in 536m² of panels

Electric range beyond belief
Batteries can store enough energy to drive the Türanor for three days – and that's at a speed of 7.5 knots. Go slower and it can run for up to 15 days. Circumnavigating the Earth will see it cover 34,000 miles!

Carbon fibre for light weight
The Türanor weighs 95 tons – by boat standards, this is very light. It is because the hull is constructed from a carbon fibre sandwich. This is made up of 20.6 tons of carbon fibre, 23 tons of epoxy resin and 11.5 tons of structural foam.

Low drag, high speed
The Türanor is a multihull catamaran yacht. This helps it slice through the water using as little energy as possible; it is an efficient, low hydropneumatic drag method. Catamarans can also help reach higher speeds.

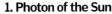

Rivendell

How does a solar cell work?

The theory of solar electricity generation is 'literally' exciting – it's all thanks to the effect of light on certain elements and was investigated by several physicists, including Einstein

Solar cells convert sunlight into electricity through the photovoltaic effect on a semiconductor. This is where electrons are emitted from a material that has absorbed energy from electromagnetic radiation such as sunshine. These are photoelectrons. Photovoltaic cells work on the same principal, but work on any light source, not just sunlight.

Individual solar cells are connected together in a module. These are then interconnected to other modules, forming an array. This is covered by a protective material to create a solar panel. Depending on the materials used, such panels can be highly flexible.

Electricity produced is used to power most objects that run on electric – from lights to cars. Consumer solar panels are often connected to batteries. This ensures the power that is not immediately used can be stored for later use, so it is not wasted. Efficiency of today's solar panels is, however, only around 10-20 per cent. This will improve in the future.

1. Photon of the Sun
Sunlight contains photons: these hit the solar panel and are absorbed by the semiconducting materials it is constructed from – a common product here is silicone.

3. One-way road
The composition of the p-n (positive-negative) junction means electrons can only flow in one direction. The arrangement of the solar cells channels these atoms into an object that consumes them.

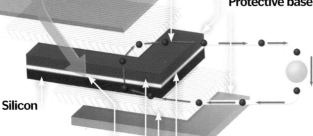

Silicon

Protective base

Silicon

2. The photon barge
The absorbed photons 'knock loose' negatively charged electrons from atoms within the structure.

4. Semiconducting solar
Electron transfer occurs at the p-n junction. This is what makes the solar cell a semiconductor.

5. Influential doping
A p-n junction is created within the silicon lattice by 'doping' – that's introducing a section of impurity within the otherwise pure structure. This changes the electrical composition and is where the electronic action occurs.

6. Digging the hole
The work of the photons creates a 'hole' in the covalent bond between atoms. Atoms therefore move sideways to fill this hole. This flows through the lattice.

The route...

Efficiently circumnavigating the globe in a boat means working with the waves. Energy can be conserved if you go with the tides rather than against them, so following the path of 'least resistance' around the world is the way to go.

To maximise publicity, the Türanor is stopping over in cities such as New York and Abu Dhabi. The route therefore hugs the US coast and takes a direct route across the Atlantic to minimise distances.

New York
San Francisco
Abu Dhabi
Singapore
Darwin

As wide as an Airbus

The wingspan of the Solar Impulse is so broad, it equals an Airbus A340. There are 12,000 photovoltaic cells covering a 200m² area: they boast an efficiency rating of 12 per cent. The energy density of the battery is 240kWh/kg. The accumulators weigh 400kg: more than a quarter of the entire plane!

The Statistics

Solar Impulse

Length: 21.85m
Wingspan: 63.40m
Height: 6.40m
Weight: 1,600kg
Motor power:
4x10hp electric engine
Solar cell count: 11,628
Average flying speed: 70km/h
Max altitude: 8,500m

The Impulse's wingspan compared to that of an Airbus A340

Constant watch

The batteries need thermal insulation to retain its heat: at 8,500 metres, it can be subjected to a temperature of -40°C. The plane is in constant air-ground communication and hundreds of parameters are observed by the management system.

Solar Impulse

The Solar Impulse has been designed to fly around the globe under solar power alone – day AND night

Electric motor props

Propulsion comes from four pods beneath the wings, each containing a 10hp electric motor and polymer lithium-ion batteries. A gearbox limits the rotation of each 3.5m twin blade propeller to 400rpm.

Carbon fibre rich

Carbon fibre is an integral construction material. The upper wing is a skin of encapsulated solar cells, using 145-micron monocrystalline silicone. Beneath the wing there is a flexible film: these two surfaces encase 120 carbon fibre ribs, which give the aerodynamic profile.

A simulator will modify routes to help the ground team work around air space restrictions

The route...

The route is essential to ensuring the plane finds itself in clear, cloud-free skies at sunrise, to charge the batteries. The exact route will only be decided a few days before the run, based on meteorological information. A simulator will examine 5,000 key parameters – winds, temperatures, air humidity and turbulence – before selecting the route. The simulator will propose modified routes for the plane in 'real-time'.

Hawaii
Spain
China
Florida
Persian Gulf

DID YOU KNOW?

Solar-powered car (plant)
Seat plans to design a car plant that could one day be entirely powered by solar energy. The roof of the Martorell plant is covered in solar panels as Spain looks to become independent of fossil fuels by harnessing the Sun's energy.

DID YOU KNOW? The hemp used to construct the Eco Elise is grown near Lotus's East Anglia factory

Solar cars

Cars have used all sorts of energy sources, but the Sun hasn't been one of them. Until now...

Solar-powered cars don't offer the flexibility of battery-electric or hydrogen power, but they are a tantalising prospect. If structures can be made light enough, and solar panels efficient enough, solar power could provide a useful complementary source to other means. This has been driving enthusiasts for decades, but now, international competitions have reached the mainstream.

Australia's World Solar Challenge, for example, has been running since 1987 and demands competitors cover 1,877 miles between Darwin and Adelaide. Battery capacity is limited to 5kWh, and the PV area to 6m². Batteries can weigh no more than 21kg and the cars are run on public highways so must be fast enough!

Solar ability
The body is covered in pyrite solar film, which harnesses electricity to power the operating electronics and recharge the battery.

NLV Quant
The electric car with the self-charging body

Solar efficiency
Using digital prototyping, NLV invented an iron-sulphur semiconductor. This offers an average efficiency of 38 per cent and peak efficiency of 50 per cent.

Luxury car
The four-seater Quant will soon start trials.

In-wheel electric motors
Four 150kW in-wheel electric motors are powered by a modular battery running down the centre of the car – various chemistries can be installed.

The Statistics
NLV Quant

Manufacturer: Koenigsegg
Weight: 1,680 kg
Class: Electric vehicle
Body style: Gullwing
Power: 600kW (4x150kW), 800bhp
Top speed: 377km/h (234mph)
Price: TBA

Flexible solar panels
Two solar panels on the hemp roof power the electrical systems (heater and air con), so charge doesn't have to be drawn from the battery.

The Statistics
Lotus Eco Elise

Manufacturer: British Lotus
Weight: 828kg
Class: Sports car
Body style: Roadster
Power: 134bhp
Top speed: 204km/h (127mph)
Price: TBA

Lotus Eco Elise

Innovative sports car maker British Lotus is thinking green with the Eco Elise

Petrol engine
It uses a conventional petrol engine but weight reductions mean it is more efficient.

The plan
In time, the whole combustion engine could be replaced by a battery-electric setup.

Get the hemp
Most of the body panels are made from renewable hemp while all paint is water-based.

> "A combustion engine operates by harnessing the energy of intermittent explosions"

Internal combustion engines

A metal box of fiery explosions that has transformed the entire globe

The internal combustion engine (ICE) continues to power the world over 100 years after it became mainstream. In fact engineers still haven't found a viable way to better it. Combustion engines comprise a cylinder, within which is housed a piston and connecting rod. The piston is attached to a crank at the bottom, and as it moves up and down in the cylinder, the crank rotates. Importantly, this is how power is transferred to the wheels.

The force driving the piston is created at the top of the cylinder, in the combustion chamber. A combustion engine operates by harnessing the energy of intermittent explosions, lots of them in succession every minute. This converts a tiny drop of fuel into a force that turns the road wheels, driving the car. Most engines run these explosions right on the cusp of them becoming uncontrollable – that's where maximum power is produced.

Through a series of valves, a fuel and air mix enters this chamber, and is compressed. It is then either ignited (petrol) or spontaneously combusts (diesel); the resultant explosion kicks the piston back down in the cylinder.

Engines are made of several cylinders, whose individual pistons are connected to a common crank. This duplicity means biggest 'bang for buck', though car makers must balance fuel usage. More cylinders usually means more fuel used, and the optimum is four cylinders in a line, but they can also form V-arrangements or horizontally opposed layouts.

Engines are measured by various means – in Europe, litres or cubic centimetres ('cc') are familiar, while the United States use cubic inches. All measurements refer to an engine's displacement: the total volume swept by a piston in a single movement. Often, instead of adding more cylinders, engine power is increased by boosting this swept volume. It's the difference between a 1.6-litre and a 2.0-litre four-cylinder engine. ✦

The crankshaft transfers the linear motion to rotary

Piston
Transfer forces from expanding gas in the cylinder to the crankshaft via a piston rod or connecting rod.

© Daimler AG

V8

Connecting rod

Crank
Translates the linear motion from the pistons into rotation.

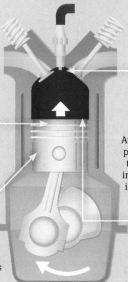

Oil pan

Converting fuel to drive

The principle of a combustion engine is straightforward – converting the potential energy of a fuel into mechanical energy by releasing it through combustion – but hundreds of components must work in unison to achieve it. That such complicated mechanisms are mass produced is further proof of the brilliance of the concept.

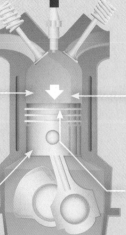

STAGE ONE
Induction stroke 'suck'

2. Inlet opens
A cam rotates and opens the inlet valve, letting a fuel-air mix enter the combustion chamber.

1. Piston plunge
The piston is pulled down within the cylinder by a conrod connected to a rotating crank.

4. Inlet closes
As the piston reaches the bottom of its travel, the intake valve closes.

3. Fuel/air trapped
The exhaust valve is closed, meaning the fuel-air mixture cannot escape.

STAGE TWO
Compression stroke 'squeeze'

2. Pressure rises
As the inlet valve is also now closed, the chamber is shut off – so the rising piston will compress the mixture.

1. Piston rises
Now, the rotating crank is pushing the piston back upwards in the cylinder.

4. Spark plug
At the top of the piston's stroke, the spark plug in the chamber is primed with electricity.

3. Heat rises
As pressure increases so does heat in the chamber.

1. Fiat 500 0.9 TwinAir two cylinder – 69mpg
Dual cylinder engine is 30 per cent more efficient than same-size four cylinder units thanks to low internal resistance and cutting-edge technology.

2. Fiat 500 1.2 16v – 59mpg
A regular 1.2 engine, with no clever gadgets but a low production cost for mass market sales across the globe.

3. 500 Abarth 1.4 T-Jet 16v 160 Esseesse – 43mpg
1.4-litre turbo is tuned for all-out performance, producing an incredible 160bhp in the tiny city car.

DID YOU KNOW? *Some scientists say we will never see the end of the internal combustion engine*

Fuel injector

Combustion chamber
Where the fuel is ignited and burned.

Exhaust manifold

Spark plug
Ignites the compressed fuel by means of an electric spark.

Cylinder   **Valve**

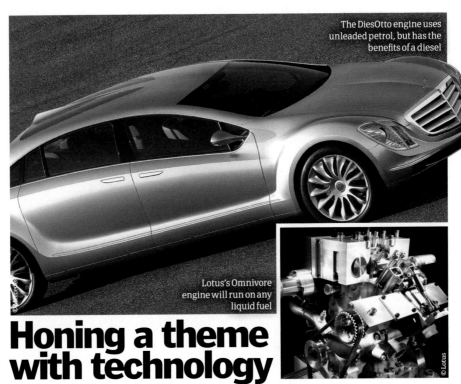

The DiesOtto engine uses unleaded petrol, but has the benefits of a diesel

Lotus's Omnivore engine will run on any liquid fuel

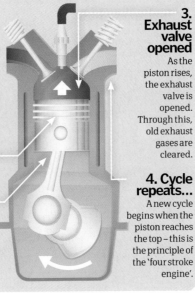

Honing a theme with technology

Direct fuel injection is becoming popular – this injects fuel straight into the combustion chamber during the compression stroke. It maximises the cooling effect of fuel and allows the engine to run a higher compression ratio – economy and power both improve.

Combining direct injection with a turbo is a further efficiency: it combines a turbo's bang while eliminating its characteristic compression ratio. Some makers even include variable valve timing as well – these super-high tech engines are in showrooms now, proving they can be made for a competitive price.

Further afield are variable displacement engines. In their most basic form, these 'turn off' engine cylinders in low-demand situations.

Makers will develop this concept in the future with more intelligent solutions.

Several firms are exploring the DiesOtto concept. This mixes a diesel's compression ignition in a lean mode, with the spark of a petrol engine when more power is needed – in the same powerplant. Units are already undergoing testing, by firms such as Volkswagen and Mercedes.

Lotus is working on a two-stroke engine called Omnivore. Using charge compression with a moveable section cylinder head, this alters the compression ratio from 10:1 to 40:1. Valves are in the cylinder walls, and fuel is injected direct into the cylinder. It's called Omnivore because it can use a variety of fuels.

Moving the fire outside the walls

An external combustion engine works through heating up an internal fluid by an external source. Think of a steam train: an open fire heats up fluid through a heat exchanger – the expansion of this fluid drives an engine. This fluid is then cooled back down again, before being reheated and expanded. The principal is why steam trains require lots of water coolant.

More in for more out

A simple route to more performance is to make the engine capacity bigger. This allows it to burn more fuel. You can do it either by adding more cylinders, or making individual cylinders bigger.

Increasing the compression ratio also produces more power, but this cannot be done limitlessly. More accuracy in injecting fuel also ups efficiency.

Adding a turbo forces more air and fuel into the cylinder, at higher pressure. And with turbo engines, cooling incoming air with an intercooler means greater expansion upon compression.

Perfecting what's already there also increases performance – polishing inlet and exhaust ports allows air to flow easier, which can give huge gains.

STAGE THREE
Power stroke 'bang'

1. Spark plug fires
The electricity in the plug produces a spark that ignites the compressed fuel-air mix.

2. Mixture ignites
The mixture quickly ignites, rapidly increasing heat and producing exhaust gas.

3. Pressure peak pushes piston
The pressure of the hot gases forces the piston back down in the chamber.

4. Crank rotates
This force is transferred to the crankshaft, turning it – which eventually turns the road wheels.

STAGE FOUR
Exhaust stroke 'blow'

1. Heat drops
Heat in the chamber will have dropped as the piston reaches the bottom of its travel again.

2. Remaining heat transferred
Any remaining heat is transferred to the engine water coolant, as the piston starts an upward stroke.

3. Exhaust valve opened
As the piston rises, the exhaust valve is opened. Through this, old exhaust gases are cleared.

4. Cycle repeats…
A new cycle begins when the piston reaches the top – this is the principle of the 'four stroke engine'.

RED BULL AIR RACE

RAF RED ARROWS

US NAVY BLUE ANGELS

Aerobatic stunt flying

Display pilots are real-life Top Guns.
Read on to find out how they can
manoeuvre their aircraft with
such extreme precision

216

2x © Red Arrows / © Jvrg Mitter/Red Bull Content Pool / © US Navy

Red Bull Air Race

The ultimate motorsport?

The Red Bull Air Race markets itself as the ultimate motorsport. It's similar to car auto-testing, in that the pilots follow a route through and around a series of obstacles. 20m (65ft) tall air gates are used for the 5-6km (3-4mi) course. These hollow tubes are held erect by air compressors and are quite delicate so as to avoid damaging the aircraft. Some gates must be flown between normally, and some must be negotiated while flying at 90° to horizontal. Time penalties are added for bad form, breaking rules, or clipping gates. The course is three-dimensional, so vertical turns (loops) are included.

The two aircraft that fly in the race – the Edge 540 and the MXS-R – are very similar in specs. Both are made from carbon fibre, their engines produce up to 350bhp, and the race rules limit them to a maximum of 12g during manoeuvres. The Red Bull pilots must wear special g-race suits and recline their seats by up to 40° to cope with the extreme gravitational forces. The pilots are all active aerobatic air show display pilots, and must fulfil minimum criteria set by the Red Bull Air Race Committee.

A plane in action at the Red Bull Air Race World Championships 2010, EuroSpeedway, Germany

Pilots must avoid obstacles on the course

Dream teams around the globe

Aerobatic stunt teams come from all over

- Frecce Tricolori (Italian Air Force)
- Red Arrows (Royal Air Force – United Kingdom)
- Blue Angels (United States Navy)
- Snowbirds (Canadian Forces)
- Cartouche doré (French Air Force)
- Saudi Hawks (Royal Saudi Air Force)

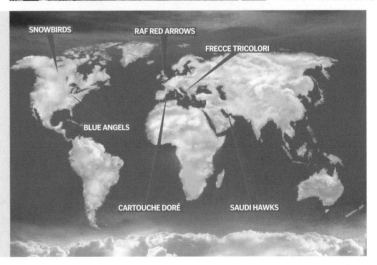
SNOWBIRDS   RAF RED ARROWS   FRECCE TRICOLORI   BLUE ANGELS   CARTOUCHE DORÉ   SAUDI HAWKS

Very few of us will have been lucky enough to fly a jet aircraft, and fewer still have had the privilege to do so professionally. Of the thousands of people around the world who are pilots, only the best of the best are trusted to represent their profession or their country as display pilots. Thrilling the crowds by flying unbelievably low and fast while pulling huge g-forces, the highly skilled display pilot is able to take an aircraft to the very edge of what it, and the pilot, can withstand with such precision that they can do it in tight formation with their team mates. Every death-defying display is planned, rehearsed and scrutinised in minute detail, with the pilots and their aircraft optimised

for their display role. Advanced simulators are also used to rehearse the displays, which is both safer and less expensive than real flying.

The Royal Air Force Aerobatic Team, (The Red Arrows) and the United States Navy Flight Demonstration Squadron (The Blue Angels) are two of the most respected air display teams in the world. Similar in many ways, they both use the diamond as their signature formation, and have a pair of solo aircraft to perform the more aggressive stunts.

To be a Red Arrows or Blue Angels pilot requires more than 1,500 and 1,250 flying hours respectively. In both teams, the display pilots are chosen for their above-average flying abilities and outstanding personal attributes. The aerobatic displays are

actually flown by the formation leader in each team, who guides the group around the sky and signals over the radio when to make turns. The other aircraft concentrate on staying in precisely the right position off his wingtip by lining up visual cues, such as wing edges, aircraft features and letters or symbols, and maintaining this exact picture to ensure they are in exactly the right place. The pilots develop a sense of where everyone is at all times, through rehearsal and repetition. They also develop a sense of where dangerous slipstreams (jet washes) are, as the jets generate turbulent air behind them. Standard procedures place the responsibility on each pilot to avoid collision in a specific order (the leader avoids nobody, they avoid him), adhering to

217

"Aircraft modifications are made to comply with the demands of aerobatic flight"

▶ clear exit instructions and routes, which are practised in real flight and on special simulators.

Aircraft modifications are made to comply with the demands of aerobatic flight. The Red Arrows have a modified fuel delivery system to improve engine response time, while the Blue Angels fit a control stick spring system that gives the pilot far more feel and precision of control, by applying a significant resistive force to his inputs, and requiring the pilot to maintain a substantial 18kg (40lbs) rearward force on the stick to maintain level flight. Both teams also modify their aircraft to generate spectacular smoke trails for the display. To achieve this effect, oil is sprayed into the jet exhaust from special tanks fitted where there would normally be a gun.

The most obvious difference between the two teams is the aircraft they fly. The Red Arrows use the single engine BAe Systems Hawk T1A, which is the current fast jet training aircraft used by the Royal Air Force. The Blue Angels fly the aircraft carrier-based Boeing F/A18 Hornet, which is a current frontline combat aircraft with two afterburning engines. The Hornet has far greater performance than its counterpart. It is larger, more powerful, has an advanced flight control, radar and weapons system, and when not displaying, is almost twice as fast as the radar-less Hawk. ❁

The Blue Angels have flown several different aircraft in their 65-year history. Today they fly F/A-18 Hornets

Anatomy of a Red Arrow

The BAe Systems Hawk T1 has been flown by the Red Arrows since 1979, and has some unique modifications

Pilot
The Red Arrows Hawk T1A is not just for entertaining crowds. If required, the Red Arrows are capable of fitting a pair of AIM-9 Sidewinder missiles and a 30mm cannon.

Cockpit
The tandem cockpit is arranged so that the rear seat is higher than the front, giving the instructor a clear view. The Red Arrows fly their displays with rear seats empty.

Altitude
Able to reach a maximum height of 14,545m (48,000ft), the Red Arrows rarely fly so high, as most flights are within UK airspace and so are relatively short.

© Alex Pang

Supersonic
The Hawk reaches Mach 0.88 in level flight, but can achieve Mach 1.15 in a dive, which allows trainee pilots to experience the transonic (sound barrier) region of flight.

Airframe
The aluminium alloy airframe of the Hawk T1A is heavily engineered to handle a lot of abuse. In Red Arrows service it performs 7g manoeuvres, but it can go to +8g and -4g if required.

How to perform...
A Red Arrows gypo break

The gypo break is a spectacularly fast, disorientating, four-aircraft manoeuvre with coloured smoke, performed while heading directly towards the audience

1. Formation
Four aircraft, in line abreast but staggered slightly, fly directly towards the centre of the crowd. From the ground their position makes them appear very close together.

2. Smoke
The four aircraft begin injecting diesel and coloured dye into their jet exhausts to create the red and blue smoke trails behind them.

3. Go!
The inner two aircraft pull up and turn towards each other, crossing paths before performing barrel rolls in opposite directions.

4. Roll
The outer two aircraft maintain straight and level flight, but perform simultaneous 360° rolls away from the inner aircraft.

5. Crossover
The two innermost aircraft cross over again, and appear to miss each other by millimetres. This is an optical illusion, however, as there are actually several metres between them.

6. Break
Rolling 90° towards each other, the outer pair also cross in a 7g horizontal turn, with all four aircraft seeming to occupy the same spot for a moment.

How to perform...
A Blue Angels echelon roll wit sneak pass

Breaking all of the rules by rolling an echelon left formation the wrong way, this classic sequence has a surprise ending

2. Uncomfortable
To maintain formation, the rearmost aircraft must perform a negative g. inverse barrel roll, unpleasant as it forces your blood to pool in your head.

3. Attention
Continuing their slow roll, the echelon draws everyone's attention away from the solo aircraft approaching on the left.

Say cheese
1 A photographic team ensures that every Red Arrows' training and display flight is filmed for safety and training purposes. They also take still images.

Servicing
2 Every Hawk aircraft is dismantled, meticulously inspected and tested every winter, which takes anything between 4 and 16 weeks per aircraft.

Smoke trails
3 Not just for effect, the smoke trails emitted by the aircraft are used to estimate wind direction, not to mention spot other Red Arrows during manoeuvres.

No copying
4 The Red Arrows' perfectly symmetrical diamond nine formation epitomised the team so well, it became registered as an official trademark.

All in the name
5 The name 'Red Arrows' wasn't a spontaneous choice. It was chosen to combine two earlier team names, the Black Arrows and the Red Pelicans.

DID YOU KNOW? During a Diamond 360 formation, four aircraft fly with only 45.7cm (18 inches) of separation between them

Eject
The Martin-Baker Mk10B zero-zero rocket-assisted ejection seat can fire both front and rear pilots to safety, even when the aircraft is stationary on the ground.

Engine
The single Rolls Royce Adour engine produces 23.2kN (5,200lbs) of thrust and does not have an afterburner fitted. It is modified for Red Arrows use with an improved fuel delivery system to spin up more quickly.

Smoke
Attached to the central underbelly, the smoke and dye pod sits where the 30mm ADEN cannon would be fitted in times of war.

Dye
The centre pod holds seven minutes' worth of smoke-generating oil. It also contains enough coloured dye to change the white smoke to red or blue for one minute apiece.

Airbrake
The airbrake can be opened to create drag and slow the aircraft down, or to maintain speed with high engine power applied. Closing the airbrake gives instant acceleration.

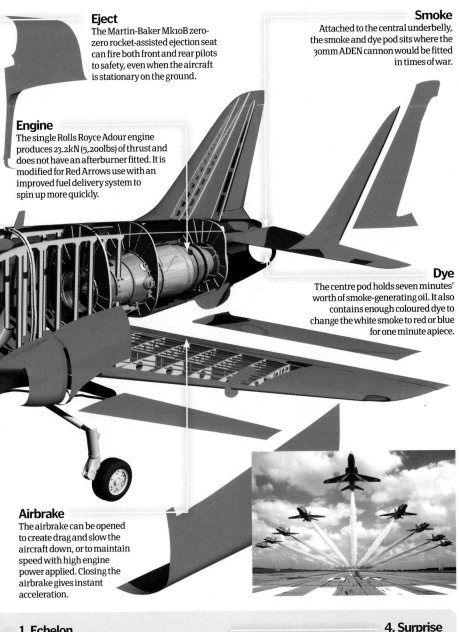

1. Echelon
The 'book' says that you cannot roll an echelon left formation to the left, as it is a high negative g move. In an incredibly difficult and technical manoeuvre, this is exactly what the Blue Angels do.

4. Surprise
Blasting down the runway at 15m (50ft) above the ground and almost at the speed of sound, the 1,120km/h (700mph) sneak pass is a shocker in every sense of the word.

5. Loud
Pulling up to 7g as he climbs away, the sneak pass aircraft with afterburners lit has to maintain a high-energy manoeuvre that causes lots of drag, such as a maximum rate turn, or he will accelerate through the sound barrier.

6. Encore
Not to be outdone, the sixth aircraft thunders in from behind the crowd at full afterburner, and pulls up into a string of vertical aileron rolls that are 4.8km (3mi) high.

INTERVIEW
Flight Lieutenant Juliette 'Jules' Fleming

2011 Hawk display pilot
Jules has been in the RAF since 1999, and has deployed to both Iraq and Afghanistan, flying the Tornado GR4 ground attack aircraft. She now demonstrates the solo Hawk display aircraft at airshows

How It Works: How did you become the solo Hawk display pilot?
Juliette Fleming: I was at the squadron several years ago during my training, and I would take the spare display aircraft to various airshows. When I was posted back to the squadron as an instructor, I put my name forward to be the next display pilot. Five of us had to complete a flying display sortie with the boss, presenting our sequences, and then after interview I was selected from the five.

HIW: What is the best and worst thing about being a display pilot?
JF: The best thing is the people I meet. The flying is awesome, taking the jet to different places and being responsible for the aircraft and people, but meeting the kids and inspiring them is the best, full stop. The worst is the long hours you work, and living out of a suitcase.

HIW: Do you get nervous during the display?
JF: I have been competing in horse riding events since I was three years old, and I've been a racing driver. Flying the display is the same feeling for me, and it's what it's all about – the anticipation, adrenaline, that nervous feeling as you run in for the first manoeuvre. Then the nerves go as you focus on the display, and putting the jet where it needs to be.

HIW: What does it feel like inside the aircraft during the display?
JF: When we start work up to the season, you really notice the g-forces when you are flying, but this goes away after a while as you have to focus on the technical aspects, like assessing the weather, where the jet is relative to the crowd, and putting the jet where it needs to be in a safe manner. I don't notice the g-forces any more.

HIW: What advice would you give to any of our readers who want to be a display pilot?
JF: Keep hold of your dreams, and have goals to work towards or you will end up bumbling through life. Mould your career to get where you want to be, and be prepared to work on the ground with people to make the opportunities to fly. You need to show that you have that little bit extra compared to the person next to you. Dedication is really important, as you must be prepared to give up your weekends.

"In modern, commercial jets, autopilots are the central hub of the craft's flight management system"

Autopilot

How does this system fly the plane automatically?

An autopilot system consists of three main elements: a computerised guidance program that plots the aircraft's course and compares its real position to its virtual one, a series of motion and position sensors such as airspeed indicators and gyroscopes to deliver real-time feedback, and a selection of servomotors to actuate the craft's engines and alter its flight-altering components when changes are necessary. By syncing these three elements autopilots can not only stabilise an aircraft's pitch, yaw and roll movements – greatly relieving pilots on long-haul flights – but also handle, in poor visibility conditions, automatic runway approaches and landings.

In modern, commercial jets, autopilots are the central hub of the craft's flight management system, a grouping of sensors such as GPS and INS (inertial guidance system) that help calculate the current positioning and course of the aircraft without need for external reference. The feedback from these systems are equalised and, in the case of accuracy discrepancies, resolved through a multi-dimensional Kalman filter, a mathematical model for mitigating random variations in feedback values. The most common filter is a six-dimensional one, receiving and processing information for the aircraft's pitch, yaw and roll, but also its altitude, latitude and longitude. The latter values are specifically important for modern day passenger aircraft, as they must run to specific schedules and on courses with certain rated performance factors, with set minimum velocity, altitudes and time factors to be met.

Cutting-edge advanced autopilot systems may also include an autoland sub-system, however these are usually only available at major international airports, which have various ground-based systems to communicate with the autopilot flight management system on board to help alignment and ratify its current and potential approach and landing course. The International Civil Aviation Organization categorises autoland systems dependent on the visibility level at the runway and degree of automation capable by the autopilot. For example, a simple CAT I system requires pilots to have a decision height of 60 metres and a forward visibility range of 550m to engage an automatic landing, while a complex CAT IIIb system allows pilots to engage the system with a decision height of less than 15 metres and a forward visibility of just 75 metres. ✿

The first autopilots could only control how level a plane was flying

Autopilot fundamentals

Autopilot sensors and systems would be useless without the system's servomotors to control the aircraft's physical components

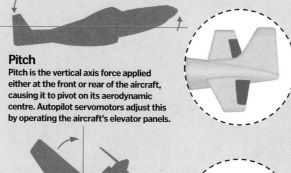

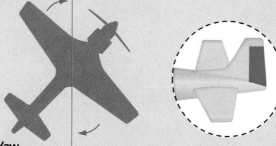

Pitch
Pitch is the vertical axis force applied either at the front or rear of the aircraft, causing it to pivot on its aerodynamic centre. Autopilot servomotors adjust this by operating the aircraft's elevator panels.

Yaw
The yaw axis is vertical and is defined to be perpendicular to its wings. Yaw motion is the movement of the aircraft's nose from side to side on a horizontal plane. Servomotors control this by adjusting the aircraft's rudder.

Roll
Roll defines the plane's movement in relation to the longitudinal axis that passes through its body from nose to tip. Autopilot servomotors compensate for roll by adjusting the aircraft's ailerons.

5 TOP FACTS AUTOPILOT

1 Oily times
Autopilots, while made famous by aeroplanes, are actually used to automatically control all sorts of vehicles, including cars, trucks and boats. In fact, the first ship to use a basic autopilot was the JA Moffett oil tanker in 1920.

2 Eight days
The first pilot to fly around the world solo, the famed Wiley Post, used a Sperry Corporation autopilot in his record-setting eight-day journey in 1933. Sperry is credited as the company to have officially invented the autopilot in 1912.

3 Under pressure
Autopilots are used on board spacecraft to counteract minor disturbances caused by micrometeorites, radiation pressure from the Sun, and minor irregularities in the gravitational fields of nearby planetary bodies.

4 CAT-egories
The International Civil Aviation Organization breaks down autopilot landings into five categories, dependent upon visibility levels and the degree of automation. Categories range from CAT I through to CAT IIIb.

5 Failure
Autopilots are built to be fail-safe, with manual overrides always given precedent over the system's actions. The major cause of autopilot failure is with an aircraft's servomotors, the machines that physically adjust its components.

"Oh no, how do I restart the engine?"

"Once billed as the next generation of transportation"

Hovercraft

How do these incredible machines traverse both land and sea?

The ability of hovercraft to cross dry land as well as water has seen them employed in the military and tourism sectors for many years. Although once billed as the next generation of transportation, they have somewhat decreased in popularity over the last decade. Despite this, their usefulness is still readily apparent.

The core principle of a hovercraft is that the hull of the vehicle is suspended on top of a giant cushion of air, held in place by flexible rubber that allows it to traverse difficult terrain or choppy waves without being torn apart. At the centre of a hovercraft is a huge fan that fires air downwards, pushing the hull off the ground as high as two metres (6.5 feet). Smaller fans on top of the hull push air backwards, giving the hovercraft forward momentum. Rudders direct this flow of horizontal air to allow a hovercraft to change its direction.

Traditional hovercraft have an entirely rubber base that allows for travel on land or sea, but others have rigid sides that, while suited only to water, can have propellers or water-jet engines attached for a quieter craft. ✿

© Alex Pang

Hovercraft have been in use for over 50 years

© Andrew Berridge

Cargo
Most modern hovercraft are used for military purposes, like this Landing Craft Air Cushion (LCAC), which can transport vehicles and troops with ease.

Skirt
This flexible and inflatable barrier traps the cushion of pressurised air beneath the hull, in addition to increasing the height of the hull to allow it to move over obstacles.

The air cushion

Storage
Air is stored until it's needed to give more lift, when air escapes through the hovergap.

Lift
Transfer of air into the plenum chamber increases pressure and allows the craft to rise.

Air flow
Air is sent down into the plenum chamber of the hovercraft from the main fan.

Plenum chamber
The region of trapped air underneath the craft is known as the 'plenum chamber', which controls the escape of air to create a high-pressure environment and thus a circulation of controllable air.

5 TOP FACTS
HOVERCRAFT HISTORY

Sir John Thornycroft

1 The first patent for a hovercraft design was made by Sir John Thornycrof in 1877, but he could not solve the problem of air escaping from underneath the vehicle.

Sir Christopher Cockerell

2 Esteemed British engineer Sir Christopher Cockerell began work on the first hovercraft in 1953, completing his first working model by 1955.

Channel crossing

3 The first hovercraft to cross the English Channel was the SR.N1, completing the journey on 25 July 1959, reducing the time of the trip to just half an hour.

Retired

4 Cross-channel hovercraft were expensive to run, especially with degradation caused by sea salt, and the last trip was made in October 2000.

Military

5 Since their invention, hovercraft have been regularly employed by the military. The Griffon 2000 TDX Class ACV, is currently in use by the Royal Marines.

DID YOU KNOW? American Bob Windt holds the record for the fastest hovercraft speed, reaching 137.4km/h (85.38mph) in 1995

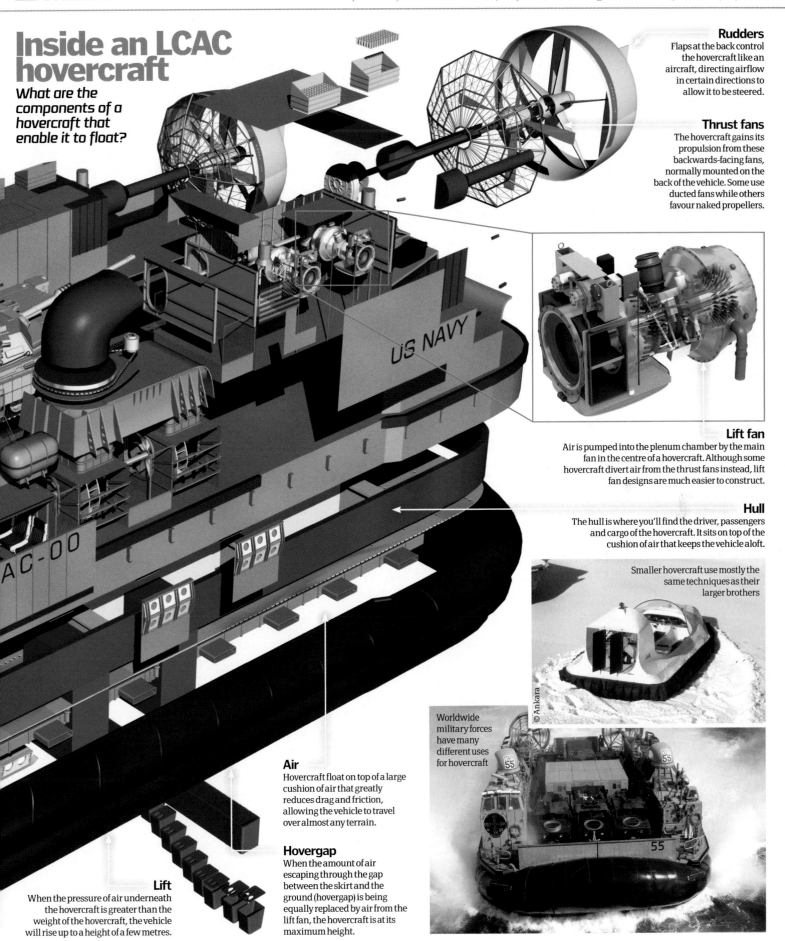

Inside an LCAC hovercraft

What are the components of a hovercraft that enable it to float?

Rudders
Flaps at the back control the hovercraft like an aircraft, directing airflow in certain directions to allow it to be steered.

Thrust fans
The hovercraft gains its propulsion from these backwards-facing fans, normally mounted on the back of the vehicle. Some use ducted fans while others favour naked propellers.

Lift fan
Air is pumped into the plenum chamber by the main fan in the centre of a hovercraft. Although some hovercraft divert air from the thrust fans instead, lift fan designs are much easier to construct.

Hull
The hull is where you'll find the driver, passengers and cargo of the hovercraft. It sits on top of the cushion of air that keeps the vehicle aloft.

Smaller hovercraft use mostly the same techniques as their larger brothers

© Ankara

Worldwide military forces have many different uses for hovercraft

Air
Hovercraft float on top of a large cushion of air that greatly reduces drag and friction, allowing the vehicle to travel over almost any terrain.

Hovergap
When the amount of air escaping through the gap between the skirt and the ground (hovergap) is being equally replaced by air from the lift fan, the hovercraft is at its maximum height.

Lift
When the pressure of air underneath the hovercraft is greater than the weight of the hovercraft, the vehicle will rise up to a height of a few metres.

223

Landing a plane

Find out how pilots get tons of metal down safely to the tarmac

Landing a plane is the most delicate part of a flight. It involves turning a flying craft into a ground vehicle, bringing hundreds of tons of mass to earth without incident, while shedding speed along the way. Aircraft will naturally fly all day long. So long as they have sufficient fuel, aerodynamics are designed to keep them moving. To alter this, pilots not only have to reduce engine power, they also must slowly adopt a 'dirty configuration', using aerodynamic drag to reduce speed.

The landing procedure begins miles away from the airport. During this time, changes in altitude,

speed, direction and overall aircraft setup must be completed. This is mainly conducted in dedicated 'step down airspace' defined by air traffic control. Passengers are told the landing procedure is due to commence, and are instructed to return to their seats and fasten their seat belts.

Furthermore, at night cabin lights are dimmed before the landing procedure commences, and window blinds raised. Why? So, in an incident, passengers will be less disorientated. Dimming the lights reduces glare and means eyes will already be adjusted to dim conditions. It will also let some light into the cabin and allow passengers to spot dangers.

Landing is a two-stage process; the approach to landing, and landing itself – which will only be good if the approach is good. During the approach phase, pilots slow the plane from cruising speed to an approach speed, from which they can descend gently to a landing speed. A stated aim of pilots is to allow the plane to contact the ground with the lowest possible vertical and horizontal speed.

As throttling back is insufficient to fully slow an aircraft, the additional configuration changes are filtered in at defined approach points. These include gradually raising flaps and, later on in the procedure, extending the landing gear. Indeed, such

1. Kai Tak
HONG KONG

Hong Kong's Kai Tak 'Runway 13' demanded pilots dodge mountains and skyscrapers, pass over a harbour, then turn 47 degrees prior to landing.

2. RAF Gibraltar
GIBRALTAR

Gibraltar Airport is the world's closest airport to the city it serves. What's more, a main road passes across its main runway. The road is closed each time a flight lands.

3. Madeira
PORTUGAL

Madeira's runway is situated on a mountainside, making enlargement tricky for years. 180 columns, 70m high, eventually gave it the crucial extra length.

DID YOU KNOW? Heathrow Airport is used by more than 90 airlines which fly to 170 destinations around the world

Visual guide to a cockpit

Backup in background
Backup dials are positioned less prominently but offer an additional readout in case of main dial failure.

Glass act
Modern jets use glass cockpits. Instead of hundreds of individual instruments, readouts are shown on VDU computer screens.

Flight management systems
Flight management systems are cutting-edge flight technology. Pilots enter the flight plan through them, so they can control speed, navigation and so on.

Mode control panel
A mode control panel allows the pilot to mastermind heading, speed, altitude, vertical speed plus vertical and lateral navigation.

Engine indication
Engines are monitored in great depth, with fuel flow and temperature, electrical functions and other parameters analysed.

Basic six
The six instruments to keep an aircraft in flight are: airspeed, artificial horizon, vertical speed indicator, altimeter, directional gyroscope and turn altitude.

The air control tower can help guide a plane down onto the runway

entering the centre airspace; they blend all together, with the required separation, into a separate channel for final approach to the runway.

Final approach requires stated clearance from ATC. Sometimes, a landing must be aborted at the last moment, either because of an emergency alert from ATC, or an override by the pilot. This is called a go around: the aircraft will pitch up sharply, full power will be applied,

emergency calls in the process. Holding patterns are predefined and dictated by ATCs in the control tower.

When it's busy, ATC will sometimes specify a defined airspeed for pilots to maintain, usually within an accuracy of +/- ten knots. This keeps the aircraft in sequence with those in front and behind – it is how the rate of approach to crowded airports is controlled.

ATC allows two forms of instructions to pilots, which will be stated before the

"The pilot's target is to reach the runway at a precise point"

is the drag created in doing this, some engine power must actually be reapplied to compensate.

The pilot's unquestionable target is to reach the runway at a precise point, and they are able to quickly form a mental picture of the destination landing strip as all runways are given a number from 01-36. This is their heading – where 36 equals 360 degrees, or due north. It enables pilots to quickly visualise the landing direction, and judge how wind

conditions may affect this. Runways can have two numbers, for example 34 and 16. They are separated by 18 because it is the same runway operating in two directions.

The final approach procedure is initiated in a 30-50 mile radius. Air traffic controllers (ATCs) on the ground receive 'their' approach aircraft from fellow en-route ATCs. The controller's job is to find a space for the approach aircraft at a safe separation from others

landing gear and flaps will be tucked away and a very steep climb will be felt.

This can be alarming for passengers but it's a specific procedure for which pilots are trained. It usually occurs either because a plane is still occupying the runway, or the pilots do not have sufficient visual references to land safely. Passengers will be familiar with delays from being kept in a holding pattern. This is for their own safety and ensures the pilot has the time and space to complete their landing procedures – avoiding 'go around'

procedure commences. The descent itself can be under specific altitude instructions which pilots must obey – this is to further help in traffic separation. Alternatively, the aircraft is cleared to descend at the pilot's discretion. This means they themselves decide speed and rate of descent – the only proviso is that once they leave an altitude, they cannot return to it.

On the technical side, landing procedures are managed by an instrument landing system (ILS). This uses radio beacons situated on the ▶

"Just before an aircraft touches the ground, the nose will be raised so the wheels touch the ground first"

ground to precisely guide a plane down with immense accuracy. An ILS follows a specific glide path that helps the plane follow an ideal three-degree angle to the runway.

ILS radar is often supported by an approach lighting system (ALS): lightbars, strobes and so on, which are situated at the start of the runway. They are a major aid for pilots, helping them switch from instrument flight to visual flight – and they can also extend the operating range of the airport because they count as part of a 'visual approach'. Pilots must be able to see three quarters of a mile to the runway: with a high intensity ALS, this can be reduced to half a mile, or more if the lights extend to parts of the runway.

The final seconds before touchdown is when many passengers hold their breath. Just before an aircraft touches the ground, the nose will be raised up. This is called a 'flare', and means the main landing wheels touch the ground first. The perfect landing will see the wheels touch the ground just as lift on the wings completely falls away and the plane 'stalls'. To feel hundreds of tons of mass controlled in such a precise way is extremely satisfying.

When the rear wheels are on the ground, the pilot does not lower the nose – it drops of its own accord. It does so because as the aircraft loses speed, the flight controls continue to lose effectiveness so gravity can take over. Once all wheels are on the ground, the aircraft is in rollout mode.

Here, the flying machine is turned into a ground machine – and must be stopped before the end of the runway. On large jets, the first method of doing this is to raise more flaps to increase drag, and engage reverse thrust on the jet engines. As forces build, pressure on the landing gear increases.

Once there's enough mass pressing down on the wheels, the pilot can apply the brakes. Passengers feel this two-stage deceleration in landing – first, the engines will roar, and then there will be a slight jolt as the brakes come on. The length of this rollout process depends on the weight of the plane, the runway's gradient, condition and elevation, ambient temperature, brake effectiveness and pilot technique.

Autopilot can actually perform the complete procedure right up to touchdown and rollout. What autopilot cannot do is control the ground taxi process; this will always be done by the pilot, using guidance from ground control. On the ground, the aircraft will taxi to its final position, where passengers will disembark. ✿

Monitoring each flight's progress is essential for avoiding any mid-air collisions

That's a big pile of instructions... has he had any training?

Localiser array

Inner marker beacon
The inner marker beacon, shown by a white light, indicates the arrival of the runway threshold. It enables the pilot to check they are at the correct height.

Missed approach
The runway should be in sight when the middle marker beacon sounds; if the pilot is uncertain for any reason, a missed approach procedure should be carried out at this point.

Runway

Ideal descent
The glide path is designed to provide an ideal descent slope of three degrees.

Glide slope array

Point of intersection

Middle marker beacon
A middle marker beacon uses an amber warning light and indicates the aircraft is within 1.2km of the runway.

Multitasking ILS
Several planes can use the ILS at the same time – this leads to the famous evenly spaced Heathrow landing stack.

Morse code secret signal
The ILS can issue Morse code signals, to reassure pilots they're working, and confirm they're approaching the correct airport.

Glide path extended

60m

900-1,200m

6-11km

Instrument landing system explained

An ILS is installed at most important airports, helping land planes accurately, safely and efficiently

Based on the ground, the instrument landing system is a standardised system that communicates with the aircraft and guides it to ground using radio signals. It uses two components to determine a plane's path; a localiser, that controls lateral guidance, and a glide path for vertical guidance.

Localiser antennas emit dual signals of different frequencies, either side of the runway. A receiver on the aircraft measures any difference between them and adjusts the approach accordingly. The glide path antennae, situated to one side of the runway, does a similar job for the vertical route.

LONGEST

1. Qamdo Bangda
Higher runways need more space due to thinner air – and at 4,344m above sea level, Tibet's Qamdo is the highest in the world. That's why the runway is 5,500m long...

SHORTEST

2. Honduras
Just 2,163m long, the Honduras airport can handle Boeing 757s – just. Close mountainous terrain reinforces its status as one of the world's most dangerous.

SCARIEST

3. St Maarten Airport
This Caribbean airport runway is so short, aircraft have to virtually skim the surface of Maho Beach.

DID YOU KNOW? The runway of Ulyanovsk Vostochny Airport in Russia is the world's widest, with a width of about 105m

Approach and landing
A step-by-step guide to how you end up safe and sound on the runway

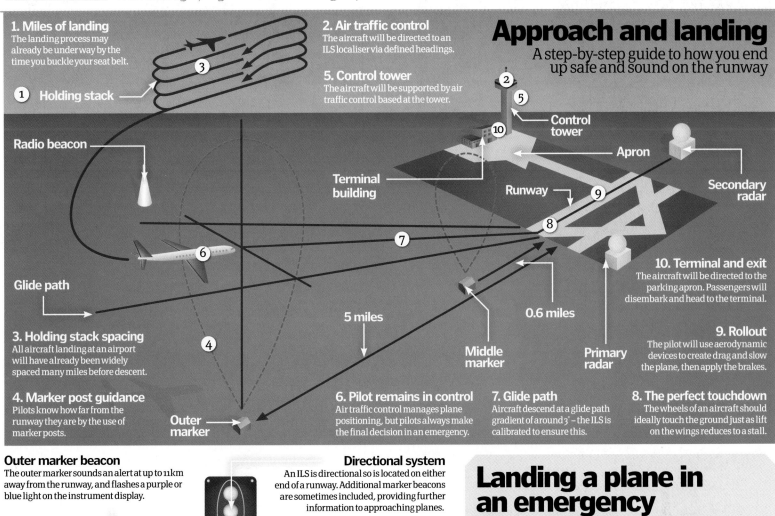

1. Miles of landing
The landing process may already be under way by the time you buckle your seat belt.

2. Air traffic control
The aircraft will be directed to an ILS localiser via defined headings.

5. Control tower
The aircraft will be supported by air traffic control based at the tower.

① **Holding stack**

Radio beacon

Control tower

Apron

Terminal building

Runway

Secondary radar

Glide path

5 miles

0.6 miles

10. Terminal and exit
The aircraft will be directed to the parking apron. Passengers will disembark and head to the terminal.

3. Holding stack spacing
All aircraft landing at an airport will have already been widely spaced many miles before descent.

4. Marker post guidance
Pilots know how far from the runway they are by the use of marker posts.

Outer marker

Middle marker

Primary radar

9. Rollout
The pilot will use aerodynamic devices to create drag and slow the plane, then apply the brakes.

6. Pilot remains in control
Air traffic control manages plane positioning, but pilots always make the final decision in an emergency.

7. Glide path
Aircraft descend at a glide path gradient of around 3° – the ILS is calibrated to ensure this.

8. The perfect touchdown
The wheels of an aircraft should ideally touch the ground just as lift on the wings reduces to a stall.

Outer marker beacon
The outer marker sounds an alert at up to 11km away from the runway, and flashes a purple or blue light on the instrument display.

Directional system
An ILS is directional so is located on either end of a runway. Additional marker beacons are sometimes included, providing further information to approaching planes.

ILS establishment
Aircraft need to come within 2.5 degrees of the localiser course in order to become established on a final approach route.

Localiser modulation frequency

ATC lead
Air traffic control directs aircraft to the localiser using defined headings – this keeps good and even spacing between planes.

0.7°

Glide slope modulation frequency

3.0° - 6.0°

3° above horizontal

Landing a plane in an emergency
Let's hope you never have to use this...

No time to make notes!

Pilot passed out? No worries, help is at hand. Just follow these simple steps and a successful emergency landing can be achieved.

Sit in the pilot's seat; this is the one positioned on the left of the cabin. Before touching anything, check the altitude instrumentation in front of you. The altitude indicator (often referred to as the virtual horizon) is the circular display that shows a W-shaped representation of the plane's wings in relation to the Earth and sky.

Next check whether the autopilot is engaged. If it is and the plane is level, don't touch anything. If the wings are not level, adjust any bank or pitch using the yoke (stick).

Now phone-in the emergency on the radio. Air traffic control will guide you to a runway, but you'll have to make the landing yourself. Pull back on the throttle (handled lever on pilot's right side) to reduce power, and push down on the yoke to drop the nose. Drop the landing gear and just as you are about to touch down raise the nose so the main wheels touch down first.

Finally, when on the tarmac engage the reverse thrusters (movable bars behind the throttle), pull the throttle down to its 'idle' position and apply pressure to the top of the rudder pedals (down by your feet) to brake.

HISTORY
Discover how things worked

categories explained

🏛 Ancient world · 🗼 Buildings & places · 🏭 Industry · ☎ Inventions · 🗡 Medieval times · 👑 People & Places · 💣 Weapons & War · 📖 General

HOW IT WORKS
HISTORY

244
Mallard steam
locomotive

240
The planet's
biggest dinosaurs

246
Roman forts

249
Viking warriors

252
Tudor houses

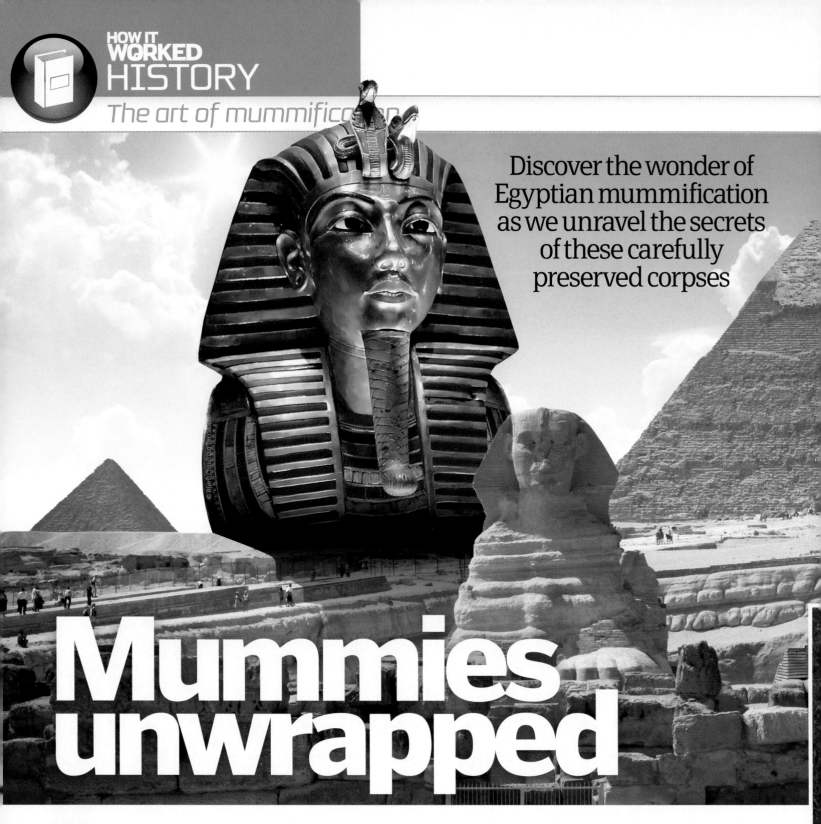

Discover the wonder of Egyptian mummification as we unravel the secrets of these carefully preserved corpses

Mummies unwrapped

 Mummification was a process undertaken by the ancient Egyptians. They believed that by preserving a body, its soul could live on in the afterlife. Embalmers offered various packages, which included a basic, standard and luxury version. Even so, it was only the rich that could afford to mummify their dead and thereafter place them in an elaborate tomb. Ordinary civilians were buried in pit graves, and some of these bodies were naturally dried.

Mummification was an elaborate and lengthy process that took 70 days. The violation of the body was abhorred, so the first incision performed on the corpse was made by a 'scapegoat'. He was then ritually stoned and chased from the embalming chamber. Afterwards, the intestines, lungs, stomach and liver were removed – these were mummified and placed in special containers called canopic jars. The brain was pulverised with a long narrow instrument and drained through the nose or the back of the skull. The heart, which was then known as the seat of learning, was left inside the body. During the mummification process the priests would venerate the dead; they would light incense, recite prayers and invoke aid and protection from ancient Egyptian gods. Once cleansed, the body was then ready to be dried.

The ancient Egyptians placed the body in natron salts, which absorbed all its moisture. After a period of 40 days it was removed and packed with herbs, oils and spices, which were known to cleanse and preserve the cavities. If extra body parts were needed the corpse was equipped with false wooden limbs, or eyes made of obsidian. It was then ready for bandaging. Each limb was carefully tended to; fingers and toes were treated individually, and golden caps were placed on the nails. In order to protect it, a large number of amulets were left on specific parts of the body. Often, garlands of leaves or berries, which were thought to have rejuvenating properties, were placed around the neck. The hair was dressed with oils and jewellery. Due to heat and lice, the ancient Egyptians shaved their heads, so elaborate wigs (made of human hair) were placed on the deceased. Makeup was applied, and it was dressed in fine clothes and adornments. While women were buried with combs and pottery, men were armed with daggers or swords. These were placed either on the body or within the wrappings.

At the beginning of the 20th Century, Egyptology was in its infancy. Many early excavators ignored

5 TOP FACTS
MUMMIES

Mummia
1 The term 'mummification' comes from 'mummia', an Arabic word that means pitch or resin. This dark, viscous liquid was used in the later stages of mummification.

Ramesses II
2 Ramesses II was one of Egypt's greatest rulers. When he was moved to Paris for scientific exams, he had a passport that described him as 'King (deceased)'.

Healing the sick
3 'Mummia' is described by Shakespeare in Romeo and Juliet. Until the 20th Century people took mummia to cure ills such as stomach upsets, headaches and arthritis.

Making a mummy
4 Artist Robert Lenkiewicz inherited the body of a tramp and mummified the remains. Hotly pursued by Plymouth City Council, he hid the remains in a drawer.

Tutankamun
5 While most mummies are in museums, the remains of Tutankhamun were kept in his tomb. Discovered in 1922, the body still lies in the Valley of the Kings.

DID YOU KNOW? In 1975, an organisation known as Summum began to practise ancient Egyptian embalming techniques

human remains. The first archaeologists were more interested in treasure than mummies, and even the body of Tutankhamun was subjected to trauma. Although Howard Carter was a brilliant excavator, he could not have imagined the wonders that the dead could reveal. Nor did he envisage that innovations in science would enable us to make important new discoveries about ancient Egyptian mummies. Despite this, the world was now fascinated. Even in Victorian times, the unwrapping of an Egyptian mummy (which often took place in affluent drawing rooms) would be followed by tea, cake and polite conversation.

Thankfully, times have changed and the first scientific unwrapping of a mummy took place in Manchester when Margaret Murray examined the two brothers, Khnum-Nakht and Nekht-Ankh, in 1908. Manchester continues its strong association with the scientific study of mummies. It is here that Professor Rosalie David conducted many innovative investigations into ancient disease. In 1979 she established

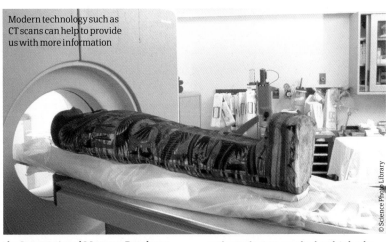
Modern technology such as CT scans can help to provide us with more information

the International Mummy Database, which employs endoscopy and serological studies, x-ray examinations and MRI scans. Perhaps the most important investigation into ancient mummies was undertaken in Paris between 1976-1977, when the mummy of Ramesses II was met at Orly airport and treated like a visiting head of state. A team of over 100 scientists, including botanists, microbiologists and anthropologists, worked on his body and published startling new evidence about mummification techniques.

Examinations that employ DNA sampling are now used in mummy studies. While the practice is still limited, it can enable Egyptologists to identify, establish and study family groups. We are now able to shed light on the everyday life of the ancient Egyptians, going on to analyse dental hygiene, hair dyes and makeup. When examining mummies we are now able to study textiles, jewellery, oils and even head lice – the oldest 'nits' in the world were found on a Manchester mummy. From these examinations we can learn a great deal about the diseases, afflictions and the general aches and pains of all classes of people, and we can even identify trauma wounds, arthritis and polio. With the invention of new scanning techniques, the destructive process of 'unwrapping' a mummy is now a thing of the past. What remains constant, however, is that mummies continue to fascinate, excite and inspire us. ✿

"Only the rich could afford to mummify their dead and place them in an elaborate tomb"

The well-preserved, naturally mummified body of a figure known as the 'Tollund Man'

King Tutankhamun, discovered by Howard Carter in 1922

TYPES OF...
MUMMIES AROUND THE WORLD

1 Ice mummies
Dated to the Pazryk culture, the Ice Maiden and her contemporaries are dated 6th to 3rd Centuries BC. These mummies were buried with elaborate funerary equipment – in the case of the Ice Maiden, there were six horses and a symbolic last meal. Her body is covered in a series of beautiful blue tattoos which depict mythical animals.

2 Mummies of the Canary Islands
The Guanche mummies were found on the Canary Islands in the 15th Century, when they were discovered by Spanish invaders. Little is known of them – many were pulverised and used as medicinal powders to aid stomach complaints. Dried in the Sun, the mummies were packed with sand and wrapped in animal skins. They were then placed on mummy boards and left in caves.

3 Inca mummies
Inca mummies, found in Peru and Chile, are approximately 500 years old. The remains are those of young children sacrificed on the mountains of the Andes, in order to honour the gods. Other mummies include those known as the 'Cloud People', which are found in northern Peru. These mummies were mummified in the driest areas of the jungle.

4 Mummies of the King's Capuchin Catacombs
Dated between the late-16th and 20th Centuries, the mummies of the King's Capuchins Catacombs are magnificent examples of the art of embalming. Thousands of bodies were dried here in 'strainers' (cells that are situated in the passageways of the catacombs). After eight months they were removed and soaked in vinegar. Adults and children are placed on display in coffins, niches and on the walls.

"The embalming process was an urgent and bloody activity"

The art of mummification

1 Bog bodies
Waterlogged peat holds very little oxygen, and this means that the microorganisms that cause decomposition cannot survive. The acidity in the bog, along with sphagnum moss, also helps to preserve the body. While the skin, hair and internal organs are remarkably well preserved, the bones are softened.
The body begins to take on a dark, leathery appearance.

2 Self-mummification
Self-mummification was practised by the Sokushinbutsu, a group of Japanese Buddhist monks. For several years, the monks would live on a diet of seeds and nuts and would drink the sap of the Urushi tree, which would cause vomiting and loss of body mass. They would seal themselves in a tomb and die – if the body had mummified, it was regarded as a holy vessel.

3 Desiccation
When left in the open, water, insects and heat will rapidly destroy the body. If the body is buried in sand or salt, moisture in the flesh is absorbed and the corpse is preserved. More importantly, in the case of Egyptian mummies the removal of internal organs aids this process, preventing internal bloating and decay.

4 Ice mummies
Ice prevents decomposition of the body and inhibits the growth of bacteria. It also preserves pollen and dust grains. Ice is an excellent and effective agent, so ice mummies seem very lifelike. Their hair, eyelashes and body decorations are often astounding. Ice mummies have even been discovered with votive offerings and grave goods.

Ötzi the Ice Man is a famous natural ice mummy

© South Tyrol Museum of Archaeology

Death chamber

We open the doors to the eerie and mysterious world of the embalming chamber, to explain how the process was performed

Although the House of the Dead was occupied by priests and their servants, it was also regarded as a place of dread. The sight or smell of the embalming chamber was viewed with fear and repulsion. Inside the House of the Dead, there would often be a long queue of bodies waiting to be embalmed; they would be placed on sloping beds so that body fluids and blood would drain into vats. Flies, inexperience and heat could make the work difficult. As we have explained, the embalming process was an urgent and bloody activity – when rushed, the embalmers often lost or severed limbs. The morality of the morticians was also regarded with suspicion; they were often associated with robbery and corruption. On the other hand, morticians were viewed as mystics and magicians, and a sense of secrecy surrounded their art.

Howard Carter discovered Tutankhamun's tomb

© Marie-Lan Nguyen

Coffins
Large, rectangular coffins were decorated with magical texts and painted eyes – believed to enable the dead to look out and survey surroundings.

Preparation
Before a corpse could be embalmed, it was placed on a sloping table so bodily fluids could drain away.

Carrion birds
The Egyptians both revered and feared birds of prey. They were often depicted in funerary contexts, and were associated with death on the battlefield.

© DK Images

Mourners and priests
A group of mourners and priests accompanied the body to the mortuary. After death, the body was quickly removed.

Reception area
The body was received in this small, holy vestibule. Here, priests conducted prayers and spells to aid the deceased's journey into the next life.

FROM DEATH TO THE TOMBS

1. The death scene
This bed is a traditional funeral bier (stand), which can be found among ancient Egyptian funerary equipment. It was designed to represent the body of a lion.

2. Embalmers at their work
Several priests attended the body of the deceased; while some worked on the body, others would recite prayers and perform magical incantations.

3. Bandaging and anointing
Many metres of linen bandages were used on mummies, where each finger and toe was wrapped individually. The body was anointed in protective oils and resins.

4. Placement in coffin
Coffins differed over the years, both in style and decoration. The coffin was made of wood and gilded with precious metals. It was inscribed with magical texts.

OLD

1. Sir John Franklin
In 1847, explorer Sir John Franklin and his crew of 129 disappeared on an expedition to the Arctic. The mummies of Torrington (21), Hartnell (25) and Franklin (61) were found in good condition.

OLDER

2. Juanita the Ice Maiden
Juanita, or the 'Ice Maiden', was sacrificed to mountain deities when she was 13/14 years old. She was found on a mountain by anthropologist Johan Reinhard.

OLDEST

3. Tutankhamun's children
Included in the category of rare Egyptian mummies are two foetuses, thought to be the children of Tutankhamun. They are believed to be twins.

DID YOU KNOW? Plastination and cryogenics are two more modern methods of preserving the body

Science of embalming

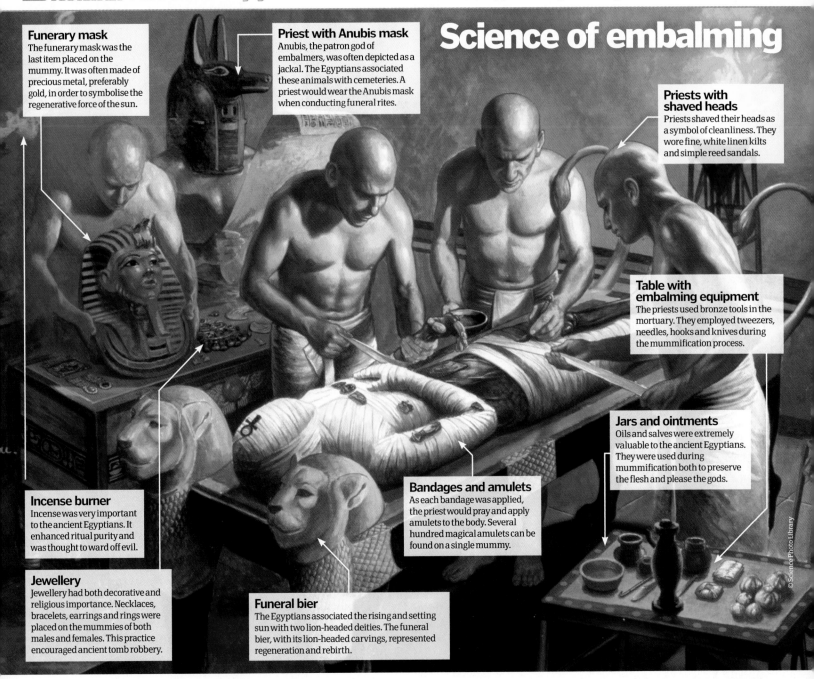

Funerary mask
The funerary mask was the last item placed on the mummy. It was often made of precious metal, preferably gold, in order to symbolise the regenerative force of the sun.

Priest with Anubis mask
Anubis, the patron god of embalmers, was often depicted as a jackal. The Egyptians associated these animals with cemeteries. A priest would wear the Anubis mask when conducting funeral rites.

Priests with shaved heads
Priests shaved their heads as a symbol of cleanliness. They wore fine, white linen kilts and simple reed sandals.

Table with embalming equipment
The priests used bronze tools in the mortuary. They employed tweezers, needles, hooks and knives during the mummification process.

Jars and ointments
Oils and salves were extremely valuable to the ancient Egyptians. They were used during mummification both to preserve the flesh and please the gods.

Bandages and amulets
As each bandage was applied, the priest would pray and apply amulets to the body. Several hundred magical amulets can be found on a single mummy.

Incense burner
Incense was very important to the ancient Egyptians. It enhanced ritual purity and was thought to ward off evil.

Jewellery
Jewellery had both decorative and religious importance. Necklaces, bracelets, earrings and rings were placed on the mummies of both males and females. This practice encouraged ancient tomb robbery.

Funeral bier
The Egyptians associated the rising and setting sun with two lion-headed deities. The funeral bier, with its lion-headed carvings, represented regeneration and rebirth.

© Science Photo Library

A step-by-step look at the mummification process, from deathbed to the grandeur of the tomb

© DK Images

5. Mourners
The coffin was placed on a bier and dragged by oxen to the tomb. It was accompanied by priests, mourners and relatives.

6. Opening of the mouth
A priest, dressed in leopard skin, would 'open the mouth' of the deceased with an instrument called an Adze. This allowed the spirit to fly free from the body.

7. Placing goods in the tomb
The ancient Egyptians believed that you could indeed 'take it with you'. Their tombs were filled with goods that were needed in the next world.

8. Priest leaving the tomb
At the culmination of the funerary rituals, the priest would leave the tomb. As he retreated, he would sweep away his footsteps from the dust.

9. Weighing of the heart
The heart is weighed before Osiris, god of the dead. If found wanting, the deceased would be devoured by a crocodile-headed monster.

Lancaster bomber

Famed for its prowess, and entrenched in popular culture by The Dam Busters film of 1955, the Lancaster bomber played a crucial role in securing an Allied victory during the Second World War

Arguably the most famous heavy bomber of World War II, the Avro-built Lancaster bomber undertook some of the most dangerous and complex missions yet encountered by the RAF. Primarily a night bomber but frequently used during the day too, the Lancasters under Bomber Command flew some 156,000 sorties during the Second World War, dropping 609,000 tons of bombs. Among these bombs was the famous 'bouncing bomb' designed by British inventor Barnes Wallis, a payload that would lead the Lancaster to remain famed long after 1945. **How It Works** takes a look inside an Avro Lancaster to see made it so successful. ✿

Lancaster bombers dropped 609,000 tons of bombs

Inside a Lancaster bomber

Crew
Due to its large size, hefty armament and technical complexity, the Lancaster bomber had a crew of seven. This included: a pilot, flight engineer, navigator, bomb aimer, wireless operator, mid-upper and rear gunners. Many crew members from Lancasters were awarded the Victoria Cross for their heroic actions in battle, a notable example being the two awarded after a daring daytime raid on Augsburg, Germany.

Turrets
As standard the Lancaster bomber was fitted with three twin 7.7mm turrets in the nose, rear and upper-middle fuselage. In some later variants of the Lancaster the twin 7.7mm machine guns were replaced with 12.7mm models, which delivered more power. The rear and upper-middle turrets were staffed permanently by dedicated gunners, while the nose turret was staffed periodically by the bomb aimer when caught up in a dogfight.

Bomb bay
The bomb bay could carry a great payload. Indeed, the bay was so spacious that with a little modification it could house the massive Grand Slam earthquake bomb, a 10,000kg giant that when released would reach near sonic speeds before penetrating deep into the Earth and exploding.

Fuselage
The Lancaster was designed out of the earlier Avro Type 683 Manchester III bomber, which sported a three-finned tail layout and was similar in construction. While the overall build remained similar the tri-fin was removed in favour of a twin-finned set up instead. This is famously one of only a small number of design alterations made to the bomber, which was deemed to be just right after its test flights.

High calibre
1 While 7.7mm machine guns were standard on Lancaster bombers, selective later variants were fitted with twin 12.7mm turrets in both tail and dorsal positions.

Slam-dunk
2 Lancaster bombers often had their already-large bomb bays modified in order to carry the monumental 10,000 kilogram Grand Slam earthquake bombs.

Busted
3 A selection of bombers became famous after Operation Chastise, a mission to destroy dams in the Ruhr Valley, which inspired *The Dam Busters*.

Collateral
4 Between 1942 and 1945 Lancaster bombers flew 156,000 sorties and dropped approximately 609,000 tons of bombs on military and civilian targets.

Black label
5 The lager company Carling used footage of Lancaster bombers to create a parody of *The Dam Busters* in which a German soldier catches the bouncing bombs.

DID YOU KNOW? A single Lancaster bomber cost £50,000 in 1942, roughly £1.5 million in today's currency

Over 7,000 bombers were built

Powerplant

The Lancaster bomber was powered by four Rolls-Royce Merlin V12 engines. These were chosen by the Lancaster's chief designer Roy Chadwick due to their reliability, as the incumbent bomber – the Avro Manchester – had adopted the Rolls-Royce Vulture and had been troubled by engine failure consistently when in service.

The Statistics

Lancaster bomber

Crew: 7
Length: 21.18m
Wingspan: 31.09m
Height: 5.97m
Weight: 29,000kg
Powerplant: 4 x Rolls-Royce Merlin XX V12 engines
Max speed: 280mph
Max range: 2,700nm
Max altitude: 7,160m
Armament: 8 x .7.7mm Browning machine guns; bomb load of 6,300kg

©John Batchelor / www.johnbatchelor.com

©Bluemoose

The bouncing bomb

One of the most famous parts of the Lancaster's heritage is its role in carrying and releasing the 'bouncing bomb' payload, as glamorised in the 1955 film *The Dam Busters*. The bomb was designed by Barnes Wallis – who was also the creator of the Grand Slam and Tallboy bombs – and was special in its ability to bounce along the top of a surface of water, much akin to skimming a stone. It was designed to counteract and evade German defences below and above the waterline, allowing Allied forces to target German hydroelectric dams and floating vessels.

In May 1943 the bouncing bombs were utilised in Operation Chastise, an allied mission to destroy German dams in the Ruhr Valley. The aircraft used were modified Avro Lancaster Mk IIIs, which had much of their armour and central turret removed in order to accommodate the payload. Despite eight of the Lancasters being lost during the operation, as well as the lives of 53 crew, a small number of bouncing bombs were released and they caused two dams to be breached, one to be heavily damaged and 1,296 civilians to be killed.

That's a real dam buster...

"The development of cast iron cannons brought down the cost of production"

Looms

Integral to the art of weaving, the loom is an ancient but highly refined machine

Looms, while appearing rather complex, are actually fundamentally simple machines that work by holding two sets of parallel threads within a frame that alternate with each other as a cross thread is filtered through them carried by a shuttle (a wooden block in which thread can be stored pre-weave). By doing this cloths and fabrics can be weaved on a large scale quickly and in far greater numbers than if undertaken freeform by hand.

Since their initial construction in the 5th Century BC, the basic mechanics of looms have remained unchanged, with only a long succession of improvements introduced to the system. The most notable addition was the introduction of a drive-shaft power source, allowing for mechanised looms to be mass-produced and slowly evolved to the point of complete automation. Indeed, today it is argued by historians that the power loom was central to the development of the Industrial Revolution and has contributed greatly to the proliferation of large and high-quality fabrics worldwide. ✿

Warp
The set of length-wise yarns through which the weft is woven.

Heddle
A heddle is a cord or wire divider used to separate the warp threads for the passage of the weft.

Shed
The temporary separation between the upper and lower warp yarn through which the weft is woven.

Yarn
This is a continuous length of interlocked fibres suitable for weaving.

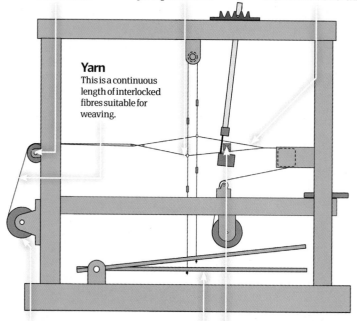

Weft
The weft is the yarn that is drawn through the warp to create a fabric.

Treadle
Operated by foot to produce a reciprocating motion in the heddle.

Shuttle
A small tool that stores weft yarn while weaving. Shuttles are passed back and forth through the shed and between the threads of the warp.

MOST MECHANICAL

1. Power loom
Edmund Cartwright created the first power loom in England way back in 1785.

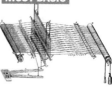

MOST BASIC

2. Hand loom
The loom of choice before the industrial revolution, the hand loom allowed cloth and fabrics to be woven on a large scale.

MOST CLASSICAL

3. Warp-weighted
Similar in mechanics to the back strap loom, apart from the fact that it is arranged vertically and uses physical weights to keep the thread taut.

Torch-hole
Gunpowder or a fuse is placed in the torch hole and ignited to fire the cannon.

Gunpowder
In the late-15th Century water was added to gunpowder to form granules or mill cakes, making it easier to store and more efficient.

Cannonball
Spherical, solid cannonballs were made from dressed stone, lead or iron.

The cannon
The weapon that changed the nature of warfare

Early cannons were crude affairs with barrels made from wooden or wrought-iron staves held together by iron hoops. If the explosive mixture was too powerful it was likely to destroy the weapon rather than fire a projectile at the enemy.

Barrel-making techniques were replaced by bell-making technology, with the production of cast brass cannons. Improvements in the casting of bronze cannons in the mid-14th Century meant that more powerful gunpowder mixtures of sulphur, charcoal and saltpetre could be employed with more deadly effect.

In the mid-16th Century, the development of cast iron cannons brought down the cost of production and enabled an even wider deployment of this weapon.

The use of cannons meant that castles and fortified buildings were no longer able to withstand long sieges. Large and complex star-shaped fortifications were introduced to cope with this danger; this had the effect of centralising power as only the richest could afford them. ✿

The development of the cannon continued through the centuries

Wadding
Hemp oakum wadding rammed into the barrel either side of the cannonball keeps it firmly in position.

Ramrod
When loaded, the ramrod is used to pack the wadding and cannonball firmly against the gunpowder. If not packed properly, the powder will burn instead of exploding.

Ready, aim, fire!

5 TOP FACTS
WHISKY

Old
1 The earliest direct account of whisky being made in Scotland dates from 1494, when cereal grains were mashed together crudely before being fermented.

Global
2 Despite the home of whisky typically credited to Scotland, the liquor is in fact produced worldwide, with large industries in Ireland, Canada, Japan and America.

Life
3 The word whisky is an anglicisation of the Gaelic 'uisge beatha', or water of life. This is the same as the Latin 'aqua vitae', which translates as the same.

Prohibition
4 During the prohibition era in the US in the late-Twenties and Thirties, the only form of alcohol made legal was whisky as prescribed by licensed pharmacies.

Sun
5 Japan's primary producer of whisky is Suntory Holdings Limited, one of the oldest distribution companies in the country. It was established in Osaka.

DID YOU KNOW? *The earliest recorded reference to bagpipes dates from the 9th Century*

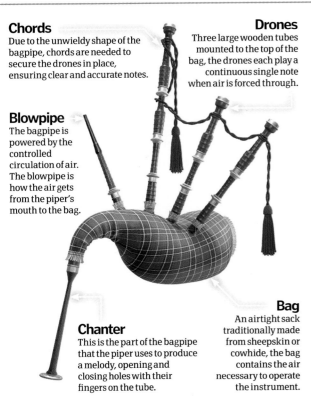

Chords
Due to the unwieldy shape of the bagpipe, chords are needed to secure the drones in place, ensuring clear and accurate notes.

Drones
Three large wooden tubes mounted to the top of the bag, the drones each play a continuous single note when air is forced through.

Blowpipe
The bagpipe is powered by the controlled circulation of air. The blowpipe is how the air gets from the piper's mouth to the bag.

Bag
An airtight sack traditionally made from sheepskin or cowhide, the bag contains the air necessary to operate the instrument.

Chanter
This is the part of the bagpipe that the piper uses to produce a melody, opening and closing holes with their fingers on the tube.

Bagpipe breakdown
How does this odd-shaped instrument work?

 A bagpipe is a wind instrument consisting of multiple reed pipes, which are set in motion by the passing of pressurised air. The air is delivered into a central bag via a blowpipe and, once the bag is squeezed, forces the air through the chanter (a melody pipe) and usually a set of drones (cylindrical tubes that play a single note). As air is continuously forced through the chanter and drones, bagpipes produce a continuous sound, which is articulated as a melody by the piper's opening and closing of holes in the chanter.

Whisky production
Discover the complex, multi-stage process involved in making this age-old alcoholic drink

 The first main stage of whisky production is malting, a process of soaking barley in water for days. This increases the moisture content of the grains and causes germination, which converts the starch in the grains into fermentable sugars. The grains are then separated from the heated water and dried.

Next, the dried malt is crushed into grist and added to water, heated to 60°C in a mashing process. This step creates a sugar solution (wort), which is then separated from the grains. The grains are disposed of and the wort is sent for fermentation in a series of wooden containers called washbacks. After two to three days in a washback, the wort generates a low-alcohol liquid, or the wash.

Distillation follows, a complex process of evaporation and condensing of the wash in stills. This enriches the alcohol content of the wash and produces a high-alcohol liquid that can then be matured into drinkable whisky. Finally, maturation is achieved by depositing the young whisky into oak casks.

2. Vapour
Vapour is carried to a second column, the rectifier. Deposited into the cool top of the column, it condenses and falls through perforated copper plates, re-heating as it gets to the heated bottom.

4. Impure
Low-alcohol content vapour and impurities are evaporated at the top of the rectifier, before being dumped back into the analyser. These go up through the column and condense back into liquid form. This waste is then siphoned off.

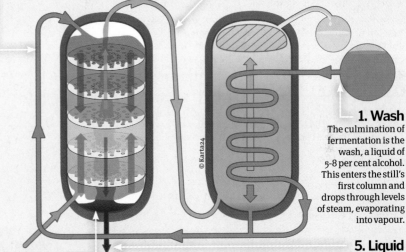
© Karta24

1. Wash
The culmination of fermentation is the wash, a liquid of 5-8 per cent alcohol. This enters the still's first column and drops through levels of steam, evaporating into vapour.

3. Enriched
At each plate, parts of the condensing liquid reach their transition stage, returning to vapour, while others with lower boiling points progress downwards. Turned vapour is enriched by the higher alcohol content liquid.

5. Liquid
The remaining alcohol-rich liquid is drawn out through the bottom of the rectifier. Only the middle cut of this spirit goes on to filling and maturation, with the initial foreshot and tail cuts diverted back into the stills. The middle cut has an alcohol content of about 75 per cent.

Gunpowder What is it and how is it made?

 Gunpowder – also referred to as black powder – is made from potassium nitrate (75 per cent), sulphur (11 per cent) and charcoal (14 per cent). When these three materials are ground finely and combined, the resultant mixture burns quickly and produces a mix of gaseous and solid by-products. The mixture is relatively insensitive to shock and friction, requiring high levels of heat to be ignited. However, when ignited in a confined space – such as in the breech of a weapon – the released gases generate enough pressure to launch projectiles, hence its widespread use in armaments. While still used today in ignition charges, fuses and primers, gunpowder is no longer widely used as a propellant for guns and cannons, being replaced with smokeless powders that grant higher muzzle velocities due to their progressive burns (they generate more and more gas pressure throughout the combustion process).

Potassium nitrate (75%)
Gunpowder is made from a mix of materials
Charcoal (14%)
Sulphur (11%)

The Mayflower

Discover what conditions were like living on board the world-famous cargo ship that took the Pilgrim Fathers across the treacherous ocean to America

The Mayflower is one of the most famous ships associated with English maritime history. After transporting the Pilgrim Fathers to a new life in America during 1620, the Mayflower was often regarded as a symbol of religious freedom in the United States. Originally, however, the Mayflower was a simple cargo ship that was used for the transportation of mundane goods – namely timber, clothing and wine. While statistical details of the ship have been lost, when scholars look at other merchant ships of this period they estimate that it may have weighed up to 182,000 kilograms. It is suggested that the ship would have been around seven metres wide and 30 metres in length.

The ship's crew lived on the upper decks. All in all, 26 men are believed to have manned the Mayflower on her legendary journey. The Master, or Commander, was a man called Christopher Jones: he occupied the quarters situated at the stern of the ship. The regular crew lived in a room called the forecastle, which was found in the bow – accommodation was cramped, unhygienic and highly uncomfortable. It was constantly drenched by sea water and the officers on board were fortunate in that they had their accommodation in the middle of the ship.

During the historic voyage, the Mayflower carried 102 men, women and children – these Pilgrims were boarded in the cargo area of the ship, which was deep below deck where the living conditions led to seasickness and disease. The Mayflower set sail from England in the July of 1620, but the ship was forced to turn back twice because a vessel that accompanied it began to leak water. Many problems affected the Mayflower and her crew during the voyage. There were serious threats from pirates, but it was storm damage that was to prove problematic on this journey. In the middle part of the expedition, severe weather caused damage to the wooden beam that supported the ship's frame. But, fortunately, it was repairable.

Several accidents also occurred, including the near drowning of John Howland who was swept overboard but then rescued. Less fortunate was a crew member who died unexpectedly – considered by all as 'mean spirited' – his demise was viewed as a punishment from God. A child was also born during the voyage: Elizabeth Hopkins called her son Oceanus.

The ship reached Cape Cod safely on 11 November 1620. The religious community, who were hoping to start a spiritual life in the New World, thanked God for their survival. ✿

"The Mayflower set sail from England in 1620, but was forced to turn back twice"

Forecastle
Accommodation for the common sailors, the men slept here when not working on deck.

Beakhead
The beakhead is the protruding part of the foremost section of the ship.

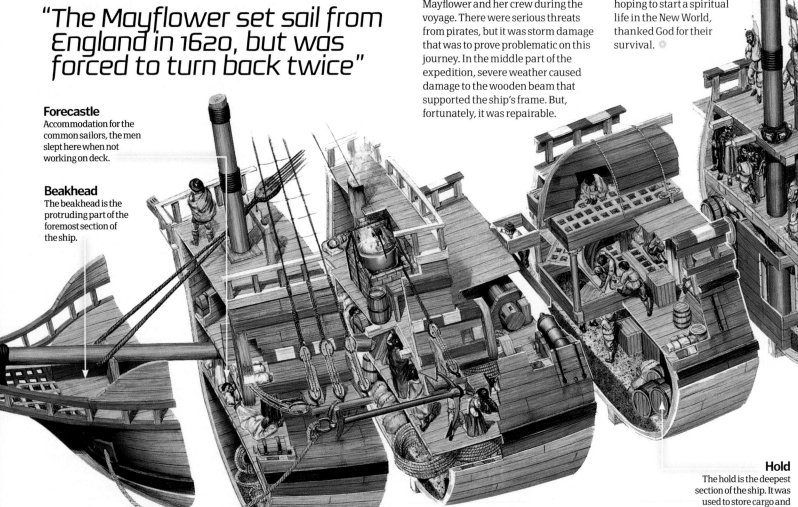

Hold
The hold is the deepest section of the ship. It was used to store cargo and accommodate passengers.

Old turkey

When the Pilgrims arrived in America, the natives taught them how to make canoes, grow maize and establish tobacco plants. They also introduced the newcomers to turkey, which was a native species of North America. For this reason the turkey became a traditional dish eaten at Thanksgiving.

DID YOU KNOW? *It's thought that upon her return to England, the Mayflower was likely scrapped for her timber*

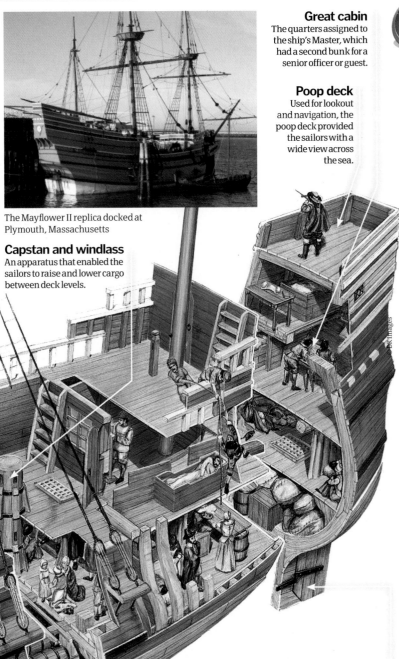

The Mayflower II replica docked at Plymouth, Massachusetts

Great cabin
The quarters assigned to the ship's Master, which had a second bunk for a senior officer or guest.

Poop deck
Used for lookout and navigation, the poop deck provided the sailors with a wide view across the sea.

Capstan and windlass
An apparatus that enabled the sailors to raise and lower cargo between deck levels.

Whipstaff
A pole that was attached to the tiller. It was used on 17th Century ships for steering purposes.

ON THE MAP

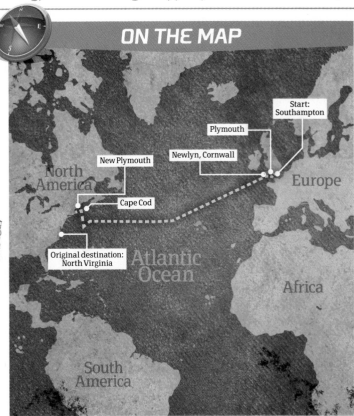

Start: Southampton
Plymouth
Newlyn, Cornwall
New Plymouth
Cape Cod
North America
Original destination: North Virginia
Atlantic Ocean
Europe
Africa
South America

The Mayflower arrived at the internal fish hook of Cape Cod

Inside the Mayflower

The Mayflower was a cargo ship that could be divided into three levels, which included the deck with masts, lookout and rigging, and the lower decks, which contained the staff quarters, gun rooms and storage areas. Below this, the hold contained passengers.

 Learn more

To discover more about this historic ship, visit Passengers of the Mayflower (**www.mayflowersteps.co.uk**), Mayflower Ship of Pilgrims (**www.thanksgiving.org.uk**), or check out the book *Mayflower: The Voyage That Changed The World* (2005), Christopher Hilton, History Press.

Pilgrim Fathers

In 1620 a group of puritans arrived on the Mayflower destined for the New World. They were known as the Pilgrim Fathers. The Pilgrim Fathers were disillusioned with the ungodly and hedonistic behaviour of their native Englishmen and believed that America was a land of opportunity where they could start a new religious community.

They landed in New Plymouth, and began to build houses, but it is believed that half their population died during the first year of occupation. The New World was seen as a dazzling land and a second Garden of Eden, but in reality the environment was harsh and unforgiving. Some natives were helpful and taught the settlers how to survive this wilderness, and in 1621 they produced their first successful harvest. This was celebrated with the first Thanksgiving – in turn, this became a traditional feast day – and it is still observed as an American national holiday.

"Palaeontologists have wondered why dinosaurs grew to be so large"

World's biggest dinosaurs

With fossil brush in hand, we unearth the massive behemoths that ruled over land, air and sea millions of years ago

Stegosaurus
Stegosaurus was slightly larger than a shipping container, but its brain was only the size of a walnut.

Flexible
Despite all this support holding the sauropod together, the design still allowed the creatures to remain surprisingly flexible.

Standing
The placement of the tendon in the vertebrae allowed sauropods to hold their necks and tails upright with minimal effort.

Brachiosaurus
The brachiosaurus used its staggering 16m (52.5 feet) height to reach tall vegetation.

© Science Photo Library

5 TOP FACTS
SMALLEST DINOSAURS

Microraptor
1 This tiny raptor, resembling an odd-shaped pigeon, lived in the early cretaceous period. It was no more than 30cm from head to tail and weighed less than a kilogram.

Raptorex
2 60 million years before T-rex, raptorex is the smallest tyrannosaur discovered so far, weighing less than 70kg (154lb), much less than its famous cousin.

Europasaurus
3 Sauropods are considered to be extremely large, but the under-a-ton europasaurus was comparable in size to a modern ox, averaging about 3m (10ft) in length.

Nemicolopterus
4 This is the smallest known 'flying dinosaur'. It had a wingspan of 25cm (10in) and weighed 0.1kg (0.2lb). It came about 50 million years before the quetzalcoatlus.

Lariosaurus
5 Lariosaurus is the smallest marine reptile discovered to date. It was about 0.6m (2ft) long and weighed 9kg, becoming extinct at the end of the Triassic period.

DID YOU KNOW? The biggest animal ever known to have lived on Earth, including dinosaurs, is the blue whale

Pterosaur
The hollow bones of a pterosaur ensured it remained light enough to achieve flight, even when reaching the size of a small plane.

It's somewhat frightening to imagine what it must have been like to wander around the plains of Africa and Argentina 100 million years ago. Whereas today you'd be hard-pressed to encounter a beast any bigger than yourself, back then you'd be running for your life as bus-sized creatures roamed free, some remaining largely peaceful and distant, others full of aggression.

The biggest land-based animal alive today is the African bush elephant, with the largest weighing a measly 13.5 tons and measuring 10.6m (34.8ft) long and 4.2m (13.8ft) high. Argentinosaurus, the current official record-holder for largest dinosaur of them all, would have been at least four times the size. It was a sauropod, dinosaurs of the Jurassic and Cretaceous period that were mostly herbivores and known for being very large. Indeed, many other types of sauropod would have stood tall above the African bush elephant, as would carnivores, raptors and pterosaurs ('flying dinosaurs').

Of course, the dinosaurs inhabited the Earth for much longer than any modern animal, from 251 to 65 million years ago, allowing plenty of time for certain species to develop into the giant hulks of flesh we now so revere. The biggest dinosaurs discovered to date have largely been determined to live in the Late Cretaceous period, 99.6-65.5 million years ago, before they faced extinction.

For a long time, though, palaeontologists have wondered why dinosaurs grew to be so large. While impressive, size can also be a hindrance. Not only does a large animal need a much higher rate of metabolism, but it must also develop much stronger bones and skeletal structures to be able to hold itself upright. Many of these gigantic animals were also cumbersome and slow, leaving themselves open to attack from large predators. Why did dinosaurs continue to grow for millions of years, then?

One train of thought is that there was a huge surplus of carbon dioxide in the atmosphere during the age of the dinosaurs. This meant that vegetation flourished, and herbivores such as the sauropods simply had an over-abundance of nourishment available to eat. While somewhat of a burden in terms of manoeuvrability, their size would certainly have helped to some extent when fending off smaller carnivores. This leads to another proposal from palaeontologists, namely that some dinosaurs grew in size over millions of years as a form of self-defence.

However, others think that these giant dinosaurs were cold-blooded, which was directly responsible for their size. Indeed, warm-blooded animals simply wouldn't be able to sustain such mammoth sizes, somewhat backed up by the lack of mammals larger than a few tons today. Huge cold-blooded sauropods, weighing in at up to 100 tons, would have been almost self-sustainable, as they could store heat throughout the day for the colder nights, maintaining a fairly unchanged body temperature and prolonging their survival.

Turn over for a look at the truly humongous beasts that would wreak endless havoc if they roamed our planet today.

How were they supported?

We examine the anatomy of a sauropod, to see how these huge creatures were able to keep upright

© Science Photo Library

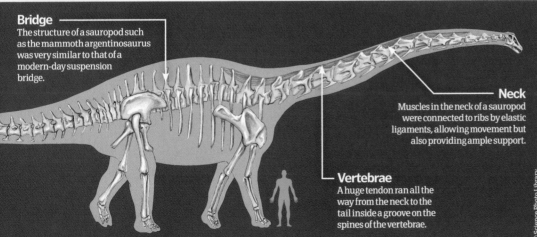

Bridge
The structure of a sauropod such as the mammoth argentinosaurus was very similar to that of a modern-day suspension bridge.

Neck
Muscles in the neck of a sauropod were connected to ribs by elastic ligaments, allowing movement but also providing ample support.

Vertebrae
A huge tendon ran all the way from the neck to the tail inside a groove on the spines of the vertebrae.

© Science Photo Library

BIGGEST OVERALL

Argentinosaurus

Argentinosaurus is the largest-known dinosaur to have ever lived, based on fossilised evidence. Weighing in at over 100 tons and measuring as much as 45 metres (148 feet) in length, this herbivore was wider and longer than a basketball court and was as heavy as a fuel-less jumbo jet.

The vertebrae of the argentinosaurus were very broad, with small peg-and-socket articulations above the spinal cord that kept the backbones of these animals sturdy and rigid. In addition, the ribs of the argentinosaurus were hollow, possibly allowing for greater manoeuvrability. Although the skull, neck and tail of an argentinonsaurus have never been found, measurements made from a shinbone can estimate the size of the various features of this colossal creature. Each hind limb of the argentinosaurus would have been about 4.5 metres (15 feet) long.

The statistics...

Argentinosaurus

Weight: >100 tons

Length: <45m (148ft)

Height: 21m (70ft)

Date:
Late Cretaceous (99.6-65.6 Ma)

Group: Sauropodomorphs

Bigger than: A basketball court

Tail
The spinosaur's tail was incredibly strong, with huge muscles at its base allowing it to be potentially used as a weapon.

BIGGEST CARNIVORE

Spinosaurus

The spinosaurus is often overlooked as the largest carnivorous dinosaur in favour of its more famous cousin, the tyrannosaurus rex. However, the spinosaurus would have dwarfed the popular movie star, measuring 16m (52ft) in length compared to 12m (39ft) for a T-rex. That being said, the characteristic features of the spinosaurus – namely its fin-like spinal protrusion – make it one of the most recognisable theropods. In the late-Cretaceous period, this 12-ton creature would have been fairly common, with its sail-like spine adding to a fearsome display and possibly helping to regulate its body temperature.

Sail
Tall bony spines growing upwards from the vertebrae of the spinosaur supported its characteristic sail-like structure.

Teeth
Within its crocodile-like snout, an unusual feature for a theropod, were rows of conical teeth for hunting and killing fish and average-sized land-based dinosaurs.

Feet
At the base of the strong hind legs of the spinosaur were three long, forward-facing claws.

The statistics...

Spinosaurus

Weight: 12 tons

Length: 16m (52ft)

Date: Late Cretaceous (99.6-65.6 Ma)

Group: Theropods

Bigger than:
A double-decker bus

The other contenders

There is some contention among paleontologists as to what the largest dinosaur of all time was. Currently the official record-holder is the 100-ton behemoth that is argentinosaurus. However, there have been several other claims to the throne over the years. In the late-19th Century, a paleontologist known as Edward Cope claimed to have found part of a vertebra that suggested he had unearthed a sauropod dinosaur (known as 'amphicoelias') measuring a massive 62m (203ft). Mysteriously, however, this bone 'disappeared' shortly afterwards, leading some to believe he had falsified the claim to get one over on his chief paleontological rival at the time, Othniel Marsh. It will be interesting to see if any more evidence of this giant creature is unearthed in future. Another contender about which little is known is bruhathkayosaurus, which may possibly be the heaviest dinosaur ever discovered, coming in at up to 220 tons.

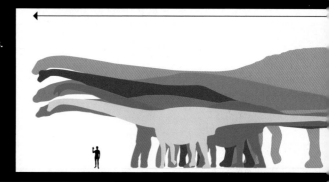

PILOSAUR

1. Liopleurodon
A 25-ton sea-dweller, the liopleurodon reached lengths of up to 15m (49ft) when it ruled the waters in the late-Jurassic period.
© Nobu Tamora

HADROSAUR

2. Shantungosaurus
A dinosaur of the hadrosaur genus, this duck-billed herbivore was very common in the late-Cretaceous period. It was about 15m (50 feet) long and weighed up to 50 tons.
© John Conway

RAPTOR

3. Utahraptor
Weighing in at a sizeable 680kg (1,499lb) and measuring 6m (20ft) in length, the utahraptor was the biggest raptor of all time.
© Nobu Tamora

DID YOU KNOW? *Despite its giant wings, some research has suggested that quetzalcoatlus was unable to fly*

The statistics...

Quetzalcoatlus

Weight: <250kg

Wingspan: 12m (39ft)

Date: Late Cretaceous (99.6-65.6 Ma)

Group: Pterosaurs

Bigger than: A small plane

BIGGEST PTEROSAUR

Quetzalcoatlus

Although not technically regarded as 'dinosaurs', pterosaurs were around at a similar time and are often (somewhat incorrectly) referred to as 'flying dinosaurs', much to the ire of some palaeontologists. Nevertheless they were impressive creatures, and none more so than quetzalcoatlus, the largest flying animal of all time. Its huge 2.5m (8ft) skull housed an elongated mouth that was used to hunt land animals including dinosaurs and other vertebrates. Despite its size quetzalcoatlus was comparatively light as its bones comprised a series of air sacs, a useful feature for such a colossal creature aiming to take to the skies. While most other pterosaurs fed on fish, quetzalcoatlus was somewhat unique in its hunting of land animals, no doubt useful nutrition to fuel its giant metabolic needs.

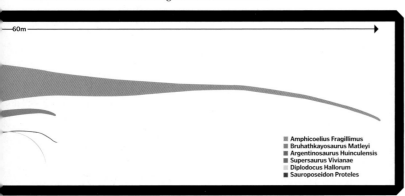

60m

- Amphicoelius Fragillimus
- Bruhathkayosaurus Matleyi
- Argentinosaurus Huinculensis
- Supersaurus Vivianae
- Diplodocus Hallorum
- Sauroposeidon Proteles

Dinosaur identification

Mike Benton, Professor of Vertebrate Palaeontology in the School of Earth Science at the University of Bristol, UK, explains how palaeontologists can estimate the size of a dinosaur from fossils and other techniques

How It Works: Can you describe your current role within the world of palaeontology?

Mike Benton: I work in a 50:50 teaching and research position – I teach undergraduates, both geologists and keen palaeontologists, and especially I teach Masters and PhD students. Every year, some 20-25 new Masters students and four-five new PhD students come from all parts of the world to work with us, and I really enjoy working with them to help them develop their careers. In research, I work on several topics by myself, on others with my students, and on others with collaborators around the world.

HIW: Could you briefly summarise the key methods and techniques used in the identification of prehistoric creatures?

MB: Palaeontologists identify fossils based on the existing knowledge of living and extinct forms. The fossils are often incomplete, and usually show only the hard parts, such as shells and bones. But, if there is a living relative, these parts can be identified, and a fair attempt made to identify what the fossil is. Usually, palaeontologists have many fossils of the same animal or plant to work with, and they can compare these.

HIW: Can you describe some of the challenges involved in identifying a dinosaur?

MB: Dinosaurs are all extinct, and their closest living relatives, the birds, are so different that it is hard to make useful comparisons in many cases. But, when complete skeletons are known, all the bones can be identified from knowledge of living forms, and the skeleton can be reconstructed. This usually shows basic things, such as whether the animal walked on all fours or on its hind limbs only, what it ate (are the teeth sharp or not?), and whether it could have used its hands for grasping things.

HIW: How are paleontologists able to discern how large a dinosaur is, and how can they estimate its diet?

MB: The dinosaur skeleton will itself be large or small. The best guide to body weight for a fossil form is to measure the leg bones. The femur (thigh bone) is particularly useful – because weight (= mass) is a three-dimensional measure, we look for something that increases and decreases in proportion to mass, and that is the diameter of the femur. So you get a good relationship between femur head diameter and body mass from living birds, crocodiles and mammals, and dinosaur body weights can then be estimated from this regular relationship. Diet is determined from overall tooth shape – curved and pointy for meat-eating, and broader for plant-eating. It's hard to be more precise, because we don't have the data set of comparative information to tell exact plant food from wear marks and scratches on the tooth enamel (used for determining the exact diet of mammals).

HIW: What, in your opinion, are the most important discoveries made in the past 50 years?

MB: Well, first, the realisation that dinosaurs were active and dynamic animals, dating from the work of John Ostrom in 1969 on deinonychus, and Bob Bakker in the Seventies on dinosaur warm-bloodedness. Second, the paper by Luis Alvarez and colleagues in 1980 that showed the first evidence that the Earth had been hit by an asteroid 65 million years ago. This has been much confirmed since then, and even the crater has been identified, all showing the key role of this in causing the extinction of the dinosaurs.

The Mallard steam locomotive

Beautiful, sleek, powerful, and to this day the fastest steam train on Earth. Introducing the Mallard steam locomotive...

A new double chimney aided the train's efficiency

© Phil Sangwell

Double chimney
Before the Mallard, traditional steam trains had been fitted with just one chimney, which limited their exhaust rate.

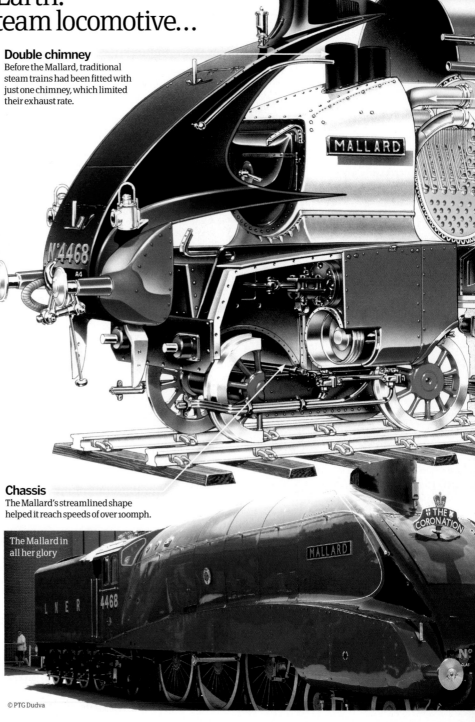

Chassis
The Mallard's streamlined shape helped it reach speeds of over 100mph.

The Mallard in all her glory

© PTG Dudva

Steam engines use coal-powered boilers to generate steam, which is funnelled under pressure down a series of pipes, known as a steam circuit. This steam moves pistons that are attached to the train's wheels, and this is what drives them. The exhaust steam is then released via the funnel at the front of the train. The system is effective, but if the boiler is put under too much pressure it can explode, devastating the engine and killing or injuring the crew. Likewise, the exhaust has to be as efficient as possible, drawing steam and exhaust fumes out to both minmise pressure in the system and to allow more steam to be drawn through at a greater speed.

This is where the Mallard excelled; everything about this locomotive was designed for speed. The streamlined body, tested in a wind tunnel, meant it could run at over 100mph for extended periods of time. However, the secret of its success lay in its double chimney, which allowed for faster venting of exhaust gases at speed and its Kylchap blastpipe. Mallard was the first locomotive of her type to be fitted with this system from new. Its four linked exhaust pipes draw more exhaust gas through the system at a greater speed and with an even flow, minimising wear and ensuring that the boiler, steam circuit and pistons could work at maximum efficiency.

Mallard was literally built for speed, and on 3 July 1938 it reached 125.88mph on East Coast Main Line, south of Grantham. Mallard still holds this record, making it the fastest steam locomotive in the world, not to mention one of the most beautiful. ✿

FAST

1. Mallard
The fastest steam train in the world, the Mallard's top speed was a record-breaking 125.88mph due to pioneering technology.

FASTER

2. Shanghai Maglev
Opened in 2004, China's Shanghai Maglev transport system reaches speeds of up to 268mph.

FASTEST

3. The bullet train
Japan's bullet train, or Shinkansen, a network of high-speed railway lines, can reach travel at up to 275mph.

DID YOU KNOW? The Mallard steam locomotive operated from 1938 until 1963, when it was withdrawn from service

Inside the Mallard
The technology behind this speedy machine

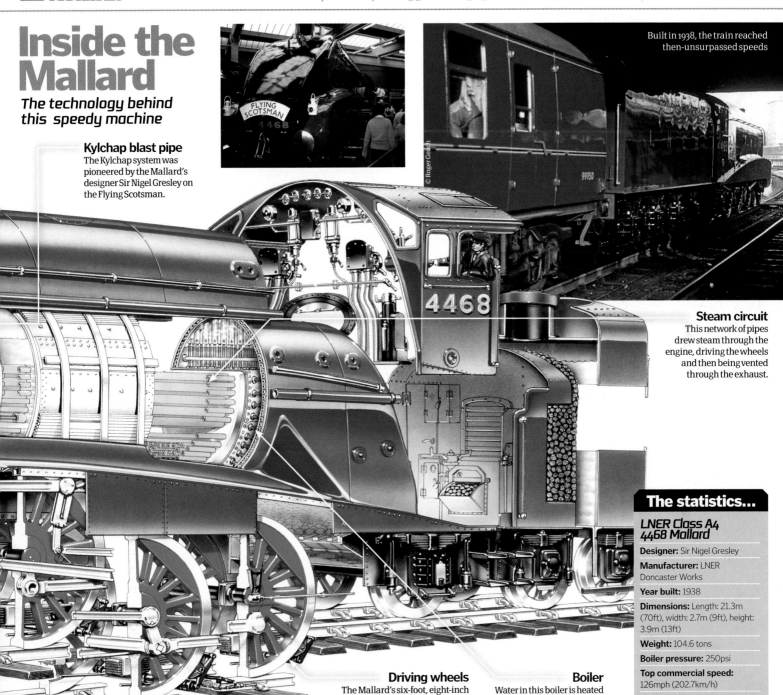

Kylchap blast pipe
The Kylchap system was pioneered by the Mallard's designer Sir Nigel Gresley on the Flying Scotsman.

Built in 1938, the train reached then-unsurpassed speeds

Steam circuit
This network of pipes drew steam through the engine, driving the wheels and then being vented through the exhaust.

Driving wheels
The Mallard's six-foot, eight-inch drive wheels meant that the maximum revolutions per minute for the engine could be reached, again maximising its speed.

Boiler
Water in this boiler is heated into steam and drawn through the steam circuit to drive the pistons that in turn drive the wheels.

The statistics...

LNER Class A4 4468 Mallard

Designer: Sir Nigel Gresley

Manufacturer: LNER Doncaster Works

Year built: 1938

Dimensions: Length: 21.3m (70ft), width: 2.7m (9ft), height: 3.9m (13ft)

Weight: 104.6 tons

Boiler pressure: 250psi

Top commercial speed: 126mph (202.7km/h)

Top speed record: 125.88mph (202.5km/h)

Status: Museum exhibit

The Kylchap blast pipe

The Kylchap blast pipe used four stacked nozzles, the first taking exhaust steam, which fed into the second, where the exhaust steam was mixed with gas from the smokebox. This flowed into a third that added more exhaust gases and this mixture, then into a fourth, which led to the engine's chimney. This meant that the flow of gas was more even through the engine and greatly increased its efficiency.

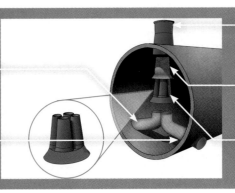

1. First blast pipe
This pipe carried exhaust steam directly from the boiler.

2. Second blast pipe
That steam was mixed with gas from the engine's smokebox here.

5. Chimney
The mixture complete, it was vented through the engine's exhaust chimney.

3. Third blast pipe
More exhaust gas was introduced to the mixture in this blast pipe.

4. Fourth blast pipe
The fourth and final blast pipe to combine the mixture led up to the chimney.

245

Inside a Roman fort

Ditch
The ditch was designed to prevent enemy warriors from gaining access to the fort.

Stables
The Romans kept horses in stable units. It is thought that most forts had stables alongside a central manure pit.

The principia
The administrative building. It was situated before a large parade yard, where the commander addressed his troops.

Gates
The Romans would build four gates at each side of the fort. They consisted of large, recessed doors made of thick, strong timber.

Rampart
The rampart was an effective barrier against the enemy - they would often build causeways to breach Roman defences.

© DominicZ

Roman forts

Discover how the Roman invaders constructed their many strongholds around Britain

When the Romans invaded Britain, they monopolised native strongholds. As time passed, they built base camps that allowed their armies to travel safely through the country. At first they fortified these camps with timber, then from the 2nd Century AD they used stone. The Romans were expert builders and had perfected the art of masonry by creating a revolutionary new material that was known as 'opus caementicium' – a concrete made of rock, rubble or ceramic tiles. Walls were built by placing mortar and stone in large wooden frames, and the result was a facing that has endured centuries. Opus caementicium was regarded as an innovative

discovery, enabling the Romans to create complex structures such as the arch and the dome.

Engineers built their forts on modified terrain – often chosing the summit or the side of a low hill, near a river or stream. Roman strongholds were built by a specialist corp that included a chief engineer; much of the manual work was undertaken by soldiers. Officers known as metatores were sent to mark out the ground for an encampment, using a graduated measuring rod known as a decempeda. Each fort was erected with a wide ditch, and also included a stockade or defensive barrier made of timber posts or stone. The Romans used the residue earth from the ditch to create a rampart. While

tradition dictated that each fort had four stone gateways, it was equipped with watchtowers that could reach an impressive nine metres (30 feet) high.

The fort worked on many levels – it served as a barracks, hospital, workshop, granary and stables. Every structure included a main street that ran unimpeded through the camp. In the centre was a parade yard and a commander's headquarters.

The Romans placed great emphasis on cleanliness, and so sanitary conditions were especially important. Forts had public baths and private latrines, consisting of rows of seats situated over a channel of running water. Drinking water, meanwhile, came from wells. ✿

Gods of War
1 We can learn a lot about the Roman religion by looking at portable altars found at forts. British finds include images of Minerva, the goddess of righteous warfare.

The hospital
2 This was a rectangular building that could house up to 60 wards. Hospitals are thought to have contained small hearths, used for the sterilisation of instruments.

Cleanliness
3 Large forts had bath houses in the central area of the camp. Places of relaxation and gambling, they often contained an altar dedicated to the goddess Fortuna.

The games continue
4 The Romans erected amphitheatres near forts; the most famous British one was at Caerleon. Combat between humans and animals was viewed here.

On parade
5 Soldiers adhered to several official festival days. The most important festival was at the beginning of the year, when they renewed their oath to the Emperor.

DID YOU KNOW? *The Romans even had a fire brigade. Cooking fires and beacons meant the fort was at risk of being set ablaze*

Granary
Raised above ground in order to allow a free flow of air, the granary stored grain, wine, meat, vegetables and cheese.

© DK Images

Barrack block
A series of long rectangular buildings. Each sleeping quarter had two rooms, one for the soldier's use and the second to store his equipment.

Early use of concrete was widespread throughout the Roman Empire

Roman soldiers lived according to a strict timetable

A soldier's life
The buccina (a type of trumpet) marked the start of every new day. The soldiers were highly disciplined – military aspirations and a strict code of honour dominated their lives. They practised sword fighting, hand-to-hand combat and military manoeuvres. Roman soldiers endured a gruelling regime that included running, swimming and marching over long distances. The day of a soldier could be divided into phases that revolved around 'the watch'. There were a series of eight, three-hour watches, known as the 'vigilia', and each change of watch was signalled by the buccinator (buccina player). Sometimes soldiers were ill or sustained injuries, so the Romans instituted a permanent medical corps and hospital in the fort. The fort could also act as a trading station where vendors sold crafts, animals and food. It was here that liaisons, both romantic and political, were established.

Housesteads Roman fort

Vercovicium
Housesteads (or Vercovicium, which means 'hilly place') is a fort situated high up in the north-west of England.

Hadrian's Wall
Housesteads is the best preserved of the 16 forts along the length of Hadrian's Wall.

Garrison
This fort would have been the home of a garrison of around a thousand soldiers.

Evidence
Housesteads fort was built around AD124. The archaelogical remains here are very impressive.

© Science Photo Library

The Bastille

Stormed during the opening days of the French Revolution, the Bastille epitomised the power of France's ruling Bourbon monarchy

The storming of the Bastille on 14 July 1789

The Bastille was originally built by Charles V, as a fortified gate to the Paris city walls in the mid-14th Century. It was originally intended to aid the defence of Paris from English attack, as hostilities between the nations were at a heightened peak. However, by the 17th Century, the gate had been transformed into a full-blown military fortified armoury and prison, used by the French monarchy and nobility to detain political troublemakers and convicts.

Holding on average 40 enemies of state at any one time, the prison became synonymous for the state's authority and fascism, with people interned by a simple lettre de cachet (a direct arrest warrant that could not be challenged), which was signed by the King. Further, under the reign of Louis XIV, the Bastille became a place of judicial detention, where the lieutenant de police could hold prisoners. It also became a storage facility for any prohibited books and pamphlets (usually political or religious) deemed undesirable by the state.

The structure of the Bastille focused around eight, 30m (98ft)-high towers, linked by massively reinforced stone walls. The walls, which were 3m (10ft) thick at the base, were surrounded by a 24m (79ft)-wide moat, which itself was surrounded by a series of other smaller fortified walls and structures. The positioning and circular shaping of the towers not only vastly increased the defensive resistance of the Bastille but also gave the soldiers mounted on top great 360-degree vision, capable of viewing the interior courtyards and surrounding territory easily. The linked nature of the towers also allowed soldiers to move from tower to tower, without having to descend to ground level first.

The interior of the Bastille consisted of two main courtyards, offices, apartments for lower-status officers, a council chamber for interrogation, multiple armament stores, dungeons, cells, dwellings for turnkeys, a kitchen and a small chapel. Cells varied in type dramatically, ranging from dark dungeon rooms filled with rats and water through to spacious apartments with stoves, chairs and beds, up to cramped and supremely cold tower rooms, where moving freely was incredibly difficult. The type of room that a prisoner was interned in depended on their social class (nobility were allowed the better rooms and even outside guests), amount of money and seriousness of crime committed.

Execution was handled in three main ways within the Bastille: hanging by the gallows, beheading by the axe, or burning at the stake. Nobles were the only class of person who had a say in how they died, given the chance to opt for beheading, which was seen as the proper way for them to be executed by the aristocracy. Interestingly, due to the vast public interest and attendance at beheadings, they were never scheduled on the same day as a theatre premier.

In general, the Bastille delivered a far greater level of comfort than most other prisons in use at the time. However, due to its housing of many political activists and enemies of the state, it became a symbol of the monarchy's decadent and fascist regime. This came to a head on 14 July 1789, when revolutionaries approached the Bastille in order to ask its governor, Bernard Rene Jourdan, to release the large amounts of arms contained within to aid their cause. Jourdan was evasive; angered by his seemingly pro-monarchy actions, the revolutionaries subsequently stormed and captured the Bastille. ✿

Inside the Bastille

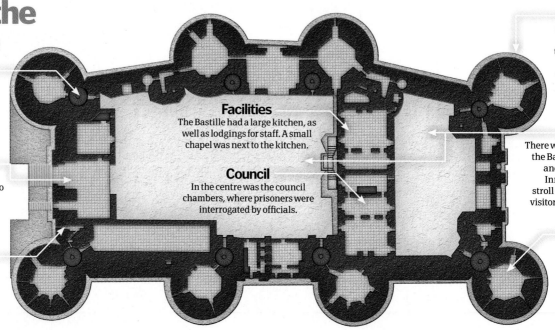

Armament
The Bastille was constantly stocked with armaments for use against prisoners, and in warfare if Paris was attacked.

Entrance
Originally there was more than one entrance to the Bastille. However, by the 18th Century it was only accessed by guarded drawbridge.

Apartments
Immediately to the right of the entrance were apartments for lower-status officers and, if class/money allowed, prisoners.

Facilities
The Bastille had a large kitchen, as well as lodgings for staff. A small chapel was next to the kitchen.

Council
In the centre was the council chambers, where prisoners were interrogated by officials.

Dungeons
Sat under the bases of the four towers were the Bastille's dungeon prisons. These were cold, damp, filthy and filled with rats and insects.

Courtyards
There were two courtyards in the Bastille, a large primary and a smaller secondary. Inmates were allowed to stroll the courts and receive visitors there if they wished.

Towers
The Bastille's eight towers were installed with spiral staircases and rooms on each floor. The topmost room was incredibly cramped and freezing cold.

5 TOP FACTS
VIKINGS

Ahoy!
1 Due to their penchant for plundering, burning and killing, 'Viking' was a word used to describe a pirate in early Scandinavian languages.

Having Olaf
2 The last Viking chief in the old independent tradition was Olaf II Haraldsson of Norway. Other chiefs and bands were absorbed into the army as a warrior caste.

Go east!
3 While the Viking raids of the 10th and 11th Centuries were mainly in western Europe, small bands of men travelled to the east, reaching as far into Asia as Constantinople.

Horny issue
4 It's a misconception that all Viking warriors wore horned helmets. On the contrary, most Viking helmets probably featured little ornamentation.

Son of God
5 The most famous Viking was Ragnar Lodbrok. He's best known for his assertion that he was a descendent of Odin, the foremost God in Norse mythology.

DID YOU KNOW? *Vikings were also referred to as Norsemen and Northmen*

Responsible for mass pillaging and sacking over western Europe throughout the 9th to 11th Centuries AD, Vikings were fearsome warriors

Viking warriors

From the earliest reported raids in the 790s AD, the Vikings – Scandinavian explorers, warriors, merchants and pirates – wreaked havoc among western Europe, sacking towns, besieging cities and conquering nations. Indeed, it wasn't until the Norman conquest of 1066 that the Viking age was finally extinguished, a period of time that left a marked, lasting imprint on the continent – one that is still evident today.

Foremost of these echoes are the burial mounds of their warrior kings, tombs laden with the treasures, armour and weaponry that they won and possessed during their conquests. Gigantic axes capable of splitting a man's head in two, swords with jewelled hilts and blades over a metre long and intimidating masked helmets have been unearthed, telling a story – albeit incomplete – of the lives and battles these humans lived. A great example of this custom can be seen in the burial complex at Sutton Hoo, Suffolk, England, an outstanding undisturbed ship burial that relinquished a wealth of Anglo-Saxon artefacts.

Other traces of this warrior culture have transcended the ages via runestones, these markers were left by Vikings to commemorate great victories, exhibitions or disasters that befell them on their travels. One of the most notable examples, and one that best helps us to understand the travelling-band nature of Viking forces, is the Ingvar runestones located in modern-day Sweden. This series of 26 stones was erected as a monument to fallen members of Ingvar the Far-Travelled's 1036-1041 expedition to the Caspian Sea. The stones tell of a great battle (probably the battle of Sasireti, Georgia) where many men died. One of the most poignant reads: "Þorfríðr raised this stone in memory of Gauti, his son. Gauti met his end in Ingvarr's troop."

This was the fundamental polarisation of the Viking way of life. Their exploratory nature and fierce combative skills won them much during early-medieval Europe, with great cities and cultures ravaged by their roving bands. However, as they eventually learned in 1066, if you live by the sword, you die by it also. ✿

Primary weapon
Vikings carried axes predominantly, which held their own distinctive crescent shape. These weapons could be used in mêlée combat, as well as a thrown projectile. Wealthier, more important warriors carried double-edged swords however, often with blades over 90cm.

Helmet
Viking helmets tended to be constructed from iron, with a round or peaked cap made from four separate metal plates. Eye spectacle protectors and nose guards were common.

Secondary weapon
Most Vikings also carried a smaller, secondary weapon for use if their primary was unavailable. These were usually seaxes, small straight knives that could be used in combat as well as utility (skinning animals, etc). Spears and bows were also carried.

Chain mail
Unlike later medieval knights, Vikings tended to wear just a mail shirt to aid mobility, rather than the full-body suits that became popular in the 12th and 13th Centuries. In terms of length, it would cover down to both the knees and elbows, being worn over thick fabric clothing.

Shield
Shields were circular and were constructed from lime, alder and poplar woods. Shield size varied massively however, ranging from 18 inches up to a gargantuan 48 inches. Shield graphics also varied, ranging from single colours up to complex Norse symbols.

Warrior wear

©York Archaeological Trust JORVIK 2011

©IanJH140

A replica of the famous Viking ceremonial helmet excavated from Sutton Hoo

The galleon became a major fighting ship

Man of war

Highly versatile and powerful ships capable of trade, diplomacy and combat, the man of war was the most prominent of armed ships from the 16th to 19th Century

Spanning a whole variety of ship designs from the 1500s to 1850, but typified by the galleon and ship of the line class of vessels, man of war ships were exemplars of ship-building expertise, delivering high manoeuvrability, storage capacity and firepower. They worked by taking the roundship and cog ship designs that had been the staple for European trade, transport and warfare since medieval times – both were powered by oars instead of sails – and added multiple masts, decks and cannons as well as more advanced rudder systems. These additions meant that long-scale voyages were now possible, opening up the largely uncharted world to nations and merchants looking to exploit the Earth's natural resources – events that lead to the great Age of Discovery.

One of the most notable man of war ship designs was that devised by Sir John Hawkins, treasurer and controller of the British Royal Navy for Elizabeth I, and a key player in defeating the Spanish Armada in 1588. Hawkins' man of war – a name chosen by Henry VIII – was adapted from the Spanish galleon and Portuguese carrack and had three masts, was 60 metres long and sported a maximum of 124 cannons, four at the front, eight at the back and 56 on each side. Powered by sail and with a high (for the time) top speed of nine knots, Hawkins' man of war proved to be incredibly successful through the 17th and 18th Centuries. It was chosen and adapted by Sir Francis Drake on numerous expeditions.

The last man of war ships to be designed were the grade-one listed ships of the line in the late-18th and 19th Centuries. These were colossal warships designed to be used in line of battle warfare, a naval tactic where two columns of opposing ships would try to out-manoeuvre each other to bring their largest cannons into range of the enemy. They were built primarily for combat and – as was demonstrated on Lord Nelson's well-known flagship HMS Victory, which sported a massive array of 32, 24 and 12-pounder cannons – were incredibly well-armed. For these first-rate ships of the line, trade was merely an afterthought, coming behind transport, diplomacy and combat in both functionally and priority.

HMS Victory: one of the finest man of war examples

5 TOP FACTS
MAN OF WAR SHIPS

Caravel
1 The man of war developed from the Portuguese trading ship the caravel, designed by Prince Henry the Navigator for exploration and to expand trade routes.

Galleon
2 During the 15th Century the caravel was adapted by the Spanish into the larger galleon type. These ships were more heavily armed than their predecessors.

Henry VIII
3 The first English man of war was named by Henry VIII in the 16th Century, who used the ships to travel while performing diplomatic missions abroad.

1588
4 Heading up Henry VIII's navy was John Hawkins, the ship builder and slave trader who went on to be knighted after the Spanish navy was destroyed in 1588.

Drake
5 The versatility of the man of war didn't go unnoticed; Sir Francis Drake adapted its design to develop a smaller more agile ship referred to as the frigate.

DID YOU KNOW? The man of war replaced the European cog as the main trading vessel in the 16th and 17th Centuries

Inside the man of war
What made this ship design so dominant for so long?

Masts
Common to man of war ships was a two- to four-mast design. These included the rear mizzen mast, central main mast and forward foremast. Not all man of war ships were square rigged, however.

A galleon had plenty of firepower at its disposal

Quarterdeck
The quarterdeck was the area of the ship where ceremonial functions took place and, while in port, the central control point for all major activities.

© DK Images

Cargo
Early man of war ships were primarily used for exploration and trading even though they were armed. Their cargo was diverse due to the exotic locations they visited and included foodstuffs, precious metals and slaves.

Cannons
While various types of cannons were used on man of war ships, 2,540kg demi-cannons were popular thanks to their 490-metre range and six-inch calibre. Demi-culverins and sakers were also installed in various quantities.

Anchor
Due to the large size of the ships used – with much room needed for their extensive cargo, cannons and crew members – the size of the anchor was also massive, requiring many men to winch it up from the ocean floor.

Man of war evolution
Follow the chronological development of the man of war

15th-16th Century (caravel)
A small, highly manoeuvrable sailing ship developed in the 15th Century by the Portuguese, the caravel was the predominant exploration and trading vessel at the time operating in Europe and Africa. It was also used in naval warfare.

15th-16th Century (carrack)
A three or four-masted ship used in Europe, the carrack is considered the forerunner of the great ships of the age of sail. Slightly larger than the caravel it could undertake longer trading journeys. It was armed with few cannons.

16th-18th Century (galleon)
Used for both trade and warfare, the galleon evolved from the carrack, and included a lowered forecastle and elongated hull for improved stability and manoeuvrability. It had multiple cannons on multiple decks and became a major fighting ship.

17th-19th Century (frigate)
Smaller than galleons, frigates were similar to ships of the line but were faster and lightly armed. They were often used for patrolling and escort missions as well as protecting trade ships and trade routes with their cannons and crew.

17th-19th Century (ship of the line)
The largest ships built in the great age of sail were ships of the line, massive warships designed to engage with each other in line warfare. These were primarily combat vehicles and sported monumental firepower.

"Daub is a primitive form of plaster, made from a mix of wet soil, sand, clay, straw and animal dung"

Tudor houses

Despite retaining the medieval taste for a Gothic style, the Tudors drove change in how houses were constructed through the late-15th and 16th Centuries. Read on to find out how the process worked…

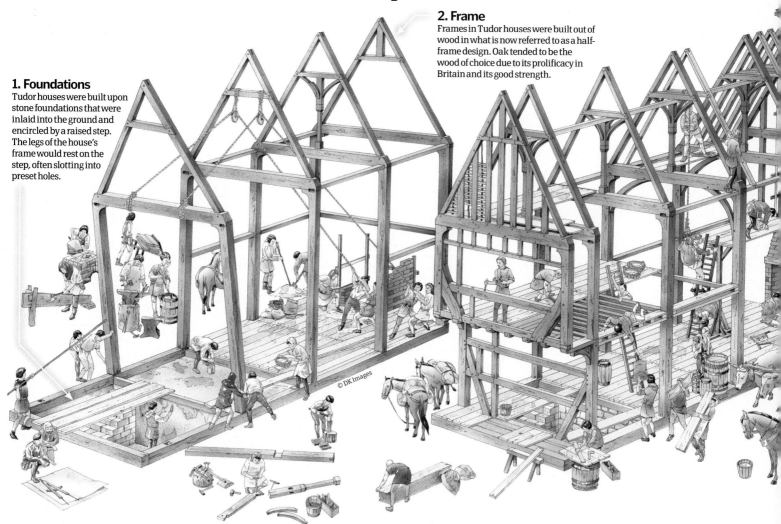

2. Frame
Frames in Tudor houses were built out of wood in what is now referred to as a half-frame design. Oak tended to be the wood of choice due to its prolificacy in Britain and its good strength.

1. Foundations
Tudor houses were built upon stone foundations that were inlaid into the ground and encircled by a raised step. The legs of the house's frame would rest on the step, often slotting into preset holes.

© DK Images

 Tudor houses were built following a half-timbered design. First, stone foundations were laid and encircled with a raised, hole-filled step into which timber frames were slotted. The original frame was hoisted into place by manpower alone and then used as a lifting platform to pull up the next frame with ropes. The frames were typically made out of oak, as the wood was common in Britain at the time and strong considering how easy it was to cut by hand. Due to the beams being cut by the hands of human carpenters, they were often rather uneven and – as can be seen today – led to a slightly bumpy, off-kilter finish.

Second, the house's chimney was installed, which for the time was revolutionary. Before Tudor architecture became standard in the 16th Century, buildings tended to be heated using the 'great hall' design, where a single large room would house an open fire and disperse smoke through holes in the upper walls and roofing. This led to a heated but smoky main room and was impractical in anything other than hall-sized areas. The enclosed fireplace and chimney structure allowed Tudor houses to disperse smoke efficiently, allowing for smaller rooms to be heated. During this stage the first floor was boarded and stairs were installed, both made from wood, and the jetty support beams prepared.

Once the building's frame, chimney and floorboards were fitted, the gaps in the timber frames were filled with wattle panelling and then water/wind-proofed with daub. Wattle panelling is characterised by a latticework of thick wooden sticks interwoven to create a flat surface. Daub is a rather primitive form of plaster, made from a mix of wet soil, sand, clay, straw and animal dung. When combined, these completed the walls of the Tudor house.

The building was then roofed, either in thatch – which was common for secular buildings at the time – or crudely tiled, as well as having its windows installed. Glass creation in the Tudor period was

5 TOP FACTS
TUDOR CONSTRUCTION

6,000
1 The wattle-and-daub used to build Tudor houses has been used for over 6,000 years as a building material, ranging from North America to Western Asia.

Wonky
2 Wooden frames tended to be common in England at the time. They would often warp, leading to many original Tudor houses to appear wonky.

Herald
3 The Tudor house's adoption of modern chimneys and enclosed fireplaces marked the decline of the medieval staple of a great hall, a large room heated by an open fire.

Trust
4 In Britain, most large-scale, original Tudor houses are owned by the National Trust, which is dedicated to maintaining the quality of the structures.

Dung
5 A main ingredient of the daub glue material that covered the wattle lattice was animal dung, which was mixed in with wet soil, sand, clay and straw.

DID YOU KNOW? *Victorians coated Tudor houses' wooden beams with tar to make them waterproof*

Building a Tudor house

3. Chimney
Replacing the medieval great hall system of dispersing smoke, Tudor houses introduced enclosed fireplaces and chimneys to channel the smoke out of the building.

5. Daub
Daub is a sticky, binder substance made from wet soil, sand, clay, straw and animal dung, which Tudors used in conjunction with wattle panelling. The daub helped fix the wattle in place and provided a paste-like material to create wind/waterproof walls out of.

6. Windows
As glass was still in its infancy as a material, large panes could not be created for Tudor houses. To create windows, multiple smaller pieces were held together with lead lattices and supported by dedicated wooden beams. Window frames were also made from wood.

Little Moreton Hall, a 15th-Century Tudor manor house located in Cheshire, England

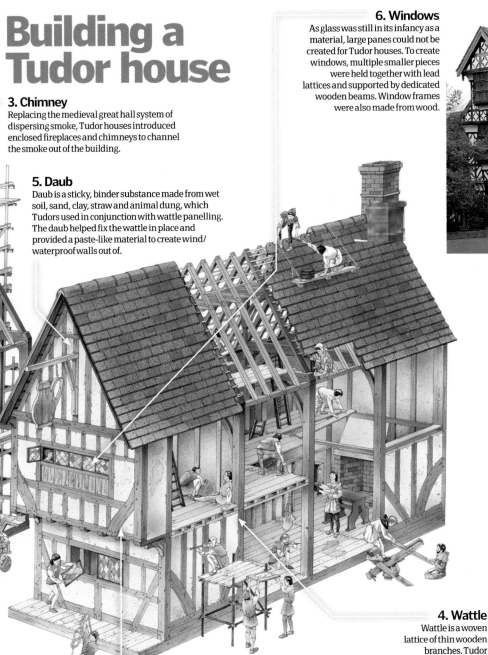

A good example of how daub was used on top of a wattle lattice to create wind- and water-proof walls

4. Wattle
Wattle is a woven lattice of thin wooden branches. Tudor houses used wattle to fill the holes between the timber frames. To affix it in place it was used with daub.

7. Jetty
Due to space considerations in cities, many Tudor houses were built with a jetty, which allowed the first floor to overhang the street below.

A sheet of wattle under construction

primitive compared with today's modern standards and craftsmen were unable to create the necessary large single panes. Tudor windows were therefore constructed from numerous smaller panes which were held together in place by an iron latticework in a tall, thin frame. Due to the combined weight of iron lattice and thick glass, the wooden window frames needed to be supported by a dedicated wooden beam which was positioned underneath.

Finally, the external trim and decorations were completed, which due to the influence of the renaissance on 16th-Century Britain, led to big changes in artwork, carvings, doors and also

window frames. A good example of these changes can be seen in the oriel; this is an overhung, multi-sided window cantilevered out from either the building's first or second floor. Daub tended to be coated in an ochre-coloured pigment while the wooden beams of the building remained exposed.

The archetypal tar black beams and whitewashed daub was not actually widespread during the Tudor period, but more a product of a movement of Victorian romanticisation of the Tudor period later in the 19th Century, with many traditional and mock houses being repainted to give them the effect we still often see today. ✿

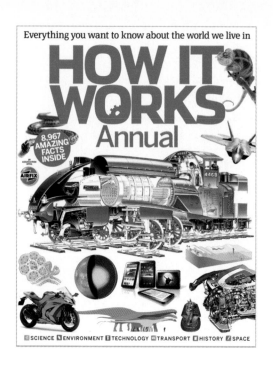

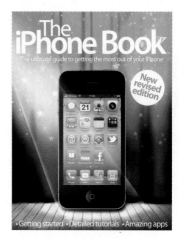

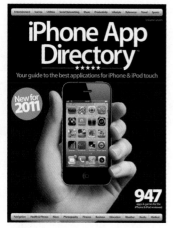

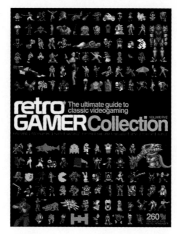

The iPhone Book vol 1
Whether you are new to the iPhone or have had one for a little while, The iPhone Book is the ultimate resource for getting the very best from your Apple device.
SRP: £9.99

iPhone App Directory vol 7
The latest collection of iPhone apps are reviewed right here, including the very best available for the iPhone 4, with every single App Store category featured inside.
SRP: £9.99

Mac for Beginners 2011
Starting with the basics, this essential guide will teach you how to master all aspects of switching to Mac including OS X, Snow Leopard, Mail and Safari.
SRP: £12.99

Retro Gamer Collection vol 5
An unmissable selection of in-depth articles featuring timeless games and hardware. From *Zelda* to *Asteroids*, this book covers all the classic games from days gone by.
SRP: £9.99

The world's best cre
to collect and keep

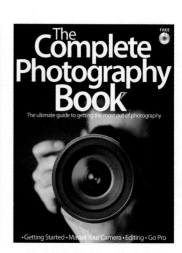

iPhone for Beginners
Everything you need to get started on your iPhone. With step-by-step tutorials, the 100 essential apps and a troubleshooting guide, this is a must-have for iPhone owners .
SRP: £9.99

The iPad Book
The ultimate guide to iPad and iPad 2, this comprehensive book brings you a wealth of productivity, entertainment and lifestyle tips, along with all the top apps to download.
SRP: £9.99

The Complete Photography Book
With fantastic shooting ideas and a wide variety of practical tips, this tome is the only resource for digital photographers.
SRP: £12.99

iPhone Tips, Tricks, Apps & Hacks vol 5
Step-by-step tutorials and in-depth features covering the secrets of the iPhone and the ultimate jailbreaking guide make this a must-own book.
SRP: £9.99

Prices may vary, stocks are limited and shipping prices vary
Order online www.im

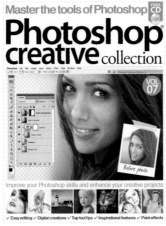
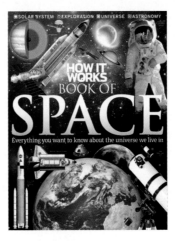

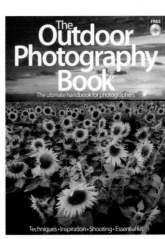

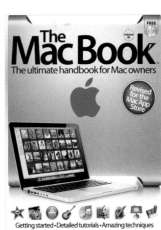

Not just for dummies

Over 400 expert hints and tips

FREE

Mac for Beginners
volume 13

Everything you need to know to get started with your Apple Mac

✓ Setting up your Mac
✓ Get the most out of iTunes
✓ Learn about iLife & iWork
✓ Master Safari, Mail and more

Android for Beginners™

All you need to get started with your Android device

Tutorials & guides for all Android devices

⟳ All the essential apps
⟳ Setting up your device
⟳ Learn about Gmail & Maps
⟳ Full guide to Android Market

Over 300 expert hints and tips

iPad for Beginners

Everything you need to know to get started with your iPad

Setting up
Best apps
iTunes tips
FAQs answered
Essential advice

for Beginners™

A clear, comprehensive series for people who want to start learning about iPhone, iPad, Mac, Android and Photoshop

Also in this series

Photoshop for Beginners   iPhone for Beginners

Bookazines
eBooks • Apps
www.imaginebookshop.co.uk